Richard Collier was born in Croydon, London. He joined the RAF in 1942 and became War Associate Editor of Lord Mountbatten's *Phoenix Magazine* for the Forces. After the war, he joined the *Daily Mail* as a feature writer and wrote fifteen major works of military history.

Also by Richard Collier

Eagle Day
1940
1941
1944-45

1944-45
THE FREEDOM ROAD

RICHARD COLLIER

CANELOHISTORY

First published in the United Kingdom in 1983 by Hamish Hamilton as

The War That Stalin Won

This edition published in the United Kingdom in 2023 by

Canelo
Unit 9, 5th Floor
Cargo Works, 1-2 Hatfields
London SE1 9PG
United Kingdom

Copyright © Richard Collier 1983

The moral right of Richard Collier to be identified as the creator of this work has been asserted in accordance with the Copyright, Designs and Patents Act, 1988.

All rights reserved. No part of this publication may be reproduced or transmitted in any form or by any means, electronic or mechanical, including photocopy, recording, or any information storage and retrieval system, without permission in writing from the publisher.

A CIP catalogue record for this book is available from the British Library.

Print ISBN 978 1 80032 595 1
Ebook ISBN 978 1 80032 594 4

Cover image: 'Raising a flag over the Reichstag' by Yevgeny Khaldei. Taken on 2 May 1945. This file comes from the websites (mil.ru) of the Ministry of Defence of the Russian Federation and is copyrighted. This file is licensed under the Creative Commons Attribution 4.0 Licence, and is accessible here https://commons.wikimedia.org/wiki/File:Raising_a_flag_over_the_Reichstag.jpg

Cover design by Phillip Beresford

Look for more great books at www.canelo.co

Printed and bound in Great Britain by Clays Ltd, Elcograf S.p.A.

For Anne and Sewell Junior,
Elizabeth and Jonathan
that they may understand

*Man has walked by the light of
conflagrations, and amid the sound of
falling cities, and now there is darkness
and long watching until it be morning.*

> —Thomas Carlyle, 'Characteristics', Essays, III, 32.

*Every age is fed on illusions, lest
men should renounce life early and the human
race come to an end.*

> —Joseph Conrad, *Victory*.

1

"The Devil's On My Side, He's a Good Communist"
1 January–29 February, 1944

Even for December the night was cold, yet they were sweating.

Five hundred yards off the coastline of Normandy, a British Landing Craft Navigation (LCN) had noiselessly weighed anchor – strategically short of the wheeling beam of the Pointe de Ver lighthouse. Momentarily, the golden swathes of light spotlit surreal images: the village of Ver-sur-Mer, huddled like a black cardboard silhouette to port, the windscreen of the 36-foot craft, studded with jewels of water under the driving rain. Beside the skipper, Lieutenant-Commander Nigel Clogstoun-Willmott, two men clad like Martians in clumsy wet suits, padded at the knees and elbows, rubberised at the wrists and face, awaited the word of command.

"Off you go," Willmott whispered, but he might have been addressing wraiths. The whites of their eyes shining from blackened faces, they had vanished into the churning maelstrom of water.

On this dark and turbulent night, neither of the two – 24-year-old Major Logan Scott-Bowden and Sergeant Bruce Ogden Smith, an irrepressible 22-year-old – viewed themselves as pioneers. Breasting a turbulent Scale 5 sea in a sub-zero temperature, sweating and seasick after a thirteen-hour journey from Portsmouth Harbour, they were in no shape to focus the thought. Only dimly there came the realisation that a routine operation they had previously carried out on the Channel Islands of Sark and Alderney might be a dress rehearsal for the real thing: a day as yet undisclosed when almost 7,000 ships would loom in the dawn off this 65-mile stretch of water, the Bay of the Seine, to land 250,000 men on five beaches code-named Utah, Omaha, Gold, Juno and Sword.

It was on this beach at Ver-sur-Mer – later Gold Beach – that Scott-Bowden and Ogden Smith were carrying out a pioneer survey

– for aerial reconnaissance had lately revealed broad dark stripes suggesting peat workings, fatal to the passage of tanks. The final words of Brigadier E. T. "Bill" Williams, the tall donnish intelligence chief of 21st Army Group, remained clearly in Willmott's mind: "If you only find out what those stripes mean – nothing else – it will be worth it."

Both men were well equipped for the task. The pockets of their wet suits were crammed with paraphernalia specially designed for members of Willmott's COPP (Combined Operations Pilotage Parties) teams: waterproof torches, underwater writing tablets, meat skewers, augers for boring holes, sachets for storing samples, even cyanide capsules in event of capture. At each man's left breast was a reel of fine sand-coloured fishing line, studded with a bead every ten yards – fashioned in the workshops of Ogden Smith's father, whose firm had supplied fishing tackle to the gentry of St James's since 1763.

Slowly, methodically, their senses attuned to the firefly flicker of sentries' torches farther inland, they began the survey that they would ultimately carry out on twenty-six beaches – many of them dummy runs designed to camouflage their mission. Working from the water's edge, they first skewered their fishing lines, boring holes one foot deep, secured the cores in a waterproof bandolier, then moved on. Ten yards inland, a tell-tale bead signalled the time had come to extract a second sample. Thus they would proceed until the beach was charted, twelve samples in all – establishing that the alarming stripes were not peat bogs but firm hard rock.

It was Ogden Smith, glancing at the luminous dial of his wrist watch, who realised suddenly that this was not as other nights. The time was one minute past midnight, and this was 1 January, 1944.

Snaking forward on his belly, he tapped the startled major on the shoulder. "What?" Scott-Bowden whispered, for torchlight was dancing very near and both men had frozen beneath the sea-wall.

"Happy New Year, sir," Ogden Smith whispered back.

Almost 1,500 miles south-west of the Normandy beaches, Premier Winston Churchill had chosen a strange background for a major tactical decision. All through the night the drums throbbed from the Medina and flutes cried, thin and sinuous in the moonlight. On the Djemma el Fna, the main square of Marrakesh, Morocco, acrobats and dancers spun and whirled through the *ahouach* dance of the High Atlas Mountains – capped now, on 1 January, by drifting snow. Yet on this same night of the Arab New Year festival, in the Villa Taylor, his winter retreat on the city's outskirts, Churchill was absorbed in one of World War Two's riskiest gambles – one to recall a Churchillian disaster of another war, in 1915, at Gallipoli.

Clad in a padded silk Chinese dressing gown, embroidered with blue and gold dragons, the Premier, who only three weeks earlier had almost died from virus pneumonia in Carthage, was tonight in seventh heaven. Oblivious to the heady scent of orange blossom, the lizards scuttling on the terraces, he bustled from room to room among a staff of naval planners, overseeing the last stages of Operation Shingle – a joint Anglo-American invasion force of two divisions, destined to hit the Nettuno beachhead at Anzio, Italy, in exactly three weeks.

His reasons were manifold. The campaign on the Italian mainland, launched with high hopes in September 1943, had become less of a battle against the Germans than against geography. The sunny autumn days in Calabria had degenerated into a soldier's purgatory: a land of knife-edged cliffs, of pelting rain that turned fields into quagmires, of cold so paralysing that despatch riders had to be lifted bodily from the saddle and massaged until circulation was restored. Since mid-October, the British Eighth Army and the U.S. Fifth Army under General Mark Wayne Clark, a tall hawk-featured man like a Wild West sheriff, had been halted before the Germans' Gustav Line – in the words of a carping British M.P., "like an old man approaching a young bride, fascinated, sluggish, apprehensive".

Thus, Churchill reasoned, a pile-driving amphibious assault of 110,000 men behind the German lines at Anzio might well put Rome and all northern Italy within the Allied grasp – mopping up the stagnant Italian campaign and freeing perhaps seven divisions for the Balkans, meeting the Red Army in central Europe to check their advance from the east.

It was a project which President Franklin D. Roosevelt and his Chiefs of Staff had long and stubbornly resisted, since it called for the retention of 56 LSTs (Landing Ships, Tank), 350-foot landing craft which could discharge their cargoes on a beach, scheduled for Operation Overlord – the Allied invasion of France, which Scott-Bowden and Ogden Smith were just then pioneering. "The destinies of two great empires seem to be tied up in some God-damned things called LSTs," Churchill had growled, for as a battalion commander of the Royal Scots Fusiliers, who recalled the World War One devastation around Ploegsteert and Armentières, he had been at all times distinctly cool on Overlord.

"Let us take care that the waves do not become red with the blood of American and British youth," he had more than once cautioned; it was with reason that Roosevelt's Secretary of War, Henry Stimson, had warned the President: "The shadows of Passchendaele and Dunkerque still hang too heavily over the imagination of these leaders."

Reluctantly – on the understanding that the LSTs would revert to Overlord by the end of February – Roosevelt had given his assent to Anzio. This, after all, would not be contrary to the spirit of Tehran.

To Churchill, the very mention of the Tehran Conference, held in the Iranian capital between 28 November and 1 December, 1943, was anathema. Brushing aside the fact that until this moment Marshal Josef Stalin, through his Ambassador to Sweden, Madame Kollontay, had for months been negotiating a secret peace with an emissary of Germany's Foreign Minister, Joachim von Ribbentrop – a fact reported by Britain's Sir Walter Monckton in January, 1943 – Roosevelt had gambled everything on two improbable factors: the Soviet Union's need for peace and Stalin's conversion to democracy.

This dream of a Grand Design, one shared by his Secretary of State, the ailing 72-year-old Cordell Hull, ensured, as one eyewitness put it, that "Roosevelt and Stalin were on the same side in any disagreement". Unwilling to dismiss the wartime alliance as no more than a marriage of convenience, Roosevelt now viewed the Soviets equally as partners in peace.

Accepting Stalin's offer of quarters in Tehran's Soviet Embassy – ostensibly on the grounds of security – Roosevelt had thus become the first U.S. President to be waited on by NKVD (secret police) servants. As the conference proceeded he had virtually allowed Stalin to dictate how the Allies should wage the last eighteen months of the war: an all-out invasion of north-west Europe, to chime with a simultaneous invasion of southern France, Operation Anvil, with scant priority for Italy or the Balkans. To the U.S. Chiefs of Staff, acutely conscious of commitments in the Pacific, this, too, made rock-ribbed sense.

At Tehran, Churchill had sought a private luncheon party with Roosevelt in vain – an attitude firmly abetted by the President's Russophile Special Adviser, the lanky unkempt Harry Lloyd Hopkins.

"Sure, we are preparing for a battle at Tehran," Hopkins told Churchill's personal physician, Lord Moran, truculently, "You will find us lining up with the Russians". On 24 November, the Premier's plea for an advanced co-ordination of Anglo-American tactics was met with an ill-mannered handwritten rebuff: "We, my dear sir, are playing poker – and years ago I learned that three of a kind beat two pair".

Unknown to Churchill, Roosevelt, who would seek a fourth Presidential term in November 1944, was playing not poker but politics. "The better I get to know that man the more superficial and selfish I think him," Field Marshal Sir John Dill, heading the British Military Mission, reported from Washington, but just how selfish Churchill had yet to learn. "We should probably find FDR ... doing things we should not like too much," the British Ambassador, Lord Halifax, warned, after a later talk with Hopkins, "lease-lend, dollar balances, trade, palling up with U. J. (Uncle Joe, the Allied nickname for Stalin), partly in order to destroy any impression that he was in our or your pocket..."

At Tehran even formal dinner parties were marred by Stalin's constant heckling of the British Premier on a firm date for Overlord, and the naming of a Supreme Commander. And when Churchill, badgered beyond endurance, had mumbled, "With God's will," Stalin taunted him, "God is on your side? Is He a Conservative? The Devil's on my side, he's a good Communist."

It was a conviction that Churchill profoundly shared. "Although I have tried in every way to put myself in sympathy with these Communist leaders," he minuted his Foreign Secretary, Anthony Eden, "I cannot feel the slightest trust or confidence in them. Force and facts are their only realities". Moreover, Churchill suspected even Stalin's motives in pressing for Overlord – "they will have the means of blackmail, which they have not at present, by refusing to advance beyond a certain point, or even tipping the wink to the Germans that they can move troops into the west".

Not without reason had *Izvestia*, on 6 December, proclaimed, "The fate of the war has been decided once for all," for as Lieutenant-General Sir Alan Brooke[1], Churchill's Chief of the Imperial General Staff, commented presciently, "Stalin's shrewdness, assisted by American short-sightedness, might lead us anywhere". Brooke could see logic, too, in Stalin's zest for Anvil: "His political and military requirements could now best be met by the greatest squandering of British and American lives in the French theatre".

Hence Churchill's overriding sense of urgency as January dawned, for an audacious and full-blooded Operation Shingle might ultimately render the unlooked-for Operation Overlord null and void.

This sense of urgency was apparent to no one more than Wing Commander H. B. "Dad" Collins, the pilot of Churchill's private plane, a four-engined York, code-named Ascalon – the name of the spear with which St George had slain the dragon. No sooner had General Sir Henry Maitland "Jumbo" Wilson, Supreme Commander, Mediterranean, been flown in from Cairo than Ascalon was diverted to Algiers, to ferry Churchill's representative with the Free French, Alfred Duff Cooper and his wife, Diana, to Marrakesh.

In the next two weeks, others came and went under their own steam: General Sir Harold Alexander, commanding all Allied forces in Italy, the didactic abrasive General Sir Bernard Law Montgomery, slated to command all ground forces in the invasion of France, Admiral Sir John Cunningham, Naval C-in-C, Mediterranean, and his R.A.F. counterpart, Air Marshal Sir Arthur Tedder. The Lord Privy Seal, bustling little Max Aitken, Lord Beaverbrook, arrived from London in a Liberator. Once Churchill's Military Secretary to the Cabinet, Brigadier Leslie Hollis, had arrived with a cypher staff of six WAAFs, Captain Richard Pim, R.N., set up a Map Room in the library.

For a man who four years earlier, on becoming Premier, had already qualified for his old age pension, Churchill set a killing pace – as none knew better than Captain Manley Power, R.N., Cunningham's Deputy Chief of Staff. Summoned post-haste to Carthage during Churchill's convalescence, on Christmas Eve, Power had spent almost two weeks commuting between his office in Algiers, London and Marrakesh, rounding up the disputed LSTs. In the end, Churchill had more than had his way: no less than 84 LSTs were diverted from Overlord and a mooted 24,000 troops had grown to 110,000.

Ordered to draw up a position paper demolishing Cunningham's objections, Power had refused; his loyalty to his chief forbade it. Furious, Churchill had drafted an order cancelling the appointment and transferring Power to his own staff. When Power again protested, Churchill responded drily, "Protest as much as you like, but write."

It was a daunting task, for on this day, 7 January, a full-dress staff meeting was to be held to finalise Anzio. But by noon, Power had drafted an up-to-date appreciation so thorough that Churchill invited him to lunch in the garden, along with his wife Clementine, his daughter, Sarah Oliver, Moran, Beaverbrook and Hollis. It was an experience Power never quite forgot. When a Moroccan waiter filled Power's glass with water, Churchill, whose prowess as a bibber was renowned, remonstrated indignantly: "Take that nasty stuff away. When the time is ripe for wine, let those who wish for wine have wine. Those who wish for water – should there be any such – can surely fill themselves at any time at any tap!"

Of all those who came and went to the Villa Taylor, one man received the shortest possible shrift: Brigadier Kenneth Strong, intelligence officer at Allied Forces Headquarters, Algiers. A British officer, Strong was opposed to the whole Anzio project; not only did he judge German forces in Italy too numerous but he knew, moreover, that Rome for Adolf Hitler was a major political prize. All roads to Rome would thus be bitterly contested.

"Well," Churchill said, as Strong prepared to voice his objections, "we may as well hear the seamy side," but this was a polite formality. Plainly, the die was cast: on 22 January, the first contingents of 36,000 troops and 3,000-plus trucks would reach Anzio.

As always, dismissing the conference, Churchill had had the last word. "I do hope, General Alexander, that when you have landed this great concourse of motor lorries and cannon you will find room for a few foot soldiers – if only to guard the lorries!".

—

As 1944 dawned, one factor was plain: though Britain's status as a supreme world power was ended, the Allies had started to break the Axis.

From Tokyo, in the Premier's official residence, Japan's Hideki Tojo, heard, if only distantly, the thunder of retribution: he had lost the Aleutians (August 1943), the Gilbert Islands (November 1943), the southern half of New Guinea (January 1943), and most of the Solomon Islands, including Guadalcanal (February 1943). Still within his grasp were Rabaul, Truk, Borneo, the Celebes, the Philippines, Java, Sumatra, Formosa, Burma and the whole coast of China – but less than six months after Pearl Harbor, on 6 June, 1942, an air-sea battle with U.S. Task Forces 16 and 17 off the tiny coral atoll of Midway, had cost Japan four of her finest carriers and more than 300 aircraft. From that day on Tojo's dominion in the central Pacific had ended.

For Adolf Hitler, Führer and Chancellor of the Third Reich, it was the blackest New Year since Versailles. In the area designated Security Zone One – which Hitler called the *Wolfsschanze* (Wolf's Lair) – a fortified compound in the pine forest of Görlitz, a few miles from Rastenberg, East Prussia, the charts in the panelled Map Room told a sombre story. In October 1942, the German armies had been virtually within sight of Suez – until the British Eighth Army under Montgomery had won a crushing victory over *Feldmarschall* Erwin Rommel near the desert whistle-stop of El Alamein. Then, early in November, a joint Anglo-American task force had invaded Axis-held North Africa; by 13 May, 1943, Alexander was cabling Churchill: "Sir, it is my duty to report that the Tunisian campaign is over ... we are masters of the North African shores."

Three months later, with Pantelleria and Sicily lost, the Allies were poised to strike for the Italian mainland; promptly the Fascist Grand Council deposed *Il Duce* of Fascism, Benito Mussolini. But although SS troops under *Hauptsturmführer* (S.S. Captain) Otto Skorzeny had staged a daring commando-style rescue operation from a mountain eyrie, Mussolini's writ now ran no farther than the puppet "Salò Republic,"[2] he had set up on Lake Garda, 500 miles from Rome. Long before New Year's Day, a new Italian government under Marshal Pietro Badoglio, had declared war on Germany – and the *Wehrmacht* were still stalled on the 25-mile Gustav Line, 80 miles east of Anzio, huddled round the monastery town of Cassino.

On the eastern front, the picture was as bleak. Again in 1942, Hitler's armies had been only 600 miles east of Kiev, the capital of the Ukraine; as 1943 ended, they were retreating slowly towards Minsk, the capital of White Russia, almost 300 miles north. It was a débâcle that had begun soon after 30 January, 1943, when *Feldmarschall* Friedrich Paulus surrendered the German Sixth Army at Stalingrad after five months of the greatest military bloodbath in recorded history – an estimated loss of 400,000 dead, 500,000 prisoners.

The lesson was not lost on the small nations of Europe, whether Axis satellites or uneasy neutrals. In Ankara, the Turkish Premier, Sükrü Saracoglu, called a 50-minute press conference to outline his country's stance: Turkey was still sympathetic to the Allied cause though not yet ready to fight for it. In Madrid, the *Caudillo*, General

Francisco Franco, had likewise embarked on a cautious crab-crawl towards the Allied camp, to ponder limiting exports of wolfram – 20,000 tons in January alone – to Germany. (An ore, which converted ordinary steel into high-grade, it was currently fetching £7,500 a ton on the Iberian Peninsula). But unlike the State Department's angry old Cordell Hull, who demanded a complete embargo, the British Ambassador, Sir Samuel Hoare, counselled finesse: "We shall best weaken Franco by not turning him into champion of Spanish dignity ... if we wish to make Spanish neutrality effective and benevolent to our policy, the worst possible method to adopt is the method that has turned most of Spain against the Germans."

It was a harder road for the satellites to travel. Hungary's ambivalent Regent, 73-year-old Admiral Nicholas Horthy, had twice in 1943 put out peace feelers, through emissaries in Stockholm and Ankara; hoping to quit the war without penalty, he stressed that either a British or American invasion would be equally welcome. Michael of Rumania, the 22-year-old King, was in a quandary; while he and Queen Helen, the Queen Mother, espoused the Allied cause, Premier Ion Antonescue was an unrepentant Hitlerite. For the time being they compromised, taking pains to visit all U.S. airmen who had been shot down and imprisoned. Finland, which had sided with Germany to regain territory lost to the Russians in the winter war of 1939, was likewise hopelessly divided – between those backing the Social Democratic Party's pro-Axis Väinö Tanner and those who sought the best terms Russia would give.

But it was in the Bulgarian capital of Sofia that the Balkan nations heard the authentic voice of Tehran, the conference which had settled the fate of eastern Europe for good and all. From Moscow, Bulgar Georgi Dimitroff, onetime secretary of the Communist International, took space in *Pravda* to warn his countrymen of the likely fate awaiting them: "The national policy of Bulgaria, from the viewpoint of her future, demands loyal co-operation with her neighbours ... only by breaking with Germany at once, and assisting in the defeat of Germany, will Bulgaria save herself from catastrophe."

–

Not only occupied Europe was divided. To many observers, it seemed that the free world, too, was riven asunder: the millions who were waging or had yet to wage war, the millions already attuning themselves to peace.

In much of the United States, the war's end seemed only a matter of time. Rosie the Riveter, with her overalls and dinner pail, that patriotic symbol of U.S. woman at war, whose Norman Rockwell portrait had graced *The Saturday Evening Post* cover of 29 May, 1943, was now an anachronism; war plants were closing down at a record rate. In Louisville, Kentucky, one plant had switched overnight from emergency production to the manufacture of 30,000 minnow buckets; another received Washington's sanction to produce 250,000 vanity cases. Near Rosemount, Minnesota, wrecking crews tackled the multi-million dollar Gopher Ordnance Works with orders to level it to the ground. On Wilshire Boulevard, Los Angeles, Sunday afternoon traffic had returned to its peacetime norm, tainting the air with a blue smog of exhaust fumes.

In Florida, the race-track at Hialeah, Miami, was netting $1 million a day and in Manhattan, inflation was rampant; $25 for two stalls for *Oklahoma* at Broadway's St James Theatre, $120 for a case of Black Market Scotch. With twenty railroad unions planning a strike, and 3,000 dissident coal mines taken over by the government, the St Louis *Post-Dispatch* saw the new national anthem as "My Country 'tis of *Me*"; in his fireside chat of 11 January, Roosevelt was moved to lash out at "the whining demands of selfish pressure groups". The pundit Walter Lippmann commented sourly: "No one has ever worked out a just system of economic payments for the Marines on Tarawa" (where 1,000 had died in November 1943).

Even occupied Paris had become a city of little bread but many circuses, featuring four opulent fashion-shows a year; the Flea Market was now a speakeasy for costly groceries, and half an hour after its box office opened the Opera sold out. England had long been a khaki-clad island, and from January onwards 750,000 GIs would flood into her ports, "straphanging across the Atlantic," as one source had it; soon the southern coastline would be a no-go area from King's Lynn on the Wash to Land's End.

But England, in this fifty-third month of war, was equally a land of bone-tired war workers, queuing in the black-out for jam-packed buses, of 40-deep lines outside Lyons' teashops for one rasher of bacon and one off-the-ration egg: a nation grown increasingly weary of exhortations to "Make Do And Mend," to beware "The Squander

Bug," and of 1s.2d, worth of meat per week. Fully 3,696,000 working days would be lost through disputes – 249,000 of them by striking miners – and in January a shipbuilders' strike was to put landing craft production twenty per month behind schedule.

The nagging question – When would the Second Front dawn? – was still subordinate to another: When would the blackout be lifted? A popular song of the hour *I'm Going To Get Lit Up When the Lights Go on in London*, dubbed the capital's best-known bottle hymn, caught the mood of a longed-for peace:

> When the nations lose their war-sense,
> And the world gets back its horse-sense
> What a day for celebration that will be.
> When somebody shouts 'the fight's up!'
> And 'It's time to turn the lights up!'
> Then the first thing to be lit up will be me…

On 28 December, those who studied their newspapers closely enough noted that a Supreme Allied Commander had finally, after Stalin's nagging, been appointed for Europe, but as yet it was not a name that had caught the public's fancy. Even *Life* Magazine, impeccably factual, had once contrived to render it as "Colonel D. D. Ersenbean".

—

West of Piccadilly, the streets were silent. A yellow-grey fog, rolling in from the Thames, blanketed the glistening miles of London's rooftops. Only the footsteps of a few late revellers, shuffling in search of bus-stops, broke the unnatural quiet. It was 11 p.m. on Friday 14 January, 1944.

At Addison Road Station, West London, a private military train, code-named "Bayonet" slid to a halt at a coal siding. Through wraiths of fog a group of gangers huddled round a coal brazier saw four men duck from the train to exchange salutes with a WAC driver waiting beside an American Packard staff car. Then the car nosed forward down the long drab Kensington Road, heading for a more salubrious destination: Hayes' Lodge, in Chesterfield Street, off Berkeley Square.

General Dwight David Eisenhower – whose name *Life* Magazine would hereafter record with due respect – had arrived to mastermind D-Day.

It was a task some critics felt he had been awarded by default. Early in December 1943, Roosevelt – backed strongly by Harry Hopkins and Secretary of War Stimson – had plumped for General George C. Marshall, the aloof frosty U.S. Army Chief of Staff, as commander of the D-Day forces. Eisenhower would thus remain in Washington to function as Acting Chief. Yet at 54, "Ike" Eisenhower's fame rested chiefly on his command of the 1942 North African landings. Not only was his concept of global strategy hazy; he lacked prestige with both Congressional and military leaders. His relationship with the flamboyant Lieutenant-General Douglas MacArthur, commander in the South-West and South Pacific, was soured by mutual contempt.

Facing these facts, Roosevelt had finally sighed, "Well then, it will be Eisenhower."

A canny open-minded Kansan, who enjoyed dialect jokes and would cheerfully sing "Abdul Abulbul Amir" to the thirty-eighth verse, Eisenhower's prime quality was his likeability; one observer thought him as worthy of a Norman Rockwell cover as Rosie the Riveter. Yet plainly this quality was a plus for a man destined to direct a coalition unique in war. As overseer and co-ordinator of more than 250,000 American, British and French fighting men, Eisenhower must also harness talents as diverse as those of his Chief of Staff, the ulcer-racked Major-General Walter Bedell Smith, his deputy, the taut smart Air Chief Marshal Tedder and the 21st Army Group's cocky confident Montgomery, whose Canadians dubbed him "God Almonty". He had also to gentle along the First Army Group's Lieutenant General Omar Bradley, whom one observer saw as "unruffled as an Ozark lake on a dead-calm day," and Bradley's total opposite in temperament, the Third Army's General George S. Patton Jr – "a foul-mouthed bully who looked like a rural dean," in one man's estimation.

From a large two-windowed office at Norfolk House, St James's Square, fitted with a wall-to-wall carpet speckled with red, green and brown, Eisenhower now set out to finalise a plan which had been in the melting-pot since March, 1943 – when "Overlord" had been the province of one man, Lieutenant General Sir Frederick Morgan, tersely briefed by Alan Brooke, as C.I.G.S: "It won't work but you must bloody well make it."

From the first "Ike" was to prove a popular figure. His ready grin, warm handshake and self-effacing approach – "Good morning, my name's Eisenhower" – were a hit with GIs and Tommies alike, and so, too, was his palpably-punishing schedule; in four months from February on, he was to visit twenty-six divisions, twenty-four airfields, five ships of war and countless depots, workshops and hospitals. "If I could give you an exact diary account of the past week," he wrote to his wife Mamie in White Sulphur Springs, West Virginia, "you'd get some idea of what a flea on a hot griddle really does!"

But all through the weeks that followed one problem was to plague Eisenhower above all: security. In all the months of planning, the Normandy beaches had been known only as "The Far Shore," but several hundred personnel, code-named "Bigots," knew key facets of the overall plan – and how could you conceal for months on end the presence of more than 250,000 fighting men and close to 7,000 ships?

As the long January days dragged by, Eisenhower didn't know.

–

On the face of it, all Eisenhower's fears were justified. His cover was already blown.

Early on the morning of 15 January, while the Supreme Commander was still sleeping soundly off Berkeley Square, *Major* Hermann Sandel of the *Abwehr* (German military intelligence) was arriving at his office on Hamburg's Sophien Terrasse. There an unsigned ten-word telegram awaited him.

It read: "*Hoerte, dass Eisenhower am 16 Januar in England eintreffen wird.*" (Heard that Eisenhower will arrive in England on January 16.)

Sandel was electrified. Eisenhower's flight from Washington to Prestwick, Scotland, on 13 January had been in true cloak-and-dagger tradition; the stars had been removed from his overseas cap, and those on his shoulder covered by his overcoat collar. Only on the afternoon of Sunday 16 January did the B.B.C. break the news of his arrival. Yet somehow Sandel's most reliable agent in Britain, A3725, Wulf Dietrich Schmidt, a young Danish industrial draughtsman, known also as Hans Hansen, had severed the web of secrecy. Most remarkable of all, Schmidt had contrived to remain at large in England since September 1940; this was his 935th message.

And a message of special import, for one day earlier the Russians had launched a major offensive against *Feldmarschall* Georg von Küchler's Army Group North, on a front stretching more than 100 miles from the Leningrad sector to Novgorod. After 880 days of siege – the longest ever endured by a modern city – two elite units of the Red Army, the Forty-Second Army and the Second Shock Army were striking simultaneously to relieve beleaguered Leningrad. Now, to Sandel, Eisenhower's arrival suggested an imminent attack on Hitler's *Festung Europa*.

"Many thanks for excellent No 935," Sandel replied promptly. "Keep us posted on Eisenhower's movements in context of invasion preparations."

Time was now of the essence. From Sandel A3725's message, marked SSD (very, very urgent) was passed post-haste to Zossen, the concrete warren of bunkers outside Berlin that housed the Army General Staff. The new recipient was *Oberst* Alexis von Roenne, senior intelligence chief of the department *Fremde Heere West* (Foreign Armies West).

Roenne, in turn, was encouraged. The crunch questions – where would the invasion come and when? – were still unanswered. Yet here was a pointer that A3725 was a man with impeccable high-level contacts.

As indeed he was. At 11:15 a.m. on Monday 3 January, two of them, Colonel Noel Wild, 11th Hussars, the head of Eisenhower's Anglo-American Deception Unit, along with Lieutenant-Colonel "Johnny" Bevan, head of the London Controlling Station, had passed through the modest entrance of No 58 St James's Street, London, the Headquarters of M.I.5., ascending to a third-floor conference room. Grouped round a board room table, a dozen men were awaiting them – among them the chairman, John Masterman, a don from Christ Church, Oxford, Helenus (later Mr Justice) Milmo, a brilliant barrister, and the art historian, Anthony Blunt.[3]

This was the Double-Cross Committee, now celebrating its second anniversary as co-ordinating body for deception tactics used by all German agents who over four years had been "turned" by "B" Division of M.I.5. Known to all of them, by reputation if not by sight, was their prize pupil, code-named "Tate," Major Sandel's A3725. Caught twenty-four hours after parachuting into England with a transmitter on 19 September, 1940, Wulf Dietrich Schmidt had, for four years, radioed his German paymasters exactly what the British wanted them to hear.

On 3 January, Schmidt had again featured high on the agenda – for Colonel Wild had outlined a plan of how the twenty-three tame agents[4] available could be deployed on an omnibus plan of D-Day deception. In this plan, it soon became clear, one of the most vital roles would be played by a tempestuous 29-year-old Russian-born redhead named Lily Sergueiev.

—

Midway through January, Lily Sergueiev was a bitterly disillusioned woman. The goal for which she had laboured for three years now seemed no longer worth the winning.

Yet at first it had all promised so well. An *Abwehr* agent from early 1942, Lily Sergueiev had needed no "turning" by M.I.5. In Lily's logic, working for the *Abwehr* had been just the first step towards a clandestine journey to England, before defecting to the British Secret Service. Her *Abwehr* code-name, "Tramp" was an apt summary of her life to date; at 17, hitch-hiking from Paris to Warsaw, she had returned as a stowaway on a German freighter. A free-lance journalist and illustrator, she had even obtained an interview with *Reichsmarschall* Hermann Göring, head of the *Luftwaffe*, in Berlin. The outbreak of war had found her in Beirut, on the first stage of a cycling tour of Indo-China – but following the fall of France she at once returned to Paris.

Chance, in the shape of a dubious Baltic journalist, Felix Dassel, an *Abwehr* recruiting agent, brought her to the notice of *Major* Emil Kliemann, a dilatory Austrian sybarite, the second in command at *Abwehr* headquarters in the Hotel Lutetia, on the Boulevard Raspail. Kliemann's screening took the novel form of intimate hand-kissing lunches at La Maisonette and Les Deux Magots, appointments for which he was often an hour late, but by early 1942, Lily had passed his test. She was in.

"You will not betray us – never," Kliemann told her thoughtfully, "because your parents have remained in Paris – *in Paris*."

This was true, for Serge and Natasha Sergueiev, both in their fifties still resided in the Porte d'Orléans quarter. Yet this was a gamble Lily had to take. In July 1943, Kliemann, after furnishing her with cover addresses in Stockholm and Barcelona, writing tablets, orange sticks tipped with secret ink and 20,000 escudos in expenses, sent her to Lisbon, since her English was fluent, to spy on the British colony in Estoril. Lily, stopping off at Madrid, checked in at the British

Consulate. After hearing her story, the head of the Secret Intelligence Service in Madrid, Kenneth Benton, at once contacted London. All this was in accordance with Kliemann's plan; that Lily, with a cousin in Cambridge and friends outside Bristol, should apply for a visa to England and once there report on troop movements in the vital Salisbury Plain area.

What followed were months of wearisome negotiations, as the authorities checked and re-checked her story, before Lily, under the alias "Dorothy Tremaine," finally reached England by flying boat on 5 November, 1943. One week later, after five days of unrelenting interrogation in Holloway Gaol, she was installed in a "safe" flat at 19, Rugby Mansions, facing Olympia, West London, and lunching with M.I.5.'s Colonel Thomas Robertson.

"We look on you as a trump card in the intelligence game," Robertson enthused. "Worth more than an armoured division. There is no doubt that the German Intelligence people have complete confidence in you, and so we are in an unique position to feed them with false information. We can pull off what is known in the trade as an 'intoxication' – the sort of thing Intelligence men dream about."

And Robertson elaborated further. With Lily's help, the Anglo-American Deception Unit could go one better than an elaborate security screen – "We can make them think that we have made our preparations to invade an area which in fact we have no intention of going anywhere near. If we succeed ... the Germans will concentrate their troops in the worst possible places to cope with the landing when it is finally launched."

From that moment on, Lily Sergueiev, like Wulf Schmidt and others before her, had a double identity: the *Abwehr*'s "Tramp," M.I.5.'s much prized "Treasure".

Yet this was the moment when everything seemed to go sour. She hated the cold blackened brick façade of Rugby Mansions, its sparsely furnished impersonal rooms. After months in Lisbon and Madrid, the creeping yellow fog, the shabbiness of the Londoners in the streets depressed her – "worn-out overcoats, shiny sleeves, dowdy clothes." She longed for her wirehaired mongrel Babs, detained at Gibraltar by British quarantine regulations, despite Benton's promises that rules could be twisted, and Robertson would take no steps to recover the dog. She found the English "cold ... undemonstrative, impenetrable." "I want to love and hate; to be alive," she wrote in her diary.

On Christmas Eve, 1943, she collapsed, desperately ill, and was rushed to a private room at St Mary's Hospital, Paddington. Two doctors, Ranald Handfield-Jones and Donald Page, examined her and broke the news. Lily had stones in both kidneys. An immediate operation was necessary.

Lily refused. "I don't want to die in England," she told Robertson. "I don't want to be buried in damp soil. I should like to see the end of the war."

In the face of such stubbornness, Robertson could only shrug. Lily was discharged, to do the best she could.

From the Allied viewpoint, her best was more than good enough. Equipped with an American Halicrafter "Sky Rider" radio by M.I.5.'s Radio Security Services Officer, Ronnie Reid, she settled in with old friends Mary and Edward Yeo, in the country village of Wraxall, eight miles from Bristol. It was an ideal location, for in this vast web of trickery now being spun across Europe from the North Cape to Cairo, from Moscow to Algiers, a trusted agent in the West Country was vital to the Germans. Any invasion pointed at Normandy would call for troop movements to all the ports of Devon, Dorset and Cornwall. Kliemann had asked Lily to log all such movements in secret ink, mailing them to her cover addresses.

Three times a week on Tuesday, Thursday and Saturday she listened mechanically for her call-sign and coded instructions, turning the tuner through the 8650 metre waveband at mid-day and the 5000 band at midnight. Using her orange stick she drafted out in block letters the material that Robertson's aides provided: information that to her meant nothing at all. In Bristol she had seen soldiers wearing a badge like a tricoloured isosceles triangle, yellow, blue and red. She had seen American soldiers wearing a large black "A" on their sleeves.

Designedly, her reports were mainly negative in contrast to the frantic movements of a mythical Army Group ostensibly commanded by Lieutenant General George S. Patton and concentrated in East Anglia and Kent. Their obvious target: the Pas de Calais.

Yet plainly the amorous Kliemann was satisfied. On 23 January, M.I.5. deciphered his message: "Information very interesting – Letters arrive well – Continue – You are very charming."

Then, out of the blue, on Friday 18 February, came a call from Robertson's aide, Mary Ward.[5]

"How do you feel?"

Lily was still seething over Babs. "Why this solicitude?" she asked coldly.

"Would you like to travel?"

"Don't tell me you're concerned with what I want! Where to?"

"To Portugal."

"Aren't the letters sufficient?"

"We cannot wait that long."

Next day, in a new "safe" flat at 39, Hill Street, Mayfair – less than a block from Eisenhower's hide-out – Lily heard the worst news yet. "The War Office want you to go to Lisbon, meet Kliemann, and bring back a transmitter." It was probable, Mary Ward explained, that soon nobody would be able to communicate with the European mainland by letter.

Lily's heart sank. For three months, despite her antipathy, she had lived among a people who fought without hating. She, too, was almost too tired to hate. Now she must once more meet up with the Germans, and the lies, the bluff, the deceit would begin all over again.

Mary Ward was watching her. "Will you do it?"

"Of course."

It was a perilous decision. At any moment her kidneys might fail altogether, and then uraemia would set in. Both Doctors Handfield-Jones and Page had been quite explicit: at best Lily Sergueiev had six months to live.

—

Despite the death sentence, Lily Sergueiev knew one advantage. Like Sergeant Bruce Ogden Smit – who on 18 January swam ashore at St Laurent to reassure General Bradley that the shingle of Omaha Beach was based on solid rock – Lily had a fixed purpose in life. But in mid-January countless thousands of men and women were still waiting impotently in the wings of history. As yet their tasks in the months ahead were impalpable, shrouded by uncertainty.

In London, from an office on Grosvenor Square, Lieutenant-Colonel Saul K. Padover, of the U.S. Army's Psychological Warfare Division, had one basic project: "to penetrate the Siegfried Line which Göbbels[6] built round the (Third) Reich." Yet faced with such a blanket assignment, where did a man begin?

At 39, Padover, a stockily-built 5ft 6ins, with what he described as "snapping brown eyes," was a latecomer to the field of combat;

until 1943 he had worked as an assistant to Roosevelt's Secretary of the Interior, Harold Ickes. Born in Vienna, the son of an American merchant, Padover had lived in Austria for the first fifteen years of his life, briefly visiting Germany in 1920, before the family moved to Detroit, Michigan. In 1936, on a Guggenheim fellowship, he had once more returned to Austria – two years before the *Anschluss*.

Of Hitler's Germans he had only second or third-hand knowledge – yet of the PWD team under Colonel Clifford Powell that would one day cross the German frontier, Padover was deemed the unchallenged expert on all things German. The team's reasoning seemed flawless, at that: Padover had once published a biography of the Emperor Joseph II.

At Aldbourne, Wiltshire, Private Donald Burgett was more certain of his own role: as a member of A Company, 506 Regiment, 101st Airborne Division, the "Screaming Eagles," he knew that he and his buddies would one day spearhead the invasion of Europe to soften the path of the infantry. A tall dark-haired 18-year-old, who hailed, like Padover, from Detroit, Burgett knew that his job would be to kill Germans rather than understand them, but inwardly he felt no qualms.

Nor was this surprising. Death had been almost a part of life ever since he had volunteered for the paratroops in April, 1943, when an instructor at Fort Benning, Georgia, had told them coolly: "Most of you will die in combat." To ensure that only motivated men stuck it out, their training had been merciless from the start. The slightest infraction of rules prompted a bellow of "Gimme twenty-five!" – and the hapless rookie, dropping to a prone position, pumped out the twenty-five push-ups ordered. Nine-mile runs, before a breakfast of cornflakes and black coffee, were routine, spurred on by the instructors' stentorian cries of "Hubba-Hubba". A day that began at 5 a.m. ended only at 5 p.m. – with more push-ups.

Yet Burgett had not once been tempted to "sign the quit slip," as opting out of training was called. Before reaching England by way of Northern Ireland, Burgett had soldiered on through the whole gamut of training: the packing and re-packing of the T5 parachute assembly, the practice drops from the 250 ft tower, the first jump from a C-47, which was equally the first time he had boarded a plane. Even two men who failed to make it were, in death, enrolled in the ruthless training programme; every survivor like Burgett was compelled to handle their bloodied boots.

Now, daily compelled to face death as in a mirror, Burgett and the others, marching to day and night assault practice, irreverently mocked that prospect with the paratroopers' song, "Blood Upon the Risers," sung to the tune of "The Battle Hymn of the Republic":

There was blood upon the risers, there were brains upon the chute;
Intestines were a-dangling from this paratrooper's boots;
They picked him up, still in his chute and poured him from his boots.
He ain't gonna jump no more.
Gory, Gory, What a Helluva way to die
Gory, Gory, What a Helluva way to die
Gory, Gory, What a Helluva way to die
He ain't gonna jump no more.

Meanwhile, D-Day for the one invasion on which Churchill had set his heart was fast approaching.

The Tyrrhenian sea lay calm. Somewhere above the moonlit clouds Allied planes throbbed persistently. Two miles to the east of the first landing craft, now churning towards the frosty eroded beaches of Anzio and Nettuno, the black mass of the Alban Hills dominating Rome was dimly visible. It was 2 a.m. on Saturday 22 January, 1944.

Aboard the ships carrying the 36,000 men of the first assault force, the chatter was tense and muted; non-coms were issuing last minute instructions: "Don't be afraid to shoot ... cross the first street and cut right ... building with a tall tower." Davits creaked faintly, barely audible above the quiet thud of screws; the clang of boots on steel rungs died abruptly, as the assault troops swarmed down rope ladders to the bobbing landing craft. Fiery lanes streaked the darkness, "like flaming zip-fasteners," as almost 800 five-inch rockets, fired in salvoes of 70 at a time, streaked for the shore, triggering tall stalagmites of water. The irate voices of British Naval Landing Officers cut the night: "Don't stand about like a half-plucked fowl. Cast off!"

Incredibly, the surprise seemed total. On shore, a German mining engineer, *Leutnant* Siegmund Seiler, whose task was to render the port of Anzio useless, was puzzled by a steady purring from the sea, growing by degrees to a rasping hum. Taken prisoner by the first Americans ashore, Seiler marvelled from a ringside seat as bulldozers and quarter-ton trucks, pre-loaded to drive straight to the front line, poured ashore – "like a big business, without confusion, order or muddle."

At 3 a.m. Major-General John P. Lucas, commanding U.S. VI Corps, the spearhead of the assault, radioed the 5th Army's commander General Mark Clark: NO ANGELS YET CUTIE CLAUDETTE. Translated, this meant that tanks had not yet arrived, but attacks by the British 1st and 3rd Divisions were going well. Against all the odds, Winston Churchill's Anzio gamble, designed to negate "Overlord," was paying off.

"Only a miracle can save us now!" was the first reaction of the normally-optimistic *Feldmarschall* Albert Kesselring, *Wehrmacht* Commander-in-Chief, Southern Command. Yet for 127 days and nights thereafter the Germans kept the Allies pinned to the Anzio beachhead – a beachhead that expanded only with the maddening deliberation of sand trickling through an egg-timer. From a perimeter seven miles deep and sixteen miles long, it had grown, by 25 January, to ten miles in depth; to fourteen miles deep, congested with 110,000 men and 18,000 vehicles, by 3 February – "highly organised insanity," Churchill growled. It was small wonder that German propaganda posters were soon picturing a snail, its horns adorned with the Union Jack and Old Glory, creeping up the toe of the Italian boot.

The plan had seemed simplicity itself. From the beaches the troops would advance not northwards to Rome but eastwards, to cut the Frosinone and the coastal roads behind the Germans at Cassino. Simultaneously, the bulk of the Fifth Army would launch a mass frontal attack on the Cassino ridge. Caught in a nutcracker, the Germans would pull back to find themselves blocked from the rear. And as they retreated they would be destroyed piecemeal around Frosinone in the valley of the Liri River.

What had gone wrong?

Much of the trouble lay in hasty cobbled-up planning, a Churchillian decision to use two divisions to salvage something from the wreckage of Tehran – "the landing force was initially weak," Kesselring was to comment, "only a division or so of infantry". Another critic put it more trenchantly still: "It was a job for a full army, or it was no job at all". Major-General William Penney, of the British 1st Division, recalled the entire planning technique as "fantastic ... we assembled and the G.3 put up a board giving an outline plan. If it was not acceptable he pulled it down and put up another". Yet at the outset the burden of blame fell squarely on the shoulders of one man: the American Major-General John P. Lucas.

A pleasant mild-mannered officer, who affected a corn-cob pipe, Lucas was self-confessedly an old man at 54, the exact age of Eisenhower – "I am afraid I feel every year of it," he noted on his birthday in mid-January. His nickname "Foxy Grandpa" was a misnomer – for Lucas was cautious rather than cunning. Lacking faith in his own judgement – "I am just a poor working girl trying to get ahead" – he equally lacked faith in the Anzio gamble – "the whole affair has a strong odour of Gallipoli."

Though Lucas, after landing, rarely left his wine-cellar headquarters, his officers found his pessimism profoundly infectious. Offered the use of No 9 (British) Commando, Lucas's response was typical: "I'll be glad to have anyone who can even heave a rock." "I have never fought a battle before," he told the startled Gordon Highlanders – untruthfully, for he had led VI Corps with distinction at Salerno – but his innate defeatism cast a creeping pall over the beach-head. "Say, Brigadier," he told the commander of the 168th (British) Brigade, "I am mighty glad to see you. You are the last pea in my pod."

It was an hour when boldness was all, for until 24 January, Frosinone, even Rome itself, lay naked to attack, yet Lucas, awaiting a German counter-offensive, cautiously consolidating his beachhead, stayed put until Kesselring had ringed the perimeter with six divisions. "Don't stick your head out, Johnny," Mark Clark had counselled, perhaps unwisely; Lucas had needed no second bidding.

"If we succeed in dealing with this business down there, there will be no further landings anywhere," Hitler told *General der Artillerie* Alfred Jodl, Chief of the Operations Staff, on 29 January, and thus on that same day, when Lucas, after constant urging, agreed to attack, Kesselring was ready. Major-General William Penney always recalled that decisive conference as "a travesty, pathetic and tragic"; after listening in silence to his commanders' submissions, Lucas, turning to Major-General James Eyles of the 45th (U.S.) Division told him vaguely, "O.K., Jim, you go give 'em the works."

The two days of slaughter that followed were a tragic sequel to a three-day attack launched across the Rapido River, south of Cassino, on 20 January by Major-General Fred L. Walker's 36th (Texas) Division. Designed to divert attention from Anzio, it had cost the 36th 1600 casualties, and the Rapido was still unforded. Now in Lucas' abortive counterattack, one unit alone, Colonel William O. Darby's famed U.S. Rangers, lost 950 men. Banishing his staff from his farmhouse headquarters, the iron-willed Darby broke down and wept.

From 2 February on, at least one unit kept the Germans on tenterhooks until the end: the 1,800 Americans and Canadians of Brigadier-General Robert T. Frederick's 1st Special Service Force, whom the Germans called "The Devil's Brigade". Holding a quarter of the entire Anzio perimeter between them, the Force soon penetrated 1,000 yards into the German lines to improve their positions, taking over the deserted village of Borgo Sabotino, re-naming it "Gusville," after Lieutenant Gus Heilman, and hoisting the Force's red flag with its black dagger and a white shield above the rooftops. Here, within sight of the German guns, they ran horse races, set up a volley-ball court, or took time off to visit "Walkmeister's Portable Whorehouse," four cheerful prostitutes whom Sergeant Jake Walkmeister had smuggled in from Pozzuoli, near Naples, inside an ambulance.

Indefatigable pillagers, "The Devil's Brigade" raided for cows, eggs, chickens, even seed corn, farming the land or sleeping by day, patrolling by night. Often advance scouting parties surprised Frederick's freebooters with a batch of German prisoners, pressed into useful service: one man toteing a bed and mattress, a second a large crate of chickens, a third pushing a baby carriage of potatoes. In truth, such prisoners were lucky; those who met the Force on night patrol often lay dead in the dawn light, a German-language paper sticker gummed to their foreheads: "THE WORST IS YET TO COME."

They were a notable exception. In later years, even after Mark Clark, on 23 February, replaced Lucas with Major-General Lucian B. Truscott, the gravel-voiced commander of the 3rd Infantry Division, most men recalled Anzio for the total sense of stalemate and frustration.

Beyond the pine forests that bordered the Mussolini Canal, the grey lonely Pontine Marshes stretched for miles, laced with creeks and drainage ditches. Closer to the beaches, on slippery slopes festooned with thorns and brambles, the troops had settled to a troglodyte life, in dug-outs, roofed with logs, planks and rammed earth; some, with rare ingenuity, had equipped them with bed-springs, or with reading lamps salvaged from jeep headlights. Yet Anzio was a battlefield unique in Europe: there were no safe places, no refuges, no rear echelon. It was with reason that men adopted the hunched shoulders and crouching gait called "The Anzio Amble," for nowhere on the beaches could a soldier escape from "Popcorn Pete," the German pilot who showered the sands with strings of anti-personnel mines, or from the shells of "Anzio Annie," the 280 mm railroad gun that sneaked back inside a tunnel.

Even hospitals, at first sited in tents, moved by degrees to canvas-covered cellars scooped from rock and sand, for the casualties were mounting daily. Major James Ross, of No 14 Casualty Clearing Station, was one of many surgeons swift to recognise the commonest danger-signals: the loud snoring breathing that bespoke a head wound, the legs drawn up in rictus that told of a perforated abdomen, the lung cases who sat bolt upright on their stretchers, coughing and straining. In truth, as Hitler, like a maddened gambler frustrated by a roulette wheel, poured in yet more troops, until in all Italy twenty-three German divisions were confronting twenty-eight Allied, the pressure on other fronts diminished, but at a fearful price. Almost 75,000 casualties – 35,000 fighting men, 40,000 noncombatants – would in time be shipped out of Anzio.

By day, men brooded in their dug-outs for hours, reading and re-reading K-Ration labels to stave off aching boredom. Gunner officers with money to burn organised a daily Anzio Derby, with beetles painted in bright colours jockeying to break out of a six-foot circle; a champion beetle might change hands for more than £7. All were distractions to blot out the heavy cloying fungus smell rising from discarded tins of bully beef, the sight of bodies wrapped in blood-stained bed sacks or ponchos, bound with Signal Corps wire, their throats torn open by scavenging dogs. As General Marshall's stepson, Second Lieutenant Allen Tupper Brown, put it, following a solicitous query from his mother: "There are no *boys* in Italy now."

For every man as the weeks dragged by, the name of the game was survival, and for all ranks the dogface cartoon soldiers, Willie and Joe, drawn by Sergeant Bill Mauldin for *Stars and Stripes* epitomised the basic truths of Anzio: the cold stinging rain, the crab lice, the mindless misery. "Just gimme a coupla aspirin," Mauldin depicted Willie telling a medic. "I already got a Purple Heart." In another, Willie made good a promise: "Joe, yesterday you saved my life, an' I swore I'd pay you back. Here's my last pair of dry socks."

But it was after dark that the Anzio beach-head came alive, in a Walpurgis night of sound: the hiss of shrapnel, the swift searing whine of bullets, the snarl of spandaus, the clatter and scream of cranes working the port, grenades bursting far off "like cactus dahlias". Only at 11 p.m. did both sides settle to dug-out radios to hear the sleepy insidious voice of "Axis Sally," broadcasting from Radio Roma: "What are those smart GIs doing to your English women while you are fighting and getting killed over here? Easy to guess, eh?". Scare tactics would follow: "Heard about Private Fox? Went on patrol and stepped on a shoe mine ... all his guts were blown away." Finally a chuckle, and the pay-off line: "Go easy, boys. There's danger ahead."

Night was also the time when senses grew keener, and the deadly proximity of the enemy became apparent to both sides; only six paces separated some Allied weapon pits from the German trenches. The Hebrew chaplain of the 3rd and 45th (U.S.) Divisions, Morris Kertzer, before holding a Passover *Seder* near the Mussolini Canal first begged the men to eat their *Matzah* quietly. The sound of 500 crunching jaws, he thought, might be all too audible.

Yet in time a wry camaraderie was born of the nearness: both sides recognised that even in a world of teeming rain and tasteless rations certain civilities should prevail. One British subaltern, Lieutenant Charles Newton, maddened by constant hammering as the Germans constructed an outpost, yelled at the pitch of his lungs: "*Ruhe da, wir konnen nicht schlafen!*" (Shut up, we can't sleep!) At once the hammering stopped.

So close were the German positions that the relief of one British platoon might take up to two nights, and this ultimately proved too much for one of Kesselring's officers. In impeccable English he called from his trench: "For God's sake, hurry up with your relief, you've kept me awake for two nights!" And the British duly obliged.

Such was the climate of tolerance in the Anzio stalemate of 1944.

—

On Tuesday 15 February, in an effort to resolve the Anzio-Cassino issue once for all, the Allies stooped to barbarity – one of many to tarnish the reputations of all contenders in this fourth year of war.

Above the Rapido River valley, looming 1700 ft high, was sited perhaps the world's most famous monastery: a vast breath-taking flying buttress of cream-coloured Travertine stone, at one point 220 yards long, its bronzed roof gleaming under the winter sun. Founded by

St Benedict in 529, it had boasted, since the seventeenth century, a beautiful baroque church with gold mosaics, frescoes, and a wonderful door of bronze.

For two generations, how to assault the Cassino massif, dominated by the 6,000 ft Monte Cairo, had been the $64,000 question in Italian military text-books; the sole access was a zig-zag shelf of roadway corkscrewing for five miles along the southern face. Yet until now, no one had ever propounded the solution of Major-General John Cannon, U.S. tactical air commander in Italy: "Given decent weather, I'll whip out Cassino like an old tooth."

This wanton vandalism stemmed from the stubborn – and wholly unjustified – belief of Lieutenant-General Sir Bernard Freyberg, V.C., commanding the New Zealand Corps, that the monastery was a German observation post. General Mark Clark, for one, dissented hotly. "I was never able to discover," he said, "on what (Freyberg) based his opinion."

In truth, as the 80-year-old Lord Bishop and Abbot, Gregorio Diamare, was to assert on 15 February, no German soldier had ever been stationed within the monastery precincts. Prompted by Pope Pius XII, Kesselring, as early as December 1943, had established a 400 yard no-go area around the monastery, enforcing it with a military police guard.

Back in the previous October, further stringent precautions had been taken – this time on the initiative of *Oberstleutnant* Julius Schlegel, chief of the Maintenance Section of the Hermann Göring Panzer Division. Fearing the risk of damage from random shells, Schlegel persuaded the Lord Bishop to collaborate on a wholesale evacuation of the monastery's priceless treasures. Thus, in the weeks that followed, a convoy of 120 German trucks had transported 70,000 priceless volumes, 1,200 original documents, Pompeian vases, Titians, Raphaels, Tintorettos and the *Leda* of Leonardo da Vinci, over the perilous mountain roads to the neutral safety of Vatican City.

On the morning of 12 February, while Mark Clark was absent at Anzio, "Tiny" Freyberg, a ponderous giant of a man, delivered a flat ultimatus to Clark's Chief of Staff, Major-General Alfred Gruenther. Prior to an assault on the ridge by the 4th Indian Division he wanted "the convent" attacked. "You mean the Monastery?" Gruenther queried. "The Monastery is not on the list of targets." Freyberg was unyielding: "In any event, I want it bombed."

Now bitter controversy arose. Not only did Clark oppose the bombing – "an unnecessary psychological mistake in the propaganda field ... a tactical military mistake of the first magnitude" – but Major-General Geoffrey Keyes, U.S. II Corps commander, as well as his subordinates, shared this view.

The problem was that Freyberg was virtually his own man. Responsible only to the New Zealand Government, he was, in effect, an autonomous ally: a general who could not be ordered, even by Clark, his superior, only asked. Further, his demand hid a thinly veiled threat – "any higher commander who refuses to authorise the bombing will have to be prepared to take the responsibility for the failure of the attack."

As commander of all Allied forces in Italy, outranking both Clark and Freyberg, General Sir Harold Alexander was in a quandary. "If Freyberg were an American commander," Mark Clark told him flatly, late on 12 February, "I would refuse to authorise the bombing." And he added a rider: it was highly doubtful that the Germans were in the monastery – "but they will certainly be in the rubble after the bombing ends."

Alexander, a handsome, courteous officer, was, as so often, anxious to effect a compromise. If Freyberg felt it was a military necessity, he must urge – but not order – Clark to authorise it.

At 9:30 a.m. on 15 February, a force of 229 Flying Fortresses – backstopped later by 26 Mitchells – droned towards the mountain, hawk-shadows following the hard and frosty line of Highway Six, which ran straight as a stretched ribbon, from Rome to Naples. As the first of 576 tons of bombs spilled from the bomb-bays, one man recalled "a hollow rumble as of thousands of tons of gravel dropping into a steel barge." Sudden bursts of orange rose above the Monastery's 15-ft thick outer walls; the southern and western slopes flickered with flashes, then the central courtyard collapsed. The great bronze dome vanished, and black smoke whirled 1,500 ft high blotted out all sight of the buildings.

Then – incredibly – nothing happened.

Hours passed – and the Allied infantry, sited far back beyond the bomb-line, failed to move up. Not until nightfall was a piecemeal assault by the 4th Indian Division, piece by piece turned back; the following night, almost thirty-six hours after the first bombardment, the Royal Sussex, after losing 130 men, in turn fell back. The hardy warriors of *Generalleutnant* Richard Heidrich's First German Parachute Division, after taking cover in caves and cellars, now emerged with sighted machine guns trained upon their foes. Allied tanks that followed up to support the infantry found themselves blocked by cataracts of rubble 15 ft high.

Along with a party of 40 survivors, the Lord Bishop pulled out on 17 February, leading a 25-mile refugee trek to Piedimonte, but the legacy of bitterness was incalculable. When the U.S. Chargé d'Affaires to the Vatican, Harold Tittman, pledged American funds to reconstruct the building, the Papal Secretary of State, Cardinal Maglione, replied bitterly: "Even if you rebuild it in gold and diamonds, it still isn't the Monastery."

At dusk on 17 February, advance units of *Generaloberst* Heinrich von Vietinghoff-Scheel's Tenth Army were already setting up posts in the ruins: the lynch-pin of a revised military complex. The road to Rome would remain blocked for many months to come.

It was all too much for Winston Churchill. His plan to "drag the hot rake of war up the length of the Italian peninsula" lay in shreds – and while the Anglo-American force stood hopelessly stalled, the Red Army was lancing towards Europe, poised for the capture of Pskov, the railroad gateway to the Baltic States. Already the total destruction of the German Eighth Army in the Ukraine seemed a certainty.

Late on 29 February, Churchill was to deliver this blistering broadside to Alexander in Caserta, damning the whole Anzio-Cassino débâcle: "We hoped to land a wild cat that would tear out the bowels of the *Boche*. Instead we have stranded a vast whale with its tail flopping about in the water!".

2

"We Are Putting The Whole Works On One Number"
1 March–28 April, 1944

Around noon on the day that Cassino was bombed, a khaki-coloured staff car marked with R.A.F. rondels, slid past the iron gates of Headquarters No 11 Group, Fighter Command, in the market town of Uxbridge, Middlesex. A stocky dark-haired officer descended to return the driver's salute. Squadron Leader Roland Beamont was arriving for a luncheon date with Air Vice-Marshal Hugh "Dingbat" Saunders, the leathery empirical Air Officer Commanding.

At 22, the stubbornly confident Beamont was one of a generation recalling 1914: a youngster who had known no other trade than war. A veteran of the 1940 Battle of France, later of the Battle of Britain, his valour as a Hurricane fighter pilot was known to Britons and Germans alike – attested by the Distinguished Flying Cross awarded in 1941 and later by 10 confirmed victories.

He was a pilot whom Saunders, a shrewd South African, held in deep esteem – and for more reasons than his courage in the air. Beamont's probing mind queried established practices – everything from gunsights to cockpit panel lights – more often than some top brass thought healthy, but this had led to some vital redeployments of the fighter arm. As a night-fighter pilot with No 87 Squadron, Beamont had cavilled at patrols that rarely spotted a German bomber, designed to soothe public morale – "politician patrols," he called them. His quiet nagging soon saw 87 switched to a night intruder role, zooming across the Channel to shoot up German-held airfields.

Always eager to learn more, Beamont, after 800 hours on Hurricanes, had gladly gone to school all over again. As a test pilot with the Hawker Aircraft Company, at nearby Langley, his priorities had been neatly reversed; the company's concern was with the plane, not the pilot. The first reaction of a fighter pilot in trouble was to bale out; a test pilot's job was to stick with the plane until the fault was righted. After a spell commanding 609 (Typhoon) Squadron, Beamont was once more attached to Hawker's – determined to pinpoint a fundamental flaw in the Typhoon's tailplane.

In Saunders' ground-floor office, the two men chatted easily, until out of the blue Saunders asked: "You've been flying the new Tempest at Hawker's. How do you like it?".

Beamont liked it very much. At 420 mph, the Tempest, with its 24-cylinder Napier Sabre engine and four 20 mm Hispano cannon was, as Beamont put it, "the fastest thing there is, I think."

Saunders nodded reflectively. "Good". Then, swiftly: "How do you feel about forming the first Tempest wing?".

Beamont was stunned. "I'd been thinking of asking you for a Tempest *squadron*, sir."

"Fine," Saunders replied equably, "Now you'll have three." But he added one proviso: at first Beamont would have to operate with just two squadrons of Tempests, plus one of Spitfires. Almost too casually, he asked, "What is the range of the Tempest?".

Suddenly Beamont knew in his bones that there was much more to this luncheon invitation than he had ever suspected. "About 500 miles, sir," he replied.

"In that case," said Saunders, crossing the room, "I shall want you within 170 miles of the Seine," and as he spoke he tugged gently at a curtain. It slid aside, and for one subliminal moment Beamont was staring at a relief map of the Bay of the Seine, territory he had time and again crossed on fighter sweeps: the deep indentation of the Orne River and the white needle-point of Ouistreham Lighthouse, the rocky bluffs by Points du Hoc, the harbour at Port-en-Bessin.

"You haven't seen this!" Saunders said drily, "Forget it." Once more the curtain blotted out the view, and Beamont realised that he was now "a very high security risk indeed".

"What do you know," Saunders asked, "about the pilot-less weapons?".

Beamont was hesitant. "Only what I've read in Signals Intelligence, sir." And this, in all conscience, was vague enough. All through 1943, teamwork by the French Resistance network "Agir," under an alert ex-Army officer, Michel Hollard, and the R.A.F.'s Central Interpretation Unit at Medmenham, on the Thames, had identified up to 100 sites, supposedly capable of launching "a cigar-shaped missile with wings".

Attacks by U.S. and British planes had proved disappointing: the ramps were too small to be satisfactory targets, visibility was minimal, the omnipresent flak often lethal. Thus as recently as 14 December, the Deputy Chief of Air Staff had warned: "The launching pads on the sites in the Pas de Calais and in the Somme-Seine area are oriented on London."

"We don't quite know what form they'll take," Saunders admitted now, "but you'll be best placed down *there*." Turning to another map, his pointer indicated four sites in the south-east, two in Sussex, two in Kent: "I'm sorry there are no permanent sites available, but you can take your pick of these." All, Beamont noted, were advanced air strips with metal track runways, laid over farmland.

The newly-promoted Wing Commander Beamont now lost no time. Within days he had chosen Newchurch, on Romney Marsh, once the haunt of derring-do smugglers, as the airfield for his Tempests; typically, of all those on his list, it was the nearest to France. But now a snag arose. Only five Tempests were immediately available.

Beamont rang 11 Group to protest. "I *know* there are more," he said, "at least twenty left Langley last month while I was there."

The Chief Engineering Officer was unhelpful. No doubt the planes were held in storage by the R.A.F.'s Maintenance Command – which might mean at any depot in the West Country.

It was a challenge Beamont relished; sitting behind a desk waiting for things to happen had never been his way. As March dawned he set off on a whirlwind tour, determined to make No 150 Tempest Wing a tangible reality. If Hitler's secret weapons *did* exist, there was surely no time to lose.

–

One man had no doubt that the secret weapons existed. In his first-floor study at Villa Orsoline, on Lake Garda, where two porcelain stoves kept the temperature sweltering in the eighties, Benito Mussolini was still hard put to it to suppress an involuntary shiver. For five months now, ever since Hitler had contrived his dramatic mountain-top rescue, fear of those weapons had governed every decision *Il Duce* had made.

The creation of the puppet Salò Republic, for one. When he and Hitler had conferred on 14 September, 1943, in the bright airy Tea House at Rastenberg, the Führer had heaped bitter reproaches on his head. "What is this Fascism," he asked with irony, "that it melts like snow under the sun?". Mussolini had listened in silence, hoping that the diatribe would soon end.

Then, with unusual brevity, Hitler had come sharply to the point. "We cannot lose a single day," he said energetically. "It is essential that by tomorrow evening you make a radio announcement that the monarchy is abolished and that an Italian Fascist State with powers centred upon you has taken its place."

When Mussolini gestured feebly – he would need a few days in which to reflect – Hitler's voice, rising sharply, cut him short, "*I* have already reflected – and enough. You'll proclaim yourself Duce once again."

And Hitler had stipulated other ruthless conditions. Most of the 28-strong Grand Council who deposed Mussolini on 25 July, 1943, knowing the war to be lost, had fled from Italy. But five men[7] had been seized by loyal Fascists, and a sixth – Mussolini's own son-in-law, the former Foreign Minister, Count Galeazzo Ciano – was held by the Germans.

"I am returning him to you," Hitler told his appalled junior partner, "because it is preferable that the death sentence should be carried out in Italy." Mussolini had protested vigorously. "This is the husband of Edda, whom I adore, this is the father of my grandchildren," was his shocked reaction. Then, Hitler replied implacably, Ciano deserved punishment all the more – "not only because he betrayed his country, but also his family". Almost pityingly he added: "Duce, you are too good – you can never be a dictator."

Typically, Mussolini sought to duck responsibility. He no longer, he told Hitler, had any personal ambitions. Fascism was beyond all mortal aid. He could not assume responsibility for unleashing a civil war. With near-clairvoyant vision he divined what the future held in store: one "Category A" military telephone line, by courtesy of the Germans, an SS bodyguard dogging him day and night, the cruel neurotic Marshal Rodolfo Graziani, "The Butcher of Libya," thrust on him as Minister of Defence; for his Party Secretary, Alessandro Pavolini, a gutter Robespierre whose repressive Black Brigades drove thousands into the partisan camp.

Hitler was barely listening. "I must be very clear," he said, when Mussolini fell silent. "If the Western allies had been able to exploit it, the Italian betrayal might have brought about an instant collapse of Germany. My intention was at once to give a terrible example of punishment in order to intimidate our other allies."

On that note of suspense, abruptly, at 4 p.m., he broke off the talks.

Was Hitler bluffing? At 9:15 a.m. on 8 January — a day of paralysing cold — as nine black-robed judges filed into Verona's moated Castelvecchio, it seemed to the six accused men huddled in the well of the court that he was in grim earnest. But when the hatchet-faced Ernst Kaltenbrunner, head of the Reich Security Service, ventured that the Führer was virtually condemning Giano to death, Hitler only laughed harshly. "My dear Kaltenbrunner," he retorted, "Mussolini will never permit the father of his beloved grandchildren to be put to death. It's all just a bit of thundering Italian bluff."

But Hitler had reckoned without a cadre of old-guard Fascists led by Verona's Prefect, Pietro Cosmin, an ex-naval officer stricken with lung cancer, and Major Nicola Furlotti, the Federal Police commandant. Both men were resolved on one thing: to demonstrate that the Salò Republic meant business, the six gentlemen of Verona must die. If Ciano was acquitted, Mussolini notwithstanding, he would perish at Furlotti's hands in the prison van taking him from Castelvecchio to Verona Gaol.

The stratagem proved unnecessary. Although Tullio Cianetti was narrowly acquitted, having changed his Grand Council vote at the last moment, five others, including Ciano, died before a firing squad in Verona's Forte San Procolo at 9:20 a.m. on 11 January. In the small hours of that morning, their plea for clemency addressed to *Il Duce* had been skilfully blocked by Cosmin.

It was, in any case, a fate that Mussolini had been powerless to avert. Looking back over five months of puppet government, he still recalled how at 11 a.m. on 15 September he had returned to the Führer's Tea House. There, in harsh spare syllables, Hitler spelt out the fate that awaited Northern Italy if Mussolini withheld his consent.

Harking back to his revelation of a Reprisals Air Fleet in July, he defined them as "devilish arms," designed for the destruction of London. Clenching his right hand slowly into a fist, Hitler all at once snapped wide his fingers to symbolise this reign of terror. "It is up to you," he challenged Mussolini, "to decide whether these weapons

... are to be used on London, or tried out first on Milan, Genoa or Turin."

Never once, the Duce maintained, did Hitler allow him any other choice. It was a punitive plan in embryo – due to be carried out the very hour Mussolini disappointed his longtime friend. "Northern Italy will envy the fate of Poland if you do not agree to honour the alliance," Hitler wound up.

Thus, some time before noon on that day, Mussolini told the Führer: "I'll take in hand the direction of Italian affairs in that part of the country which has not yet been invaded."

The annihilation of London, he supposed, could only be weeks away – yet at least, in one last attempt to bolster his crippled self-esteem, he had "created a shield for the protection of Italy."

There was a time, his aides acknowledged, when Adolf Hitler had walked taller. The Führer who, on 23 February, left the Wolf's Lair for Berchtesgaden, his chalet-style retreat perched high in the Obersalzberg, was a tired broken man, his eyes glazed and reproachful, his left hand at times trembling uncontrollably. When his mistress, Eva Braun, commented on his stooping walk, Hitler came up with alibis – "It's the heavy keys I'm carrying in my trousers pockets" or "It's so I suit you better – you wear high heels."

Sometimes, unguardedly, he came closer to the truth: "That's because of the burden of worries I'm carrying all the time." Secret worries, even more than secret weapons, loomed largest in Hitler's mind.

Despite all contrary evidence, he still clung to the belief that Russia's strength was waning. It was the back-sliding satellites that plagued Hitler above all, and with reason. On 13 March, the first envoy extraordinary, Prince Barbu Stirbey of Rumania, a 70-year-old roué and longtime lover of the late Queen Marie, furtively boarded the Taurus Express in Ankara, Turkey. As the train rolled through the moonlit mountains, the Prince remained locked in his *wagon-lit*, a small red dispatch case chained to his wrist. At the Levantine frontier, control officers who saw his British *laisser-passer* moved hastily on. Prince Stirbey was en route to Cairo, for special talks with Allied diplomats.

The starred item on his agenda was a coup: granted favourable peace terms, the National Peasant Party's Juliu Maniu would undertake to topple Hitler's favourite Balkan dictator, General Antonescu. In Cairo, and later in London, the inconclusive chaffering was to drag on for months – complicated by Stirbey's insistence that an Allied airborne division should swoop on the capital, Bucharest, on the day of the rising.

In this same week, other peace feelers were in the air. In Helsinki's handsome granite Diet Hall, 200 Finnish forefingers pressed their electric voting buttons and rejected, by 160 to 40 votes, Russia's armistice terms. Yet the onetime Minister to Sweden, Juho Kusti Paasikivi, still had hopes of reaching a settlement with Sweden's Russian Ambassador, the urbane Madame Alexandra Kollontay – whose demands were known to include the internment of German troops.

When word came that Hungary, too, was wavering, the alarm signals at Berchtesgaden rang loud and clear. On 7 March, the Red Army was barely 100 miles from Hungary's border, and Hungary's oil, bauxite and manganese were vital to Germany's war effort. Hitler decided to act.

On 15 March, a curt invitation went to the Regent, Admiral Nicholas Horthy, to join Hitler at Schloss Klessheim, near Salzburg, on Saturday 18 March.

Horthy didn't like it. The journey would entail leaving on a Friday; as an old sailor he had always sweated out Friday, waiting for eight bells to herald a new day. In the end, against the advice of his Premier, Nicholas Kállay, he decided to go, along with the Chief of the General Staff, the Foreign Minister and the Minister for War. Beset by a premonition, Horthy, at the last moment, packed his revolver, twice slipping it into his pocket then twice removing it, on the journey. In the end, indecisive to the last, he left it in the compartment.

No witness was present at the stormy meeting which ensued in Hitler's study; Horthy, whose German was fluent, had no need of Interpreter Paul Schmidt. As Horthy later recalled it, Hitler was brutally clear from the outset: since Hungary was contemplating a change of front, he must take "precautionary measures" to guard against another Italian-style "betrayal".

Now tempers flared hotly. Both men pounded the table. "If by that phrase you mean military measures," Horthy shouted, "or in other words the occupation of an independent and sovereign state ... that would be an unspeakable crime."

Then, as Hitler grew progressively more excited, Horthy cut in: "If everything has been decided upon already, there is no point in protracting this discussion. I am leaving."

In the hall of the great castle, Paul Schmidt, chatting to some colleagues, beheld an unlooked-for sight; as the door of the conference room flew open, the aged Horthy, red as a turkey's wattles, came rushing out, taking the stairs to his private suite two at a time. In his wake ran an angry Hitler, shouting unintelligibly. With an innate sense of diplomacy, the tall lean *chef de protocole*, Freiherr von Dörnberg, blocked the path of the runaway Regent until Hitler could catch up. Wrangling heatedly, the two men disappeared towards Horthy's suite.

It was a strange charade that followed. As Schmidt recalled it, the castle suddenly became "as active as a disturbed beehive"; no sooner had Horthy shouted for his private train than an air-raid siren wailed and a smoke screen simulating a mass bombing attack blanketed the castle. The telephone line to Budapest was reported "badly hit," cutting Horthy off from the outside world. Unaware that this was a Hitlerian ruse to prolong the discussion, Horthy grudgingly assented to join a silent luncheon party where Hitler picked nervously at his buttered vegetables.

All that Saturday afternoon, the play-acting continued. At one stage, Hitler even summoned *Generalfeldmarschall* Wilhelm Keitel, the haughty handsome Chief of the Armed Forces, to ask whether the occupation could not be countermanded. Too late, Keitel replied, the troops were on the march. Hearing this, Foreign Minister Eugene Ghyczy sent a telegram to his deputy in Budapest: "Tell my wife I am well" – meaning "The Germans are coming".

Viewing the proceedings with a jaundiced eye was *General der Artillerie* Walter Warlimont, Deputy Chief of Hitler's Operations Staff. As with Anzio, so now with Hungary, a Replacement Army would bleed the Western front of fully eleven divisions.

In the end, as Hitler had known he must, Horthy gave in. He agreed to replace the peace-oriented "unreliable government" of Nicholas Kállay with a new administration under General Döme Sztójay, his ambassador in Berlin. But Horthy, like Mussolini on Lake Garda, believed he had averted greater evils. A German occupation was preferable to one by Slovaks and Rumanians – a course which Hitler had favoured but which the SD, the SS Security Service, had condemned as provocative. And with the Hungarian Army still under

Horthy's orders, the fanatic Nazi-oriented Arrow-Cross Party could not gain power.

Towards 8 a.m. on Sunday 19 March, Kállay, who later took refuge in the Turkish Embassy, met Horthy's train at Kelenföld Station, outside the city. The Regent, he recalled, was "deathly pale," and understandably; flanking him as closely as warders at a trial were General Edmund Weesenmayer, the new German Minister to Budapest, and the new Premier, General Sztójay. Drawn up on the platform was a German honour guard under *Generaloberst* Maximilian von Weichs, head of the Balkan Army Group.

Already the take-over was accomplished fact. Across the Franz Josef Bridge and along Andrássy-utca, the Wehrmacht phalanxes in field-grey goose-stepped triumphantly, swastikas flying, bands playing – through a city as silent as Troy. The crowds lining the pavements made no move and gave no sign; only sullen disbelief was mirrored in their faces. No handkerchiefs were waved, no cheers sounded, not one hat was tossed into the air.

All they could hope for now was a Russian "liberation".

–

The rape of Hungary passed the sentence of death on one community above all: the country's 800,000 Jews.

At Marmaros Sziget, Transylvani – a Rumanian province Hitler had awarded to Hungary in 1940 – Dr Gisella Krausz was one of many who saw the unimaginable future taking shape overnight. A dark intense gynaecologist, in her late thirties, Gisella and her husband Francis were deeply respected figures in the little town, 240 miles east of Budapest; since many doctors were serving with labour battalions, their sanatorium at 43, John Mihalyi Street had been inundated with patients. Yet somehow Gisella Krausz had always made time for the more gracious aspects of life: her tasteful green salon was noted for its musical evenings, when Gisella recited poems by Heine and Lessing and her son, 17-year-old Emeric, a keen amateur musician, played Hubay's "Violinist from Cremona".

It was a strictly orthodox Jewish life, with fasts observed on all the Holy Days, when the salon trembled in the wavering light of the Hanukka candles, following the tradition of the ancient Macca-bees. A self-confessed homebody, Gisella found time, too, to work alongside her young housekeeper, Elizabeth, bottling jams and jellies and preserves.

On 20 March, 1944, this gracious leisurely existence was shattered like a crystal vase.

Arbitrary orders and *diktats* multiplied. All Jews must sew a yellow Star of David, the size of a side-plate, on their clothing. A curfew was clamped down; travel was prohibited. Gestapo men swarmed through the house, wrenching open closets and wardrobes, demanding gold and silver, looting any item they fancied – "unmindful of our presence as though we were already dead".

The trek to the ghetto was the next stage of Gisella Krausz diaspora.

At the far end of Marmaros Sziget, one of a row of tumble-down shacks lining a narrow muddy street became the Krauszs' new home, along with Gisella's parents, Maurice and Fanny Perl, her three brothers, Herman, Alexander and David, and her sister Cecilia. Great possessions now scaled down to a skimpy bundle of bare necessities: toothbrushes, combs, underwear. Yet when the Gestapo ordered Gisella to establish a hospital and maternity ward in the ghetto, she was transformed. Hurrying from shack to shack, begging for cotton wool, a towel here, a sheet there, she told herself that a hospital spelt hope. Within days a small apartment had been transformed into a clean white ward.

"Why should they tell us to organise a hospital," she reasoned with Francis and Emeric, "if they intend to deport us? Maybe they intend to keep us here in the ghetto until the war is over."

Both of them agreed. The hospital was an earnest for all their futures.

Two weeks later, a wholesale deportation order for the entire ghetto arrived from Berlin.

From that moment on, time was no more than a blur for Gisella Krausz. Herded to the railway station, she and her entire family were packed into cattle cars crammed with almost one hundred people per car. For eight days they travelled by day and by night towards an unknown goal. At the Polish frontier, when black-clad SS guards took over the train, they knew there was no hope – but neither was there any longer food or water. The children whimpered with cold and hunger; some men went insane; women gave birth on the wooden floor, among the brimming buckets of excrement.

On the eighth day, the train ground to a halt. The sealed doors slid open, and to harsh cries of *"Raus! Schnell!"* the prisoners piled out. Beyond a sign that read ARBEIT MACH FREI (Work Brings Freedom) lay an unforgettable sight: a vista of manicured lawns and trim flower-beds that abruptly gave way to an infinity of barracks covered with green tar paper, where watch towers loomed every forty yards above barbed wire fences. Wasted figures in zebra-striped burlap by degrees became visible. But all this paled beside the spectacle of five giant chimneys, topped with sharp red gouts of flame, trailing at first into grey ribbons of smoke which gathered slowly into a black and ominous cloud. A thick nauseous smell like burning goose fat hung over the compound.

Then a name was whispered from cattle car to cattle car, and the name was AUSCHWITZ.

—

Dr Gisella Krausz could hardly know it, but even now deliverance was possible – if the Allies would pay the price.

In the week before she arrived at Auschwitz, two men met over coffee at 8 a.m. in the Opera Café, on Budapest's Andrássy-utca. Jószi Winniger, a German *Abwehr* agent, who extended a helping hand to Jews if the price was right, had news that left his companion, Joel Brand, gasping: "Matters are reaching a critical stage. Today you have to go and meet Eichmann. You know who Eichmann is?".

This morning, 25 April, Joel Brand was celebrating his thirty-eighth birthday – and a meeting with Eichmann was hardly the present he would have chosen. *Obersturmbannführer* (S.S. Lieutenant-Colonel) Adolf Eichmann, head of Department IVb of the Reich Security Office, was the man entrusted by *Reichsführer* Heinrich Himmler, the mild-mannered ex-chicken farmer who headed the Gestapo and SS, with the liquidation of the European Jews. Since 1941, using the interlocking disposal methods of the gas chamber and the cremat-orium, Eichmann's "industrial genocide" had reportedly wiped out five million Jews.

At first glance, Joel Brand markedly lacked the steel of an Eich-mann. Stocky and red-haired, an immoderate drinker, he had lived as a rolling stone all over the United States – shovelling snow in New York, washing dishes in Cincinnati, finally signing on as a seaman. Rarely settling in one job for long, he had drifted back to Germany to work for his father's telephone company before opening a Budapest weaving shop with his wife, Hansi. Yet as a leader of the *Waada* (a quasi-illegal Hungarian Jewish relief and rescue organisation) he was the man whom Eichmann had summoned — and thus the man who would sound Eichmann out.

Once, the *Waada* knew, Eichmann had favoured a wholesale Jewish emigration to Madagascar: had he now, with the Red Army sweeping west, seen the writing on the wall? Was he trying to seek a general amnesty for himself and his friends?

At 9 a.m. Brand, still rooted with trembling knees to his chair in the Opera Café, saw a black Mercedes jerk to a halt on the opposite side of the street. It was the signal he had been told to await. An SS sergeant sprang out: "You are Herr Brand? Please get into the car."

In a ground floor room at the Hotel Majestic on Karthauzi-utca Brand now had his first sight of Adolf Eichmann: a slim anonymous forty-year-old in a well-cut uniform, "who might have been a clerk in an office". Two features only were unusual: the hard steely blue eyes and a voice like the clatter of a machine gun, rapping out a few words before pausing abruptly.

It was in this unnerving and staccato manner that Eichmann opened the interviews: "I expect you know who I am. I was in charge of the 'Actions' in Germany and Poland and Czechoslovakia. Now it is Hungary's turn…"

Brand was prepared for all this — but not for what followed. "I have got you here so we can talk business … I have verified your ability to make a deal … I am prepared to sell you one million Jews. Not the whole lot — you wouldn't be able to raise enough for that. But you could manage a million. Blood for money — cash for blood."

As if hypnotised, Brand still stood there. The voice was hammering on: "You can take them from any country you like … Hungary, Poland, from Auschwitz, wherever you like. Who do you want to save? Men capable of procreation? Women who can bear children? Old people? Children?

"Sit down, Herr Brand, and tell me."

—

Long before the Prime Minister's speaking time, the House of Commons was packed and restive. Not in five months had British

M.P.s heard from the man who more than any other could cast events in "scale, structure and proportion." Now, on his red leather bench, Churchill shuffled his notes, twice rising in a false start before the Speaker gave him the sign. Then, for one hour and eighteen minutes, Churchill reported to the nation. It was just after 2 p.m. on 22 February, 1944.

The Premier's broad canvas was torn and tattered Europe – and on the face of it, the only certainty he had to offer was the vast uncertainty. Yet perceptive listeners were not slow to detect a new trend. A reluctant convert to the *realpolitik* forced on him by Tehran and the Red Army's advance, Churchill was now prepared to accept the price of Communist partisans that victory would exact.

This was a giant step for a man who had once congratulated Mussolini's Fascists on their "struggle against the bestial appetites of Leninism". A prominent figure in this day's peroration was "an outstanding leader, glorious in the fight for freedom," Josip Broz Tito, a Communist whose Anti-Fascist Council had in November 1943, proclaimed him President, Secretary of Defence and Marshal of the Partisan Army at one stroke. Holed up in a mountain cave lined with red parachute silk near Drvar – "more like the *nid d'amour* of a luxurious courtesan than the office of a guerilla leader," reported Churchill's son, Randolph – the 51-year-old Tito now changed his Marshal's uniform four times a day, worked on his tan with a sun lamp and practised his signature for hours on end.

Yet one truth was plain. The Ćetnik leader, General Draža Mihailović, whom the British had backed since 1941 and were now to disown, had sought accommodation with the Axis. Tito's partisans, living on bread crusts soaked in bacon fat, often without boots, socks or topcoats, were tying down 360,000 German troops.

The decision to back Tito had been taken in full knowledge of the facts. Back in 1943, Brigadier Fitzroy Maclean, of Britain's clandestine Special Operations Executive, had parachuted to meet Tito in the field and then reported to Churchill: any post-war system that Tito created would be on Soviet lines. "Do you intend," Churchill asked bluntly, "to make Yugoslavia your home after the war?". When Maclean replied no, Churchill responded, "Neither do I. And, that being so, the less you and I worry about the form of Government they set up the better."

Thus, 1944 would see 9,000 tons of supplies air-dropped to Tito, in addition to seaborne cargoes – prompting one disgruntled Scottish

M.P., to charge: "The Prime Minister has, in my estimation, now become Stalin's Charlie McCarthy[8]."

Only one factor marred this rosy picture: the imminent arrival, in Suite 324–326, at Claridge's Hotel, London, of the exiled King Peter II of Yugoslavia, a brash and dapper 20-year-old. As a devout monarchist, Churchill had backed Peter to the hilt – yet the disgraced Mihailović had functioned as Peter's Minister of War in the field. Now Churchill nourished two hopes: that Peter would dismiss him and form a new government and that Tito would acknowledge Peter's constitutional sovereignty.

"If I judge the boy aright," Churchill wrote emotionally to Tito, "he has no dearer wish than to stand at the side of all those Yugoslavs who are fighting the common foe." Tito's reply was cautious. As a qualified pilot, Peter's best hope might be to join a partisan squadron forming under R.A.F. auspices – but only the Anti-Fascist Council could pronounce on his return to Yugoslavia.

An almost identical problem loomed in Greece, where the National Liberation Front (EAM) had spawned a Greek Popular Liberation Army (ELAS) of 20,000 men – in deadly rivalry to the National Republican Greek League (EDES) 5,000 strong under the monarchist Colonel Napoleon Zervas. Only once – in October 1941 – had the two armies ever co-ordinated an attack against the Germans; even SOE officers in the field deemed the Communist ELAS "95% cowardly, unwilling or inefficient." No man opposed ELAS more hotly than Churchill – "there seems to be no limit to (their) baseness and treachery" – yet in March arms supplies were resumed all over again, for in all occupied Europe short-term military expediency was to triumph over long-term political interests.

The Greek dilemma was heightened by another intermittent resident of Claridge's, King George II of the Hellenes, who retained a comfortable office-suite, Rooms 111–112. Exiled from 1923–1935, and again since 1941, the short (5ft 2ins) stiff-backed King was something of an anachronism, a man so wedded to white tie and tails that diners-out once mistook him for Claridge's head waiter. Known to his subjects as *O Aghelastos* (He who does not laugh) he was, in fact, the grandson of a nineteenth-century Danish prince, George, appointed as King by the Big Three of the day (Britain, France and Russia); predictably, he commanded no loyalties, for George of Schleswig-Holstein-Sonderburg-Glücksburg had no drop of Greek blood in his veins.

Opposition to the King's return was the strongest popular weapon that EAM/ELAS wielded, and though Churchill backed King George as fervently as he backed King Peter, observers in Cairo counselled caution: once Greece was liberated, a plebiscite should decide the King's fate.

In the fractious two-day debate that followed Churchill's summing-up, another group of displaced persons loomed large on the agenda: the Polish Government in Exile. For Churchill, a settlement of the Polish question was "a touchstone of Anglo-Soviet relations," for in 1939, when Germany had attacked Poland, all Britain could do, after guaranteeing Poland's security, was to declare war and stand helplessly by. Yet every attempt to resolve the Polish issue had resulted in impasse.

From their roomy headquarters in Kensington Palace Gardens, the twelve-man Cabinet, under the affable diffident Premier Stanislaw Mikolajczyk, stood fast on one issue: a total restoration of Poland's borders as they had been before Germany and Russia, as quondam allies, had divided the country in 1939. In Moscow, Josef Stalin and his Foreign Minister, Vyacheslav Molotov, stood as firmly on another demarcation point: the Curzon Line, an armistice boundary between Poland and Russia set up in 1920, named after the British Foreign Secretary, Lord Curzon.

The Poles' indignation was understandable: the line, which had run some 200 miles from the Western Dvina River, on the Latvian border, to just north-west of Minsk had never been acceptable to them. Resuming the war with renewed ferocity, they had dictated a peace at Riga in 1921 which won another 40,000 square miles of territory.

What irked the Poles still further was a curt demand from Moscow that they purge the more violently anti-Soviet members of their government – notably the die-hard General Kasimierz Sosnkowski, commander of all Polish forces. In vain, Churchill and Foreign Secretary Anthony Eden laboured to draft soft Polish answers that would assuage Red wrath. For Poland to refer publicly to "losing half her territory and more than 11 million of her population" was "very unfortunate". A Polish opposition paper that constantly attacked Russia had its newsprint supply cut off. For with each passing week, Russia's sickle developed a sharper cutting edge – "the *émigré* Polish Government not infrequently displays its imperialist pro-Fascist tendencies in its policies," ran one barbed statement.

Sympathisers were not lacking. "The real choice before us," Sir Owen O'Malley, Ambassador to the London Poles, minuted Eden, "seems to me, to put it brutally, to lie between on the one hand selling the corpse of Poland to Russia and finding an alibi to be used in evidence when we are indicted for abetting a murder and, on the other hand, putting the points of principle to Stalin in the clearest possible way…" One M.P., Major Duncan McCallum, wrote in similar vein: unless Stalin fell in line with the rest of the Allied nations, "the latter will have to reconsider the whole question of Lend-Lease supplies". In the margin, Eden scrawled peevishly in red ink: "Curiously enough we still want to defeat Germany".

On 10 January – and again on 20 January and 2 February – Churchill had laboured to impart the harsh facts of life to Mikolajczyk and his Ambassador, Count Edward Raczynski. On 4 January, he hammered home, the Red Army had already crossed the old Polish frontier and taken Rokitno. Only Russia could liberate Poland; militarily, the British could do nothing at all. "Great Britain," Churchill told the Poles bluntly, "will not go to war to defend Poland's eastern frontier".

Mikolajczyk was unmoved. With impeccable foresight, he charged that the Russians sought "not to revise their border but to Communise the (Polish) nation". On the question of their eastern frontier, the Poles would not yield. "In that case," Churchill lashed back, "the situation is hopeless. No agreement could be reached on such a basis, and the Soviets having occupied the whole of your country will impose their will."

On 24 February, 600 M.P.s learned for the first time what the London Poles had suspected for weeks: all Churchill's labour had been labour lost. In Russia, a Soviet-sponsored Polish National Council stood ready to make full-fledged claims for all Poland. In the bitter world of power politics, Britain would cross Russia no further. That high-minded gesture of 1939 belonged to history.

–

Hands clasped behind her head, Lily Sergueiev stretched out on the cherry-red silk counterpane, gazing with unseeing eyes at the gilded ceiling. Certainly, Room No 61 at the five-star Avenida Palace Hotel, on Lisbon's bustling Rua 1° de Dezembro was the last word in civilised comfort – a far cry from the hated Rugby Mansions. But her contentment ended abruptly there. Which organisation, she wondered, took the palm for crass inefficiency – Britain's M.I.5. or Germany's *Abwehr*?

At best, Lily knew, her cover-story had been painfully thin. Through influential friends, the story ran, she had obtained a job with Sidney (later Lord) Bernstein in the Ministry of Information's cinematographic department. Since the MOI was planning documentary films to be shown in the first countries liberated after D-Day, Lily was in Lisbon to contact refugee French and Belgian film producers – men who could inject a note of stark realism into the scripts.

Beyond that – virtually nothing. Bernstein, her radio officer, Ronnie Reid, had told her, was "tall, quite young, with a broken nose and good teeth ... nearly always wears tweeds". But Lily had never met Bernstein, and her sole glimpse of the Ministry, lodged in the University of London, was when Mary Ward drove her past it in a staff car. The basement canteen, Mary said, trying to be helpful, did tea and scones and a dish of eggs for 1s 6d.

Much worse was to follow. On 3 March, Lily had arrived in Lisbon, to check with M.I.5.'s Captain Barratt at the British Consulate. Her next port of call was the Embassy's Press Section, on the Rua San Domingo, to present a War Office letter of introduction to the Attaché, Michael Stewart.

After reciting her cover story, Lily asked him, "How does that sound?".

"It would be perfect," Stewart replied blandly, "if our director of cinematographic propaganda didn't happen to be in London just now."

Lily was beside herself. "Oh, hell! A thousand hells! There's my alibi gone!". Surely, she fumed, Robertson, Reid – *somebody* – could have had the native wit to check that her cover was foolproof.

So where, Lily pondered, did she go from here?

By degrees she devised a plan. The MOI had slipped up: French refugees no longer came to Portugal but were routed to North Africa via Gibraltar (which was true). Therefore Stewart must – ostensibly – write to his counterpart in Madrid, and any trip that Lily made to Spain would have to be authorised by London. All these supposed letters would take time – and time was what Lily needed, to somehow spirit Major Kliemann and that vital transmitter to Lisbon.

So next she must take up the *Abwehr* contact that Kliemann had given her: Herr Rudolf Morgener, located on the third floor of No 9,

Rua Antonia Augusto de Aguilar. Morgener, a tall rugged man with brown crinkly hair, was less than receptive.

"Who are you?"

"Does 'Solange' mean anything to you?" It was the name with which Lily signed all her letters and messages.

"No."

"Do you know 'Octave'?" All those letters and messages were routed to "Octave".

"Never heard of him."

"Kliemann?"

"No."

With a sense of black frustration, Lily spelt it out. "All right, I suppose nobody has bothered to let you know. There it is. Now this is what I would like you to do. I am 'Solange'. I work for somebody called Kliemann. I come from London. He is in Paris. He must come at once. He ought to be here already."

This was true, for through M.I.5. Lily had sent Kliemann a coded letter imploring him to stand by for a rush trip to Lisbon, bringing a transmitter.

Morgener stared at her, saying nothing. Finally he muttered, "I haven't the slightest idea what you are talking about ... If you will be on the Praça Pombal tonight at 9 p.m., behind the statue, I might enquire in the meantime and perhaps give you an answer..."

That afternoon Lily rested, silently reviewing the shortcomings of both her employers, before dining early in the hotel restaurant. Then, retiring to her room, she took off her black silk dress, slipping on a brown pullover and a tweed skirt. The Praça Pombal, a wide palm-fringed square with a children's sandpit, better known as the Rotunda, was within walking distance.

At this hour the square was in darkness. Even the statue of the Marques da Pombal, creator of modern Lisbon, was swallowed up into the blackness of the sky. Circling its base, Lily was painfully conscious of the grating sound of her own footfalls; between the serried ranks of the palm trees, nothing moved, a desert of whispering shadows. The luminous dial of her watch showed 9 p.m.

The car shot very fast from a side street, with a scream of cornering tyres, its headlights dimmed to a pinpoint glow, passing so close to the pavement that it almost grazed her. Then the brakes slammed on and the lights cut out; a door flew open, a hand wrenched at her arm, dragging her bodily inside onto the back seat. The car jerked forward, and nobody said a word.

Two men, but she could not distinguish either of their faces. At last the man beside her spoke in German: "Which language do you want to speak in?".

"English or French."

"English then. What do you want?"

Lily repeated the gist of what she had told Morgener that morning – only later realising that Morgener was the driver. "Solange is in Lisbon. She must see Octave at once. He *must* bring the suitcase."

"All right. The message will leave tonight. Is that all?"

It was far from all. With all the vehemence at her command, Lily spat out her fury against the dilatory Kliemann. "To have a man like that in the service is a disaster! I don't risk my neck for someone who doesn't give a damn. Two weeks ago, I gave him a rendezvous in Lisbon, *and he is not here!*"

Suddenly, she became aware of an incredible almost ludicrous coincidence! The man sitting beside her was an old acquaintance: Captain Bücking, of the German Merchant Marine, one time master of the tramp steamer, *Adel Traber*, outward bound from Hamburg. Years ago, in her roving foot-loose life, Lily, returning from Latvia, had been his only passenger on a six-day voyage from Danzig to Rouen.

"You! Good gracious! I would never have thought it possible!" Bücking exclaimed, squeezing her hands affectionately, and Lily knew a small glow of triumph: this chance contact from the past would do as much to establish her *bona-fide* as anything could. "They wouldn't take me back in the Navy," Bücking explained, "too old. So I got into Intelligence."

At 9:55 p.m. the car halted again on the Praça Pombal. Once he had contacted Kliemann, Bücking promised, he would ring the hotel with a coded message: Lily's aunt had come, or was coming, and was in good health.

Back at the Avenida Palace, Lily laughed softly as she undressed, folding away her well-worn sweater and old skirt. It was all coming right now, but it had seemed well to be practical; she had worn those clothes tonight quite deliberately.

It would have been a pity, after all, to have a new black dress scored with bullet holes or torn with a knife.

Lily's "aunt" arrived finally at 5 p.m. on Sunday 19 March, dressed in a neat dark-blue suit and felt hat, striding beside Captain Bücking across the Praça Pombal. He apologised to Lily that he had been ill, but otherwise gave no details.

In the days preceding his arrival, Lily had wasted no time. In Bücking's tiny bachelor quarters, in a run-down apartment house of creaking staircases and blocked drains, she had undergone a course in ciphering under a German radio officer named Hoppe, a pale thin-faced twenty-three-year old who opened each session with a curt "Heil Hitler!".

It was in this apartment that Lily and Kliemann conferred on that Sunday evening, after negotiating stairs littered with orange peel and dirty paper. Though he looked older and worn, Kliemann still probed for details; the rent of Lily's mythical flat in Old Brompton Road, what she paid for lunch at the MOI, how she had acquired her Skyrider radio, trading it for jewellery with a U.S. airman.

Lily had even hit on a ruse for smuggling the transmitter back to England. It would pass for a second-hand radio, and to help her dodge Customs duty Michael Stewart would send it to London in the diplomatic bag.

"You are very clever," Kliemann remarked thoughtfully, "very, very clever."

Next day, in Bücking's apartment, the long awaited transmitter was a sore disappointment: a cheap, old-fashioned converted American radio which Lily wouldn't have accepted as a gift. Carefully Hoppe showed her how to dismantle and re-assemble it, to memorise the five crystals hidden in a dummy valve, each of them corresponding to a different frequency.

To take back a keyboard would be too risky, but Hoppe explained how Lily could construct her own, using a small wooden board pierced with a nail anchored to two wires of an electric light flex.

Once more Kliemann stressed the urgency of reporting any build-up of troops between Bristol and Salisbury Plain. "I don't think that any woman has ever had the same opportunity to alter the course of history," he said with great emphasis.

Only one question remained before Lily returned to London: the £1,500 in expenses which Kliemann had promised her. On 23 March, lunching in a restaurant by the Tagus River, he whispered confidentially, "It's for you". Puzzled, Lily saw that on the chair beside him he had deposited a bulky package the size of two shoe boxes.

"You're joking?" she said incredulously.

"No. You find it a bit bulky?"

"*A bit!* I'll say. How much is there?"

Kliemann was sheepish. "£1,500... in one pound notes."

"I'll carry it under my arm," Lily said gaily, and when Kliemann protested, "You don't expect me to hide it in my brassiere, do you?"

At the last moment, speeding four agents to banks all over Lisbon, Kliemann contrived to change it into £500 worth of ten-pound notes, the balance made up with Portuguese escudos and a diamond bracelet.

But at least, as she boarded the plane, Lily knew the answer to the question she had asked herself three weeks earlier. When it came to sheer mindless inefficiency, the *Abwehr* beat M.I.5. hands down.

—

Spring had come to Washington D.C., wet and cool, like a swimmer fresh from the sea; in Rock Creek Park, early morning horseback riders sniffed the air appreciatively, and pink clouds of cherry blossom engulfed the capital's Tidal Basin. Only in the White House was there no sense of a world reborn. A small group of Roosevelt intimates – his daughter, Anna Boettiger, his negro valet, Arthur Prettyman, his secretary, Grace Tully – shared an unspoken secret. All was far from well with the President.

Even in the morning hours he seemed woefully lethargic; since Tehran, he had complained of headaches each evening. Once he blacked out halfway through signing a letter, leaving a long spidery scrawl. Ever since Pearl Harbor, his blood pressure had risen steadily; even a year earlier he had asked Grace Tully to buy a coffee cup twice as big as his normal one, so that his trembling hands could raise it to his lips without spilling.

The White House physician, Admiral Ross T. McIntire, an ear, nose and throat specialist, was concerned, too – yet strangely reluctant to raise the issue with the President. Worried, Anna Boettiger talked him into consulting her mother, Eleanor Roosevelt. Finally, at 11 a.m. on 27 March, Roosevelt was driven to the United States Naval Hospital at Bethesda, Maryland, for a long overdue check-up.

It was an eleventh-hour decision; the man assigned to the case, Lieutenant-Commander Howard G. Bruenn, who ran the Electro-Cardiograph Department, didn't even have time to examine the patient's medical records. At first sight, the man entering the hospital seemed the Roosevelt of legend, spinning his wheel-chair down the corridor, bakelite cigarette holder gripped between his teeth, waving and trading wisecracks with nurses and patients. Only as Roosevelt left the White House had McIntire seen the mask drop. "I feel like hell!" the President told him.

Soon enough, Bruenn knew why. Roosevelt was grey in the face, moving and breathing only with difficulty, convulsed by coughing. His blood circulation time was $22\frac{1}{2}$ seconds – as against an optimum 17. Under the stethoscope, rales – denoting fluid in both lungs – were plainly audible. Most serious of all: while the heartbeat was regular, the heart itself was dangerously enlarged.

At the heart's apex, Bruenn found "a blowing systolic murmur". The second aortic sound was "loud and booming". A normal blood pressure reading might have been 150/90; Roosevelt's was 186/108. At 62, Roosevelt was "a very old man with few life-sustaining forces left" – suffering from hypertension, degeneration of the vascular system, and congestive heart failure.

"I cannot live out a normal life-span," Roosevelt had once raged to Eleanor, "I can't even walk across the room to get my circulation going."

Two days later, unknown to the President, Admiral McIntire called a top-secret medical conference of seven prominent physicians. It was not long under way before Commander Bruenn, reporting his findings, sensed a closing of ranks. With each damning scintilla of evidence, the faces round the table seemed to harden. When Bruenn wound up, there was a clamour of dissent – both at the gravity of his diagnosis and against his prescribed programme. This included digitalis, fewer cigarettes, rest after meals, which should be confined to the White House, ten hours' sleep, a low-fat diet of 2,600 calories, gentle laxatives to avoid straining.

Bruenn heard the dissentients out in silence, then stood his ground. If his suggestions were not adopted, he would withdraw from the case.

The consultants were now in a cleft stick. To be sure, Bruenn could be sworn to secrecy and sent back to Bethesda. But if the President died, the Commander's fateful diagnosis and prognosis could create a scandal to rock the world of medicine. Finally, Dr James A. Paullin of Atlanta, and Dr Frank Lahey, of Boston's Lahey Clinic, pressed Bruenn to hold his fire. Both would see the President after lunch and ask for a re-examination.

Even then, on 30 March, both consultants hedged their bets. No one could deny those X-rays, showing a dilated and tortuous aorta – yet while now agreeing with Bruenn in principle they, at the same time, disagreed. Congestive heart failure was in too early a stage to justify digitalis – too early, even, to justify telling either Roosevelt or his family.

Bruenn was politely inflexible – digitalis was mandatory to remove strain from the tortuous aorta – and Dr Paullin, his hands clasped judicially, was the first to give in. Digitalis *could*, of course, be administered – but without the knowledge of the patient or his family.

It was a classical medical cover-up. Roosevelt, as all agreed from the first, was every doctor's dream: a model patient. Cheerfully swallowing the little green pills, he never once asked what they contained. He slept ten hours a night, cut his always modest liquor-consumption to one and a half highballs each evening, his cigarettes from up to thirty Camels daily to five. As a month-long guest at the Hobcaw, South Carolina, plantation of his old friend, the financier Bernard Baruch, he upped his sleeping time to twelve hours a day.

By May, when he returned to the White House, he was still doing just what the doctors ordered: keeping to his bed for eighteen hours a day, putting in four hours desk work, with one hour apiece allotted for lunch and dinner.

Bruenn was sure of one thing: the President of the United States was no longer in any shape to remould the world after his own image.

—

Commander Bruenn excepted, Franklin Roosevelt had one thing in common with his doctors. He believed what he wished to believe, adjusting the inconvenient facts of a world he sought to reshape as subconsciously as an addict excusing a tolerance pattern.

The mote that all but obscured his vision was Russia. "I know you will not mind my being brutally frank," he wrote to Churchill as early as March, 1942, "when I tell you that I think I can personally handle Stalin better than either your Foreign Office or my State

Department." The true reality was summed up by Lieutenant-General Sir Alan Brooke at Tehran: "This Conference is over when it has only just begun. Stalin has the President in his pocket." Oblivious to the unbridgeable gulf between Russia and the United States, Roosevelt's concept of a brave new world headed up by the two super powers was now near-paranoiac. It was small wonder that Stalin exploited this gullibility to the full. If Roosevelt believed that the Politburo had no more plans for world dominion, and that Communists were as other men, why disillusion him?

But on one score even Russian pleas failed to move the President: the doctrine of Germany and Japan's unconditional surrender. On 24 January, 1943, winding up a Big Three conference at Casablanca, Roosevelt, to the astonishment of Churchill and Stalin, had announced this as joint Allied policy to the world's press. Typically, he had muddled the historical allusion – Lee, he pointed out, had surrendered without conditions to Grant at Appomatox[9] but the damage was done. At Tehran, Stalin had again questioned the wisdom of this: to leave the surrender terms unclarified merely united the Germans still further. Russia was fighting Hitlerism, not the German people. On 14 January, Molotov had pressed for more precise wording; late in March, the Soviet Ambassador, Andrei Gromyko, urged a modification, in line with the thinking of both Eden and Cordell Hull. In reply, Roosevelt scrawled: "No – the British Foreign Office has always been part of this and it is N.G.".

As the pressures grew – from the State Department, from the Joint Chiefs of Staff, from Eisenhower, who privately condemned the policy as "very difficult and silly"[10] – Roosevelt, with fanatical tenacity, clung to his original dictum. "The harshness of the phrase," ran one typical objection, from Brigadier-General Carl A. Russell of the War Department, "aids propagandists in stiffening and prolonging resistance, which in turn is costly to the Allied nations in lives and resources". He added rationally: "It is not sentiment with me – just good business." Roosevelt was unrepentant. "Please note that I am not willing at this time to say that we do not intend to destroy the German nation," he minuted the Joint Chiefs on 1 April – two days after Bruenn's crucial meeting with the consultants.

Roosevelt's distaste for the Foreign Office ran deep; it was too closely linked with the colonialism he was determined, with Stalin's help, to stamp out: the British Empire, no less than the French and

Dutch overseas empires. To his ideals, British imperialism posed a far greater threat than Russian expansionism; he wanted the British to give up Malaya, Burma and Hong Kong, the French to pull out of Morocco, Indo-China and the New Hebrides. "For every dollar that the British, who have been there for two hundred years, have put into Gambia, they have taken out ten," he openly and revealingly told a White House press conference in February 1944. "It's just plain exploitation of those people." At times, this bias was so marked as to defy logic: even Churchill's aid to the Communist Tito was seen as covert colonialism.

In truth, logic was a quality conspicuously lacking in Roosevelt's world-plan. By January 1944, the Free French, under the imperious General Charles André Marie de Gaulle, numbered 400,000 men, all of them armed and equipped by America at a cost of $700 million. But while twenty-six nations acknowledged de Gaulle as leader, Roosevelt steadfastly refused to do so. De Gaulle had been a notable absentee from the Tehran Conference, for Roosevelt was convinced that the CFLN (Comité Français de Libération Nationale) intended to install de Gaulle as a dictator once France was liberated. The Committee's claim to be the provisional government of France was thus ignored – against the advice of Churchill, Eden, Hull and Eisenhower.

"I am not more enamoured of him than you are," Churchill had written to the President of de Gaulle in July 1943, "but I would rather have him on the committee than strutting about as a combination of Joan of Arc and Clemenceau." Eden was in full agreement. "President's absurd and petty dislike of de Gaulle blinds him," he noted in his diary on 4 March. But Roosevelt, unyielding in his dislike for "The Prima Donna," was deaf to reason; even when D-Day dawned, no agency existed for the civil administration of France. In mounting exasperation, Sir Alexander Cadogan, Permanent Under Secretary to the Foreign Office, complained: "Roosevelt, P.M. and – it must be admitted – de Gaulle all behave like girls approaching the age of puberty."

Roosevelt's enthusiasms were now as irrational as his hates. For almost three years he had backed the corrupt Kuomintang regime of China's Generalissimo Chiang kaí-shek in their struggle against Japan – a clique combining "some of the worst features of Tammany Hall and the Spanish Inquisition," one critic noted. It was a move prompted in part by an emotional haze of missionary propaganda, in part by a concept of China, with 400 million potential customers, one day supplanting industrial Japan – but this post-war vision of a democratic China emerging as an Asian leader was a gross idealisation.

As far back as September 1943, Chiang, like Stalin, had been ready to pull out of the war, for his entire policy consisted of one aim: to hold on to power. If Japan withdrew from Chinese territory, Chiang had agreed, he would sever with Britain and America. Only on a matter of timing had the talks broken down; Japan had insisted on the severance before undertaking withdrawal.

What Roosevelt failed to grasp was that Chiang was much keener on killing Chinese Communists than Japanese. All his best troops were sited in China's north-west, confronting the forces under Mao-tse-tung and Chou-en-lai. Far from being a sound investment, Chiang's China was an economist's nightmare: goods indexed at 100 in 1937 had soared to 125,000 by 1945. His unwieldy army had swollen to 327 divisions – though many units were kept understrength, enabling officers to siphon off the pay of non-existent soldiers.

To backstop this tatterdemalion force, Roosevelt had dispatched, as Chiang's Chief of Staff, Lieutenant-General Joseph W. Stilwell, "Vinegar Joe," a crabbed 58-year-old who proposed, literally, to re-write history: to prove by personal leadership that the Chinese soldier was the finest in the world. Dressed like a dogface soldier, and a slovenly one at that, chewing on a private's rations, often leading from the front like a platoon commander, the acerbic Stilwell was now poised to end Japan's blockade of China for good and all – pressing through north-central Burma to seize the towns of Mogaung and Myitkyina, forging on to China's southern border at Yunnan province.

Of all Roosevelt's global misconceptions, it was this China delusion that would cause the most futile toll of Allied lives in the weeks to come.

-

In the heart of eastern India there was a railroad. Built before the turn of the century, in peacetime it had been a slow and sleepy line: the 250-mile long Bengal and Assam Railway, manned by native crews and turbanned engineers, hauling tea from the plantations of Assam to the *godowns* of Calcutta.

By 1944, all this had changed. Now the railroad was a vital link in Roosevelt's grandiose plans for China – ferrying up to 1,500 tons of supplies a day to the airfields of Assam, whence they were flown over The Hump to Kunming. Until the 478-mile-long Ledo Road was completed in 1945 – by 17,000 engineers at a cost of $148 million – the Bengal-Assam was also "Vinegar Joe" Stilwell's sole lifeline in his advance to northern Burma.

On Saturday 1 April, the line was irrevocably threatened. Ten divisions of Japanese, 100,000 men of Lieutenant General Renya Mutaguchi's 15th Army had forded the muddy Chindwin River and were advancing on the railhead at Dimapur. All that lay between them and "Vinegar Joe's" supply route were the tiny British-held hill towns of Imphal, the capital of Manipur State, and Kohima, 50 miles south.

It was a campaign Churchill had hated from the first. For him, the notion that China was a great power was "an American illusion"; the British role in sustaining that illusion nugatory. "For the South-East Asia Command, there appears to be no role at all," noted the Political Adviser to the Supreme Commander, Lord Louis Mountbatten, "except to cover General Stilwell's supply route, and to employ British forces at the maximum disadvantage to themselves with minimum effect upon the enemy." For the sake of Allied amity, Churchill was willing enough to launch amphibious operations, but the whole concept of jungle fighting appalled him – "like going into the water to fight a shark." This was a war where men slept with wires attached to their big toes – one pull would awaken them, for nobody spoke above a whisper; a war of humid forests and acre-deep hedges of thorn, where trees loomed 100 feet high above the green twilight; a war beset by leeches and malaria, dysentery and scrub typhus.

Now, willy-nilly, the British were caught up in the path of the Japanese advance.

At 7:30 p.m. on that Saturday night, the scene at Dimapur Junction was one of near-hysterical confusion; on 29 March, the 31st (Japanese) Division of Lieutenant-General Kotuku Sato had cut the road between Kohima and Imphal. Now the first relief troops of the 2nd (British) Division, wiry sun-bronzed men in jungle green, were at that moment arriving by train. Gangs of pioneers were hacking at slit trenches; haggard coolies stumbled through darkness with top-heavy loads. One supply officer, pressed for mortar ammunition, cried out in pious horror, "Dear God, I didn't come here to fight a war!".

Nor was this surprising. Even in 1944, all three communities – Dimapur, Imphal, Kohima – were garrison towns, staffed by non-combatants. Officers knew the green valley of Imphal for the finest pheasant shooting east of Suez; twice weekly, their sturdy little polo ponies, twelve hands high, thundered across the plain. At Kohima, 87 miles north, a township of red corrugated-iron roofs 5,000 feet up in the Naga Hills, the black-out was an unknown factor; the smell of wood fires lingered pleasantly on the evening air and the Deputy Commissioner, Charles Pawsey, still made his daily rounds with two spear-carrying Naga orderlies clad in red blankets. Even Kohima's landmarks somehow harked back to Kipling: Naga Village, Hospital Ridge, Jail Hill, and the Ladies' Mile, a narrow bridlepath where the *memsahibs* of peacetime had taken their gentle constitutionals.

On 23 March, when Colonel Hugh Richards, a fair-haired 50-year-old flew in from Delhi to take over Kohima, he was shaken by what he found. The town lay on three levels, hilly, broken, biscuit-coloured terrain; clumps of alders and fine oaks limited the fields of fire. What little barbed wire had existed had gone forward to Imphal – which Mountbatten had further reinforced by pirating 30 C-47s from the Hump run to airlift in the entire 5th Division.

The weapon pits were too wide, manned by down-in-the-mouth scratch troops who had never even fired a riffle. The sole artillery was one 25-pounder used for training – and there was scant prospect of getting more.

Richards made a snap decision. Until now, four widely dispersed "boxes" had made up the defence plan; these must be scrapped. What counted was Kohima's winding Ridge, more than one mile long and 400 yards wide, with steeply wooded slopes. It commanded the terrain to the south and the east; thus Sato must secure it before reaching Dimapur.

On 3 April, Richards gave his sector commanders orders no man in Kohima had ever thought to hear: "Collect your bedding and get into your trenches". That night, under a brilliant moon, Kohima seemed to hold its breath; only the clink of picks working far into the night on Transport Ridge broke the silence.

It was a siege to go down to history. Imphal, too, was beleaguered, but General Mutaguchi's troops never advanced closer than twelve miles to the valley, an investment which dragged on, punctuated by reliefs, until July. But of Richards' 2,500 men, only 1,500 were combatants, men of the calibre of Lieutenant-Colonel "Bruno" Brown's 1st Battalion, The Assam Regiment, or Lieutenant-Colonel "Dan" Laverty's 4th Battalion Royal West Kents whose emblem, a white horse rampant, had seen service at El Alamein.

On 5 April, artillery of a sort did arrive: four 3.7 inch howitzers of the 20th Mountain Battery, Royal Indian Artillery. But that was all.

"It was a private's battle," one officer recalled later with truth, for only rock-steady morale in the ranks was proof against the twenty-five major attacks which followed. On 5 April, the Japanese seized Transport Ridge, the southernmost defence point; next day, working north, they secured Jail Hill, named after the small, red-roofed civilian prison. The box had now shrunk to an area 900 yards long by 400 yards wide. On 6 April, too, Sato's men cut off the water supply; the defenders were now down to a daily mugful per man, drawn from standpipes.

There were many acts of suicidal courage. On Detail Hill, Lance-Corporal John Harman, of the Royal West Kents, sprinted thirty-five naked yards towards a Japanese bunker, under a glinting stream of machine-gun bullets, crouched at its mouth with bullets passing inches above his body, tossed in a lethal four-second grenade, then walked calmly back carrying the machine-gun. Killed before the siege was lifted, he won a posthumous Victoria Cross. It was on Detail Hill, too, that Harman's company commander, Captain Donald Easten, chanced on a solid brick bakery with the Japanese entrenched between six cast-iron bread ovens. Between them, he and an engineer lieutenant, John Wright, plastered an abandoned door with slabs of gun cotton then slammed it against the bakery wall. As the igniter exploded, the bakery went sky-high; curtains of bren gun fire cut down the escaping Japanese.

From 8 April, Kohima became the sole battlefield of World War Two to focus on a tennis court: a solid asphalt court 20 yards wide constructed below Deputy Commissioner Pawsey's bungalow by the Burmah Oil Company. Now the Royal West Kents under Major Tom Kenyon lobbed off volleys of grenades where Slazenger balls had once bounced, often all through the night, to a mounting crescendo of bugle calls and high-pitched *banzais*.

Little by little, night alarms eroded the defenders' nerves to snapping-point. A grenade exploded amongst a dump of tar-barrels, sending flaring jets of tar into the darkness; the drumming of hoofbeats triggered a panicky rumour of stampeding elephants. At dawn, the defenders eyed one another ruefully, not trusting themselves to speak: beyond the thorn stockade, a dozen cows lay riddled.

It was a time when the British needed all the shrugged-off courage they could muster. "Have a cuppa char, sir," a Kentish soldier greeted

Captain Donald Elwell, of the Assam Regiment, as he slid into a dug-out, "Sorry the missus isn't in." Wounded officers, it was noted, now kept their revolvers close at hand – just in case. On 13 April, Richards issued a Special Order of the Day that smacked of a bygone more chivalrous age – an order spirited from trench to trench by men creeping between splintered trees, received by hands stretching tentatively from the torn earth.

In part it ran:

"I wish to acknowledge with pride the magnificent effort which has been made by all officers, NCOs and men and followers of this Garrison in the successful defence of Kohima … Put your trust in God and continue to hit the enemy hard wherever he may show himself. If you do that, his defeat is sure…"

By the night of 17 April, the perimeter had shrunk still further. All were now crowded into a space measuring 350 yards long and wide on Summerhouse (now Garrison) Hill, beneath the Deputy Commissioner's bungalow. Word had reached Richards that a relief column was on its way – but the crucial question was, When?

Beside him, at his command post, a simple trench roofed with corrugated iron and rubble, a young private soldier shifted nervously in the first hours of his all-night stand-to. The words came very softly on the still night:

"Sir, can I ask you a question?"

"Of course, what is it?"

"When we die, sir, is that the end or do we go on?"

That was the spirit of Kohima, at dawn on 20 April, when the 1st Battalion Royal Berkshire Regiment, spearhead of the relieving 6th Brigade, rounded a bend on the mountain road to sight the lunar landscape that was now The Ridge.

It had cost over 4,000 casualties, but the railroad was saved. The siege was over.[11]

In southern England, by late April the countryside was transformed. For ten miles inland along a 550-mile long coastal strip, only those with special identity cards might now go. The grass verges of the roadsides had vanished, swallowed up beneath vast stands of ammunition. Wayside signs loomed large on aluminium tanks – "Do not drink this water without halogen tablets" – or cautioned truck drivers: "Know your distances. This is sixty yards from the last sign". Red crosses shimmered through woods misty with bluebells: hundreds of tents, hundreds of ambulances, waiting to bring the first wounded back.

Parachutes blossomed in the spring sky as airborne men rehearsed the last desperate act. Endless convoys – tanks, jeeps, bren gun carriers – lurched through the pale green of the countryside. On countless stony beaches in the west country, assault troops splashed wearily ashore.

Everyone sensed that the big push was coming. The question was: When?

In a tin-roofed brick-built office twenty feet square, lit by flickering fluorescent tubes, the man who carried most of the answers in his head was working late. On the night of 28 April, at the new headquarters of the Allied Expeditionary Force, Bushey Park, near Kingston, Surrey, General Dwight D. Eisenhower was a desperately worried man.

To the myriads of troops whose hands he shook daily – seeking, but never finding, a man from his hometown, Abilene – he gave no hint of strain: the cheery infectious smile, the easy approach, seemed inbuilt. So, too, did the self-effacement; on a lunchtime visit to "Willow Run," the mass-production officers' mess in Grosvenor House, "Ike" had pushed aside a half-eaten meal of pork chops and spinach, until an escort pointed to a cautionary chit: "Eat all you take on your plate or explain by endorsement hereon". Pink with embarrassment, muttering "Doggone if I'm risking a reprimand," Eisenhower manfully polished his plate.

It was at night, in his comfortably shabby home, Telegraph Cottage, once a link in a semaphore network, that his "family" – Lieutenant-Colonel James Gault, his British Military Assistant, his orderly, Sergeant Mickey McKeogh, his driver, WAC Lieutenant Kay Summersby – saw the real signs of stress. Ostensibly, this was the time when "Ike" relaxed over highballs, clad in a checkered shirt, an old suede and leather jacket, GI slacks and battered Filipino straw slippers. Yet he was now smoking more than three packs a day; his hand was so crippled with pressing the flesh and drafting memos that he wrote home to Mamie in soft lead pencil. Frantic with fatigue, he complained of a constant ringing in his left ear.

All too often his temper flared like a blowtorch. "I am tired of dealing with prima donnas," a visitor heard him rage at Tedder, when a wrangle between staffers arose, "By God, you tell that bunch that if they can't get together and stop quarrelling like children I'll tell the Prime Minister to get someone else to run this damn war. I'll quit."

The pressures of planning the greatest seaborne and airborne armada in history were beginning to tell.

Much had long been decided by a process of elimination. If Calais, closest to England and to Europe's finest port, Antwerp, seemed obvious to the Allies, it was apparent to the Germans, too; defences in the Pas de Calais area were formidable. Thus Normandy, with a serviceable port, Cherbourg, close to Portsmouth, and the Norman town of Caen, with its road and rail network to Paris, seemed a sounder choice. The beaches were firm, as Sergeant Bruce Ogden Smith was ably demonstrating, and behind them there were good road networks.

Despite Lily Sergueiev's reports, Hitler opted for Normandy as the target – "How many of those fine agents are paid by the Allies, eh?" he had demanded shrewdly. But his generals were less certain – and the defences that much less advanced.

Choice of time was as complex as choice of place. D-Day must be an assault at low tide – so that Allied engineers could neutralise steel obstacles sited to rip out the bellies of landing craft. It must be a near-dawn attack, so that men and ships could cross under cover of night. A full moon was too risky – yet some moonlight was needed for paratroopers like Donald Burgett to function. The attack must come late enough for troops to complete their training – yet early enough to give the Allies four months of good weather after landing.

In the spring of 1944, these conditions pertained only three times – in the first few days of May, the first and third weeks of June.

How many men should take part? As planned by Lieutenant-General Sir Frederick Morgan in the old Norfolk House headquarters, the initial estimate – three divisions – had been entirely too modest. It was Montgomery, whose troops would storm the British sector beaches, who had beefed up the assault, while visiting Churchill in Marrakesh – "This will not do. I must have more in the initial punch." By 10 January, he had been more positive still: "Give me five divisions or get someone else to command."

Now, due to Montgomery's insistence, five divisions would land on the first tide, the essential elements of two more on the second tide, and both Americans and Britons would go in on their own separate fighting fronts.

The technology involved was the least of Eisenhower's worries; British know-how had been working overtime. There were the new-fangled innovations of Montgomery's brother-in-law, Major-General Percy Hobart, collectively known as "Hobart's Funnies" – Sherman tanks whose Duplex Drive equipment enabled them to swim ashore, mine-clearing Shermans, called Flails, their rotors powering wire-cutting knives, Crocodiles filled with 400 gallons of flame-throwing fuel. Since Cherbourg promised stubborn resistance, the British fell back on an early concept of Commodore John Hughes-Hallett, the Royal Navy's senior planner – "if we can't capture a port we must take one with us." On the day appointed, £25 million worth of artificial harbours called "Mulberries," each as large as Dover Harbour, plus breakwaters called "Gooseberries," would be towed across the Channel to shelter shallow-draught vessels unloading supplies. To save on shipping space, a 710-mile pipeline under the ocean (PLUTO) would pump one million gallons of fuel daily from the Isle of Wight to Normandy.

At times Eisenhower found the logistics almost frightening. The Navy's briefing alone – designated as "Operation Neptune" – was a 700-page document as thick as the Manhattan telephone directory "but rarer than Shakespeare's First Folio"; any man required to read it was locked in under armed guard. All told, Overlord called for 700,000 separate items[12], from Trousers, Wool, Protective to Bags, Vomit, Soldiers, For the Use Of, all ordered in quantities running into millions. Enthused by the planners' panoramic photographs, "Ike" had called for "forty sets" – meaning 40,000 – but British resources could not cope. Until the job was done, American bombers flew in 730 miles of paper and ten tons of chemicals every other day.

Even at this late stage, controversies were raging. All along, Omar Bradley had insisted that an airborne drop on the Cotentin Peninsula must spearhead the storming of Utah Beach: the exits were limited to narrow causeways perched above flooded marshland. So long as the Germans held those causeways, Cherbourg would not fall.

Then, to Eisenhower's dismay, Air Chief Marshal Sir Trafford Leigh-Mallory, the C-in-C of Britain's Fighter Command, sought to spike the plan: the low-flying C-47s would face crippling flak from the first, the Normandy hedgerows take cruel toll of gliders. "Your losses will be excessive," he told Bradley, "certainly far more than the gains are worth." Bradley was obdurate; if Leigh-Mallory killed the drop, "then I must ask that we eliminate the Utah assault." Leigh-Mallory now turned angrily to Montgomery: "If General Bradley insists upon going ahead he will have to accept full responsibility for the operation." Rapping the table like a testy schoolmaster, Montgomery wound up the argument: "That isn't at all necessary, gentlemen, *I* shall assume full responsibility for the operation."

But Leigh-Mallory did not give up easily, and his importuning was to plague Eisenhower to the end.

Softening up the terrain behind the beachhead was another bone of bitter contention. On D-Day, an air umbrella of deadly fighters – P38 Lightnings, P51 Mustangs, P47 Thunderbolts – would shepherd the invasion fleet; it was with truth that Eisenhower told the troops: "Don't worry about the planes overhead. They will be ours." And in February 1944, 3,800 American and British bombers, geared to a seven-day assault called "Big Week," had wrought such havoc among German air plants at Regensburg, Stuttgart and Schweinfurt that the Luftwaffe was powerless to hit back.

Yet all this vaunted air superiority went for nothing while the British War Cabinet havered and vacillated – appalled by the toll of French casualties that might ensue if bombs fell far inland. To cripple military movement within a 150-mile radius of the beaches, Montgomery, backed by Tedder, wanted attacks on 74 key rail centres – a prospect staunchly opposed by Churchill and Eden.

Would it "build up a volume of dull hatred in France?" Churchill had pondered, as late as 26 April, and he added, "Post-war France must be our friend". On 27 April, to Eisenhower's chagrin, almost three months of sterile argument had ended in stalemate: only centres where casualties did not exceed 150 could be attacked. Now only Roosevelt could reverse this verdict.

But the greatest bugbear of all, as Eisenhower had sensed back in January, was security. It was this problem that loomed largest in his mind on the night on Friday 28 April.

No sooner had he clinched the Utah airborne drop than a staff officer browsing through a London bookstore chanced on a manual titled *Paratroops*, by Captain F. O. Miksche, a Czech serving with the Free French. Prominently featured was a map of the Cotentin Peninsula, showing drop and landing zones almost identical to those planned. Published in 1943, the book must long ago, through neutral sources, have reached Germany.

In fact, *Generaloberst* Kurt Student, the founder of Germany's airborne forces, had read the book, found it instructive, and dismissed the Cotentin as a sand-table exercise. But Eisenhower, not knowing this, would anguish for many weeks ahead.

There had been other grounds for long and wakeful nights. Back in March, a parcel of papers stamped BIGOT, breaking open in a Chicago mail office, had caused widespread panic until the mystery was solved; a hard-pressed sergeant in the London Ordnance Supply Section had, in a moment of aberration, mailed the package not to the appropriate U.S. department but to his sister. There was the case, graver by far, of Major-General Henry Miller, an Eisenhower crony and Quartermaster of the United States Ninth Air Force; on 18 April, in Claridge's dining room, he had told a party of guests that D-Day would be accomplished fact by 15 June. For this Eisenhower could and did reduce him to Lieutenant-Colonel, shipping him back to the States – but what could he do in the case of Leonard Sidney Dawe, compiler of *The Daily Telegraph*'s crossword puzzle?

A mild-mannered 54-year-old physics teacher from Leatherhead, Surrey, Dawe was to produce five puzzles spread over five days containing five separate code-names: UTAH, OMAHA, OVERLORD, NEPTUNE and MULBERRY. Yet pressed by M.I.5. for reasons, Dawe could come up with no explanation at all. For all he knew the puzzles had been compiled six months earlier – before the code-words had even been allotted.

Now, one day previously, had come the biggest security scare of all. On the night of 27–28 April, in Lyme Bay, on the Dorset coast, a force of German E-boats had cut in against the Allied Force U on a training exercise, sinking three LSTs. More lives were lost – 197 sailors, 441 soldiers – than at Utah Beach on D-Day, but among the missing were ten Bigot officers, men who knew crucial facets of the plan.

Thus until the bodies were found and identified Eisenhower would know no peace – for if only one man fell alive into German hands and talked the entire invasion plan was in jeopardy.

It was with a growing sense of the enormity of his task that Eisenhower had written to Lieutenant-General Brehon Somervell, Chief of Supply Services in Washington: "We are not merely risking a tactical defeat; we are putting the whole works on one number..."

3

"Take Unto You The Whole Armour of God"
29 April–5 June, 1944

"Freimut, mein liebe, ich schere mich den Teufel darum!" (Frankly, my dear, I don't give a damn!)

The parting words of Rhett Butler to Scarlett O'Hara could rarely have been uttered in a stranger setting: a dining room where candle-light glowed on polished mahogany and faded Gobelin tapestries in the twelfth-century Château de la Roche-Guyon, 50 miles north-east of Paris. The narrator, the jovial *Vizeadmiral* Friedrich Ruge, naval aide to *Feldmarschall* Erwin Rommel, was regaling his chief with their nightly diversion: Ruge's blow-by-blow summary of Margaret Mitchell's best-seller *Gone With The Wind*.

Since 9 March, when he took up his quarters in the château as Commander-in-Chief of Army Group B, this had been Rommel's sole relaxation. At 53, "The Desert Fox" was, as so often, facing a race against time: the fortification of almost 800 miles of coastline from the dikes of Holland to the Brittany peninsula.

It was a question on which he was politely but firmly at odds with the Commander-in-Chief, West, the ageing patrician *Feldmarschall* Gerd von Rundstedt. For Von Rundstedt, the blockhouses, casemates and gun emplacements of Hitler's Atlantic Wall were a folly that had eaten up 3.7 billion Reichmarks, "an enormous bluff ... more for the German people than the enemy." The Wall might "temporarily obstruct" the Allied attack; it would never stop it. As Von Rundstedt saw it, the invasion, when it came, could only be defeated *after* the Allies had landed – by a mass assault of troops, held back from the coast until then, striking its inadequate supply lines and disorganised bridgeheads.

Rommel would have none of it. The only way to smash the attack was at the very outset – on the beaches. His aide, *Hauptmann* Hellmuth

Lang, always recalled how Rommel, stabbing at the sands with his black silver-topped "informal" marshal's baton, had summed up his entire credo: "We'll have only one chance to stop the enemy and that's while he's in the water ... everything we have must be on the coast." Unwittingly, he coined a phrase that went down to history: "Believe me, Lang, the first twenty-four hours of the invasion will be decisive ... for the Allies, as well as Germany, it will be the longest day."

Time and again Rommel had exerted pressure – on von Rundstedt, on Hitler's Chief of Operations, Jodl, on Hitler himself – to incorporate two divisions he wanted above all into his coastal defence system: *Gruppenführer* Witt's 12th S.S. Panzer Division in the Cotentin Peninsula, *Generalleutnant* Fritz Bayerlein's Panzer Lehr in the region of Avranches. Hitler, for one, was hostile to the concept of mobility. "Their part is to get killed behind the fortifications," he told Rommel coldly, on 20 March, "So they've no need to be mobile."

Then, too, there was still the vexed question: where would the invaders strike? The main strength of Rommel's Army Group B, the Fifteenth Army, was still concentrated in the Pas de Calais. Only as late as 7 May was a weak compromise reached. Three Panzer Divisions – the 2nd, the 21st and the 116th – were at Rommel's disposal. But four remaining Panzer Divisions were still held far inland as a High Command reserve.

But Rommel was no man to acknowledge defeat. "I'm raising plenty of dust," he wrote cheerfully to his son Manfred, for his whirlwind tours of the coastline, which complaisant officers came to dread, had one object in view: to refashion the Atlantic Wall after "The Devil's Gardens" which had so nearly defeated the British at El Alamein.

"Let me see your hands," Rommel ordered one strongpoint commander in the Contentin, *Leutnant* Arthur Jahnke – and only when the officer stripped off his gloves to reveal bloody callouses scored by barbed wire did he nod, satisfied. "Well done. The blood on an officer's hands from fortification work is worth every bit as much as that shed in battle."

For what Rommel sought now was a hitherto undreamt-of barrier of minefields, six miles wide, along the entire Atlantic Wall: 65,000 mines to a square kilometre, 200 million mines in France alone. Always single-minded, the Wall in time became a kind of obsession for Rommel. Persuaded to visit the famous porcelain china works at

Sevres, he had remained blind to the works of art. "Find out if they can make waterproof casings for my sea mines," was his only comment.

His ingenuity was boundless – "the greatest engineer of the Second World War," enthused his fortifications expert, *General* Wilhelm Meise. Among Rommel's deadliest obstacles were the Elements C, great iron gates 15 feet long and 12 feet high, set 300 yards from high water mark, with powerful legs bracing them firmly against tidal pressure. There were "hedgehogs," wooden or steel triangles four feet high, with mines or old French shells primed to explode on contact; curved rails; ramps fitted with Teller mines and blades to disembowel landing craft; concrete pyramids called tetrahedra, fitted with fused shells. Inland, to foil gliders and parachutists, he had planted what the French called "Rommel's asparagus" – wooden poles up to 12 feet high, embedded two feet deep, spaced thirty yards apart and mined at the apex.

The troops at Rommel's disposal lent urgency to this problem. "Many a man here has been living a soft life," Rommel grumbled, but many were all too frail to have lived otherwise. While the average age was thirty-one, many were as old as fifty-six, split, for administrative efficiency, into units which bespoke their disabilities: "ear battalions" of deaf men, "white bread divisions" of men with stomach ulcers. Others were ill-trained assortments of Russian prisoners-of-war – like Infantry Regiment 987 of the 276th Division, whose soldiers spoke 34 separate dialects from Armenian to Tartar.

By 11 May, 517,000 beach obstacles – 30,000 of them fitted with Teller mines – had been rammed or pile-driven into position, and Rommel, on a visit to Fifteenth Army, had solemnly distributed accordions as prizes to the most dedicated divisions. Only in Normandy was the work lagging behind, but Rommel did not worry unduly. He told himself there was still time.

"When they come it will be at high water," Rommel had told *Leutnant* Jahnke on one inspection trip, and this mirrored the earlier thinking of *Admiral* Theodor Krancke, Naval Group West, who had predicted that the Allies would come by moonlight, at high tide, both to observe and float over the obstacles, in the neighbourhood of a large port. They would need visibility of 5000 yards, winds of no more than 30 mph, and wave heights no greater than seven feet. Around 11 May, though, Krancke had confused the issue, warning of a landing at low tide.

At the fine Renaissance desk in his ground floor office, dominated by the portrait of the Duc de la Rochefoucauld, the seventeenth-century maxim writer whose castle this had been, Rommel set down his hopes and fears in letters to his wife, Lucie. "Still no signs of the British and Americans," he wrote on 6 May, "I am looking forward to the battle with confidence." On 15 May: "Still nothing doing ... I'm convinced that the enemy will have a rough time when he attacks." On 19 May: "I'm waiting to see whether I shall be able to get away for a couple of days in June."

And if possible one of those days would be Tuesday 6 June, Lucie's fiftieth birthday; her present, a pair of handmade grey suede shoes, size five and a half, had already been purchased in Paris. This would mean leaving La Roche-Guyon for the Rommel home in Herrlingen, Germany, no later than the early morning of 4 June.

The Allies were coming – but Rommel, like a neglectful host, would not be there to greet them.

—

At Zossen, outside Berlin, *Oberst* Alexis von Roenne, who had so warmly welcomed the news of Eisenhower's arrival in mid-January, was a puzzled man. As senior intelligence chief of the department Foreign Armies West, Roenne's task was to slot the reports of agents like Wulf Dietrich Schmidt and Lily Sergueiev into a coherent pattern – yet by mid-May the messages pouring in were as shrill and confusing as static in the ether.

The Allies, it seemed, were assembling armies at all points of the compass. The 21 miles of water between Calais and Dover had never seemed so wide.

All told, some 250 largely-conflicting messages had to be evaluated – pointing not only to Normandy and the Pas de Calais but to Denmark, Belgium, even the Balkans. And why was the British Fourth Army, under Sir Andrew Thorne, with headquarters in Edinburgh Castle, encamped on the east coast of Scotland? Reportedly numbering 250,000 men, their landing craft had been spotted by high-flying reconnaissance planes on the Firth of Forth, their twin-engined bombers on airfields near Glasgow. Reports of Fourth Army dances and football games featured almost weekly in the Perth and Dundee papers.

Plainly their destination must be Norway, so to repel them seventeen divisions were to stand to all that summer from Kristiansand to Tromsö.

Only much later did it emerge that Fourth Army was a brilliant phantom, consisting of twenty officers, squads of "indiscreet" radio-operators, and diligent camouflage artists creating rubber tanks, wooden aeroplanes and an "invasion fleet" made up of wood, canvas and chicken wire.

Of this world of double, even triple cross, Lily Sergueiev remained an ever more reluctant part.

Trouble started as early as 25 March, when Lily, resting up at 39, Hill Street, had a visit from Colonel Robertson and Mary Ward. How had Kliemann come by those ten-pound notes in Lisbon? Robertson wanted to know.

When Lily explained, Robertson broke the news: "Thirty-nine of the fifty banknotes are false."

Lily was nonplussed. "False?"

Robertson's pink moon face was impassive. "Do you think that Kliemann knew? Do you think that it could be a trap?"

Lily did not think so. "What could be the aim?"

"He might want to know how you react."

Still Lily could not see it. "The first time I tried to change a note I would be arrested! There would be an enquiry and Kliemann would quite probably lose his agent. No, that doesn't make any sense at all!".

"You might be right," Robertson agreed reluctantly. "Let's leave it at that."

From that moment on, Lily sensed that her standing with the *Abwehr* was the subject of much debate in St James's Street. Finally it was decided the risk must be taken – but the cyphering, transmission and encoding would all be under the supervision of a young radio officer, Russell Lee.

Unknown to Robertson, Lily was nursing a secret. In Lisbon, she had arranged a positive check with Kliemann, to indicate a message sent under duress: two dashes between her call-sign and the first words would mean that she had been arrested. A perfect message spelt correctly would indicate British control; only a slightly garbled text denoted the genuine article.

It was a legitimate precaution for any German agent, giving Kliemann even greater confidence – but for the moment Lily was keeping this arrangement to herself. The secret spelt power over the British: a power she knew she would never use, but the knowledge that she held it was sweet. The British had denied her the one thing that she loved above all, her mongrel, Babs; as a compromise it had been shipped to her sister, Nelly, in Algiers, then run over by a truck. Lily hated the British for that – and for the false bonhomie cloaking their cold haughty demeanour, for the way they made use of her without bothering to hide the fact.

On 10 May, from a borrowed house with a green front door in Palace Gardens Terrace, north of Hyde Park, Lily made her first successful transmission, ending with a flourish of K's – meaning "Come in". Suddenly the transmitter burst into answering life: O.K. – G.B. – SK, SK (End of transmission).

"They have answered!" Lily cried out, jubilant despite herself, for in that moment she even felt a closeness to Russell Lee and Mary Ward. It was her "own small personal victory in the tremendous entanglement of the war".

All through May she was sending an average of six messages a week, at noon on Tuesdays, Wednesdays and Thursdays. Each Thursday she took the 4 p.m. to Wraxall, resting up with the Yeos until Monday morning, nursing her strength. Each Monday afternoon she asked Mary Ward: "Where have I been this time?" Sometimes the answer was: "You stayed with a colleague from the Ministry on Salisbury Plain". Or at other times: "You have been to Cambridge, staying with a cousin." It was all immaterial: a fictional montage of trains, clubs, messes and canteens, of conversations which reaped rich harvests of badges, vehicles, tanks and planes.

By 18 May, Lily was finding the suspense unbearable. She had an uneasy feeling that Russell Lee was planning to take over her call-sign. "I would like you to know one thing," she told Mary on impulse, "You mustn't try to work without me. I didn't mean to warn you... I would have said nothing, just withdrawn... watched you bring about your own destruction. But I have told you now. You are warned."

Mary was shocked. "It would not be us alone you would harm. In France your countrymen await the liberation."

"Why, in fact, do you suppose I have told you all this?"

There was a long silence before Mary said shamefacedly, "You were very fond of Babs?"

Lily shook her head. "It's not just that; you have destroyed my faith in your country, in your honour, in your loyalty. For three years I have been fed on hatred... When I arrived here I thought it would come to an end."

"And now?"

"It's for you to decide," Lily Sergueiev told her, "My decision is taken: I shall continue to work."

All over the world now there were the small signs pointing to one ineluctable moment: H-Hour on D-Day.

In the Gothic stillness of San Francisco's Grace Episcopal Cathedral, 1000 men and women of all faiths, gathering to pray for the invasion armies, knelt on the hard stone floor to hear the British Consul-General, Godfrey Fisher, read from St Paul's epistle to the Ephesians:

> Put on the whole armour of God, that ye may be able
> to stand against the wiles of the devil. For we wrestle not
> against flesh and blood, but against principalities, against
> the rulers of the darkness of this world, against spiritual
> wickedness in high places. Wherefore take unto you the
> whole armour of God, that ye may be able to withstand
> in the evil day...

When that day came, New York City's Mayor Fiorello La Guardia announced, an open-air street service would be held in Madison Square. When that day came, Maryland's Governor Herbert O'Connor would ask all liquor stores to close down for the day in respect for those about to die.

In London's barnlike Lancaster House, overlooking Green Park, five months of dickering and dissent had also been leading towards that day: the three-man European Advisory Commission, the lanky Lincolnesque John Gilbert Winant, his poker-faced Soviet counterpart, Fedor Gusev, and the Foreign Office's bustling Sir William Strang, had charted the shape of post-war Europe before battle was even joined. Between the Elbe River and the Low Countries the British writ would run. East of the Elbe, the Red Army would control all life on earth. The U.S. would run the southern regions, primarily Catholic Baden, Württemberg and Bavaria. Berlin, perhaps all Austria, would be under a jointly-staffed three-flag occupation.

Neutral Europe took due note of these intentions. While cautiously rejecting an American offer to buy up all the ball-bearings produced by the country's giant SKF (Svenska Kullagerfabriken), Sweden prepared to cut Germany's shipments by one-fifth. Portugal was ready to ban all further German consignments of tungsten ore (wolfram). Turkey had agreed to bar all exports of chrome.

In England it was now the time when generals took to the open road, selling themselves to the troops like U.S. politicians in the primaries. In Hampshire and points west, GIs took a long cool look at 51-year-old Lieutenant General Omar Bradley descending from his black Cadillac and liked what they saw: a 6 feet tall "doughboy's general," who wore an issue combat jacket under a stained trench coat, his GI trousers stuffed into his paratroop boots. Posing questions in his melodious Missouri drawl, he seemed to share a secret understanding with his informants: the infantryman would write the final score. As senior U.S. ground-forces commander in Britain his optimism in off-the-record chats was reassuring: "This stuff about tremendous losses is tommyrot ... Some of you won't come back but it will be very few."

Soldiers surveying General Sir Bernard Montgomery took away a different picture. Always he followed a set routine; after talking to the officers, he walked up to half a mile between troops drawn up in hollow square, hands clasped behind him, piercing grey eyes in a lean beaky face peering intently at each man. Save for a distant band there would be total silence; "an atmosphere of theatrical tension," the war correspondent Alan Moorehead noted. The inspection over, Montgomery, mounting a jeep with a loudspeaker, told the troops: "Break ranks and gather round me."

Then came an astonishing moment: 5000 men in heavy boots stampeding towards the jeep like charging buffaloes. Montgomery's address, delivered up to five times a day until a million men had heard it, never varied: "I have come out here to see you today so that I can get a look at you and you get a look at me." A calculated pause – "Not that I'm much to look at" – followed by an easy ripple of laughter. "We have got to go off and do a job together very soon now, you and I... and now that I have seen you I have complete confidence... absolutely complete confidence... And you must have confidence in me."

And confidence was what they had in plenty. Politicians might look askance at Montgomery – "indomitable in defeat, insufferable in victory," Churchill had allegedly said – and even the generals never wholly trusted him. "A very good soldier, but I think he is after my job," Alan Brooke had told King George VI, who retorted, "I thought he was after mine." But among Tommies or dogface GIs, Montgomery never lacked the common touch – "Seen the paper? Here, take my copy" – "Have some cigarettes? My lady friends send them to me."

At 10 a.m. on Monday 15 May, at his old school, St Paul's, West Kensington, Montgomery for a time held the stage before a more exalted audience. If the setting was prosaic – The Model Room, a circular classroom like a cockpit, panelled in pitch-pine, with hard narrow wooden benches rising in tiers – the company was illustrious. Only King George VI and Churchill aspired to armchairs; the remainder squatted on the hard benches, swathed in topcoats or blankets, for the cold was bitter.

It was the last full-dress Overlord conference, and no man who took part in it would ever forget it. Rear-Admiral Morton L. Deyo, commander of the bombardment force off Utah Beach, always recalled how Eisenhower spoke first with a smile "worth twenty divisions". Next came Montgomery, who did not hide his admiration for his old adversary: "Rommel ... has made a world of difference since he took over ... he is best at the spoiling attack ... he will do his best to 'Dunkirk' us." General Sir Hastings Ismay, Assistant Secretary to the War Cabinet, was struck by the transformation of the stage into a vast map of the Normandy beaches, set on a slope, a Lilliputian landscape dwarfed by the giant figures of senior commanders swooping on landmarks. Admiral Sir Bertram Ramsay, the aloof silver-haired Allied Naval C-in-C, spoke of the problems of getting the troops ashore; Air Chief Marshal Leigh-Mallory spoke for the Air Forces.

Following lunch, and a brief address by King George VI, fighting a stammer – "just a grade above a moron, poor little fellow," commented Lieutenant-General George S. Patton, uncharitably – the American side of the assault came under review. Rear-Admiral Alan G. Kirk spoke for the Western Naval Task Force, Bradley for First Army, General Elwood P. Quesada for the Ninth Army Air Force. At 5 p.m., when the conference broke up, spirits had risen; there was a palpable sense of victory in the air.[13]

Ismay, for one, recalled lines from Shakespeare's *Henry V*:

...he which hath no stomach to this fight,

Let him depart; his passport shall be made,
And crowns for convoy put into his purse:
We would not die in that man's company
That fears his fellowship to die with us.

Churchill, too, was in fighting trim. "It is the Germans who will suffer very heavy casualties when our band of brothers gets among them," he had written ebulliently to Roosevelt, and now the assembly was cheered when he told them forcefully: "Gentlemen, I am *hardening* towards this enterprise."

So the world waited: for the waters to rise, for the dams to burst.

"What have you done up to now? It is a question of days, of hours. Eichmann will not wait."

On an upper floor of the Pera Palas Hotel, Istanbul, overlooking the still waters of the Golden Horn, Joel Brand, the Hungarian given a unique chance to save a million Jews, angrily confronted that city's group of Jewish Agency rescue workers.

It was Thursday 18 May, more than three weeks since Brand had had that momentous meeting with Adolf Eichmann – yet it was in vain that he now tried to instil a sense of urgency into the Agency's Istanbul chief, Chaim Barlasz, and a dozen of his co-workers.

"Get in direct touch with your people and with representatives of the Allied powers," Eichmann had told Brand, at the conclusion of that first interview, "Then come back to me with a concrete proposal. Tell me where you want to go and we'll give you the necessary permits." For this reason, Brand had picked on Istanbul, knowing the Agency had links with the Allies in Jerusalem and Cairo.

On that same evening, Brand had discussed the deal with Dr Rezsö Kastner and other *Waada* leaders and all had been unanimous: for the lives of a million Jews, Brand was empowered to offer Eichmann "a very large amount of foreign currency." But at their next meeting, this was an offer Eichmann brushed aside. Money was of no interest. What he proposed was one of the war's strangest barters: 10,000 brand-new Army trucks, equipped with spare parts, one truck for every hundred Jews, plus 800 tons of coffee, 200 tons each of cocoa, sugar and tea, and two million bars of soap.

"I can give your Allies an assurance on my word of honour that the trucks will never be used in the West," Eichmann told him. "What they are needed for is the Eastern front exclusively."

In the days that followed, Eichmann went further still. "If you return from Istanbul and tell me that the offer has been accepted," he guaranteed, "I'll close Auschwitz and bring ten per cent of the million I've promised you to the frontier." At their final meeting, on 15 May, a last-minute threat lent new urgency to the transaction: 12,000 Jews were to be transported daily from that moment on but initially to Austria and Czechoslovakia. "If you don't come back," Eichmann told Brand, "they'll all go to Auschwitz."

From the first, Brand saw it all as a figment of Eichmann's distorted imagination. Never for one moment did he think the Allies would give the Germans 10,000 trucks. Only Eichmann, so convinced that the Jews ruled the free world they could deliver anything they wanted, could have believed that. The answer must be to play for time.

To reassure the Germans, Brand had agreed that Andor Grosz, a Hungarian triple-agent who spied impartially for the *Abwehr*, the *Waada*, or whoever greased his palm should travel with him from Budapest. It was just as well. Despite advance warning the Jewish Agency had secured Brand no Turkish visa. It was Grosz, using local contacts, who had bribed them both through Immigration.

Now, in the Pera Palas, Brand saw all too plainly the answer to his question, What have you done up to now? The answer was, Nothing. Although three weeks had elapsed since the Agency cabled they were expecting him, they had put out no feelers at all. With his facile optimism, Brand had even hoped that the Zionist leader, Dr Chaim Weizmann[14], would have flown in from Jerusalem – yet not one member of the Executive was present.

"We must make some serious counter-proposal," he told Barlasz and the others desperately, "so that the negotiations can continue. Tomorrow I'll cable Eichmann and tell him that all goes well, that his offer is accepted in principle, provided that the deportations stop immediately."

Vainly he tried to make them see how precious time could be. Eichmann had offered them Jews in advance. If 100,000 Jews reached, say, the Spanish frontier, negotiations on shipping and countries of asylum could drag on for months – buying yet more time. "Every hour," Brand exhorted them, "means five hundred saved from death."

There was silence until Barlasz rose. "Joel, we all feel as you do," he said uncertainly, "we are only wondering what would be the best course to follow."

Brand felt suddenly helpless. None of these men had ever looked death in the face as the leaders of the Budapest *Waada* had done. Even a telegram to Weizmann, they argued, was out of the question – "we can never know if our telegrams have arrived on time or even whether the wording won't be garbled." All of them were parochial to a fault, obsessed with *Aliyah Beth*, the code-word for beating the British ban on illegal immigration into Palestine. They lacked even the power to secure him a Turkish visa, Brand thought bitterly, let alone to succour a million Jews.

It was Andor Grosz, a plump worldly-wise *bon vivant*, who sought to enlighten him. "Joel, you're as blind as a bat," he scoffed, "Do you really believe that Eichmann wants to free a million Jews in order to get dollars or trucks? The Nazis realise they've lost the war and they know that no peace will be made with Hitler. But Himmler thinks he can drive a wedge between the West and Russia. He wants to make use of every contact he can to start conversations with the Allies."

Contemptuously, he concluded: "The whole of your Jewish business was just a blind."

Brand stared back at him, not believing a word. His sense of mission was quite absolute now: only he could save a million Jews.

–

In Auschwitz, Prisoner No 25,404, who had once answered to the name of Dr Gisella Krausz, had no interest in salvation. Ten minutes after arriving there, she had nothing left for which to live.

At Auschwitz, the jerk of one man's thumb – the elegant well-manicured thumb of *Obersturmführer* Dr Josef Mengele, the camp pathologist – decided between life and death. As he surveyed the waiting columns, whistling, always whistling Wagner or *The Blue Danube*, a jerk to the left meant death within the hour, fuel for the five chimneys. A jerk to the right spelt a temporary reprieve: those selected would find work to do in one of thirty subsidiary labour camps.

Of all Gisella Krausz' eight-strong family, only she was directed right, to march into captivity.

Overnight she became part of a world inconceivable in Marmaros Sziget: forty square miles exclusively dedicated to the extinction of the Jewish race. Mile after mile of wooden barracks, called 'blocks', housing 1200 women apiece, where huge posters of red, black and white lice, captioned *Eine Laus, dein Tod* (a louse is your death) adorned the walls. It was a world lower than any animal kingdom, where more than 3000 women shared one communal latrine, where three-quart food bowls – used as chamber pots at night – often served up to six women by day.

This was a world where the life-span of the luckiest was often no more than ten months, but few women were so lucky: the slaughter of the Hungarian Jews lasted for 46 days on end. On peak days, 20,000 died, in batches of 1200 at a time, interleaved with conifer branches and old railway sleepers for kindling, doused with wood alcohol.

Even by night, the destruction went on; wakeful in the darkness Gisella Krausz could see the flames glowing through the barrack walls, a Gustave Doré vision of silhouettes with pitchforks, turning, forever turning, the corpses.

For Gisella Camp "C," housing 32,000 Polish and Hungarian women, became a world where survival was paramount, in great things and in small. Theft was so rife that women slept on unwiedly bundles, packed with all their possessions from shoes to feeding bowl; in the wash-house a woman held the bundle between her knees. At all costs she must avoid the fate of the *Muselmänner* (Muslims) – the bizarre nickname for men or women who sank into a zombie-like trance. Often, Gisella noted clinically, it followed a loss of one-third of their natural body-weight, and as May wore on they were dying everywhere: in the barracks, outside the barracks, in the camp toilets, at the interminable three-hour roll-calls known as *Zählappel*.

Thus, on a day which began at 4 a.m. with that same roll-call, Gisella waited with gnawing impatience for "the most important moment... the only moment worth living for" – noon, when the wail of the siren signified the dinner distribution. Almost always it was dubious greenish turnip soup – exactly ten mouthfuls, Gisella calculated – but it was warm, it was food, it stood for strength and hope.

In Block 15, the "hospital" block, staffed by five doctors and four nurses, Gisella was always busiest once the dinner hour had passed; savage fights over the soup ration meant bleeding heads to bandage, broken ribs to be taped, scratches to be cleaned. But the cages along the walls were daily filling up with grimmer cases which the doctors were almost powerless to cure: typhoid, malaria, scarlet fever, pneumonia. There were few medicines, only a few rolls of paper bandages, and no surgical instruments; operations were performed, without anaesthetics, with small pairs of rusty scissors and a sharp knife which Gisella kept sharpened on a stone.

Only in the matter of diet did the patients fare marginally better: a third of a loaf of good white bread each day, forty grams of margarine three times a week, sometimes a slice of sausage or half a tablespoon of jam. Those too weak to eat passed the rations on for exchange in the latrine mart: a piece of bread for two aspirin, fat bacon for sulphonamide. "There was only one law in Auschwitz," Gisella noted, "the law of the jungle."

Yet granted the power to heal, if only rarely, Gisella Krausz was more privileged than most. For the three million inmates of Auschwitz the only measure of time was their swiftly-ebbing vitality; for how long was a question only newcomers asked.

For them each day was as another: the harsh cries of "*Alles heraus*" that drove them to and from the Siemens and Buna work-sites, the baying of guard dogs, the blows from weighted clubs, the shriek of the circular saw slicing yet more firewood for the five chimneys, the dazzling searchlights by night, the thick clouds of black sweetish-smelling smoke by day. And always the handsome impassive Mengele, with his doctor's gold rosette and highly-polished boots, on hand to greet each trainload of death and chart the destiny of thousands: a thumb to the right, a thumb to the left.

In the West, the preparations to launch the Second Front for which Stalin had pressed so remorselessly gathered pace.

It was 3 a.m. on Sunday 21 May. In a roomy tent near the Dungeness Lighthouse, Wing Commander Roland Beamont, who three months earlier had been briefed to form the R.A.F.'s first Tempest fighter wing, was gently shaken awake by the duty intelligence officer. He reported, "Big show tomorrow, sir. They've lifted the train ban."

Although Beamont did not know it then, Roosevelt had decisively ended the British War Cabinet's interminable three-month debate on railway bombing. "However regrettable the attendant loss of civilian lives is," he had written to Churchill on 12 May, "I am not prepared to impose from this distance any restriction on military action by the responsible Commanders…"

Beamont had barely digested this news before a dispatch rider ducked beneath the tent flap. "Wing Commander Flying, sir? Form D for you, sir."

Skimming the preamble, Beamont came swiftly to the cogent paragraph:

"Intention: To attack and destroy with all available squadrons enemy rail transport from Germany to the Atlantic coast from first light 21 May. Planning routes and timing in allotted areas at wing leaders' discretion…"

By dint of combing the entire west country, using Air Vice Marshal Saunders' name with impunity, Beamont had located those missing Tempests in no short order. Within three weeks he had one and a half squadrons in training; by April all three had settled in together at Newchurch – two Tempest squadrons, No 3, under the quiet detached Alan Dredge and No 486 (New Zealand) under Johnny Iremonger, with No 56, operating Spitfire IXs, led by the urbane Gordon Sinclair.

Now at last they were ready to operate as Beamont had trained them: in small well-led formations covering an entire area, ensuring maximum destruction for minimum loss.

It was an area of which No 150 Wing by now knew every yard: a 160-mile sweep of the Pas de Calais area from Ostend through Brussels to Douai. By dawn on this chill Sunday, with fifty-plus engines throbbing to a crescendo of 2000 horse power, Beamont had divided that area into four sectors, each to be patrolled by no more than four aircraft at a time. Just as he had expected, 11 Group Control was early on the phone: why were they not flying in squadron formation?

"How have the first shows gone?" Beamont parried.

"Plenty of trains but losing some Spits," the Controller admitted.

"Naturally," said Beamont evenly. "A big formation with all that light flak in the coastal belt is asking for it. I think you'll find our system satisfactory."

In the briefing marquee, he outlined his tactics to the pilots. "Two thousand fighters are on this show, which is intended to paralyse the enemy's transport system," he encouraged them, "I see no reason why we should not top the list of scores." He recalled a final caution: "Don't forget to watch for flak wagons. They are usually on the last truck. If you do find one firing at you, leave the engine to the bloke behind. Concentrate on knocking out the gun."

Then it was all as Beamont remembered from other times and places, before the railway bombing interdiction of December 1943, when he had led the Typhoons of No 609 Squadron on the pioneer "train busting" forays. Crossing the coastal defence belt at 4000 feet over Calais, his section peeled off inland towards the Lille-Mons area, a stomach-tightening low-level swoop with the cones of flak rising to meet them, slowly at first, then faster and faster, like brightly coloured balls tossed by a juggler. Brief vivid impressions registered: the goods train at Lens, and the crackle of small-arms fire spattering at him from the long line of coaches, until his aim righted and flashes of shell-splinters sprayed its engine, as he held the burst for two and a half seconds.

Another train, at Orchies this time, recorded by his cinecamera gun film as a bellying white corona of steam. Then the landscape unreeling very fast, like a film projector out of control; the hedgerows, the permanent way, then the single locomotive near La Bouverie, one hammer-blow explosion, followed by the clawing flames from a goods-train's diesel engine.

"Pilot's time on single-engine aircraft," his log-book noted laconically, "Day, 45 minutes. Ops." So it went for two more days, until 150 Wing alone had written off or damaged 100 trains, with no losses at all, and the daily supply trains that the *Wehrmacht* needed to sustain them in France had shrunk from 100 to thirty-two.

It was all satisfyingly routine, Beamont thought, and yet...

His probing brain could never resist a mystery, and there was one strange phenomenon that still defied explanation. He could pinpoint the place -just north of Le Havre, at 10,000 feet – as well as the exact time, 2 a.m. on 8 May, the wearisome tail-end of a night intruder sortie. Below him, in the night sky, perhaps eight miles away, a bright orange glow was pulsing, travelling towards the north-west.

Curious, Beamont had given chase, all the time losing height, until he was down to 2000 feet, with the glow only a mile ahead. Then, as ephemerally as a shooting star, the orange light blotted out, lost in the Channel waters.

There had, of course, to be a logical explanation, Beamont knew. But just at this moment it quite eluded him.

For exactly twenty weeks now, the exploits of the Red Army had loomed large in the free world's headlines. Even in the United States, Lieutenant-General Douglas MacArthur's feats in the Pacific – the encirclement of Rabaul, the securing of Truk and Kwajalein, the sweep along the New Guinea coast – shared front-page space with a formidable quintet of Soviet commanders: Marshal Ivan Konev, General Rodion Malinovsky and Marshal Georgi Zhukov in the south, General Konstantin Rokossovsky and General Ivan Bagramian farther north.

Against all odds, their progress had been phenomenal. In January, which in some sectors saw the harshest winter for a century, Red Army tank crews, their *polushubki* (half-coats) stiff with frost, began each day chipping ice off their treads and gun-barrels – yet by February they were 800 miles west of Stalingrad, only 500 miles from Berlin. Harrying their foes with white-painted Stormoviks, pounding them with multi-barrelled Katyusha rocket guns, they had marked the 1002nd day of their war by swooping across the Dniester River in one night. Seven days later the *Wehrmacht* had retreated fully 850 miles from the Volga – back to the line of the Prut River, from which "Operation Barbarossa" had been launched on 22 June, 1941.

In one short week they had wrested back the Crimea and all but a tiny corner of the blazing Ukraine Peninsula, moving at 50 miles a day or better, besieging Odessa, relieving Sebastopol after seventy-two hours of bombardment. Nothing, it seemed, could stem their advance to the west.

No man watched that advance with greater interest than Captain Mikhail Koriakov, a combat correspondent attached to the 6th Red Air Force. Until 1938, Koriakov, a slightly-built bespectacled youngster of 33, had worked as a newspaperman then, tiring of the ambience, taken a job with the Tolstoy Museum. From the spring of 1941, he had been in the thick of the fighting, from Moscow onwards.

Now he nourished a curious preoccupation for a man tempered by three years of war: the restoration of God to the Russian people.

A native of the Sayan Mountains of Siberia, Koriakov had first learned about God as an eleven-year-old schoolboy; in distant Siberia, Communist placards proclaiming "Down with the priests and the imperialists!" were only finding cautious favour. As a teenager,

Koriakov had grown up largely indifferent to religion – but in the summer of 1941, the call, "We cannot retreat any further! Moscow is at our backs!" had resulted in "a spiritual landslide".

In the face of death, all material values fell away. To Koriakov, from then on, a sense of heaven became "the only vital life-giving sense". From that time on he had asked himself with ever-growing urgency, what spiritual lessons would this cataclysmic war bring about? What changes would there be in relation to freedom of conscience?

On Sunday 21 May – the same day that brought a welcome taste of action to Wing Commander Beamont – Koriakov received his dusty answer.

On that morning, stationed at Volhynia, in the north-west Ukraine, he learned with deep sorrow, through a radio operator's bulletin, of the death of Sergei, Patriarch of Moscow and all the Russians.

Koriakov had never glimpsed the Acting Patriarch of the Russian Orthodox Church, Metropolitan Sergei – yet this man had affected his entire life. The Kremlin, anxious to lull Allied fears, had permitted him a rare wartime freedom – "let the storm break," he had preached as early as 26 June, 1941, "We know that in its wake will come good as well as evil". Such words, the Politburo knew, were calculated not only to reassure the Allies but to inspire mothers sending their sons to the front, wives operating steel mills and reapers; the Church all over Russia had contributed to the cost of the Dimitri Donskoy Tank Battalion.

Few outside Russia knew that the widely-discussed *Journal of the Moscow Patriarchate* was published for export only. In Moscow, where only four churches remained open as showpieces, not one bookshop was permitted to stock a copy.

On an impulse, Koriakov strolled down the village street. Here, in Volhynia, for the first time in many months, he had seen a church open for worship, cross and cupola glistening in the sun; in most of Russia, the churches, filthy, partly dismantled, were used as *kolkhoz* (collective farm) storehouses, their altars piled with sacks of grain. "Will there be a Requiem for the Patriarch?" he asked a peasant woman at the church door. She was dubious: only the elder would know.

But the elder, an old man with a long coat and a thick beard, had not even known the Patriarch was dead. The field newspaper for which Koriakov worked, *The Country Falcon*, was still on the presses, and civilians rarely saw it. Again on impulse, he strolled back to the office, picked up a still-damp news-sheet and returned to the church. Following a colloquy with the priest, the elder returned from the altar: a Requiem would be sung immediately after the Communion.

Almost in a dream, Koriakov heard again, after so many years, the ancient words of the ritual, "the stern majestic chants". The Requiem over, the elder came forward to hand him a wafer. At this moment, Koriakov felt inexpressibly pagan; he had no idea what to do with it.

"Eat it reverently and may God be with you," the elder told him.

It was a glorious morning. Storks were building nests high in the old oak trees across the road; the air was heady with the scent of lilac blossom. Slowly munching the wafer, Koriakov felt suddenly that his old life "had snapped as if it was a dry stick cracked against a knee".

Barely an hour later, a soldier knocked at his door; he must report immediately to the news-sheet's editor, Major Rutman. Another correspondent, Lieutenant Gorshkov, had seen him leave the church and filed a complaint.

"Were you in the church this morning?" Rutman asked abruptly.

Koriakov admitted it. "I gave the elder a copy of the newspaper with the news of the Patriarch's death."

"Were you the one who ordered the Requiem?"

"No, I did not."

"Denying will not do you any good!" Rutman bellowed at him, "Go to your room and await further orders!".

It was evening when the next summons came. To Koriakov's astonishment, the Major's office was now packed from wall to wall — with fellow correspondents from *The Falcon*, with officers of the political section, with members of the 6th Air Force military court from nearby Berezhnitsa. Prominent on Rutman's table was Koriakov's Bible; his parents had promised to send it on by parcel post and Rutman had intercepted the package.

The cross-examination began immediately. From the first, Koriakov sensed that they were out to trap him; it was Captain Pronin, the major's second-in-command who led off the questioning. "When we were in Valdai (north-west of Moscow) I saw a fat book on a table in your room called *History of the Russian Church*. Do you remember it?".

Koriakov did. It was not a proscribed book; he had borrowed it from the Workers' Institute Library.

"Have you ever perused *A Brief History of the Communist Party*? Have you ever read it?"

"Yes, I have. As a matter of fact I received the highest possible mark in Leninism."

"Why haven't I ever seen *A Brief History of the Communist Party* or *The Problems of Leninism* on your table?" Pronin countered.

Without success, Koriakov sought to defend himself. It was a writer's duty to observe life in all its phases; a writer could go to church as a matter of curiosity. At once Rutman cut in triumphantly, "You did not just go to church. You ordered a Requiem!"

A babel of angry denunciation broke out: "A Soviet officer consorting with priests!…" "That a thing like that should happen in Western Ukraine!…" "You are a disgrace to the Red Army uniform!…"

Koriakov was silent. Only punishment and disgrace lay ahead, that much was certain, though what forms these would take he did not know. It was now that Rutman sought to entrap him on the Party line.

"What is your explanation of certain concessions we have made to the Church people during the war years?" he asked craftily.

Koriakov saw only one possible answer: the truth. For reasons of internal policy, because the Church could harness the patriotism of the nation – but chiefly because of foreign policy.

Smirking, Rutman turned to the other members of the court: "No one can say that he lacks political education. He reasons and writes well, whenever he feels so inclined."

It was then, with controlled and icy fury, that Rutman spelt out the Politburo's post-war intent: a truth long known to Churchill but which Roosevelt would never perceive until too late.

"Can't you understand that if at present we are forced into a coalition with a bastard like Churchill we can also seek a temporary understanding with the priests?

"Apparently you have no conception that when the war is over we intend to settle accounts with all the church-going scum."

–

As encounters were measured it was all too brief, a minor footnote in time, yet the hopes of thousands of men had pointed to that moment.

At 7:31 a.m. on 25 May, a morning of thin mist and poppies glowing in the wheat-fields, Captain Benjamin Harrison Souza, of Honolulu, was moving north from the Anzio beachhead with a platoon of engineers. Along the coastal road north of Terracina they met up with Lieutenant Francis Xavier Buckley, a carrot-topped engineer from Philadelphia. Both men eyed one another suspiciously.

"Where the hell do you think you're going?" Captain Souza growled.

"I'm trying to make contact with the Anzio forces," Buckley replied.

"Boy," Souza told him fervently, "you've made it."

Thus, after four months of toil, tribulation and terror, the Anzio beachhead passed into history. The beachhead front and the Cassino front were at last one.

It had been a bloody battle of attrition – launched as Italy's severest winter melted into a warm hazy springtime tinged with the scent of honeysuckle and ripening fruit. Promptly at 11 p.m. on 11 May, to the same code-word, "Zip," that had heralded El Alamein, 1600 guns had opened fire on the 15-mile Cassino front, a storm of 174,000 shells hosing the German positions.

From the first the Free French Expeditionary Corps, under the shy silent General Alphonse-Pierre Juin were in the vanguard – led by officers in jeeps "as reckless as New York taxi-drivers," weaving in and out of the column, heedless of shell pockets, winding up the west bank of the Garigliano River to capture and hold Monte Faito. Using seasoned mountain fighters, Moroccan colonial troops known as Goumiers, whose mule supply-trains plodded in their wake, Juin's men secured six miles of precipitous terrain in three days.

Along the Tyrrhenian seacoast, the Anzio beachhead was by contrast strangely silent. The little town leaned down to the harbour in a frozen cascade of wreckage, desolate, forgotten. But inland, tanks and infantry of General Mark Clark's Fifth Army were at last punching within two miles of Highway No 7, the Via Appia.

All that week the Allies rolled on up the shin of the Italian boot. By 14 May, Kesselring's eastern front was collapsing. At 5:25 p.m. on 16 May, monitors of Major-General Christopher Vokes's 1st Canadian Division logged a watershed telephone conversation between Kesselring and *Generaloberst* Heinrich von Vietinghoff-Scheel, Tenth Army Commander. In the Cassino area, Vietinghoff reported, only 100 tanks were now left. "Then we have to give up Cassino," was Kesselring's resigned decision.

Now came the chance that Lieutenant-General Wladyslaw Anders' II Polish Corps had so long awaited. For them, unlike the French, the world they had known could never be restored; ahead of the battle with their German foe loomed another with their Russian "ally" that history has yet to resolve. But Cassino and the mile-high rock mass of Monte Cairo remained to be taken, and on 17 May the Poles vented their pent-up frustrations in a primeval battle that raged from house to house, from room to room, among the rubble and the splintered trees, until one German battalion was reduced to using rocks for ammunition.

At 10:20 a.m. on 18 May, when the 12th Polish Lancers hoisted their red and white standard over the monastery's ruins, Anders' Corps had suffered more than 3700 killed, wounded or missing. But on 17 May, one of the last German units to pull back from the Gustav Line to the Hitler Line, seven miles north, *Oberst* Ludwig Heilmann's 4th Para Regiment, had its lead company down to one officer, one corporal, one private. Six days earlier they had joined battle with 700 men.

Now, in the lull that followed, Cassino's shattered acres, where nightingales sang each evening at dusk, became an object of daily pilgrimage for all those rear-echelon personnel who had only followed the battle from afar. Corporal Peter Llewellyn, of a New Zealand ammunition company, was impressed above all by the silence, and how "the smashed stones seemed to be able to absorb sound as quicklime absorbs water." He recalled, too, the stench "of dead houses – the stifling sweetish reek of old mortar, mice, dirty wallpaper, broken wainscots, domestic dust."

Veterans in later years retained a harsher picture of Cassino: a battle where a steak dinner was always, perversely, hated as the prelude to an assault, fighting over ground too rocky to tackle with spades, where thirst was slaked with rusty petrol-tasting water. For every combatant, Cassino had been a sub-world of cellars or caves, screened by blanket awnings, lit by guttering candles, smelling of fried Spam, Dettol disinfectant and sweat, where men moved only at night and in canvas slippers, overwhelmed by the monatstery's jagged silhouette.

One commander now saw a more elusive goal as within Fifth Army's grasp. Ever since 20 January, Major-General Fred L. Walker had smarted at the mauling that his 36th (Texas) Division had taken at the Rapido River crossing, which had cost them 1,600 casualties. With the fall of Cassino, Highway No 6, the Via Casilina and Highway No 7, the Via Appia, now lay open – and Walker believed that the 36th might redeem its jinxed reputation by knifing through the ring which the retreating Germans had drawn round Rome.

His concept was a daring one: elements of the 36th would infiltrate a gap that scouts had spotted in the German lines, cut off the German garrison in the tiny village of Velletri, then embark on a 15-mile night trek through the Alban Hills. But in the early afternoon of 30 May, both Clark and Major-General Lucian K. Truscott, VI Corps commander, were less than enthusiastic.

As Sergeant Max E. Shaffer, the division's photographer, whom Walker had summoned to his command tent, later recalled it, Walker was attempting a hard sell on both commanders, but in vain. "Fred, it won't work," he remembered Mark Clark commenting, "You will get a hell of a lot of men killed for nothing."

Walker was insistent. "I know it will work, and in fact I am so sure it will I will stake my reputation on it."

But neither commander was convinced. Truscott, before leaving Walker's tent, was quite adamant: "Fred, I won't give you permission to do this; if you do it on your own and you fail, the axe will fall." Shaffer also recalled Mark Clark adding, "Fred, I can't OK this. If you do it and succeed we are on our way to Rome; but if you fail you will have to bear the brunt of what comes with the failure, and your action will be without my approval or the approval of Truscott."

Walker, undeterred, had continued to plan, even assigning Sergeant Shaffer to the task force to compile a photographic record. Nor was his optimism misplaced. Towards 4 p.m. on 30 May, Truscott called him back with a reluctant go-ahead: "I have talked to General Clark and General Clark has Okd your project... *But you had better get through.*"

The race for Rome was on.

—

On the morning of Friday 26 May, three Army staff cars halted at the traffic lights on Harrow High Road, London, en route for Northolt aerodrome. Pedestrians in the moment of crossing briefly glimpsed a well-loved figure: a black Tank Corps beret, a fleece-lined leather jacket worn over a khaki battledress with five rows of ribbons, grey eyes alert above a clipped military moustache. As the car moved forward, a cheer burst out: "Good old Monty!"

The man who flashed them the "Monty" smile and responded with the brisk "Monty" salute was just then as frightened as he had ever been. While Lieutenant-General Bernard Montgomery lay low in his advance Portsmouth headquarters, his "double" 46-year-old Lieutenant Meyrick Clifton-James of the Royal Army Pay Corps, was embarking on the first stage of a 1,000-mile journey to Gibraltar and Algiers. A Montgomery look-alike who for years had toured the provinces as a small-part actor, Clifton-James was almost M.I.5.'s last fling of the D-Day dice.

For plainly if Montgomery was visiting Algiers, no assault across the English Channel could as yet be imminent.

Studying the general's mannerisms – the right hand weighing an invisible object when discussing a point, the slightly-nasal high-pitched voice – Clifton-James had rehearsed the role for three weeks with ever-growing doubts. But now, as the roadside cheering redoubled, it was like a first-night curtain rising; he was "on" and he was word-perfect.

At intervals he was to let drop khaki handkerchiefs initialled "B.L.M." like clues in a paperchase. He was to address Gibraltar's governor, Sir Ralph Eastwood, "Monty's" old Sandhurst crony, as "Rusty" and to be "madly indiscreet," talking of a mysterious "Plan 303". Despite the risk of snipers, he would travel always in an open car, so that German agents could train their telescopes on him. On Montgomery's insistence, he would even receive a general's pay – in the region of £8 a day – for every day on the job, but even this was scant compensation for the ordeal that would follow.

Oblivious to the danger, Clifton-James had learned with dismay that "Monty" was teetotal and a non-smoker, eschewing both meat and fish. Ahead of him stretched a forty-eight hour tobacco-free nature cure, fortified by nothing stronger than ginger ale.

-

Another M.I.5. agent was working overtime. By 2 June, from the house in Palace Gardens Terrace, Lily Sergueiev was transmitting three messages a day, always at night. True or false? Lily never knew. One item of information was intriguing: she had seen a great concourse of gliders on an airfield, painted with black and white stripes. The invasion force would definitely use towed gliders to transport men and material.

"The other day you said you could ruin our work," Mary Ward asked her suddenly, "How?"

Lily was silent. Then: "I didn't bluff. There *is* a security check."

"Perhaps we know it?"

Lily laughed. "Oh no. You can go through all my transmissions with a mathematical genius, but you won't find it."

"What is this sign?"

Again Lily was silent. "You realise that I must warn Colonel Robertson about it?"

Lily sensed her time was almost up. "I'm only surprised you haven't done it already," she said sadly.

-

Sunday 4 June, 5 a.m. In a darkened railway siding outside Southampton, General Sir Hastings Ismay, who had waited up all night on Churchill's private train, listened intently to the metallic tones of Major-General Walter Bedell Smith, calling from Admiral Ramsay's headquarters, Southwick House, near Portsmouth. There was news from the weather men and all of it was bad: their forecast for D-Day, 5 June, was uniformly pessimistic. A cloud base of 500 feet to zero and Force 5 winds would both rule out the use of aircraft and render naval gunfire ineffective.

Eisenhower and his commanders had been unanimous: without Allied air superiority, the landings posed too great a risk. A 24-hour postponement had been agreed.

Ismay, who had expected the news, promptly retired to bed; in the small hours, Churchill had remarked that nothing could be done, and on no account was he to be awakened. Half an hour later Ismay was rudely shaken awake; Churchill, after four hours sleep, had risen early and was now eager for news.

It had been a fraught decision, for every hour was crucial: how much longer could the gigantic secret be kept? Already huddles of loaded transports and supply ships were collecting at the Nore, Milford Haven, Plymouth and Southampton. Hundreds of LCTs, moving south from the Combined Operations Training Base at Inveraray, and the Clyde base of Troon, were assembled, camouflaged with netting, off the mud-flats of Portsmouth, in secluded coves at Newhaven, Lymington and Poole. On these craft the men already embarked fought a miserable retching battle against nausea and seasickness.

There were other all-too-obvious signs that invasion was imminent. On airfields from Debden in Essex to Honiton in Devon, the warning red cross of St Andrew loomed on the signals area outside every Watch Office: airfield unserviceable, landing forbidden. Scores of trains had been cancelled without notice; London's main termini now resembled huge frowsy dormitories as stranded passengers caught a few hours sleep.

Yet the whole vast enterprise must wait upon the weather.

All that Sunday afternoon the preparations continued – hoping against hope. Since before dawn, ground crews of the U.S. Eighth Air Force on England's east coast had been busy breaking open a paint consignment labelled "For the cake walk," daubing black and white stripes two feet wide on the wings and tail booms of P-38 Lightnings. By early afternoon the same camouflage instructions had reached Wing Commander Roland Beamont, as he touched down at Newchurch; all told, 10,000 aircraft would use up 100,000 gallons of paint, singling them out from Luftwaffe planes. Over the scrambler telephone, Beamont and other R.A.F. wing leaders heard the same identical instructions: "Report Tangmere 1000 hours tomorrow for A.O.C.'s briefing. Absolute secrecy to be maintained."

As the day wore on, the weather worsened perceptibly.

At 9:15 p.m., rain lashed the pine trees outside Southwick House; behind the heavy blackout curtains of the library, flurries of rain rattled like buckshot against the window panes. It was a large comfortable blue-carpeted room, dominated by a table with a green baize cloth, set about with easy chairs and sofas; dark oak bookshelves lined the walls. Tonight, every man present had been a participant in that euphoric St Paul's School conference of 15 May, when the going had seemed so easy: Bedell Smith chatting with the pipe-puffing Tedder, Montgomery in corduroy slacks and a roll-topped sweater, Ramsay and Leigh-Mallory, formally clad as always.

All of them awaited Eisenhower – and, above all, Group Captain James Stagg, the tall serious R.A.F. meteorologist.

Promptly at 9:30 p.m., trim in a dark-green battledress, Eisenhower entered. There was the faintest hint of a rueful grin – "When I die they ought to bury me on a rainy day in a ceremonial coffin shaped like a landing craft," he had joked earlier – but his face was set and worried. Shortly the three senior meteorologists, led by Stagg, reported with their briefing.

As Stagg later recalled it: "No one could have imagined weather charts less propitious." Two depressions over the North Atlantic were in themselves mid-winter phenomena, and while all three forecasters were confident that the stormy cold front would traverse the Channel overnight, none of them could predict the sequel.

"There have been some rapid and unexpected developments in the situation," Stagg told the hushed assembly. In two to three hours, the rain would cease, followed by thirty-six hours of less clear weather with moderate winds. Bombers and fighters should be able to operate on Monday night, 5 June, though hampered by cloud.

At its simplest, it boiled down to one unenviable option: tolerable weather, far below minimal requirements, would pertain for little more than twenty-four hours.

No sooner had Stagg finished than the questions erupted. Could the forecasts be wrong? Had reports been checked with all available sources? Still Eisenhower hesitated, as someone asked Stagg, "What will the weather be on D-Day in the Channel and over the French coast?". It was fully two minutes before Stagg replied, "To answer that question would make me a guesser, not a meteorologist."

It was an awesome decision for any man to take. Eisenhower looked questioningly at Bedell Smith. "It's a helluva gamble but it's the best possible gamble," Smith replied. Next it was Montgomery's turn. "I would say – Go!" was his incisive verdict.

The minutes ticked by, while Eisenhower wrestled with it. Another postponement would mean two weeks delay, with less favourable moon conditions, and thousands of troops had already embarked and been briefed. Watching his chief, Bedell Smith felt pity for his "loneliness and isolation," sitting with his hands clasped before him, staring at the green baize cloth.

"The question is," Eisenhower mused, as if to himself, "Just how long can you hang this operation on the end of a limb and let it hang there?".

At length he looked up. The decision was taken: "I am quite positive we must give the order... I don't like it, but there it is."

In the main hall, smiling broadly now, Eisenhower chanced upon Group Captain Stagg. "For heaven's sake," he told the concerned meteorologist, "hold the weather to what you told us and don't bring any more bad news."

—

Southwick House, 4:15 a.m., 5 June. As the meteorologists once again faced the commanders, the tired face of Group Captain Stagg bore the ghost of a smile. "I think we have a gleam of hope for you, sir," he told Eisenhower.

The mass of weather fronts coming in from the Atlantic was moving faster than anticipated. Everything now suggested fair conditions beginning late on 5 June and lasting until the morning of 6 June, with a drop in wind velocity, some break in the clouds, and a ceiling of 3,000 feet.

Eisenhower thought for one whole minute. Then, very quietly but audibly, he said, "O.K., let's go."

—

The word was passing. All over southern England, men hearing the news, steeled themselves for what they had to do.

Aboard the LSI (Landing Ship Infantry) *Empire Lance* in Southampton Harbour, the men of the 6th Battalion, The Green Howards, heard the Senior Naval Transport Officer's measured tones over the loudspeaker: "At 17:45 hours, this ship will weigh anchor, and, in passage with the remainder of the armada, sail for the coast of France." As this news was broken, an eerie hush fell on ship after ship. At Tangmere airfield, Sussex, following a mass-briefing from Leigh-Mallory, Wing Commander Roland Beamont passed up lunch to spend two hours immersed in the Overlord invasion orders, then commented with healthy scepticism, If only it works... At Debden airfield, Essex, Colonel Don Blakeslee, commanding the 4th (U.S.) Fighter Group, laid it on the line to his pilots; each P-51 Mustang would be outfitted with two 500-pound bombs to launch against the Atlantic Wall. Tense and tight-lipped, Blakeslee told them: "I am prepared to lose the whole group."

For the men who would form the invasion spearhead – more than 1,000 glider pilots, 13,000 American paratroopers and 4,255 British

– these last hours were among the longest they had ever known. If the British 6th Airborne Division's role was as onerous as any – the destruction of a massive four-gun coastal battery near Merville, the seizure of two vital bridges across the Orne River and the Caen canal – at least they knew the hazards. Only three days earlier, Major-General Richard Gale, the divisional commander, revealing their destination, had told them: "The Hun thinks only a bloody fool will go there – that's why I am going!".

Few men were better suited to the task. From the first, like the U.S. paratroopers, the glider pilots' indoctrination had verged on the sadistic, designed to scare off all those who couldn't stand the pace; any man nicking his chin with a razor was booked for being "idle while shaving". But to merit the coveted badge of blue wings surmounted by a lion rampant called for more than flying skills. Initiative tests were mandatory; pilots were given 2s 6d ($12\frac{1}{2}$ new pence) and forty-eight hours to achieve an impossible assignment – anything from acquiring the secret recipe for Worcestershire sauce to achieving half an hour's dual control on a steam roller. By common consent, the palm went to British noncoms George Biddlecombe and Paddy Ryan; assigned to collect the signature of the Duke of Beaufort and finding him absent they settled for that of his house guest, H.M. Queen Mary.

The airborne troops were ready too. On a score of airfields pivoting on Newbury, Berkshire, paratroopers smeared their faces with cocoa and linseed oil or with the ashes from spent fires; others carefully shaved their heads, leaving only a Mohawk scalp lock. At Honiton, in Devon, Private Donald Burgett, the young paratrooper who knew death as an old familiar, smiled wryly at one group of buddies "doing the Jolson bit, singing 'Mammy', waving their hands and blinking white-looking eyes in blackened faces". But Burgett's real concern was with his equipment. By take-off time – towards 11 p.m. – he and all the others were weighed down with packages like walking Christmas trees.

Aside from his suit of Olive Drab, worn under his jump suit, Burgett was wearing a helmet, boots, gloves, a main parachute, a reserve parachute, and a Mae West. He was armed not only with a rifle, a .45 automatic, three knives and a machete; he was further burdened with a cartridge belt, two bandoliers, almost 750 rounds of ammo, both .30 and .45, a Hawkins mine to blow the tracks off a tank, four blocks of TNT, an entrenching tool, three first aid kits, two morphine needles and a gas mask. He had nine separate grenades, five days rations, a canteen of water, a change of socks and underwear and 200 cigarettes.

It was small wonder that when the order came, "Emplane," two Air Corps men lifted Burgett and the rest of his "stick" bodily into the C-47, where many knelt as if in prayer. It was the easiest way to ride.

Though Burgett only glimpsed him, Eisenhower was briefly at Honiton – and at Welford, Tarrant Rushton, and all the airfields ringing Newbury. "If it goes all right," his driver, WAC Lieutenant Kay Summersby, had told him, "dozens of people will claim the credit. But if it goes wrong, you'll be the only one to blame." Yet nothing of this showed in the Supreme Commander's face as he moved through darkness among the black-faced troops, like an echo of Shakespeare's *Henry V* on the eve of Agincourt: a little touch of Eisenhower in the night.

"What is your job, soldier?"

"Ammunition bearer, sir."

"Where is your home?"

"Pennsylvania, sir."

"Did you get those shoulders working in a coal mine?"

"Yes, sir."

"Good luck to you tonight, soldier."

For some unit commanders, it seemed a time for exhortation. In the 101st Airborne Division Area, Colonel Howard "Skeets" Johnson, commanding the 501st Parachute Infantry Regiment, brandished his jump knife like a berserk cheer leader, rallying his troops in a frenzied chant of, "We're the best! We're the best!". In the 82nd Airborne Area, Lieutenant-Colonel Edward Krause, of the 3rd Battalion, 505th Parachute Infantry, held aloft a folded Old Glory and vowed: "Tonight… we're going to liberate the people (of Sainte Mère-Église) and fly this flag from the tallest building." By dawn on 6 June, they had done just that.

For others it seemed a time for prayer. At Broadwell, Gloucestershire, Captain John Gwinnett, a chaplain of the 6th Airborne, dedicated the divisional flag of Bellerophon mounted on the winged horse Pegasus, using as text: "Fear knocked at the door. Faith opened, and there was nothing there." At Honiton, Second Lieutenant Joshua Logan, the noted Broadway producer, after briefing the paratroopers on escape and evasion techniques, handed over to the group chaplain. Suddenly the padre's prayer tailed off in a high-pitched scream: "Get in there and kill them! Kill them! Go over there and kill 'em!"

"Scared the hell out of everybody," Logan was to recall.

The secret could no longer be kept from the world at large. At Littlehampton, on the Sussex coast, Sister Brenda McBryde, of No 75 British General Hospital, who two weeks later would herself embark for France, was one of a group who left a crowded dance floor to cool off on the flat roof; the muffled beat of the Palais Glide came faintly on the still evening air. Suddenly they were conscious of a new vibration, growing louder by the minute.

As Sister McBryde watched, a cloud of tiny specks in the sky inland fanned out and multiplied; formation after formation of planes was throbbing overhead. The noise grew deafening; dancers were flocking up from the ballroom floor, "moon faces turned up to the sky". Lancasters, Blenheims and Halifaxes thundered above them, all of them towing Horsa or Hamilcar gliders, moving purposefully across the sky, heading for France.

A great drawn-out sigh went up from all the watchers; it was, Sister McBryde recalled, "like the Ah-ah-h-h that follows a firework display".

—

In blacked-out London, one man knew a mounting disquiet. At No 10, Duke Street, in the shadow of Selfridge's department store, Captain Eugène Mamy, the night duty officer in de Gaulle's intelligence department was listening to the "Personal Messages" which the B.B.C. broadcast twice daily to the French Resistance from a studio at Bush House, Aldwych.

For two years now, the 200,000 men and women who made up the French Resistance had shared a fantasy world with the faceless Mamy. They, and they alone, could interpret a message like "the crocodile is thirsty" as a signal for sabotage, or "the doctor buries all his patients" as a motor boat's secret voyage to Finisterre. As chief of de Gaulle's Premier (Operations) Bureau, Mamy composed the bulk of these, tailoring rural phrases like "Reeds must grow, leaves rustle" to symbolise "The Green Plan," or mass railway sabotage.

At 10:15 p.m. on 5 June, Mamy was expecting no more than the usual transmission period: sixteen minutes, covering an average of thirty-five personal messages according to length. Yet now he realised that fully seventy code-messages were winging their way to France. The entire Resistance was being alerted – the peaceful south no less than the threatened north.

In the overall plan, only two phrases were common to all of France – "The dice are on the table," to signal The Green Plan, and "It is hot in Suez," cue for The Violet Plan, the sabotage of underground Post Office cables. But tonight the messages were coming thick and fast, so crowded together that resistants and Gestapo agents alike were hard put to it to distinguish their own group-message from the others. John Remembers Rita... The Compass Points North... Napoleon's hat is in the ring. Lastly, the words of an old French song, imbued with grim meaning, The children get bored on Sunday. Every resistant knew the significance of that one: get ready, distribute arms, contact your leader, report every move the Germans make.

This was the firm intention of Eisenhower's headquarters, as General Joseph-Pierre Koenig, commanding the French Forces of the Interior, had been informed that very day: since many messages were known to the Gestapo, maximum chaos would be created behind the lines by releasing all of them simultaneously.

Mamy, unaware of this strategy, was sure of just one thing: outside the invasion zone, thousands of resistants would die even as D-Day dawned.

For the war leaders there was nothing to do now but wait. In the Kremlin, Josef Stalin was sitting up late and drinking deep with Molotov and Milovan Djilas, Marshal Tito's Yugoslav emissary to Russia. A despatch had arrived from Churchill announcing the landings, and at once Stalin began to scoff: "Yes, there'll be a landing, if there is no fog ... Maybe they'll meet with some Germans! What if they meet with some Germans! Maybe there won't be a landing then, but just promises as usual."

Churchill had returned to London, to pace the Map Room of "The Hole," the six-acre honeycomb of offices below Whitehall, where one in ten of War Cabinet meetings were held. He had "hardened to this enterprise," but at this hour doubts once more assailed him. In his mind echoed the tramp of ghostly legions from A. E. Housman's *A Shropshire Lad*:

Far and near and low and louder
On the roads of earth go by,
Dear to friends and food for powder,
Soldiers marching, all to die.

It was late, and Clementine Churchill had joined him. "Do you realise," her husband asked, "that by the time you wake up in the morning, twenty thousand men may have been killed?"

—

In Italy, the Normandy beaches seemed a world away. Rome was the prize now, and all men knew it.

Before midnight on 30 May, under the fitful light of a new moon, elements of Major-General Fred L. Walker's 36th (Texas) Division, with Italian guides in the van, set off for the first objective of their long trek through the hills: the crest of Monte Artemisio. The few German sentries they met were silently despatched with knife thrusts. Breasting the hill unchallenged at dawn on 31 May, they now overlooked the garrison town of Velletri.

The one man bitterly opposed to this thrust was General Sir Harold Alexander. For Alexander, the fall of Rome, though desirable, was no more than incidental; all along his intention was to destroy the right wing of Vietinghoff's retreating Tenth Army at Valmontone, ten miles north-east of Velletri. Yet, typically, Alexander had issued no written orders to Mark Clark – merely enquiring diffidently of Clark's Chief of Staff, General Alfred Gruenther, "I am sure that the Army Commander will continue to push towards Valmontone, won't he?".

Gruenther, deadpan, reported back to Clark: "I assured him that you had the situation thoroughly in mind, and that he could depend on you to execute a vigorous plan with all the push in the world." In truth, the push for Valmontone by Major-General Lucian Truscott's VI Corps was now only a token thrust. More than the entrapment of Vietinghoff's troops, Mark Clark wanted Rome, and Alexander knew it.

Harold Macmillan, Churchill's Minister Resident at Allied Headquarters, North-West Africa and Mediterranean, never forgot meeting Alexander soon after his conference with Gruenther; Alexander's face, normally impassive, was twitching convulsively. When

Macmillan asked what was wrong, Alexander snapped back, "What is right?". Then why, Macmillan asked, when he understood the contretemps, had he not put his foot down? "Why do you talk nonsense?" Alexander raged, "How can I give orders?".

Yet as far back as February, Churchill had pinpointed Alexander's weakness as commander when he cabled regarding the Anzio stalemate: "I have a feeling that you may have hesitated to assert your authority because you were dealing so largely with Americans and therefore *urged* an advance instead of *ordering* it. You are however quite entitled to give orders..."

But Clark, who had long ago cleared his plan with both Roosevelt and General Marshall, had seized the lack of written orders as the green light. For the President and the Army Chief of Staff, suspicious of Balkan adventures, Rome was prize enough.

Thus by 1 June, white flags were fluttering over both Velletri and Valmontone; though Kesselring's armies were still technically in one piece, the way to Rome was clear. Forging in the lead as always were those scourges of the Anzio beachhead, Brigadier-General Robert T. Frederick's 1st Special Service Force, the "Devil's Brigade," their mission to secure the city's nineteen Tiber bridges before the Germans blew them. By 4:20 a.m. on 4 June, this mission was complete, though they had not neglected their propensity for pillage. Most men's sleeping bags were now snugly lined with sheets bearing the papal crest, looted from the Pope's summer residence at Castel Gandolfo.

Now the whole of Fifth Army was streaming in their wake, and along the white dusty roads leading to the capital the scarred milestones told their story: ROMA, 20 KM, ROMA, 18 KM, ROMA, 15 KM. Prominent in the lead and revelling in every moment of it was the U.S. II Corps commander, General Geoffrey Keyes. Begged by one officer to take cover from snipers, Keyes replied: "This is the first quiet spot I've seen in weeks. If I go back anywhere, they'll get me on the telephone."

It was the free world's first liberation of 1944, and appropriately church bells were pealing. On Trinity Sunday 4 June, as the first main body of troops, borne in grimy jeeps and tanks, nosed through the Porta Pia to the code word "Elefante," dusk was already falling, but still the crowd went wild, surging forward to press wine and flowers on the bearded mud-stained GIs – who responded with whole cornucopias of chocolates, cigarettes and biscuits.

Five hundred miles north on Lake Garda, Mussolini ordered three days' public mourning for the city he would never see again – at the moment that Sergeant John Vita, mounting the Duce's famous podium in Piazza Venezia, delivered a mock-Mussolinian harangue to a fusillade of revolver shots. On the Corso, Italian partisans sporting hammer-and-sickle badges paraded with Red flags. One officer still commented wryly, "I'll bet there are enough Fascist party badges in the Tiber today to make the fish sick."

Near Gestapo HQ, on Via Tasso, an impromptu conga line snaked through the streets to the chanted refrain of "Hey, *Paesano*! Have you gotta the *vino*?" Oblivious to the swaying throng, a lone GI, shepherding a lone German sniper, wound his way through them in total absorption. But this was a rare exception. Suddenly, it seemed, there were no more Fascists and no more Germans – a transition so swift some found it hard to grasp. One "Devil's Brigade" GI bedded down for a night with a prostitute; as dawn broke, forgetting the city had changed hands, she wished him *Guten morgen*. Chaplain Morris Kertzer, checking in at the Grand Hotel, was embarrassed to find German diplomats making a hasty exit via the back door. Shrugging massively, the manager told him, "In the hotel business, one must be prepared for all eventualities."

The wife of the Irish Minister, Delia Kiernan, was equally taken by surprise. Out for a stroll near the *Stazione Termini*, she spotted a cluster of soldiers, their uniforms caked with mountain mud, sprawled out on the pavement. At first she took them for Germans, until one of them, sitting up, called, "Say, sister. Come and park your arse beside me." "So then," Delia Kiernan related afterwards, "I knew I was liberated."

In the great piazza before St Peter's, fountains sparkled in the sunlight, and a vast multitude flocked in, summoned by the largest of all its bells, the eleven-ton *Campanone*. Before the gigantic tapestry of the crossed keys, Pope Pius XII gave thanks for Rome's deliverance from war. Then, with a helpless frozen smile, he submitted to his first Allied press conference, bemused by the photographers' raucous cries of "Hold it, Pope – we gotcha in focus," before receiving the profound apologies of Major-General Ernie Harmon. To Harmon's consternation, his 1st Armoured ("Hell on Wheels") Division had taken twelve ear-splitting hours to rumble past the Vatican. "Any time you liberate Rome," answered Pius with feeling, "you can make all the noise you want."

On 5 June, in a warm glow of triumph, Mark Clark – whom the Father's Day Committee of New York had just elected "Father of the Year" – set the seal on the city's rejoicing, mounting the Piazza del Campidoglio for a conference with his corps commanders. Clark's day had already been made by a quotation reported from an awe-struck GI getting his first glimpse of the Colosseum: "Jeez, I didn't know our bombers had done *that* much damage."

Already, it seemed, Rome had been returned to history. At a cocktail party, an Italian *Principessa* approached Captain George Walton, air support officer of II Corps, with an oddly double-edged compliment. "I want to congratulate you," she gushed in all sincerity, "Do you realise that you are the first of the barbarians to have taken Rome from the south?"

—

In the dining room of the Albergo Città, the newly-established British press camp by the Spanish Steps, the B.B.C's Godfrey Talbot brought his colleagues back to earth with a jolt.

"Boys, we're on the back page now. They've landed in Normandy."

4

"Do Not Be Daunted if Chaos Reigns"
6 June, 1944

Behind the Normandy beaches, a brooding silence reigned. For the citizens of Caen, Bayeux, St Lô and all the coastal towns, the night of 5 June, endured behind tight-closed shutters, was hot and airless. This night was, above all, a testing time for several thousand men and women of a Resistance network code-named *Centurie*. Scattered over 9,000 square miles between Cherbourg and Le Havre and forty miles inland, as far as Argentan, they sensed their hour had come.

On the night of Thursday 1 June, the B.B.C. had broadcast certain personal messages. The first held an ominous note: "The hour of combat is at hand!" Others were more in keeping with spring and a young man's fancy: "The flowers are very red," "Eileen is married to Joe". Then three days had passed, and still they waited for messages with meaning for Normandy.

Now, at 10:15 p.m., German Central Time on 5 June – one hour earlier than British Double Summer Time – came the string of personal messages that so distressed Captain Mamy in London. Two of them at least held significance for every Norman resistant. In the kitchen of his house on Route Nationale 13, the Paris-Cherbourg highway, Jean Chateau, a burly placid electricity board inspector, was eating an omelette with his wife, Albertine. Rigid with emotion, Chateau said, "Why – I think this is it."

In the wine cellar of his bicycle shop in Bayeux, Georges Mercader, intelligence chief for the coastal sector between Vierville and Port-en-Bessin – the region of Omaha Beach – had carefully removed his secret radio set from behind two convincingly dusty bottles of claret. "It is hot in Suez," Mercader heard them, "It is hot in Suez". To the bicycle merchant, it was heart-stopping news: more than two years after *Centurie*'s inception, in April 1942, the invasion was at last a reality.

"The dice are on the table," said the voice, "The dice are on the table". For Mercader this was enough, and he snapped off the tuner; the other messages, meaning nothing, were of no concern. "I have to go out," he told his wife, Madeleine, "I'll be late tonight." Then wheeling out a low slung racing bicycle he pedalled off to alert his sector leaders. A former Normandy cycling champion, who had represented the province in the Tour de France, the lithe dapper Mercader knew that no German curfew applied to him. Impressed by his prowess, the local commandant had given him *carte-blanche* to practise day or night.

It was in keeping with the maxim which had enabled *Centurie* to survive virtually unscathed until now: Keep it normal. Almost without exception, every agent enrolled blended in with the landscape: their head, Eugène Meslin, Chief Engineer of Roads and Bridges, the insurance agent, Pierre Harivel, Fernand Arsène, the plumber, Léon Cardron, the fisherman, who had even secured photographs of Arromanches, where the British' 'Mulberry harbour" would be sited. All of them brave unobtrusive men, with more scope for travel than most, who listened in cafés, and watched the progress of Rommel's Wall, then went quietly home to transcribe their discoveries on the small sector plans that were hidden where prudence prompted – in chicken runs and flower-pots, inside bicycle handlebars or lavatory cisterns.

These findings, smuggled to England by fishing boat or low-flying Lysander aircraft, then double-checked by the planes of No 140 (Army Co-Operation) Squadron, had weekly charted the Atlantic Wall in blueprint, even as the cement was poured.

Now the days of subtle strategems were past. It was time for action. In the darkness along the coast, teams of five men armed with charges and detonators went quietly from their houses to carry out the first instalment of "The Green Plan," railway sabotage. (Within three weeks, 3000 rail cuts had been accomplished). At Caen's *Gare Centrale*, the stationmaster, Albert Augé, and his team, first destroyed all the yard's water pumps, then pulverised the steam injectors on every locomotive. Explosions erupted along the Wall as teams led by a Cherbourg grocer, Yves Gresselin, dynamited the Paris-Cherbourg line above Carentan and the line between St Lô and Coutances. Other teams moved in, blowing the lines between Caen and Bayeux, between Caen and Vire, forty miles south.

Nor were communications forgotten. In the heathland above Omaha Beach, André Farine, the stocky red-faced proprietor of the

Café de l'Éitanville, near Grandcamp-les-Bains, split forty men into eight teams of five before they melted discreetly into the darkness. Armed with shears and other tools, they cut the mighty telephone cable that ran from Cherbourg to Smolensk at eight separate points. At St Lô, another team made ready to sever the vital military telephone between German 84th Corps and the 91st Divisional HQ near Valognes. Gresselin's men demolished the St Lô–Jersey cable and the long distance line from Cherbourg to Brest. The sluggishness of German reaction in the Cotentin Peninsula owed much to these men.

Some agents did not hear the messages; they were already in the field. Léon Dumis, a bald courteous little garage proprietor, had taken up temporary headquarters at Ifs, a small village four miles south-east of Caen; under the cover of checking the milk production of dairy cattle, he paced from farm to farm, chewing matchsticks into varying lengths: a half-match spelt 50 yards, a quarter match 25 yards. These, his primitive co-ordinates, marked the distances between German ack-ack batteries, to be passed in due time to the Allies.

On this night, Dumis was sleeping in the open, beneath a hedge, screened from the stars by a clump of elms, oblivious to the sleepy curses of German gunners 150 yards away. Through the gloom a man loomed on a bicycle, to whistle softly and Dumis struggled through the grass to meet him. "They are coming," the man said, then was swallowed up in darkness.

Dumis thought only: *Enfin*. He was too tired to know any more complex emotion before again falling asleep.

-

Five miles north-east of Dumis' resting-place, strange things were afoot. In the village of Ranville, 11-year-old Alain Doix sat up in bed transfixed; the big brass knobs of the bedpost seemed to have come alive, quivering with the brilliant light of chandelier flares. Towards the Channel, flak flickered and danced in the sky like summer lightning.

Six thousand feet overhead, a lively chorus of "Abie, My Boy" came to an abrupt halt; unseen by the Doix household, six Halifax aircraft from Tarrant Rushton, Dorset, were releasing the tow ropes of six Horsa gliders. Swooping eerily towards the earth like kestrels over a barnyard, plainly visible to Alain and his father René, the gliders were heading as if magnetised, towards two bridges.

Spanning two parallel waterways, the Orne River and the Caen Canal, still and refulgent in the moonlight, the bridges were a vital link in the D-Day plan. Whoever secured and held them could interdict any flow of German armoured reinforcements from east to west – enabling Lieutenant-General Miles Dempsey's Second Army of Britons and Canadians to swing out into open country after landing on the assault's eastern flank.

It was an onslaught so hazardous that every man in the 150-strong task force – Royal Engineers and men of the Oxford and Buckinghamshire Light Infantry under Major John Howard – was there of his own free will.

As Howard's lead glider neared the canal bridge, the night was strangely silent. No firing from the ground rose up to greet them. Next instant, in a grinding rending landfall for which no one was quite ready, more than 6000 pounds of men and glider struck the bridge head-on, swaying and shuddering, splintering like matchwood, the barbed wire that guarded the approaches snapping like twine under the impact of the 88-foot wingspan. As the perspex cockpit canopy sprayed into glittering shards, both pilots were hurled clear of the wreckage into the wire. Behind them a muffled thudding signalled the landfall of the gliders in their wake.

"Come on, lads," Howard yelled, and now men were tumbling out, some through the door, some through the buckled cockpit, pouring across the bridge. In this carefully-contrived chaos, surprise was total; some Germans, asleep in their gunpits, knew nothing until hurtling grenades blasted them awake, others came to, only groggily, staring down the glinting barrels of Sten guns. Now forty men under Lieutenant Danny Brotheridge pelted like furies for the vital far bank. As they ran a German sentry was clearly visible, Very pistol held high. Forty bren guns, fired from the hip, opened up simultaneously; even as the flare burst into the night sky the man fell dead. Seconds later, Brotheridge, too, fell, mortally wounded in the throat.

As a warning to the Orne Bridge garrison, 500 yards away, the flare was fired too late. In what Leigh-Mallory later acclaimed as "the finest piece of airmanship thus far" the pilots had crash-landed on a sloping landing zone just 300 yards long. Both target bridges had fallen as one.

By a quirk of irony, neither could have been blown, even had the Germans been alerted. Sappers surveying the scene found that though demolition preparations were completed, no explosive charges had yet been placed. They were stored in a cottage nearby.

Now there was nothing left to do but hold the bridges and wait – for the small-hours arrival of a 72-glider supply train led by Major-General Richard Gale, who to ensure good luck had brought along amulets as various as a four-leaved clover and a miniature crusader's sword plus a tin of treacle for sustenance. In a captured pillbox, Corporal Edward Tappenden was calling into his walkie-talkie radio D-Day's first success signal: "Ham and jam… ham and jam." A few enterprising souls knocked at the door of Georges Gondrée's tiny *estaminet*, nestling beside the bridge. When Gondrée, reluctantly opening up, heard the reassuring words, "It's all right, chum," he burst into tears of relief, then busied himself uncorking ninety-seven bottles of champagne hoarded against this moment.

It was 12:35 a.m., and D-Day's first battle had ended. It had lasted scarcely fifteen minutes.

On the German side of the hill, there had been no premonitions. From Paris to Brest, no man from senior commanders to soldiers in their concrete dug-outs expected anything but the quietest of nights.

There was heavy cloud; in some coastal sectors it was drizzling. A wind of Force 5–6 was churning the sea to a turbulent Scale 4–5. In his office overlooking the fine cathedral of St Lô, *Major* Friedrich Hayn, intelligence officer at HQ 84th Corps, knew for certain that the weather ruled out all chances of a landing. In his strongpoint on the east coast of the Cotentin Peninsula, *Leutnant* Arthur Jahnke was equally sanguine. The Allies would come at high water – hadn't Rommel himself said so? – and at any moment now the tide would turn.

At the Luftwaffe's Paris headquarters, the Palais Luxembourg, the chief meteorologist, *Oberst Professor* Walter Stöbe, even doubted that Allied planes would be airborne this day. On the strength of this, many anti-aircraft crews were stood down. At Cap de la Hague, Cherbourg, weather men assured *Konteradmiral* Walter Hennecke, Naval Commander, Normandy, that invasion conditions could not prevail again until the second half of June.

Oddly, Hennecke was one of the few senior commanders on the spot to hear such intelligence. Rommel, later intending to confer with Hitler, was in Germany with his wife, Lucie – as was his operations officer, *Oberst* Hans Georg von Templehof. Von Rundstedt's intelligence chief, *Oberst* Wilhelm Meyer-Detring, was on leave; *Admiral* Theodor Krancke, commanding Naval Group West, had left for Bordeaux.

And still more men were preparing to depart. At 10 a.m. on 6 June, a *Kriegsspiel* (map exercise) was scheduled to take place in Rennes, Brittany, almost 100 miles away, chaired by the paratroop general, Eugen Meindl; virtually every divisional commander was expected to attend, along with two regimental commanders. *Generalleutnant* Carl von Schlieben, commanding the 709th Division, near Valognes, had left that afternoon; *Generalmajor* Wilhelm Falley, of the 91st Air Landing Division, near Château Haut, had moved off at nightfall.

Incredibly, the message that spelt out the Allies' precise intentions had been intercepted, and decoded by 11:37 p.m. on 4 June, then filed in twenty-three separate pigeonholes – a masterpiece of bumbled bureaucracy.

As far back as 14 October, 1943, *Oberstleutnant* Oscar Reile, of the *Abwehr*'s Paris-based Section IIIF, the bane of the French underground, had filed a report based on interrogations of two captured resistants. The password for the Anglo-American invasion of France would be six lines taken from Paul Verlaine's sonnet, *Chanson d'Automne*:

Les sanglots longs
Des violins
De l'automne
Blessent mon coeur
D'une langueur
Monotone.

(The long sobbing of the autumn violins,
Wounds my heart with a monotonous languor.)

The first part of the signal, Reile reported, up to and including the word "l'automne," would be broadcast by the B.B.C. on the first and fifteenth days of given months. The second would be broadcast when the landings were scheduled for the next forty-eight hours – the time to be counted from midnight of the day of the initial transmission.

Thus on 2 June Reile had alerted his chiefs that on the day preceding, Bush House, via radio station Daventry, had repeated the first segment several times between 1:20 and 2:30 p.m.

On 4 June, Reile informed twenty-three addressees that the second part of the alert had been broadcast no less than fifteen times between noon and 2:30 p.m. on 3 June. Among the recipients were *General der Artillerie* Jodl at Hitler's headquarters, Von Rundstedt, Rommel's Army Group B, *Oberst* Meyer-Detring, and *Oberstleutant* Hellmuth Meyer, intelligence chief of the Fifteenth Army.

In some instances – as in *Oberst* Alexis von Roenne's office at Zossen – the messages were filed and forgotten. In others they were disclaimed: "the immediate 'invasion' is not yet apparent," Meyer-Detring noted as his leave began. In one instance, there was plain disbelief. *Generaloberst* Hans von Salmuth, Fifteenth Army's commander, disturbed at a bridge party, commented disdainfully, "I'm too old a bunny to get too excited about this." But as a precautionary measure he did place Fifteenth Army – well outside the invasion area – on full alert.

Almost every other move seemed destined to abet the Allies. Of the 160 serviceable fighters left in France, three squadrons of *Jagdgeschwader* 26 had now been ordered away from the coast – to Metz, Rheims and Marseilles. The wing commander, *Oberstleutnant* Josef "Pips" Priller, had been left with just two planes to stave off an invasion. In the Omaha Beach region, half the ammunition supplies of the 352nd Artillery Regiment had been moved several miles inland – to safe ammunition dumps. To the chagrin of the 709th Division they were still patrolling, as they had always done, with blanks in their rifles; their live ammo, for conservation reasons, was stowed in their haversacks.

At St Lô, the imminent target for 13,000 U.S. paratroopers, the commander of 84th Corps *General der Artillerie* Erich Marcks had other things on his mind. At dawn he, too, was departing for Rennes to take a leading role in the *Kriegsspiel*, a role which intrigued him. Marcks was to represent the Allies in the forthcoming war-game, staging an invasion in which a paratroop assault would be followed by a landing from the sea. There was no doubt that *General* Meindl had set him a thorny problem: the hypothetical invasion area was Normandy.

Unknown to Marcks, a surprise party was in the offing for his fifty-third birthday, 6 June. *Major* Hayn had secured several bottles of well-chilled Chablis, to celebrate that moment: precisely at midnight, before the corps commander left for Rennes. A shade uneasily, Hayn and the chief of staff, *Oberstleutnant* Friedrich von Criegern, were wondering how Marcks would react. An austere stern-faced man, who restricted all meals to official rations, Marcks, who had lost a leg in Russia, was in no sense demonstrative.

But as the solemn knell of the cathedral bells tolled midnight, the little group decided to go ahead. With Hayn in the lead, bearing the Chablis and a tray of glasses, they marched into their chief's room. His artificial leg creaking as he rose to greet them, Marcks peered through his glasses then gestured them to be at ease. All of them stood, raising their glasses solemnly, toasting his health.

It was 12:02 a.m. – the moment that Major Howard's raiding party, forty miles to the east, were readying for that long last glide towards the bridges.

By any criteria, Howard's men were lucky. They had gained their objectives. Due to many factors, thousands more would always recall D-Day as a night of wild terror and confusion, of muddle and fouled-up planning.

Bedevilled by low cloud, scores of pathfinder aircraft failed to find their correct drop zones. One plane load of paratroopers was dropped in the English Channel, never to be seen again. A fate as dire awaited Colonel Robert Sink's 3rd Battalion, 506th Parachute Infantry; dropping into a field ringed by burning oil-soaked barns, almost all of them were wiped out. If Colonel Howard "Skeets" Johnson's men did land in the right zone, this was purely by accident; a bundle of equipment, blocking the doorway for thirty crucial seconds, prevented everyone from jumping. When Johnson and his troops followed it into space, they were over the field assigned to them.

Some thirty men of the 82nd Airborne landed not in one of the six drop zones ringing Sainte Mère-Église but squarely in the town itself, where a hailstorm of German fire met them. One man, Private John Steele, of the 505th Regiment, hung for two hours suspended from the church steeple, so deeply in shock he never remarked the monstrous tolling of the bell. Pfc Ernest Blanchard, tangled in a tree, sawed so desperately at his harness that he sliced off the top of his thumb. It was as bad in the British sector to the east. Scores were swept by high winds into the flooded valley of the Dives River, to drown in slimy ditches seven feet deep by four feet wide. Even the luckiest took seventeen hours to fight their way out of the swamps.

Thus most Americans hit the dirt to fight battles which the planners had never envisaged – with 60 per cent of their equipment lost. Major-General Matthew B. Ridgway, commanding the 82nd Airborne, was virtually in the dark for thirty-six hours; lacking a radio, he could only estimate that 4,000 of his men were unaccounted for. Major-General Maxwell D. Taylor, of the 101st, recalled himself as "a lonely division commander who had lost or at least mislaid his division". By D-Day's end, Taylor had news of only 2,500 men.

Most of the missing, like Private Donald Burgett, were already engaged in a gigantic lethal game of hide-and-seek over a chequerboard of fields and marshes 10 miles square, identifying friend from foe only by the snapping of a toy "cricket": one snap to be answered by a double snap, then a password, "Flash," followed by "Thunder". Burgett knew accurately enough the task facing the two divisions: somehow in five hours they must carve out an "airhead" roughly 12 miles long by 7 miles wide, securing the five narrow causeways dominating Utah Beach.

The problem was: How?

From the moment the green light flashed on in his C-47, and Lieutenant Muir, the platoon leader, yelled, "Let's go," it had been like every practice drop Burgett could recall; air, solid and rushing, wrenching the parachute from the bag, battering the lungs to emptiness, the crackling of the 28-foot canopy as it unfurled, the sizzling sound of twenty-eight separate suspension lines, taut silk supporting his swaying descent, the connector links whistling past the back of his helmet. Cursing, he hit the pastureland too hard, with a force that almost stunned him. Briefed to drop them at 700 feet, the pilot had come as low as 300 feet, more intent on evading the flak.

It was a bad beginning. As Burgett struggled free of his harness, watching a sky "lit up like the Fourth of July," he sensed the vague shadowy figures of other troopers plunging downwards, men who had been dropped so low their chutes had no time to open. Almost simultaneously, seventeen men hit the soft pasture. In the mild June night they made a sound "like large ripe pumpkins being thrown down to burst".

"Dirty son of a bitch pilot," Burgett swore, close to tears.

Now he knew he was quite alone. This one he would have to play by instinct all the way.

Hours of cautious inching forward seemed to follow: through hedgerows, across the short grass of grazed-over pasture, wet with dew that soaked his knees and elbows. A long way off, ack-ack rolled like kettledrums, and machine-gun fire stitched the darkness. By degrees, the cautious snapping of Burgett's "cricket" brought welcome reinforcements from "A" Company: "Slick" Hoenscheidt, "Red" Knight and Private Hundley. It was "Red" Knight who scouted forward on hands and knees to discover a sloping cavity screened by a clump of trees. Crawling forward, the four of them prepared to lie low. All they could do was wait for the dawn and a chance to orient themselves.

Just then a German machine-gun opened up, harsh staccato bursts like an angry woodpecker, and showers of twigs and bark were raining down. "They know where we're at," came Hundley's soft southern drawl. "That settles it," Slick decided, "We've got to make a break for it."

Again they moved out in single file, seeking for somewhere, anywhere, to hole up. Huddled against a hedgerow, soaked by a light misty rain, they waited with numbed patience for the cold grey light of the false dawn. To their left loomed a lone church steeple, and their spirits rose. Any troopers worth their salt would head for that landmark.

Instinct proved them right. Breasting through hedgerows they struck a dirt road, where a group of troopers, blackened faces streaked with sweat, had assembled. Some were men from the 82nd, some from the 101st, but most reassuring of all they were reunited with Lieutenant Muir.

"Just the four of us," Burgett answered his officer's query.

"Swell," Muir enthused, "there's seven of us here; we're going to attack that town; you can come along if you want."

Somehow Burgett accepted it as all according to plan: after a long and lonely night of bewilderment, a lone lieutenant and ten dogface soldiers were off to begin the war.

Two men marched 400 yards ahead as scouts, with Burgett, M-1 rifle at the ready, serving as connecting link between them and the main body. By degrees a misty sun was rising to burn the dew from the grass. Aside from the far-off hammering sound of battle, it was like strolling a country lane in Michigan.

Half a mile on, the road curved to the left. Rounding the bend, Burgett stopped short. The scouts ahead had vanished.

The men huddled uneasily, debating the matter. Somehow the advent of daylight made the scouts' unwonted disappearance more sinister. Covered by the others, Burgett searched the surrounding fields – his stomach recoiling at his first-ever glimpse of "Rommel's asparagus" studding the meadows. But no trace of the scouts.

Feeling acutely lonely, Burgett took over as point, moving 300 yards ahead of the rest. All the time the road curved gradually right, until suddenly they had reached the outskirts of a medieval town: grey stone houses, barns, sheds, interlocked by narrow streets. A natural fortress, Burgett thought, his stomach tense for snipers.

But what materialised instead was three teen-age girls, armed with a jug of wine, crying "*Vive les Américains*," smothering him with hugs and kisses. Good-humouredly accepting their embraces, Burgett refused the wine. It could be poisoned, right? At that moment, recalling those seventeen paratroopers, the vanishing scouts, he trusted nothing, nobody.

Where were they? Lieutenant Muir wanted to know, and to help them get their bearings, the girls brought an old woman who had taught English in school. Even then the name meant nothing, until the teacher located it on Muir's map: Ravenoville.

Muir let loose a string of oaths, all of them directed at the U.S. Air Corps. "They dropped us all over the whole Cherbourg Peninsula," he raged, "Who the hell's side are they on anyway?"

Plainly, whoever secured those causeways, it would not be Lieutenant Muir's little band. "Now we've got to fight through nine towns and twelve miles of enemy country just to get to where we were supposed to land and start fighting in the first place."

–

Aboard the ships, there was no way of knowing how things were going awry.

It was hours now since most of the convoys had passed through the assembly area off the Isle of Wight, code-named Piccadilly Circus, heading for France, along five buoy-marked lanes, splitting into ten channels – two for each beach – as Normandy came closer. To all who glimpsed them they were an unforgettable sight. All told, the armada was spread out across twenty miles of Channel water – the mighty command ships, bristling with antennae, bone-white hospital ships with scalloped green lines and stacked cans marked "Whole Blood," shallow-draught landing ships 350 feet long, rusty decrepit little minesweepers, destroyers, heavy cruisers, Channel steamers and coasters, self-important little tugs fussing like ducklings on a pond.

Many, after four years of war, were already a part of history: the U.S.S. *Augusta*, flagship of Rear-Admiral Alan Kirk, which in 1941 had carried Roosevelt to Placentia Bay, Newfoundland, for his first "Atlantic Charter" meeting with Churchill; the U.S.S. *Nevada*, sunk at Pearl Harbor in that same year but now raised to fight again; the light cruiser, H.M.S. *Ajax*, which had hunted down the *Graf Spee* in Montevideo Harbour, following the Battle of the River Plate, as far back as December 1939. Heading for the British beaches in his flagship, the cruiser H.M.S. *Scylla*, was another figure from history, Rear-Admiral Sir Philip Vian; after ending "the phoney war" in February 1940 by boarding the German prison-ship *Altmark* in neutral Norwegian waters, Vian, in 1941, had led his 4th Destroyer Flotilla to put paid to the battleship *Bismarck*.

Impressions of that night would remain inescapably vivid. Aboard the 3rd (Canadian) Division ship, H.M.S. *Hilary*, heading for the British beaches, war correspondent Ross Munro recalled how "the wind howled through the wireless masts ... the sky ... black as the inside of a gun barrel, and spray and rain lashed the deck." Another man recalled the noise of the wind: "there was no room left in the air for any other noise; the noise of the wind and the water – and the low throbbing from the Diesels..." Aboard LCT 947, a British naval lieutenant, Lambton Burn, listened with fascination as Lieutenant-Colonel A. D. Cocks briefed his Royal Engineers under the single light of an electric lamp: "Look at your maps. Caen is Poland, Hermanville is Mexico... All bogus names to be destroyed tonight ... 0430h all troops to be issued tea or hot soup."

Conditions varied incredibly from ship to ship. Aboard the U.S.S. *Chase*, a solidly-built mother-ship ferrying many assault barges, *Life* photographer Robert Capa marvelled at the nonchalant way the mess boys at 3 a.m. served hot cakes, sausages, eggs and coffee wearing neat white jackets and white gloves. Aboard LST 302, Flight-Lieutenant Alan Caverhill, R.A.F. browsed idly through his D-Day phrase book – everything from "*Encore une verre du vin rouge, s'il vous plâit, Mademoiselle*" to "*Hande hoch*". On other transports, men chatted aimlessly, played cards or wrote eleventh-hour letters – though few were as optimistic as Staff Sergeant Larry Johnson, of the U.S. Rangers. Dropping a line to a former girl friend in Paris, Johnson was seeking a date – early in June.

For those in the flimsier craft, it was a never-ending nightmare. In LCT 777, Signalman Third Class George Hackett, Jr., remembered waves so high they smashed from one end of the heaving craft and rolled out the other. Sergeant Morris Magee of the Canadian 3rd Division found the wallowing of his landing craft "worse than being in a rowboat in the centre of Lake Champlain". He was so far gone he could no longer vomit. One man, Second Lieutenant Joseph Rosenblatt, Jr., remembered polishing off seven helpings of chicken à la king and never feeling better, but he was the notable exception. Most men were so racked with nausea they now longed to reach the beaches they had dreaded – "bacon and eggs, pork chops and plum pudding, they all went the same way," one survivor recalled with misery.

Only the Captains of the pitching craft, who had sweated it out on their bridges for fifty-six hours now could have put their minds at rest; they had known the timing ever since breaking the seals of the bulky "Package A" nearing Land's End. "Serial One in force," ran the cryptic message. At 3 a.m. on 6 June, this meant D-Day for the American beaches was still three-and-a-half hours distant; for the hapless British another four-and-a-half hours of suffering.

–

By 1:11 a.m. the Germans were coming alive to the danger. In St Lô, *General der Artillerie* Erich Marcks, still concentrating ferociously on the forthcoming *Kriegsspiel*, took a phone call from *Generalmajor* Wilhelm Richter, whose ill-trained 716th Division were massed on the coast above Caen. The news suggested a war game transmuted into grim reality. "Parachutists have landed east of the Orne," Richter reported. "The area seems to be around Breville and Ranville..."

Marcks and his staff were galvanised. The corps commander at once called *Generalmajor* Max Pemsel, chief of staff of Seventh Army. On Marcks' orders, Pemsel signalled *Alarmstruffe II*, Coastal Alarm – the code-word for invasion – to all Seventh Army units.

Pemsel was one man who never doubted that the invasion's main thrust was here and now. First he called his own C-in-C, *Generaloberst* Friedrich Dollmann: "General, I believe this is the invasion. Will you please come over immediately?". Next 84th Corps was again on the line: "Parachute drops near Montebourg and St Marcouf". Both were locations on the Cherbourg Peninsula. At 1:35 a.m., Pemsel alerted *Generalmajor* Hans Speidel, Rommel's chief of staff at Army Group B.

Others were less certain. From Fifteenth Army headquarters on the Belgian border, *Generaloberst* Hans von Salmuth called *Generalmajor* Josef Reichert, whose 711th Division were stationed east of the Orne. Earlier Reichert had reported British paratroopers landing with apologetic aplomb on his front lawn – "Awfully sorry, old man, but we simply landed here by accident." Egocentrically, Reichert believed his own headquarters had been singled out for airborne attack.

"What the devil is going on down there?" Von Salmuth wanted to know.

"If you'll permit me," Reichert answered, "I'll let you hear for yourself." To Von Salmuth, the distant hammering of machine-gun fire came clearly up the wire. He, too, lost no time in calling Army Group B.

But Speidel was a hard man to convince. At 2 a.m. Pemsel had called him again: naval radar at Cherbourg was picking up ships near the Bay of the Seine. "The air landings," he insisted, "constitute the first phase of a larger enemy action." Speidel thought otherwise: the action was still "locally confined". "For the time being," the War Diary noted, "this is not to be considered as a large operation".

At 3 a.m. there was still dire if understandable confusion. Among the senior officers only Pemsel was convinced that the Allied *Schwerpunkt* – the main thrust – was Normandy. The myth of the Pas de Calais, so sedulously nourished by Lily Sergueiev, died hard: supposing the paratroops were only a diversion to mask a massive thrust against Fifteenth Army?

Von Salmuth's Chief of Staff, *Generalmajor* Rudolf Hoffmann was so sure of it he called up Pemsel solely to place a bet that he was right. He proposed a really first-class dinner as a stake. But Pemsel knew it in his bones: this was the real thing.

Before disconnecting he told Hoffmann: "This is one bet you're going to lose."

—

Behind Sword Beach, the assault's easternmost flank, lying between the villages of Hermanville and Colleville, the invasion was in jeopardy before the British had even come ashore.

Three miles east of Sword, at Merville, behind a Rommel-inspired barrier of minefields, trenches, anti-tank ditches and a stockade of barbed wire fifteen feet wide by ten deep, four heavy guns, 150s embedded in reinforced concrete casements 6ft 6 inches thick, ranged in on the beach. To avert a massacre on Sword, 600 men of the 9th Battalion, 5th Parachute Brigade, under Lieutenant-Colonel Terence Otway, were to storm and destroy this battery.

It was a brilliant near-suicidal concept – at length dreamed up by Major-General Richard Gale after pondering the brilliant coup-de-main staged against Belgium's Fort Eben Emael by nine German gliders in May, 1940. As Gale envisaged it, a crushing attack by 100 Lancaster bombers, plus a follow-up ground assault by 9th Para – with three gliders crash-landing on the battery at the same moment – would overcome resistance.

But in the small hours of 6 June, Otway had bitter cause to recall the parting words of Brigadier James Hill, C.O. of the 5th: "Gentlemen, in spite of your excellent training and orders, do not be daunted if chaos reigns. It undoubtedly will!"

And undoubtedly it had. Though Otway and his batman, Lance-Corporal Wilson, had baled out near the drop zone – Wilson emerging unscathed after plunging into a greenhouse – raw R.A.F. crews had contrived to scatter the bulk of his men over 50 square miles. Thus, at 2:35 a.m., one and a half hours after the drop, only 150 out of 600 men had reached the rendezvous. Worse, an 11-strong glider supply train, bringing such vital paraphernalia as anti-tank guns, scaling ladders, flame throwers and Bangalore torpedoes had failed to arrive.

At first Otway saw nothing for it but to do the best he could with the men available – men armed only with rifles, Sten guns, grenades, twenty Bangalore torpedoes and one heavy machine-gun against the deadly obstacles and a garrison 200 strong.

Now, crouched at the edge of the battery's barbed wire, Otway saw the carefully-wrought plan, rehearsed on the Berkshire downs time and again since February, falling apart by the minute. The bombing raid had failed abysmally; not one bomb had hit the battery. The glider train was still missing. Of the three gliders scheduled for the crash landing, only two had arrived – and Otway was powerless to signal them. The crash dive was to be triggered by a star shell fired from a mortar – and Otway had neither star shell nor mortar.

Already his men had done much to redeem the disasters. With wire cutters they had sliced through the outer barricade and placed their

Bangalore torpedoes in readiness. Lacking both mine detectors and tape, a group under Captain Paul Greenway had done it the hard way: prodding for trip-wires with bayonets, denoting the cleared passage with heel-marks in the mud.

Towards 4:30 a.m. Otway saw his last hopes vanish. As the gliders circled, vainly seeking a signal, German machine-guns opened up on them with 20-millimetre tracer. Promptly, one took evasive action, landing unscathed four miles away; the second, shearing into an orchard, caught fire within seconds of the crew jumping clear.

In the aching silence that followed, Otway's second in command, Major Allen Parry, whispered, "Have you decided what to do, sir?".

"Do?" said Otway sharply, "attack in three minutes, of course. Pass it on."

Now, above the crackle of small-arms fire, the coughing rasp of mortars, one sound stood out above all the rest: the shrill evocative cry of a hunting horn, blown by Lieutenant Alan Jefferson. Seconds later came Otway's stentorian summons to battle: "Everybody in! We're going to take this bloody battery!"

Pandemonium reigned. With a searing whoosh the Bangalore torpedoes blasted the wire. Through wreathing smoke, whooping and yelling, Otway's red-bereted paratroopers hacked their way forward, firing as they went, splitting into four assault parties, headed for the guns. Piling into the anti-tank ditches, other paratroopers fought hand to hand with the Germans, kicking, gouging, lunging. Cries of "*Paratruppen, paratruppen*" grew in volume, and Private Sid Capon, surprising two men in a trench, could see why. One, raising a Red Cross box above his head in a gesture of surrender, was crying, "*Russki, Russki*"; not every man in this garrison had stomach for defending Rommel's Wall.

Inside the battery defences, bomb craters, loose wires and mines contrived to hamper the assailants. Lieutenant Alan Jefferson fell, wounded, but still the hunting horn remained at his lips, the weird haunting notes resounding amid the screams of dying men, the crump and flash of grenades. Machine-gun fire glittered in a bright stream, and Major Allen Parry felt as if "someone had kicked me hard in the leg," collapsing momentarily into a bomb crater, resourcefully using his whistle lanyard as a tourniquet. Painfully hobbling towards No 1 casemate, he beheld a scene of ultimate slaughter: the dying and the wounded, among them 70 of Otway's men, lay everywhere.

But for the most part the battle was petering out, the guns destroyed by Gammon grenades, lumps of plastic explosive encased in a stockinette bag. With almost classic British *sang-froid*, Lieutenant Mike Dowling, his right hand clasped to his left breast, reported to Otway: "Battery taken as ordered, sir. Guns destroyed." Promptly, Otway fired a yellow flare – a signal of success – from his Very pistol. Noted by an R.A.F. spotter plane, it was radioed just in time to H.M.S. *Arethusa* offshore. In little more than half an hour, *Arethusa*'s guns were slated to open up on Merville, in the hope of accomplishing what Otway's party had now achieved. Turning, Otway realised that Dowling was lying dead at his feet. Even as he made his report he had been dying.

For many who came ashore on Sword Beach, tensely awaiting a holocaust, the final landing, thanks to Otway's men, was almost an anti-climax. But on Bloody Omaha it was to be a different story.

−

It was 5:45 a.m. Off the American beaches the naval bombardment would soon begin. For the 3,000 men of the first assault wave, H-Hour was only 45 minutes distant. Aboard the flagship *Augusta*, Lieutenant-General Omar Bradley methodically plugged his ears with cotton wool, blotting out the last-minute pep-talks which every unit commander had somehow felt impelled to deliver: "Keep in line! Keep in line!"... "U.S. Rangers, man your stations!"... "This is it, men, pick it up and put it on, you've only got a one-way ticket and this is the end of the line"... "I'll do your praying for you from here on in. What you're going to do today will be a prayer in itself"... "Now hear this! This is probably going to be the biggest party you boys will ever go to – so let's all get out on the floor and dance!"

Now the invasion barges, swinging on their cranes, were descending like slow-moving elevators. Painfully, as the light broke in the east, troops laden with 300 pounds of equipment, inched their way down cargo nets, into the heaving craft. The most final of all messages passed from ship to ship: "Away all boats!". Watching them go, Bradley was sorely troubled. Before leaving England he had learned – too late – that the seasoned German 352nd Division was manning Omaha, although up to 4 June Allied intelligence had placed them twenty miles distant, in the St Lô region. Now Bradley nourished the hope that the naval bombardment, combined with massive air-cover, would neutralise that tough opposition.

5:50 a.m. Abruptly, the terrible storm of the bombardment drowned out the rattle of chains, the squeal of winches. Six miles offshore, the battleships, *Texas*, *Arkansas* and *Nevada*, the cruisers *Tuscaloosa*, *Quincy* and *Black Prince* pounded the shore batteries and the coastal battery on Pointe du Hoc, the target of the Ranger battalions, with blinding breathtaking waves of fire. Then tragedy struck. The air cover on which Bradley had pinned so much hope, 329 Lancasters, Fortresses and Liberators, confused by low cloud, hopelessly overshot their target – dropping 13,000 bombs up to three miles inland.

Ahead of the frail ranks of the first assault craft, dominating the 7000 yards of beach, Rommel's finest fortress loomed still intact: 85 machine gun posts, 38 rocket pits, 35 pillboxes, 18 anti-tank gun positions, 8 casemated batteries, 6 mortar pits and 4 field artillery positions.

Behind Omaha, in Strongpoint 62, *Leutnant* Friedrich Frerking lifted his field telephone: "Target Dora, all guns, range four-eight-five-zero, basic direction 20 plus, impact fuse". Then, "Wait for the order to fire." Behind his MG-42, *Gefreiter* Hein Severloh waited nervously; the moment must be coming, already the Americans of the first wave, tiny ant-figures, were knee-deep in water. "Target Dora – fire!" Frerking shouted, and Severloh curled his forefinger round the trigger. By noon, Severloh was only one of many to have pumped 12,000 rounds into the American ranks.

All through the shallows men fell dying, and as the tide swept them inshore they nudged with ghastly importunity against the living, as if still seeking human kinship. Everywhere off the American beaches landing craft were foundering and capsizing – ten off Omaha, seven off Utah. For the U.S. Navy's Lieutenant Dean L. Rockwell, this was an appalling moment; he and he alone had charge of the 16 landing craft from which 32 Duplex Drive amphibious tanks were to be launched – but in the pounding surf fully 27 had foundered before the first troops had landed.

From this carnage, men retained brief and awful vignettes: a man shot through the head, "spinning round like a chicken," a captain, both cheeks pierced by shrapnel, blood spouting as he rallied his troops to charge, an operator, tugged under by his heavy radio, screaming, "For God's sake I'm drowning". As they lay pinned down by withering fire, an Army lieutenant whispered to *Life* photographer Robert Capa: "I'll tell you what I see – I see my ma on the front porch waving my insurance policy."

Weird irrelevant fancies assailed the mind: Captain Carroll Smith saw his friend Captain Sherman Burroughs of the 29th Division lolling inertly in the surf and thought that never again would Burroughs be doubled up by one of his migraine headaches. He had been shot through the head.

Aboard *Augusta*, Bradley asked a group of war correspondents, "Well, do you know all about what's going on? I don't."

Aboard a torpedo boat four miles offshore, Major Logan Scott-Bowden and Sergeant Bruce Ogden Smith, who had acted as pathfinders for the Western Naval Task Force, were aghast at what they saw. "But this is bloody dangerous," Ogden Smith burst out, "they're going down like ninepins, poor devils."

Hundreds never achieved the initial slog over 300 yards of wet sand to shelter beneath the cobblestoned sea wall. Pfc Henry Meyers, a signaller, came ashore struggling with half a mile of telephone wire; his orders were to set up a telephone link somewhere inland, but so far as Meyers could see no one had even crossed the first belt of shingle.

The Army-Navy demolition engineers – 272 men under Commander Joseph H. Gibbons – whose task was to blow a path through the beach obstacles fought a losing battle from the first. Brought in minutes behind schedule they had to battle more than Teller mines and Elements C: struggling infantrymen blocked their progress and soldiers cowered behind obstacles they were scheduled to blow. Out of 16 gaps allotted to Gibbons' 16 teams, only five were ever wholly cleared and two partially; thirty minutes after they set to work, 111 of Gibbons' men were dead. Enemy fire took toll of their equipment, too. Of 16 bulldozers earmarked for Omaha, only three ever went into operation.

For the 220 U.S. Rangers, under Lieutenant-Colonel James E. Rudder, the task was marginally easier. Landing on a shingled shelf beneath the 100-foot cliffs, their task was to scale them, using ropes and extension ladders borrowed from the London Fire Brigade, and destroy the powerful battery reported by *Centurie* sector chief André Farine at Pointe du Hoc. At a cost of 135 dead and wounded they made it; within five minutes of reaching the cliff base, the first Ranger had bellied over the top – belying the jibe of one naval intelligence officer: "Three old women with brooms could keep the Rangers from climbing that cliff." But the giant guns had gone – inexplicably moved 1,200 yards back into an apple orchard.

But by noon Bradley was wrestling with a crucial decision. So great had been the devastation that for the first time he was forced to contemplate the hitherto unthinkable: the total evacuation of Omaha, the diversion of those Americans still clinging to life to Utah and the British beaches.

—

Two German commanders were completely in the dark. Sometime after 1 a.m., *Generalleutnant* Edgar Feuchtinger, whose 21st Panzer Division, once an element of Rommel's tough *Afrika Korps*, was scattered through all the villages 25 miles south-east of Caen, had had word of the British paratroop drop. At once Feuchtinger awoke the division's Panzer Regiment commander, *Oberst* Hermann von Oppeln-Bronikowski. "Imagine," he said, "*they* have landed." In a strikingly short time, officers and men had mustered, alert beside their tanks, engines revving, waiting to move out. Soon orders *must* come – to close in and drive the Allies back towards the coast. But the night ticked away, and no word came.

Precious time had thus been lost before Feuchtinger, at 6:30 a.m., acted on his own initiative; Bronikowski was at liberty to set his Mark IVs rolling. But from that moment on Feuchtinger imposed radio silence; all further orders were passed by despatch riders. There was thus no way for Bronikowski to know that he was moving against the wrong enemy. Oblivious to the fact that wave after wave of Montgomery's men were splashing ashore on the coast, Bronikowski's 120 Panzers were moving north-east – to challenge Major Howard's hold on the Orne and canal bridges.

At 5 a.m., in his blockhouse headquarters sited beneath a girls' school in St Germain-en-Laye, twelve miles from Paris, *Feldmarschall* Von Rundstedt had also decided to act. Still convinced that Normandy was a diversion, he was even so taking prudent precautions. The 12th S.S. and the Panzer *Lehr* – the two divisions Rommel had for three months sought to integrate into his coastal defence system – were both ordered to rush to the coast. Technically, both, as reserve divisions, were under Hitler's command, but Von Rundstedt thought it unlikely the Führer would impede their despatch. His teletype message requesting their release was strictly for the record.

Von Rundstedt had discounted one factor; at Hitler's Berchtesgaden headquarters, the atmosphere was what the old Field Marshal liked to call *Wolkenkuckkucksheim* (cloud cuckoo-land). Staff who received the message in the office of *General der Artillerie* Alfred Jodl decided that it was still too early to wake him. Only Jodl could clear it with the Führer, and Hitler, asleep with Eva Braun, three miles away in his mountain retreat, had not retired until 4 a.m. Nobody would disturb him for another five hours.

Nor was Von Rundstedt aware that Army Group B had not yet seen fit to alert the man most intimately concerned: *Feldmarschall* Erwin Rommel.

—

Off Utah Beach, one unknown man's unwitting error had saved thousands of lives. Blinded by the smoke from the naval bombardment, tugged by a strong current, a lone control boat officer had brought the first assault wave onto a beachhead almost 2000 yards south of the original Utah – away from the firepower of twenty-eight heavy batteries but away, also, from the two of the crucial five causeways that Private Burgett and the 101st Airborne were struggling to secure.

Brigadier-General Theodore Roosevelt, Jr. – a distant cousin of the President's – now faced a snap decision. Any moment now, wave after wave would be landing – 30,000 men, 3,500 vehicles. Should they pile into this relatively peaceful area, with its one narrow causeway – or switch back to the causeways of the original Utah? The question was no sooner posed than answered: "We're going to start the war from here."

Soon, on the one open causeway running in from the beach, two generals – Roosevelt and Major-General Raymond O. Barton, commanding the 4th (U.S.) Division – were standing side by side engaged in traffic cop duty, speeding along steady lines of men, and trucks christened "Filthy Flora" and "Ten Shilling Annie" inland to victory. The casualties on Utah had been less than 200 men.

On the British beaches, "Hobart's Funnies" were more than proving their worth: Churchill tanks carrying "Petards," short-barrelled mortars lobbing "flying dustbins," heavy high explosive charges, against concrete bunkers and casemates, other vehicles laying bundles of wood, called "fascines," in the path of any tank likely to bog down. On one half of Juno Beach, Canadians of the 3rd Division, their path thus smoothed for them, mopped up all resistance in the town of

Courseulles in two hours. On Gold Beach, at Ver-sur-Mer – site of the first Scott-Bowden-Ogden Smith survey – the going was tougher; on the western half of the beach, stalled by hedgehogs and tetrahedra, the men of the 1st Battalion, The Hampshire Regiment, took almost eight hours to knock out the defences of Le Hamel, suffering 200 casualties as they fought.

On Sword Beach, from the first, a strange élan prevailed – as if to vindicate the heroism of Otway's men at Merville. Aboard LCT 947, Lieutenant Lambton Burn watched the Commandos of Lord Lovat's 1st Special Service Brigade, in their trim green berets, striding through the surf "with shoulders hunched like boxers ready for in-fighting"; as they waded, Piper William Millin, waist-deep in water, oblivious to the scream and splash of shells, paraded up and down the shoreline, keening "The Road To The Isles" as the Commandos struggled ashore. As relaxed as a man on a holiday beach, Colonel Derek Mills-Roberts, of Lovat's Brigade, remarked conversationally to a corporal, "Seems ages since we had a dry landing. D'you find the sea cold?". Another Lovat contingent, 171 French Commandoes under *Commandant* Philippe Kieffer, were likewise in good heart. Told that he would lead the attack on the gambling casino at Ouistreham, near the mouth of the Orne, Sergeant Count Guy de Montlaur, was overjoyed. "It will be a pleasure," he told Kieffer, "I have lost several fortunes in that place."

There was cause for jubilation. On Sword, in contrast to Omaha, the timing was exactly right; at first, the senior sector engineer, Colonel R. W. Urquhart, spotting stakes and ramps topped with mines and shells just visible above the wavetops, dived overboard with his men and swam from stake to stake, cutting the mines away. But soon the arrival of an armoured breaching team, with sixteen flail tanks and eight armoured bulldozers, saw five exits clear – at a cost of machinery, not lives. Inland, the same success story was visible: signs reading "*Achtung Minen*" swiftly gave place to "Verges Clear To Twenty Feet".

From every British beach men bore away a patchwork of impressions. In the Ouistreham half of Sword, soldiers of the East Yorkshire Regiment remembered scything waves of machine-gune fire which within minutes cost them 200 dead at the waterline. Others remembered, even under fire, an almost exaggerated *politesse*. Aboard a sinking LCI off Juno, Lieutenant Michael Aldworth held back his men from disembarking prematurely with a gentle, "Wait a minute, chaps. It's not our turn". From the bowels of the craft, a voice queried, "Well, just how long do you think it will be, old man? The ruddy hold is filling up with water."

Even under a hail of fire, the British emerged as resolutely single-minded. Sergeant Henry Morris, of the 13th/18th Hussars, whose Duplex Drive tank had been launched 4,000 yards off Sword, was quite determined to make it to the beach because he wanted his breakfast; the tinned steak-and-kidney pudding in his ration pack had been no fare to tempt a sea-sick man. Company Sergeant Major Harry Bowers, of the Hampshires, fought his way forward on Gold with one object in mind; his feet were killing him and he wanted a nice soft pair of German boots. Scaling a pillbox and dropping a grenade through the firing slit, he stripped them from the first Russian prisoner to emerge.

Many remembered Sword for its astonishing atmosphere of carnival – akin to the reception the Americans were even then receiving in Rome. Heedless of the danger from mines, groups of Frenchmen crying "*Vivent les Anglais*" swarmed onto the beach, ready to hug and kiss any unwary Englishman they met. From Colleville-sur-Orne, a mile inland, the Mayor himself, sporting the big brass helmet of a fire chief, turned up to welcome the invaders. One artilleryman, Captain Gerald Norton, was even accosted by four Germans, suitcases already packed, waiting to board the first British boat available.

Already, scenting victory, the long khaki-clad files were moving inland, towards Caen, Bayeux and Périers. Only on the western flank was the issue still in doubt.

–

On Bloody Omaha, men were awakening slowly, as if from an anaesthetic. Rallying by degrees, more and more were coming to realise they must fight their way inland or perish. The commander of the 16th Infantry Regiment, Colonel George A. Taylor, voiced the basic truth: "Two kinds of people are staying on this beach – the dead and those who are going to die. Now let's get the hell out of here!"

All along the beach, officers and non-coms took their cue from Taylor – raging, swearing, urging shell-stunned men to struggle to their feet: "Get your arse on up there!" "This is what separates the men from the boys". "Let's see what you're made of". And gradually, as morning gave way to afternoon, barbed wire was cut, beach exits opened up – often so narrow, Lieutenant Franklyn A. Johnson, of the 1st Division saw, that engineers were delicately draping unexploded mines with handerchiefs and toilet tissue. "Flames everywhere," Major Stanley Bach, the 1st's liaison officer, had noted at 1:20 p.m., "Men burning alive…" But by 3:40 p.m.: "Infantry moving by us on path over crest … We get to open field – follow path – see one man that had stepped on mine; no body from waist down."

Yet by 4:50 p.m. Bach himself had reached Saint-Laurent, three quarters of a mile inland; Colleville had fallen and so had Vierville-sur-Mer. Even on Omaha, at a cost of 2,500 casualties, the Atlantic Wall was irreparably breached.

—

Now, all along the Bay of the Seine, a thin line like a high water-mark stretched for fully 65 miles: the aftermath of Overlord. Soldiers' packs and shoe-polish, diaries, socks, hand-grenades and Bibles, many Bibles. Snapshots of families who would never grow older and the last letters from home, each address neatly razored out for reasons of security. Torn pistol belts and pocket books, bloody abandoned shoes, metal mirrors and thousands of cartons of waterlogged cigarettes.

Soon the sea would erase the memory; the tide was coming in.

—

Since reaching Ravenoville, Private Donald Burgett had been as confused as any man. At the end of the day, Burgett had to grope back to think just what his outfit had achieved.

It had not taken long for the company to swell to three officers and seventeen men – nor to discover that all Ravenoville from this point on was a German fortress. But as Lieutenant Muir argued, "That's what we came here for, to kill Krauts, and from the looks of it, there are plenty to go around."

As Muir led them all in a head-on attack against a group of houses across an apple orchard, it seemed as simple as that. Yelling and screaming at the pitch of his lungs as he ran, Burgett saw his first German victim running through trees; stopping short he "took a good sight on him and squeezed the trigger." Afterwards he never recalled feeling the recoil or even hearing the shot: just the man spinning sideways and falling face down out of sight. Another German rounded the building, then stood stock-still, staring dazedly at his dead comrade. Carefully sighting on his chest, Burgett squeezed the trigger again and this man, too, fell forward.

Then the fighting grew so feverish that Burgett lost all count of his personal toll of dead; darting from house to house with a captured haul of German "potato masher" grenades, he and the others hurtled them through every door and window. The sloping fields beyond were suddenly alive with running men in shabby grey, struggling to get away. Bemusedly, Burgett learned from his buddy, Private Phillips, a Pennsylvania Dutchman who spoke some German, that they had taken seventy-five prisoners. Thirty more Germans were dead; the remaining hundred, never dreaming they faced only twenty men, had pulled out.

After that they had sown all the roads out of Ravenoville with Hawkins mines camouflaged under cowpats, breakfasted off K rations of chopped pork and egg yolks and smoked contentedly in the sunshine. Then, as the Germans began filtering back, there was another pitched battle across a blacktop road, so intense that the smell of cordite seeped into their nostrils and lay thick at the backs of their throats.

They were so close to the sea now they could see the battleships off Utah Beach, and suddenly huge shells "like boxcars twisting slowly through the air" were landing so close that shockwaves of sound were uprooting whole apple trees, spinning them like cabers across the orchard. Hastily the troopers lobbed orange smoke grenades to denote friendly troops, and the battleship, responding with an orange smoke pot, ceased fire. All of them heaved a sigh of relief.

The rest of the day "passed easily" while they consolidated, chatting about the beach landings and wondering how long it would take to meet up with friendly troops. All told, Burgett supposed, they hadn't done badly. They had captured a fortified town, taken seventy-five prisoners, and killed as many more. And now they commanded the high ground overlooking one small portion of Utah.

After shooting so many men he had imagined he might feel different, but so far he felt just as usual. Killing Germans was just a job, after all.

Again and again, Rommel's driver, *Gefreiter* Daniel, sounded the horn. Beside him in the speeding Horch, the Field Marshal was urging repeatedly, "*Tempo! Tempo! Tempo!*". Driving his gloved right fist into the palm of his left hand, he muttered bitterly, "My friendly enemy, Montgomery."

It was all too late, as Rommel had guessed it would be. Not until 10:15 a.m., still in his red-striped dressing gown, had Rommel heard from *Generalmajor* Speidel that the invasion had been launched. Now he was racing back to resume command, but the delays would be fatal. Hitler – whose only comment had been, "Well, is it or isn't it the invasion?" – had waited until 3:40 p.m. before releasing the vital Panzer divisions, the 12th S.S. and Panzer *Lehr*. Now the 12th S.S. could not hope to reach the coast before 7 June. The Panzer *Lehr*, strafed repeatedly from the air, would not make it until 9 June.

The one unit which might have exploited an eight-mile gap which British Commandos had not yet closed between Juno and Gold, the 21st Panzer, was still north of Caen – preparing to attack the wrong enemy.

Twisting round in the Horch's front seat, Rommel spoke feelingly to his aide, *Hauptmann* Hellmuth Lang. "Do you know, Lang," he said, "if I was commander of the Allied forces right now, I could finish off the war in fourteen days."

5

"What A Lot of Things Could Have Been Arranged!"
7 June–21 July, 1944

At first it was only a shadow in the sky, some seventeen feet across, half the span of a small fighter plane. To the first two men who spotted it, Ernie Woodland, a greengrocer, and Archie Wraight, a builder, both part-timers in Britain's Royal Observer Corps, there was something eerie in its progress. As it passed 2,500 feet above Post M-2, a Martello tower at Dymchurch, on Romney Marsh, coughing "like a Model T Ford going up a hill," a weird red glow was sputtering from its fuselage.

No Briton had ever glimpsed its like, but from descriptions issued as far back as April, both men knew instinctively what they saw. As Wraight swivelled his high-powered naval binoculars, Woodland was calling urgently into his handset telephone: "Mike Two, Diver! Diver! Diver! on four, north-west one oh one." Thirty miles northwest, in the Observer Corps Centre at Maidstone, Kent, the same cry echoed across the Operations Room: "Diver! Diver! Diver!"

Minutes later, falling 24 miles short of its target, London, the missile ploughed into the earth at Swanscombe, near Gravesend, gouging a shallow crater twenty feet wide by three feet deep in a cabbage patch, searing the soil for 80 yards around with blowtorch fire.

It was 4:13 a.m. on Tuesday 13 June, one week after D-Day. Hitler's "secret weapon," the pilotless two-ton *Vergeltungswaffe* (Reprisal Weapon) No 1, its warhead packed with a ton of Amatol, had been turned against the Allies.

–

Two days later, in 150 Wing's dispersal at Newchurch aerodrome – within sight of Post M-2 – Wing Commander Roland Beamont was chafing. Intermittently he and all the pilots had watched what seemed like comets with flaming tails sailing like red stars towards the capital – unaware that on 55 launching sites across the Straits of Dover the catapult rigs had yet to be adjusted for maximum results. Ahead of Londoners lay an 80-day ordeal, destroying the gulf between soldier and civilian, yet destroying also 500 houses a day and a total of 6,000 lives.[15]

Yet still the dispersal telephone remained obstinately mute; no scramble had been ordered against the strange intruders. Past patience, Beamont telephoned HQ, 11 Group, Fighter Command: "Can't we do something about these things?"

The Operations Officer was pessimistic. "What *can* you do? These are flying bombs and the radar plots show their speed at 450 m.p.h."

No man to resist a challenge, Beamont answered, "Well, at least let's have a crack at them. I'll order cockpit readiness at full squadron strength."

On the night of 15 June, the assault began. All over southern England reports flooded in to police stations and Observer Corps posts – ranging from "a noise like a motorcycle with a two-stroke engine" to "little aeroplanes with a light up their arse". Leading the wing off at dawn, Beamont was conscious of an unwonted flutter in his stomach – realising now that what he had seen as far back as the small hours of 8 May had been a V-1's trial flight. Yet surely this operation was no riskier than target practice at a drogue? A robot bomb could not retaliate; it was what the fighter pilots of the day called "a piece of cake".

Suddenly the code-word "Diver" crackled over his intercom; the wing was vectored to a line running from between Dover and Folkestone to Calais. Shadowed by his No 2, Sergeant Bruce Cole, Beamont fanned out over the Channel. At 450 m.p.h., he thought, there would be no time for a second attack – only a quick clean kill. That meant getting in close – but how close dare one get? What if the bomb exploded?

And now, drifting from cloud in mid-Channel, Beamont saw the intruder clearly for the first time: a black fleeting speck, trailing a pinpoint of light. Then it had passed him, bulleting for London like a lighted dragon, and Beamont at once gave chase, though sensing failure, for not until Maidstone did he sight it again. No chance now to close the range – so at almost 600 yards he opened fire, expending all his ammunition in one long burst. Palpably, hits on the wing were slowing it down – but it was Sergeant Cole, closing in, who delivered the *coup de grâce*. The missile tipped on its back, trailing a tongue of fire, to crash in a field near West Malling.

But still the problem remained: *How close?*

Two days later, Beamont knew the daunting truth: automaton or no, the V-1 could hit back.

He was flying alone, ten miles north of Hastings, and 1,000 feet above when he sighted his victim and at once he closed on a racing course until the bomb was almost beneath him. Putting the Tempest into a 450 m.p.h. dive, he hurtled to meet it until the flickering orange flame was square in his gunsights. But although he pressed the firing button, the V-1 still kept going.

Now the challenge was so strong that all thoughts of minimum range escaped him; the dive accomplished, he was flying faster than his target and he closed yet another hundred yards until the orange jet bulked hugely in the gunsights. A long long burst, he decided, his thumb hard on the gun button. Then the sky blew up.

The Tempest shuddered with the recoil, and Beamont found himself ducking; the wing went down and the aircraft flipped into a roll, miraculously clear of the sheet of flame that whiplashed through black bellying smoke. The heat was unbelivable; he smelt burning oil, burning paint. "This is it," he thought, feeling no emotion, no fear, only a drowsy acceptance.

Seconds later, he opened his eyes to see the Sussex coastline, incredibly, *above* him; he had flown clean through the explosion and come out upside down. Now he assessed the damage. Flames had licked through the ventilator to scorch his sleeves; the paint had risen in gross black bubbles on wings and fuselage, oil covered the windscreen like black rain. He was alive – but by how narrow a margin?

Setting course for Newchurch, Beamont decided that the phase of guesswork and light-hearted quixotry was past. Now it was time for tactics.

On 14 June – two days before Roland Beamont launched his crusade against the V-1 – one man's resolution determined the fate of France as a nation for the foreseeable future. From the bridge of a French destroyer appropriately named *La Combattante*, the Tricolour whipping stiffly from her taffrail, General Charles de Gaulle surveyed the coastline of Normandy.

For the tall (6ft 4ins) humourless General, whom the British nicknamed "Wormwood," this was a solemn hour. Four years after France had sued for peace, entrusting her destiny to the Vichy Government of 88-year-old Marshal Henri-Philippe Pétain and his Prime Minister, Pierre Laval, de Gaulle was returning to *la patrie*. In 1940, his clarion-call had rallied thousands to the cause of freedom: "France has lost a battle, but France has not lost a war". Now de Gaulle had another paramount aim: to see that France did not lose the peace.

A man of rigid dissatisfactions, de Gaulle had been in a towering rage for ten days now – ever since a notable quarrel on 4 June with the British Premier in Churchill's private train. Thanks to Churchill's stubborn espousal of Roosevelt's views, no Free French civil affairs officers had even now been appointed, and no provisional government recognised. Instead, Roosevelt had called for American military government officers to take charge, as if occupying enemy territory, and for the printing of half a billion green and purple occupation francs – "*les faux billets*" (sham money), de Gaulle had stigmatised them. And though the General had accepted as a *fait accompli* the call for a nationwide rising that had so distressed Captain Mamy, he was appalled by the resultant slaughter in fully twenty-five Departments outside the invasion zone, notably on the Vercors massif, above the Rhône River, where 2,000 men died needlessly.

Churchill had been unrepentant on every score. "Each time I must choose between you and Roosevelt I shall always choose Roosevelt," he flashed, and two days later he ordered an aide: "Go and tell Bedell Smith to put de Gaulle in a plane and send him back to Algiers – in chains if necessary. He must not be allowed to re-enter France." "What can you do," he grumbled to Sir Alan Brooke, "with a man who looks like a female llama surprised when bathing?" To Roosevelt, deploring "the faults and follies of de Gaulle," he wrote, "The feeling is that she (France) should be with us in this. But who is 'she'? When this works out in the person of de Gaulle, all the difficulties that you and I know so well, emerge…"

Many saw this long-standing feud as now totally counterproductive. From London's Dorchester Hotel, Alfred Duff Cooper penned a hasty hand-written note to Eden: "The P.M. says he will describe the whole of de Gaulle's past career (in a forthcoming House of Commons debate) and will denounce him as the mortal foe of England. If this were to occur in open session, the result would be disastrous." As the London *Economist* commented wisely: "...allowing for the worst the President can suspect, the present American attitude is calculated to bring about exactly those dangers which it is designed to prevent."

As indeed it had. A patriot who loved France with a passion akin to carnality, de Gaulle saw clearly the dangers of liberation: by mid-1943, his bitterest enemies, the Communists of Paris and southwest France were ready to proclaim a Soviet-style revolution as soon as the Germans fell back. Thus de Gaulle, working in utmost secrecy, had for nine months now been assembling a caravan of 200 French liason officers, under Colonel Pierre de Chevigné, to follow in the wake of the Allied armies, posting proclamations, appointing new officials – then moving on. Of the ten-strong team accompanying him on 14 June, clambering awkwardly into DUKWs off the beaches near Bayeux, de Chevigné made one, besides François Coulet, de Gaulle's Regional Commissioner-designate for Normandy.

The *coup d'état* worked to perfection. Chatting cordially to Montgomery, who was planning the forthcoming battle for Caen in his trailer, de Gaulle let slip that he was leaving behind Coulet to take over the civil administration of Bayeux. Coulet, in turn, was replacing the Vichy Sub-Prefect of Bayeux, Pierre Rochat, with a local Resistant, Raymond Triboulet. At Isigny and other bridgehead towns, similar appointments would be made. Montgomery took the point. "The next days will show," ran a staff memo of 19 June, "whether Coulet and Triboulet can establish themselves and win the people's confidence as the *de facto* government. Meanwhile we are treating them as such."

"We just had to present the Allies with an accomplished fact," de Gaulle commented shrewdly to his Chief of Staff, General Edmond Bethouart, as *La Combattante* hoisted anchor, "You'll see that they will say nothing."

It was a transition even smoother than de Gaulle could have envisaged. Within hours, Vichy's Rochat received an urgent summons to the Bayeux Sub-Prefecture. "*Mon cher monsieur,*" Triboulet greeted him effusively, "You can do me a service." As Rochat gaped, his successor explained his predicament: "The fact is I have no sub-prefect's uniform. We're about the same size. Would you mind giving me yours?"

It dawned on Rochat that for four years the buttons of the Vichy police uniform had sported a long-standing symbol of Fascism, a double-headed Gallic battle-axe. "*Bien sûr*," he replied, savouring the irony, "But – don't forget to change the buttons."

–

De Gaulle was quite unaware of it, but his Free French Forces had gained a new recruit: Private 75, 954 Sergueiev, Lily, ambulance orderly. In an office on London's Portman Square, Lily was recounting the story of her last stormy days with M.I.5. to Captain Vaudreuil, an intelligence officer.

"There's no objection to your enlisting in the Army," Vaudreuil had answered her initial query. "On the contrary! You couldn't tell me *why* your work with the British is finished?"

Lily could. Following her disclosure of her security check to Mary Ward, there had been one last tense unsmiling interview with Colonel Robertson and Mary at 39, Hill Street. "Mary has informed me of what you have arranged in Lisbon," Robertson told her coldly, "We have accordingly decided that you are no longer trustworthy. You will not transmit any more; we'll do that ourselves. I shall organise your return to Paris or Algiers."

"I left France without your help," Lily told him defiantly, "I'll return there in the same way."

"I suppose," Robertson said after a long pause, "that you don't wish to give us the security check?" Lily only shrugged.

But when Robertson departed, Lily was conscious of a painful struggle within her. She cared nothing for the British now, but, like de Gaulle, she cared passionately for France. If Russell Lee slipped up on a transmission, it was France, cold, hungry, despairing France, now so near to liberation, who would suffer. Six months had gone, and she was still alive; the latest X-Rays at St Mary's Hospital showed no change. If she was going to die, it would be in Paris with her conscience at last clear.

"Okay," she told Mary Ward, finally, "I'll give you the check."

"I didn't really get on with the British," she wound up her recital to Vaudreuil.

A Gaullist to the last, the Captain smiled seraphically. "I'm glad you told me all this. What I wanted to hear you say is that you didn't get on with the British."

One major problem faced de Gaulle's Regional Commissioners, waiting to forestall the Communists in liberated France. The success of their mission could only chime with the pace of the Allied advance. And the Allies were not advancing.

For six whole weeks, in a pastoral parody of the Anzio-Cassino stalemate, the British and Canadians remained stalled before Caen in the apple orchards of Normandy, for Montgomery's hope of seizing the city on the first day was, as his Chief of Staff, Major-General Freddie de Guingand admitted, "a pious hope rather than a certainty". Yet from the outset Montgomery made the best of it. "From the very beginning," he wrote to Alan Brooke as late as 27 July, "it has been my policy to try and pull the main enemy strength, and especially his main armoured strength, on to the British Second Army on the eastern flank so that our affairs on the western flank could proceed more easily..."

In truth, Caen was a "set-piece" Montgomery battle in the tradition of Alamein – careful, precise, using armour as a parry to ward off Rommel's jabs, compelling the Germans to react to his strategy, using Bradley's 1st Army in a right swing against Cherbourg (which fell on 26 June). Murderous blows from the air were a part of it, too; after one assault on 18 July, when 7,700 tons of bombs were expended to gain seven miles of ground, no German prisoners could be interrogated for twenty-four hours. All of them were temporarily stone-deaf.

All along, Montgomery faced the opposition of crack troops; to the west of Caen, the stubborn men of *Standartenführer* Kurt Meyer's 25th Panzer Grenadier Regiment held fast, along with *Generalmajor* Fritz Bayerlein's *Panzer Lehr*, which alone held ten miles of front. As a veteran of the desert war, Bayerlein knew that aside from the 51st Highland Division all of Montgomery's elite troops were now in Normandy – yet the High Command was still insisting that this thrust was "a diversion". Not until the end of July was Fifteenth Army transferred from the Pas de Calais.

At 9 a.m. on 17 June Hitler, to compound confusion, summoned Von Rundstedt, Rommel, and their two Chiefs of Staff to a conference at his reserve headquarters at Margival, near Soissons, 57 miles north-east of Paris. In a well-furnished carpeted conference room Hitler squatted on a low wooden stool, toying with his metal-rimmed spectacles, fiddling with a bunch of coloured pencils, while the Field Marshals were left to stand like schoolboys before a headmaster. Speidel, for one, was totally disenchanted with a Führer "ageing, stooping and increasingly incoherent," who resisted all Rommel's contentions that "Germany was politically isolated ... it was urgently necessary to end the war".

"Don't you worry about the future course of the war," Hitler retorted, "look to your own invasion front."

It was the same when Von Rundstedt suggested that the rigid defence of the whole Cherbourg Peninsula should give place to a withdrawal into the port itself. Using ruler and compass, Hitler triumphantly worked out the minimal number of square miles held by the Allies compared with that area of France still in German hands. "The fortress of Cherbourg is to be held at all costs," the Führer concluded.

With those words, the Field Marshals saw the future of Germany's war writ large. For months now, the phrase "promoted to Fortress" had been a standing joke at Von Rundstedt's headquarters; it was as if, by invoking the magic word, Hitler could conjure impregnable bastions out of thin air. Dunkirk was to be a fortress, no less than Calais, Boulogne, Dieppe and Le Havre; all told, some sixteen fortresses were to tie up 200,000 men, on top of 35,000 men in the Channel Islands, each island a fortress in itself.

"That Bohemian corporal,"[16] grunted Von Rundstedt, using his habitual slighting phrase for Hitler, "will try to hold everything and so in the end lose everything." The old Field Marshal was one man who would have fully appreciated the sentiments of Lieutenant-General Sir Alan Brooke: "I'd like to meet Hitler. I'd like to shake his hand ... worth forty divisions to us."

It was to be the same on the Russian front, for one week later, after a Red Army offensive burst upon the German Army Group Centre Hitler decreed that Bobruisk, Mogilev, Orsha and Vitebsk, all Byelorussian garrisons, should be elevated to last-man last-round status – detaching six divisions to enforce the order. From the débâcles of Stalingrad, Tunis and the Crimea Hitler had learned nothing at all.

These were high-level concerns. For most serving on the Caen front, the war had slowed to a waiting game, with many realising for the first time what war itself could mean. "I never wish to see again," wrote one 11th Hussar officer, "the plain of Caen with its harvest ungathered, villages smashed beyond recognition, choking dust for miles and miles..." and this sense of waste and attrition was fuelled by many images. For Sister Brenda McBryde of No 75 British General Hospital, it was the field incinerators, smoking all night, burning tattered once-proud uniforms and badges: the shoulder flashes of The Royal Winnipeg Rifles, white lettering on rifle green, the leaping black boar of XXX Corps, the blue and red flash of 21st Army Group. For Private Leslie Cornwell, of the Durham Light Infantry, it was the nerve-racking sight of the pioneer platoons, forever making white crosses ready for use before battle commenced.

For most armoured-car crews it was the ever-present bottle of "Stupor Juice," rough red wine spiked with calvados, which gave Dutch courage on each patrol. For Captain Jocelyn Pereira, intelligence officer of the 5th Battalion, Coldstream Guards, it was the omnipresence of death: "the huddled bundles in the ditch; the corpse-like attitude; the rotting uniform for a shroud; bodies curiously shrunken and frozen, gesturing like a tailor's dummy; the waxen face that knows no more surprises..."

It took the battalion's humourist, Guardsman Payne, who saw service at St Mauvieux, by Caen's Carpiquet airfield, to rise above it all: "St Mauvieux? Oh, a very quiet place. All you ever heard was cries of '*Bring another stretcher!*'"

If the war had bogged down on the western front, more than 6,000 miles away, in the Pacific Ocean, the pace was quickening. At 4 a.m. on 15 June, more than 127,000 fighting men stormed ashore on Saipan, the largest of an island group known as the Marianas.

"The war was lost when the Marianas were taken away from Japan," Prince Higashikuni, C-in-C, Home Defence Headquarters, was to avow, and this mass assault, which saw 8,000 U.S. Marines ashore in twenty minutes, was also to transform the entire life of a 20-year-old aviation cadet, Ryuji Nagatsuka.

Not that Nagatsuka made part of the battle. On 15 June, as one of a new intake of 240 *tokusos* (aspirant cadets) he was stationed at Kanumaruhara, almost 100 miles north of Tokyo. Until recently a dedicated student with the French Literature Department of the Imperial University of Tokyo under Professor Arinaga, Nagatsuka had received his call-up papers with reluctance, aware only vaguely that his homeland was in danger.

How gravely in danger, Nagatsuka had never realised until he and his fellows, in their brand-new summer uniforms, mustered before Commander Minami in front of the headquarters building. "You are no longer civilians from whom much must be hidden," Minami told them gravely, "I am going to tell you the whole truth about the present state of the war."

It was truth that Nagatsuka heard with growing disbelief – so far removed was it from the jingoistic optimism of dailies like *Asahi Shimbun*. "Attacked from both sides," he heard, "Germany can no longer hope to conquer Great Britain. And our country is compelled to fight the Allies single-handed in the Pacific. We are losing our battles. In the Central Pacific Ocean, defeat follows upon defeat."

The cadets were listening tensely, facing facts as final and overwhelming as a terminal cancer verdict. Tarawa: 4,690 Japanese lives lost. Rabaul: 127 aircraft lost within twelve days. Truk, in Commander Minami's words, had been "the Japanese Pearl Harbor"; 270 aircraft lost, 34 transport ships sunk, nine warships severely damaged, 600 men dead or wounded. Not even a glimmer of hope from the Burma front: "the chances of Operation Imphal succeeding are growing fainter and fainter."

The reversal of Japan's fortunes, Minami was making plain, rested squarely on their shoulders. "All our fighting men in the front lines are crying out for more planes and more pilots. Victory depends on mastery of the air. It is your task to regain it. Before ending my talk I wish to say only one word to you: Courage! Break ranks!"

No cadet could then conceive that worse was to follow. But at 3 a.m. on 18 June, three hours before normal reveille, a bugle sounded urgently through the dingy barracks: cadet pilots were summoned to an emergency muster in full uniform before headquarters. There Commander Minami was again awaiting them, his voice resonant in the darkness. Saipan – which Premier Tojo had decreed flatly was impregnable – had been invaded three days earlier.

The implications were not lost on Nagatsuka and his fellows. From Saipan to Tokyo was only 1,125 miles, and all of them knew that the hated new American bomber, the B-29, capable of carrying four tons of bombs, had a range of 3,500 miles. The fall of Saipan would bring the Japanese archipelago within easy range.

After that, the days seemed to drag with agonising slowness. Before graduating to the yellow-painted *Akatonbo* (Dragonfly) training planes, the cadets must spend thirty wearisome days on gliders, skimming at a puerile twenty feet above the ground. All of them yearned to get into the battle, for although forbidden to read newspapers or listen to the radio – this was pabulum for women and civilians – they daily gleaned the facts about Saipan from progress reports fed them by Ensign Sakai, the leader of Squad 4.

In truth, the 43rd Japanese Division, under Lieutenant-General Yoshitsuga Saito, which formed the core of the defence but had only reached Saipan early in June, was doomed from the first. With no defensive positions prepared, Saito, an expert on horse procurement rather than combat, was forced to tackle the Americans on the beaches rather than stall them from positions inland. And although the courageous watchword on Saipan was "Seven Lives for the Emperor" – whose 16 June message of encouragement had been burned after reading lest the Imperial word be polluted by the invaders – courage was no longer enough.

"Victory depends on mastery of the air": a truth equally known to Vice-Admiral Marc A. Mitscher, a sprightly leathery-faced gnome of a man who habitually sported a lobsterman's cap, the commander of Task Force 58. On Sunday 18 June (Monday in Tokyo and the Marianas), carriers of the Japanese Southern Expeditionary Fleet sent off virtually all their planes in a maximum-range strike against Mitscher's ships. As they drew near, Hellcat fighters soared up from the decks of the U.S. carriers to engage them in one of the war's costliest air battles – "The Great Marianas Turkey Shoot". In these furious few hours, 369 Japanese aircraft fell victim to the Hellcats – the war's biggest toll for a single day.

Most of the U.S. Fifth Fleet, of which Task Force 58 made part, then turned west, steaming under forced draft all night and much of the next day, seeking to engage a Japanese fleet now stripped of its air cover. But only two hours of daylight remained when the scout planes gave a final fix on the Japanese; this, too, was a strike at maximum range. Darkness fell; at 8:30 p.m., on 20 June, when the first planes were heard returning, Task Force 58 was blacked-out.

In the flag plot of U.S.S. *Lexington*, Mitscher, seated on a leather transom, lit his fourth cigarette in succession and said softly, "Turn on the lights. Tell 'em to land on any carrier."

It was one of the Pacific War's boldest gambles. As the Avengers and Helldivers closed in, the entire fleet below them sprouted lights – what one man described as "a sea-going Coney Island in enemy waters". Lights glowed red at the mastheads of battleships, cruisers and destroyers; star shells burst and soared; glow-lights blinked the outlines of flight decks and from every carrier a searchlight beacon thrust a beckoning finger clear into the sky.

Each plane was desperately low on fuel; some ran dry as they waited their turn to land. Their pilots ditched them in the Philippine Sea, then scrambled with their crewmen aboard rafts, blinking flashlights at the rescuing destroyers. There were some bad landings and planes were wrecked on the jam-packed decks, for many pilots chose the wrong carriers. Yet for 93 planes lost to Japanese action and "extreme range," all but 22 pilots and 27 crewmen were saved.

With more than 400 planes lost and 30 ships sunk, the outcome at Saipan was no longer in doubt. On 9 July, Nagatsuka heard the island had fallen, and that a political earthquake had shaken Japan's war structure: Premier Hideki Tojo and his entire Cabinet had resigned.

To Nagatsuka another truth now became apparent with no need of guidance from Commander Minami: in the course of a calendar year, every cadet at Kanumaruhara was fated to die in action.

–

In London now, fears were growing apace: under the day-long barrage of flying bombs, how would morale stand up? Almost a million and a half citizens were to quit the capital, for often, in a southern suburb like Croydon, nine V-1s might be seen overhead at one time. In a 27 June memo to the War Cabinet, Churchill's Minister of Home Security, the pugnacious one-eyed Herbert Morrison, who feared 100,000 deaths and 250,000 injured a month, warned: "This is not 1940–41 ... people are asking, 'Where is this air superiority they talk about?' ... the people have had nearly five years of war strain ... there is a limit, and the limit will come."

Yet faced for the first time "by a purely arbitrary fate," those Londoners remaining behind – the brave and the few – were adapting. Such traditional magnets as Lord's Cricket Ground and Speaker's Corner never lost their pull. Thousands returned to the Tube shelter life of 1940, dusting off almost forgotten tin hats; the undaunted, still pursuing a social round, found a welcome glut of taxis and unreserved tables – most notably at the Savoy Hotel, with its river view and mirror-glass decorations. Estate agents commented on a new phenomenon; flats on the south side of any large block were harder to let than those on the north. In the London parks, cratered, one man noted, "with great gaping ulcers," the rabbits had all gone to ground. The scent of sap from wounded trees hung heavily in the summer air.

London became a city of watchers and listeners – ears cocked for the squawking danger signal of a klaxon, for the ominous silence when the throaty chugging cut out overhead. They watched, too, for the silent hoisting of black wind socks on high roofs, then, following a far-off explosion, for the tell-tale signs of impact: the "huge buff plume calm and clean as sand against a pale bluish sky". Many a Londoner would have echoed Eisenhower, sitting patiently in a shelter at Bushey Park: "Every time I pray Oh Lord keep that engine going, I feel kinda mean."

To name the missiles, it seemed, was in some degree to tame them. If *The Daily Express* was first off the mark with The Buzz Bomb, *The Daily Telegraph* was swift to follow with The Bumble Bomb. To the War Cabinet they were, officially, from 19 June, the "flying bomb," but one day later the R.A.F. coined a phrase of their own, which stuck, "the doodlebugs" – unlike a ruder sobriquet, "The Farting Furies".

Despite the shrugged-off Cockney courage, there were many appalling incidents. Croydon, with 142 V-1s, was the worst-hit borough, but the miles of slate-grey roofs south of Waterloo Station – Camberwell, Wandsworth, Lewisham – fared almost as badly. The worst tragedy of all came at 11:20 a.m. on Sunday 18 June: a V-1 cutting out over the high red-brick tower of Queen Anne's Mansions, by St James's Park, fell almost vertically on the roof of the Guards Chapel, attached to Wellington Barracks, during morning service. "All the waters and the winds in the world had come together in mighty conflict," was the impression of an ATS subaltern, Elizabeth Sheppard-Jones, who survived, although paralysed for life, but 119 died, 122 were seriously injured, as the roof and heavy concrete girders collapsed "in a bellow of bricks."

To Dr R. V. Jones, hurrying to the scene from his office at No 55, Broadway, the impact was especially personal; as adviser to A.I. 1(c), the Air Component of M.I.6., the British Secret Intelligence Service, Jones had been involved in all the early appraisals of the V-1's potential. Moreover, he knew what a ton of explosive could do. Yet his first impression was a bizarre one: all Birdcage Walk, leading to the chapel, was "a sea of fresh pine leaves, the trees had all been stripped and you could hardly see a speck of asphalt for hundreds of yards."

Twelve days later, at 2 p.m. on Friday 30 June, the tail-end of the lunch hour, a V-1 struck the wide curving crescent of the Aldwych, outside the main door of the Air Ministry building – blasting a line of parked buses into scarlet scrap-metal, catapulting all those on the upper decks into the branches of a plane tree, tugging the black-out curtains from hundreds of high windows, sucking half a dozen WAAFs (Womens Auxiliary Air Force) bodily across a windowsill, to smash to the pavement below. Wardens and rescue workers arriving in the splintered canyon of the Aldwych counted a toll of 46 dead and 399 seriously injured.

At topmost level the mood was for reprisals – Geneva Convention or no. Although a World War One pacifist, Herbert Morrison urged on Churchill: "A threat to Germany to bomb to destruction as and when opportunity offers their smaller towns, if this utterly indiscriminate bombing does not cease; or the use of gas." Churchill's reply, on 4 July, was a masterpiece of understatement – "The Germans might retaliate by filling their flying bombs with gas, and this would be annoying to our civilian population" – but two days later the prospect had taken hold of him.

"I want a cold-blooded calculation made as to how it would pay us to use poison gas, by which I mean principally mustard,"[17] he minuted Ismay, "...If the bombardment of London really became a serious nuisance ... I should be prepared to do *anything* that would hit the enemy in a murderous place ... I want the matter studied in cold blood by sensible people and not by that particular set of psalm-singing uniformed defeatists which one runs across now here now there."

In the end, timing, not benevolence, clinched the issue. Ruling out gas as basically ineffective, the Chiefs of Staff looked more favourably on the use of anthrax pellets, code-named "N spores," for experiments on Gruinard Island, off the north-west coast of Scotland, had resulted in the storage of 5 million anthrax-impregnated cattle-cakes at Porton Down, on Salisbury Plain. But work on a full-scale programme, 4,250,000 anthrax bombs, to be packed inside 500-lb cluster bombs and dropped by 2,700 heavy bombers, was eight months short of completion at Camp Detrick, in Maryland – as was work on two chilling substances, 1313 (Isopropyl Phenyl Carbamate), lethal to cereal crops, and 1414 (Calcium-2 – Methyl-4 – Chloro-Phenoxy Acetate), fatal to root crops.

Plainly such long-term solutions – rendering German soil uninhabitable for generations to come – were impracticable for 1944. So the onus lay on Wing Commander Beamont and his pilots.

Since his narrow escape from that exploding V-1 – a hazard others had since shared – Beamont and his squadron commanders had debated the problems endlessly. Analysing every combat report filed, Beamont detailed his findings: in the first three days No 150 Wing had destroyed less than half the sightings reported. Most abortive attacks had been delivered at between 300–400 yards, which helped explain the failures: a V-1's wing thickness was no more than eight inches, the diameter of the fuselage three feet. Yet damage to the attacking Tempests had been limited to aircraft closing to less than 200 yards. For Beamont, this clinched it: the gunsights of 150 Wing were now harmonised to exactly 200 yards.

Another problem was the sightings: from the moment radar picked up a track barely four minutes elapsed before the missile reached the coast. And although their speeds were no more than 390 m.p.h., as against the estimated 450, the combined approach speeds in a head-on interception totalled almost 800 m.p.h. Thus, by the time a pilot had swung through 180 degrees to attack, his quarry was out of range.

Other aggressors were proving more of a hindrance than a help. Slow-paced fighters, eager to join in the fray, were blocking the Tempests' path at the vital moment. Ack-ack crews, allowing insufficient deflection, were damaging more Tempests than V-1s. On Tuesday 20 June, two days after the carnage of the Guards Chapel, Beamont flew to H.Q. 11 Group to put his case to the Senior Air Staff Officer, Air Vice Marshal Cecil "Boy" Bouchier, a dynamic little Royal Flying Corps veteran.

Bouchier listened sympathetically to Beamont's proposals. His wing should concentrate in the 50 miles between Eastbourne and Dover in a belt 7,000 feet high extending three miles out to sea. Within that area, guns should hold their fire and all fighters save the Tempest and the Spitfire XIV (averaging 375 m.p.h, at 2,000 feet) should be withdrawn. But Observer Corps posts, sited at half-mile intervals along the coastline, could play a crucial role. By firing grey smoke rockets to converge on the V-1s they would enable the pilots to spot them more swiftly.

Beamont's restrained indignation brought results. Within twenty-four hours, the Tempests had the battlefield to themselves – a battlefield which allowed no respite. All leave was cancelled. The armourers were mobilised on a twenty-four hour shift basis, for each of the 36 aircraft was firing its 20-mm cannon up to four times a day. For the first time since the Battle of Britain, pilots lived at dispersal, subsisting on tepid food brought by truck from the cookhouse. It was as hard for the ground crews, working eighteen hours a day, with time out only for sleep, for from dawn to dusk there were always eight Tempests on patrol.

Early in July, Beamont ceased what he now recalls as "pussy-footing" and surprised even himself. In one week he despatched two V-1s without firing a shot.

Three miles inland from Hastings, following a radar track above cloud, he spotted a gap in the layer, put the Tempest's nose down, then caught his breath. Sliding like a shark through the drifting wraiths, a V-1 was heading straight for him.

No time to pull out from the dive; no time to turn away. His sole hope was to cross the V-1's track before the moment of collision. In that split second he jammed the Tempest's throttle wide open, thrusting on the control column, gearing the fighter to a full power dive. For one awful moment the orange jet was swimming in his vision before the missile's nose leapt vertically past his cockpit and disappeared. Pulling the Tempest into a climbing turn, Beamont swung round to attack.

But attack what? The flying bomb had disappeared. For a moment he scanned the horizon in vain, then saw it once again: a pulsing orange corona of fire spraying smoke and chalk from the Sussex Downs. With faint incredulity, he acknowledged his victory. His slipstream had upset the missile's gyro control and sent it spinning into space.

Soon after, out of sheer necessity, Beamont embarked on a riskier venture yet.

From the Pas de Calais, the Germans were launching the V-1s in waves of six at a time, and Beamont, after shooting down one over the coast, had pursued another inland – as far as West Malling, the site of his first "kill". From 200 yards he opened fire, then the guns stopped dead. He was out of ammunition.

And now the sky was empty of fighters; there was only himself, flying impotently alongside the V-1, formating on it like a pre-war air display. He watched the deadly midwing monoplane, its single fin above the spurting jet, and a thought crept insidiously into his mind. Could he tilt the nearside wing and send it careening to the earth?

But was contact even necessary? His slipstream had done it once before – so wouldn't the airflow over the top of his own wing suffice? Slowly he edged closer to it, delicately sliding his wingtip beneath. As if polarised the wings began to yaw into contact, and Beamont kicked his rudder sharply, veering out of reach. Unscathed, the V-1 rocketed on.

Slowly Beamont nudged back into position. Both Tempest and V-1 were on a gradually converging course, streaking for London at 380 m.p.h. Dipping his wing, Beamont crept in, until its tip was poised beneath the missile. Gingerly, like a man testing his balance on a tightrope, he began cautiously to raise it: nine inches, eight inches, six.

His hands were rigid on the control column. How much longer before the wings clashed irrevocably together?

A sweating eternity, then the airflow tipped the scales. Tilting to one side, like a glider caught by thermals, the V-1 seesawed for the earth, to rip itself apart in the Kentish pastures.

Thoughtfully, Beamont headed back to Newchurch. He needed a stiff drink and a bath, and in that order. A man could get himself killed, taking risks like that.[18]

–

On Thursday 20 July, at 6 a.m., the heat was already like a blanket over the city of Berlin. Yet even at that hour, *Oberstleutnant* Graf Claus von Stauffenberg, assistant to the chief of staff of the Home Army, had weightier things than the weather on his mind. As he boarded his staff car in the lakeside suburb of Wannsee he cast one final reflective glance at his pleasant pine-shaded villa. If he returned here tonight, he would have changed the face of the world. Failing this, he would be dead.

At 37, Stauffenberg looked ill-equipped to affect the destiny of Germany, let alone the world. Although 6ft 2ins tall, dark-haired and strongly-built, his dramatic black eye-patch testified to the loss of his left eye in the desert fighting in Tunisia – an encounter that had also cost him his right forearm and two fingers of his left hand, yet these very disabilities were, in Stauffenberg's words, a passport to commit "high treason with every means at my command."

It was with good reason that a portrait of Hitler – "this proletarian megalomaniac" – loomed large in Stauffenberg's Beldlestrasse office. "I chose this picture," he had told a brother officer as far back as the winter of 1941, "And I put it up so that whoever comes here shall see the man's expression of madness and the lack of any sense of proportion." But this morning the time for plot and counter-plot, debate and counter-debate that had typified the inchoate German resistance for six years now, was past. Within hours, after killing Adolf Hitler with an assassin's bomb, Stauffenberg would signal Operation Valkyrie, a revolt against the entire Nazi regime. With the Führer gone, the military would seize the reins of government and sue for peace before it was too late.

In the city, the car stopped briefly to pick up Stauffenberg's adjutant, *Leutnant* Werner von Haeften, before turning south for Rangsdorf airfield, a forty-five minute drive. Here they were joined by a third conspirator, *Generalmajor* Helmuth Stieff, of the Army's Organisation Department, a youthful embittered hunchback. By 7:30 a.m., after boarding a twin-engined Heinkel, they were airborne. Ahead lay a two-and-a-half hour flight to the *Wolfsschanze*, where Stauffenberg would report to the Führer's conference on troops available for the Russian front.

Grappling with the straps of his bulky yellow briefcase, Stauffenberg once again checked his bomb – a two-pound lump of grey plastic folded in an old shirt. Both this and the fuse, inside a slender glass capsule, were tailor-made to an assassin's needs. Once the capsule protecting the fuse was broken, an acid inside would ooze silently over a wire holding back the firing pin. Fifteen minutes later, when the acid had destroyed the wire, the firing pin would spring forward.

Next Stauffenberg ferreted a small pair of pliers from the briefcase. With only one hand – and that lacking two fingers – he would have to use these to crush the capsule. As the Heinkel droned east, he practised the manoeuvre again and again, squeezing the pliers against a dummy metal tube. There must be no last-minute hitches. Not only was the Führer to die; that afternoon Stauffenberg must return to Bendlerstrasse to mastermind the seizure of the city.

It was 10:10 a.m. The plane was banking towards the Rastenburg airstrip. No sooner had it landed than Haeften instructed the pilot:

"See that the plane is ready to take off at any time after noon." Climbing into a waiting staff car, the three men set off on a tortuous nine-mile drive through dank pine forests to the *Wolfsschanze*, showing their passes, good for that day only, three times in all at heavily-guarded checkpoints. Around 10:43 a.m., after skirting minefields, pillboxes and many circular compounds, the car halted at the *Führersperrkreis*, Hitler's personal compound, ringed by a barbed wire fence seven feet high.

Now there was time to spare. Over breakfast in the officers' mess, Stauffenberg made a point of chatting with the camp commandant's aide, *Hauptmann* von Möllendorf, who was later to prove useful. Then, still hugging the briefcase he checked in at the office of *Generalmajor* Walter Buhle, Chief of Staff to the Armed Forces High Command, to confer on manpower. At 11:35 a.m. both men reported to *Feldmarschall* Wilhelm Keitel. But on the way in, Stauffenberg hung back – to deposit his cap and uniform belt in the empty orderly room.

"I hope you can provide the troops we require," was Keitel's greeting. "The news from Russia is bad." For answer, Stauffenberg displayed the briefcase: "I have everything here, *Herr Feldmarschall*."

At 12:27 a.m. – three minutes before the conference began – Keitel and Stauffenberg set out for the *Führersperrkreis*. Then, to Keitel's intense annoyance, Stauffenberg halted abruptly: "I forgot my cap." Hastening back to the orderly room and closing the door behind him, he unstrapped the briefcase, seized the pliers and snapped the capsule. There was no turning back. In fifteen minutes the bomb would explode.

Emerging he found Keitel barely a step away, his hand reaching for the door knob. "Hurry!" he growled ill-temperedly, "We're already late."

In the 15-by-40 foot wooden map room, its walls reinforced with brick, its roof with 4 inches of concrete, every window was flung wide to combat the relentless heat. Twenty-two men were now grouped round the long wooden map table, listening to *Generalleutnant* Adolf Heusinger, Deputy Chief of Staff of the Army, reporting on the deteriorating Russian front. Briefly interrupting, Keitel saluted Hitler, who was standing at the centre of the table, his back to the door, and explained Stauffenberg's presence. Now Keitel took his place beside the Führer. As Heusinger rambled on, Stauffenberg cast a covert glance at the map table. Where could he place the briefcase to best advantage?

The map table, he saw, was supported not by legs, but by three stout wooden slabs, running at intervals across its width. Murmuring an apology to a staff officer, Stauffenberg leant past him, to rest the briefcase against a table support barely six feet from the Führer's legs. Then he glanced at his watch: 12:39, three minutes to go. Unseen, he slipped through the door and left the map room.

Two hundred yards distant, at Bunker 88, Haeften was waiting with a car. Waiting, too, was *General* Erich Fellgiebel, Army Chief of Signals, a recent and important convert to Operation Valkyrie. When the bomb went off, Fellgiebel's role was a crucial one: to inform the conspirators in Berlin, notably *Generaloberst* Ludwig Beck, a former Chief of Staff, and Stauffenberg's chief, *General der Infanterie* Friedrich Olbricht, that Hitler was dead, and to seal the *Wolfsschanze* off from the outside world by closing down all radio and telephone networks.

Again Stauffenberg checked his watch. "Another moment," he said. But the seconds crawled.

In the map room, *Oberst* Heinz Brandt, Heusinger's Chief of Staff, moving closer to inspect the maps, had twice struck his foot against the obtrusive briefcase. Irritated, he stooped to move it – from against the inside of the heavy table support to the far side, which now served as a sturdy buffer.

Heusinger was summarising the situation facing Army Group North: "The Russians are moving considerable forces northwards, west of the Düna ... If the Army Group does not now withdraw from Lake Peipus, a catastrophe will..."

With the impact of a 150-mm shell, a shrivelling sheet of yellow flame blasted the map room. The roof collapsed in a niagara of debris. Men were pitched bodily through the open windows. To *General der Artillerie* Walter Warlimont, "there was nothing but wounded men groaning, the acrid smell of burning, and charred fragments of maps and papers fluttering in the wind." As limply as a rag doll, Hitler was pitched into Keitel's arms, blood pouring from his ruptured right eardrum, his hair and trousers on fire. "Somebody must have thrown a hand grenade," he gasped when the flames were beaten out, then, retiring to his private bunker, sat down shakily to take his own pulse.

For Stauffenberg and Haeften, speeding for the airstrip, even seconds were now a precious commodity. Twice Stauffenberg bluffed his way past checkpoints – but at Checkpoint 3, the guard commander was adamant. An alert was in progress and no one could pass.

"Ring the commandant's adjutant," Stauffenberg ordered, and was at once connected with *Hauptmann* von Möllendorf, with whom he had breakfasted so pleasantly. "*Generaloberst* Fromm (commander of the Home Army) is waiting for me at the airstrip," he lied, and Möllendorf, all unsuspecting, swallowed the bait. At 1:05 p.m. Stauffenberg and Haeften were boarding the Heinkel.

In the *Führersperrkreis*, all was still confusion. Four men were to die as a result of the bomb blast – *Oberst* Brandt, who had moved the briefcase, *General* Rudolf Schmundt, Hitler's chief adjutant, the Luftwaffe Chief of Staff, *Generaloberst* Günter Korten, and the stenographer, Heinrich Berger. Others were severely shaken, or cut about the head, like Jodl. But as yet no one had noticed Stauffenberg's departure, or connected him with the explosion. The theory was that a slave labourer from the Todt Organisation[19] had somehow planted a bomb.

Although at the heart of the conspiracy, Stauffenberg was by no means the first man to try to kill Hitler. Between September and December 1943, six attempts had been planned on the Führer's life, and all, for varying reasons, had misfired: an air raid had postponed an inspection, a conference was cancelled at the eleventh hour. Finally Stauffenberg, who had planned "Operation Valkyrie" – a contingency counter-coup by the Home Army if millions of slave-labourers in the Reich revolted – as a cover-plan,[20] swore, "I'll do the damned thing myself – with my three fingers."

Yet the senior officers surrounding Stauffenberg were by no means the brightest or the best. Rommel, approached on 9 July by *Oberstleutnant* Cäsar von Hofacker, adjutant to the military governor of Paris, appears to have balked at assassination as a means of ending the war; instead he favoured seeking Hitler's permission for a meeting with Montgomery. Still more – among them Jodl himself, *Generaloberst* Heinz Guderian, who on 21 July was appointed Chief of the Army General Staff, and *Feldmarschall* Erich von Manstein, commander of Army Group Don – balked instead at Roosevelt's "unconditional surrender" policy, and its naive and Calvinistic assumption that all Germans were equally tainted by Nazism. Again, the President's logic was faulty: a coalition with Russia, a former Nazi partner, troubled him not at all.

At 3:45 p.m., as his plane reached Rangsdorf, Stauffenberg was tense with expectancy. For two hours he had been cut off from all contacts – with Rastenburg, with the Bendlerstrasse. From the airfield, Haeften at once called Home Army headquarters. Had the "Valkyrie" orders gone out? Had they received General Fellgiebel's message? To his dismay, Haeften now heard that no orders had gone out – and no word had come from Fellgiebel. Instead, *Generaloberst* Fritz Thiele, the *Wehrmacht* signals chief in Berlin, had phoned Rastenburg – as early as 1:15 by some accounts, as late as 3:30 p.m. by others – to learn only that an explosion had taken place.

Convinced in his own mind that Hitler was dead, Stauffenberg was thunderstruck by the delay. Seizing the phone, he ordered tersely, "Issue the Valkyrie orders at once," before commandeering a car and setting off for Bendlerstrasse. Only now, at 4 p.m., did the first Valkyrie messages stutter out over the teleprinter, and in offices all over Berlin phones began to ring.

At Bendlerstrasse, General Olbricht now entered the office of his chief, *Generaloberst* Friedrich Fromm. An unmitigated opportunist, who "always heard the grass grow," Fromm had long been aware of the conspiracy – "Don't forget Keitel when you make your 'putsch'," he had cautioned them – yet had refused to commit himself until an obvious victor emerged. "Hitler has been assassinated," Olbrich told him, "To ensure the internal security of the Reich you must put Operation Valkyrie into effect and take charge of it."

Fromm wavered visibly. "How do you know the Führer is dead?"

Olbricht now attempted a fatal double-bluff. Fellgiebel, he said, had phoned to confirm it – then, certain that all communications with Rastenburg were cut off, offered to place a blitz call to Keitel.

All later evidence suggested that Fellgiebel, on seeing Hitler alive, had lost heart and taken no action to isolate the *Wolfsschanze*. ("To think that these revolutionaries weren't even smart enough to cut the telephone wires," Göbbels commented later, "My little daughter would have thought of that.") For scarcely had Olbricht lifted the phone than Keitel answered. "I have just received a report that the Führer has been assassinated," Fromm told him cautiously.

"Nonsense!" was Keitel's dismissive reply, "There has been an attempt, but the Führer is alive. He is only slightly injured."

Around 4:30 p.m., before Olbricht had time to countermand his own orders, Stauffenberg burst in. Confidently, he assuaged his chief's fears. Hitler was most assuredly dead, Keitel was merely playing for time.

Now a bitter wrangle arose. When Fromm refused to issue the "Valkyrie" orders, Olbricht revealed that they had already gone out. In a rage, Fromm sent for the staff officer responsible and placed him in close arrest. Next it was Stauffenberg's turn to incur Fromm's wrath. "Keitel is lying!" Stauffenberg maintained. "It was I who set the bomb and I tell you Hitler is dead." "*Graf* Stauffenberg, the plot has failed," Fromm retorted. "You must shoot yourself."

"This is the time for action," Olbricht shouted defiantly, "before Germany is ruined." Now all three, like unruly cadets, fell to fisticuffs, two of them grappling with the powerfully-built Fromm, who broke free to strike Stauffenberg in the face. Alerted, *Leutnant* Haeften burst in with drawn pistol; Fromm was overpowered and placed under guard in an adjacent office. *Generaloberst* Erich Hoepner, whom Hitler had stripped of his rank and forbidden to wear uniform back in 1941, now unpacked that same uniform from a suitcase and took command.

What Hoepner commanded was still an unknown quantity. In Paris and Vienna, Valkyrie troops were already moving in, occupying key strongpoints, disarming the S.S., and there was no lack of willing supporters arriving at the Bendlerstrasse – among them *Generaloberst* Beck, ostensibly the coup's commander, Count Wolf von Helldorf, the Police President of Berlin, Count Otto von Bismarck, the administrative president of Potsdam, and Hans-Bernd Gisevius, overtly a vice-consul from Zurich but in reality an agent of the U.S. Office of Strategic Services. But loyal rank-and-file troops were thinner on the ground – thanks to the intervention of Dr Hans Hagen, a part-time employee of Göbbels' Propaganda Ministry.

At Doberitz, a suburb of Berlin, Hagen had just delivered a lecture on National Socialist Guidance Problems, when orders arrived for the *Grossdeutschland* Guard Battalion, under *Major* Otto Remer: Hitler was dead and Remer's unit was to seal off the governmental quarter round the Wilhelmstrasse. Hagen, scenting a coup, borrowed a motor cycle, rode hard for the Propaganda Ministry, and bulldozed his way into Göbbels' office. One glance at the pickets in the street outside convinced the malign and dwarfish Göbbels that this was no false alarm. He ordered that Remer should report to him immediately.

Remer, whose orders had included the arrest of Göbbels, suspected a trap; he arrived with his adjutant and twenty armed men, swaggering into the Minister's office with revolver drawn and cocked. Göbbels, who was with the Minister of Armaments and War Production, Albert

Speer, was equally suspicious; minutes earlier he had pocketed cyanide capsules as a precaution.

"I must know what the situation is. I am informed that the Führer is dead," Remer demanded.

"The Führer is alive. I spoke to him only a few minutes ago," Göbbels answered truthfully. And to prove it he lifted the telephone, ordering a blitz connection to the *Wolfsschanze*. Hitler, who had only now finished entertaining Mussolini and his entourage to afternoon tea, at once asked to speak to Remer. "*Major* Remer, can you hear – do you recognise my voice?"

And indeed Remer did. Awarded the Oak Leaf cluster to the Knight's Cross for bravery, he had spent forty-five unforgettable minutes with his Führer some months earlier; the guttural tones were unmistakable. "They tried to kill me," Hitler told him, "but I'm alive. Only my orders are to be obeyed. You are to restore order in Berlin for me."

With this conclusive proof, Remer needed no second bidding. Racing back to his battalion, he now began to unravel all the work of the last desperate hours. This was a deadly blow for the plotters – for Hitler was now using the Army, not the S.S., to put down an army conspiracy. By 6:30 p.m. troops still loyal to Hitler were parading through the city armed with loud-hailers, turning back all those units that Stauffenberg had ordered in: "Back to your barracks! Hitler is alive! You are traitors if you do not turn back!"

It was a fatal backlash. At 6:45 p.m. listeners to the *Deutschlandsender* radio all over Europe heard a programme on rat extermination faded out to learn that an assassination attempt had failed. By 7:15 the Bendlerstrasse was besieged with phone calls, and Stauffenbeirg was embarking on a desperate last-minute attempt to rally officers growing hourly more faint-hearted. "The radio announcement is false... I tell you, Hitler is dead! The nation is in danger and the Army must take over." At 7:30 p.m. there was a glimmer of hope: tanks were said to be on the way.

At 7:45, *Feldmarschall* Erwin von Witzleben, the Commander-in-Chief-designate of the new *Wehrmacht*, arrived crimson with irritation. "A fine mess, this," he growled at Stauffenberg, for morale was now ebbing so fast that even the sentries manning the building were deserting their posts.

At 8:45 p.m. the *Deutschlandsender* was again on the air: Hitler was to record a message which would be broadcast later that evening. Still

Stauffenberg could not believe it. Never relinquishing the telephone, he cajoled, exhorted and threatened by turns. But where were the units from the training centres? Where were the tanks? "We can only hope that all will go well," old *Generaloberst* Beck sighed fatalistically.

All, in fact, went disastrously wrong. Towards 11 p.m., a group of officers not involved in the conspiracy, led by *Oberstleutnant* Fritz Herber and *Oberstleutnant* Bodo von der Heyde, sensed that the tide was turning; failure to offer resistance now could cost them their own lives. Armed with Tommy guns from the Arsenal at Spandau, they marched into Olbricht's office, demanding Fromm's release. Stauffenberg, chancing by, was seized and held; breaking loose and bolting down the corridor, he was shot in the left arm. A fusillade of shots rang out; the long gloomy corridors came alive with running men, shouting "For the Führer or against him?".

Fromm, now released, took over command. Prowling through the headquarters, the Hitler faction one by one rounded up Beck, Hoepner, Olbricht, Stauffenberg and Haeften, assembling them in Fromm's office. Beck, granted permission by Fromm to take his own life, failed even in this; after he had twice wounded himself superficially in the temple, a sergeant dragged him from the room and shot him in the neck. At 11:25 p.m. Fromm announced that he had called "a court martial in the name of the Führer," which had pronounced death sentences on four officers: *Oberst* Mertz von Quirnheim, Olbricht, Haeften, and "this colonel whose name I have forgotten" – Stauffenberg.

Soon after midnight, the four were led down to a court-yard. In the dim light of truck headlamps they waited impassively as a firing squad took up position. Then one long ragged volley rang out and they fell dead – Stauffenberg reportedly crying, "Long live our blessed Germany," though there was doubt even about that.[21]

Barely twelve hours had passed since Stauffenberg had set down his briefcase under a map table in the *Wolfsschanze* – 300 miles from Berlin and just six feet from Adolf Hitler's side.

–

The aftermath was predictable. It was 1 a.m. before Hitler spoke to the nation: "The circle of these usurpers is very small ... It is a gang of criminal elements which will be destroyed without mercy ... We shall settle accounts with them in the manner to which we National Socialists are accustomed."

And Hitler was true to his vow. On his orders, 400 investigators set to work to uncover every outside link with "the basest creatures that ever wore the soldier's tunic" – rendering Himmler's S.S. more powerful than ever as they usurped many Army functions. The trials of the military leaders – Witzleben, Hoepner, Stieff and others – were all over by 9 August, following forty-eight hours of screaming vituperation from the President of the People's Court, Roland Freisler, who rated a sharp rebuke from Hitler – "He is behaving like a ham actor instead of getting the trials of these common criminals over as quickly as possible." On 9 August, the first eight condemned were hanged with nooses of piano wire attached to meat hooks in Ploetenzee jail, now converted into a macabre movie-studio where whirring cameras recorded their death agonies on 200,000 feet of film. But other trials linked to the conspiracy – perhaps 600 arrests in all and 200 executions, including that of the ambivalent *Generaloberst* Fromm – dragged on until April 1945.

World reaction was predictable, too. Churchill's was jovial: "They missed the old bastard – but there's time yet." Others were suspicious; Churchill's Minister of Labour, Ernest Bevin, saw it as "a Nazi stunt to popularise H.," while his Minister of Information, Brendan Bracken, viewed it as "Göbbels' work". In America, the Office of Strategic Services embarked on a series of crack-brained ventures designed to score where the generals had failed – everything from blinding Hitler with liquid nitrogen to injecting his vegetables with female sex hormones to change him into a woman. The *New York Herald Tribune*, though, mirrored a Roosevelt-like disdain: "Let the generals kill the corporal, or vice-versa, preferably both".

Hitler's unwilling satellites found it hard to restrain their disappointments. The Vichy French Premier, Pierre Laval, after sending the Führer a warm telegram of congratulations, commented drily: "The only pity is that he wasn't killed. What a lot of things could have been arranged!" Benito Mussolini's reaction verged on delayed shock: having first goggled in awe at the smoking ruins of the map room, then sat in embarrassed silence, crumbling chocolate cake in his fingers, while Hitler, in a kind of apocalyptic rage, vowed destruction on all his enemies, Mussolini was finally, on returning to Lake Garda, reduced to hugging himself with glee.

Others, too, could endure the humiliation his Grand Council had inflicted on him on 25 July, 1943. "Even to him," he chortled, over and over again, "it can happen even to *him*."

Even as Hitler was wreaking vengeance on his enemies, the Normandy front, after weeks of deadlock, was falling apart.

On 2 July, after roundly telling Keitel, "Make peace, you fools! What else can you do?" Von Rundstedt was dismissed from his post, to be replaced by *Feldmarschall* Hans von Kluge, a wily strategist known as "Clever Hans". Seven days later, at a cost of 5,500 casualties, Montgomery at last broke through to that part of Caen west of the Orne River. Already the stage had been set for Bradley's stirring drive for Avranches, at the northern base of the Brittany Peninsula.

For the Germans, the box score of disasters was mounting almost daily. On 17 July, a low-flying Spitfire shot up Rommel's Horch *en route* to Livarot; now "The Desert Fox," flung onto the highway with a fractured skull, was out of the Normandy battle. Nor would he be replaced; Kluge himself assumed command of Army Group B. One day later, the first Americans – 100 riflemen of the 1st Battalion, 115th Infantry – battled their way into St Lô. The pivotal town of the Cotentin Peninsula, St Lô was a road junction as tactically important to the Americans as Caen to the British. Two days later, Montgomery's attack had carved through Caen itself to the south.

No commander was more bitterly disillusioned than *Generalmajor* Fritz Bayerlein of Panzer *Lehr*. On 2 July, Kluge had issued an order which to Bayerlein made no sense at all: he was to hand over his positions at Tilly, west of Caen, to an infantry division, and then, leaving behind one third of his tanks, tank grenadiers and artillery, transfer to the American front in the St Lô area.

Bayerlein was beside himself. Where was the point in splitting up a battle-worthy division? Were things so desperate in St Lô? And in truth, Panzer *Lehr* was now a division on paper only: the costly battles of the last weeks had stripped it to a third of its effective strength.

By 25 July, 2,000 bombers had reduced Bayerlein's sector to a charnel-house four miles wide and two miles deep. Trenches had caved in; anti-tank gun positions were annihilated. Stores of fuel, ammunition and supplies burned with a fierce lambent flame. At least half the 5,000 men remaining to Bayerlein had been killed, wounded or buried alive. At noon on 26 July, he pulled out his headquarters to a flea-ridden farmhouse at Dangy, three miles south – just in time to escape a further raid by 400 medium bombers.

Dead-beat, hungry and filthy, Bayerlein and his staff had not washed, shaved or tasted hot food for three days. Thus, later that afternoon, their spirits rose; a sentry reported a staff car bearing an *Oberstleutnant* from Kluge's staff. Plainly, having assessed their plight, Kluge was sending word of reinforcements.

In his immaculate uniform, the scarlet stripes of a staff officer marking the seams of his trousers, Kluge's emissary was patently embarrassed by the grimy roughnecks crowding round him. For what he brought was not a promise of help but an order.

"*Herr General*," he told Bayerlein uneasily, "the *Feldmarschall* demands that the line from St Lô to Périers be held."

All of them stared at him in silence: *Major* Kauffman, the operations officer, *Major* Wrede, head of divisional administration. Then, softly Bayerlein repeated the injunction: "The line from St Lô to Périers is to be held. May I ask with what?"

The officer ducked the question. Patiently, as if to a none-too-bright subaltern, he repeated: "What I am passing on to you is an order, *Herr General*. You've got to hold out. Not a single man is to leave his position!". Almost as an afterthought, he added, "A battalion of S.S. Panther tanks will be striking at the American flank to relieve you."

In that moment, the world of the good soldier Bayerlein fell apart. He, who had fought under Guderian on the icy road to Moscow, who had battled through El Alamein with Rommel, only to see the Afrika Korps' final dissolution in Tunisia, could bear no more. Quite clearly and irrevocably he saw how Hitler's insane refusal to yield a yard of ground spelt the end for Germany.

Hands gripping the edge of the table, his voice was low-pitched but charged with a terrible intensity. "Every one is holding out in front, *Herr Oberstleutnant*. Every one. My grenadiers, my engineers, my tank crews – they're all holding their ground. Not a single man is leaving his post. Not one! They are lying in their foxholes mute and silent for they are dead. Dead. Do you understand?"

Stepping closer, until the faces of the two men almost touched, Bayerlein's final words signalled the beginning of the end in

Normandy: "You may report to the *Feldmarschall* that the Panzer *Lehr* Division is annihilated. Only the dead can now hold the line. But if those are my orders I shall stay here."

—

Early on 20 July, around the hour that Stauffenberg was leaving his Wannsee villa, the British delivered a bombshell of their own.

Over breakfast on this overcast day, the 186,000 readers of the influential London *Times* spotted a soberly-worded but intriguing item at the top of page 2:

> A MONSTROUS "OFFER"
> GERMAN BLACKMAIL
> BARTERING JEWS FOR MUNITIONS
> FROM OUR DIPLOMATIC CORRESPONDENT
>
> It has long been clear that, faced with the certainty of defeat, the German authorities would intensify all their efforts to blackmail, deceive, and split the allies. In their latest effort, made known in London yesterday, they have reached a new level of fantasy and self-deception...
>
> The whole story is one of the most loathsome of the war. It begins with a process of deliberate extirpation and ends, to date, with attempted blackmail ... At the end of last month, 400,000 of the 750,000 Jews in Hungary had been "liquidated" ... A short time ago, a prominent Hungarian Jew and a German official, whose job obviously was to control his actions and movements, arrived in Turkey and managed to get a message passed to British officials. The Hungarian Jew said he had "every reason to suppose" that the German authorities were prepared to spare the lives of the remaining 350,000 Jews in Hungary, and even let them leave for abroad, if the British would send Germany important war stocks, including 10,000 army lorries. These stocks, he said, would not be used on the Western front...

In Cairo, that same Hungarian Jew, Joel Brand, who had sought to save a million lives in all, was horrified. As yet Brand was unaware that

The New York Herald Tribune had, one day earlier, carried an identical story; he first gleaned the news from *Davar*, a leading Palestine daily. But of one fact he was painfully aware: the British, in broadcasting the news to the world and sabotaging the deal, had proved themselves "the enemies of my race".

Since his despairing interview with the Jewish Agency's Chaim Barlasz in Istanbul, Brand – who still stubbornly rejected the double-agent Andor Grosz' contention that the million Jews were no more than a smoke screen for S.S. peace feelers – had fought a losing battle all the way. When the Zionist foreign minister, Mosoche Shertok, was refused a visa into Turkey, Brand, on his own initiative, had boarded the Taurus Express for Aleppo – intent on top-level talks with Shertok and the Allies in Jerusalem.

But the Allies were one jump ahead. On D-Day, 6 June, in Aleppo's railway station, Brand was unceremoniously seized by British civilian agents and bundled into a jeep. Two days later, following a bewildering sojourn in an Army barracks, he was driven to an Arab villa for his first meeting with the man he had all along sought: the tall middle-aged Mosche Shertok.

"You can speak quite openly," Shertok told him, and then, indicating the silent group of officers and civilians who sat in on the conference, "Our British friends here are most interested in your report and we have nothing to hide from them."

Brand was far from realising it, but the British were stalling for time. As far back as 31 May, a War Cabinet Committee on Refugees had dismissed Eichmann's proposals as "blackmail ... a piece of political warfare": if the Germans had anything to propose, the proper channel was the Protecting Power, Switzerland. Yet here again they faced a dilemma: in January 1944, Roosevelt, largely for electoral reasons, had given his blessing to a War Refugee Board, strongly backed by Treasury Secretary Henry Morgenthau, its prime object the salvation of Jews. Thus the Committee saw the red light: "a mere negative should not be opposed to any scheme which promises rescue of Jews."

Yet all the Allies' half-hearted attempt to "keep the door open" "to avoid the accusation of indifference to the whole Jewish catastrophe," as Eden put it – had been effectively killed stone-dead on 18 June, by Deputy Soviet Foreign Minister, Andrei Vyshinsky. Russia, Vyshinsky told Roosevelt's Ambassador in Moscow, William Averell Harriman, "deemed it neither expedient nor permissible to negotiate with the German government regarding the problem mentioned."

From this moment on, Joel Brand was no more than a pawn in a devious game of world power politics.

Brand was quite unaware of this – then, and even later. "I am here as the delegate of a million people condemned to death," he told Shertok passionately. "Their lives depend on my return." Even Shertok's promise to fly to London to confer with Eden failed to appease him: he was appalled, too, by the British decision that he himself must proceed further south to Cairo, via Beirut and Haifa, for further interrogation. All of this would take time, and time was no longer on the side of those million anonymous Jews.

From a large well-furnished cell in Cairo's Security Intelligence Headquarters, Middle East, a room made gracious by flowers, fresh fruit and books, Brand tried daily to impress that urgency on his interrogator, Lieutenant W. B. Savigny. For eight hours a day, for two weeks on end – from 16 June to 30 June – Savigny, perched on a dais eight inches above the floor of the sunlit interrogation room, listened politely, sometimes sceptically, to Brand's impassioned monologue. And day after day, it seemed to Brand, the same questions recurred as remorselessly as a fugue.

"Do you think the whole business could be a private deal by Eichmann...? Or has it got the backing of the German government?"

"I don't know about the German government, but I'm quite sure these people are acting with Himmler's authority."

At times, the scepticism was all too apparent:

"Do you really imagine that we would deliver ten thousand lorries to the Germans in the middle of the war?"

"I've already said a dozen times that we don't *want* any of your lorries. Give me a promise – a promise that you'll never have to keep – and on the strength of that alone I can save a hundred thousand lives."

At such times, the British distaste for the logistics involved became apparent too:

"But the Allies will have to take these hundred thousand people at some neutral frontier and then put them on ships. Have you any idea what such an operation would mean in wartime, how much shipping would be required?"

For here, indeed, was the crux of the matter: the Jews were a worldwide embarrassment, like poor relations laying siege to a rich man's door. "What on earth are you thinking of?" a high official whose name he never knew was to ask Brand later, in the garden of the Anglo-Egyptian Club. "What should we do with a million Jews? Where should we put them?" If the logical answer was Palestine, this too, the British, standing fast on the White Paper of 1939, which limited Jewish immigrants to a blanket 75,000, steadfastly rejected – "if ... Middle Eastern oil and Middle Eastern communications are indeed vital to us, then it is essential to follow a different policy which will not alienate the Arab people," Eden was to stress by mid-September.

"Brand gives the impression of being a very naive idealist," Savigny reported to his chief, Brigadier R. J. Maunsell, a verdict few could dispute. For as autumn approached the high ideals of 1940 were now yielding to political expediency; many panaceas would be pondered, nothing would be done. "Must I?" Eden minuted plaintively, on learning that Shertok and Chaim Weizmann sought an interview concerning Brand; in the end the responsibility was shunted to his Minister of State, George Hall. Even Churchill, who for three decades had espoused the cause of Zionism, blew now hot, now cold.

When the bombing of Auschwitz was first mooted, Churchill was all enthusiastic – "You and I are in entire agreement," he told Eden. "Get anything out of the Air Force you can and invoke me if necessary." But when Air Secretary, Sir Archibald Sinclair, objected that bombing was "technically impossible," the Premier tamely acquiesced – although from March 1944 on the Allies had ruled the skies over Europe. In the United States, the same apathy was evident; three times in all, Assistant Secretary of War John J. McCloy rejected the War Refugee Board's pleas for the bombing of Auschwitz.

This bland indifference to the Holocaust was prompted in part by Britain's post-war plans for an Arab Palestine – "a disproportionate amount of the time of this office is wasted on dealing with these wailing Jews," commented one Foreign Office satrap, Armine Dew. Thus the Vyshinsky veto, delivered on 18 June, came as a godsend to the irresolute Allies; since the Soviet Union now called the tune in almost every theatre of war, their word should be law here, too. "We have discussed this matter with the Soviets, and that's it," Churchill's secretary, John Martin, told Weizmann tersely.

By 20 July, Brand, now permitted to mingle, although under escort, in Cairo society, saw the logical outcome of this policy: by leaking his mission to the world's press, the British had at one and the same time negated it and kept the Germans at arm's length. Ironically, although twenty-eight nations were fighting Hitler, not one of them was pledged to rescue the Jews. Thus the lives of millions would be sacrificed on the altar of "unconditional surrender".

For Brand, that "very naive idealist" it was a blow almost too bitter to contemplate; three months of planning and strife and anguish had gone for nothing. He had embarked on a giant step in the service of his race – and he had failed.

Only months later did the concept, like a shaft of light through storm clouds, break through: if the Allies were not pitting their might against the total evil of Nazism, why, then, were they fighting? In that crusade, to save even one life was a moral imperative – yet while the Allies had, however tentatively, debated the issue, once the Soviets had rejected it out of hand, the Allies had tamely followed suit.

In the end, even this negative conclusion brought comfort of a sort. It was not he, Brand, who had failed the Jews. It was the West who had failed humanity.

6

"Paris Is Worth 200,000 Dead"
22 July–September, 1944

"Well, Douglas – where do we go from here?"

"Mindanao, Mr President, then Leyte – and then Luzon!"

In the ground-floor room of a cream-coloured stucco mansion, converted to a Navy rest centre, on Waikiki's Kalaukau Avenue, President Franklin D. Roosevelt, wielding a long bamboo pointer before a giant map of the Pacific, cast a challenging eye upon General Douglas MacArthur. Flanking the President, Admiral Chester W. Nimitz, naval commander in the Central Pacific, sagely kept his counsel. It was soon after dinner on Wednesday 26 July: in the soft blue Honolulu night, the booming of the surf on Waikiki Beach was plainly audible. It was a night to go down to history; on the agenda was the whole future of the war against Japan.

For MacArthur, as Commander in the south and south-west Pacific, more was at stake than mere victory. Back in June, Fleet Admiral Ernest King, Roosevelt's crusty Chief of Naval Staff, had formulated a plan – supported by Nimitz – of bringing Japan to her knees from bases to be established in the Marianas: a plan which involved both the capture of Formosa and a direct attack on Kyushu, southernmost of the four main Japanese islands. Any such plan, they pointed out, would involve by-passing the Philippine Islands.

MacArthur was stunned. In March, 1942, following a direct order from Roosevelt, he had reluctantly left the island fortress of Corregidor, on Manila Bay, in a PT boat bound for Australia – three weeks before 7,000 of his troops surrendered to the Japanese on the Bataan Peninsula. On 17 March, arriving at an air strip near Darwin, he had vowed, "I have come through, and I shall return" – and from that time on his entire war had been dedicated to this end. His first headquarters, at 401, Collins Street, Melbourne, had duly been code-named "Bataan" – and in November 1943, when he moved on to New Guinea, Government House, at Port Moresby, like the General's private plane, was inevitably christened "Bataan," too.

It was a crusade with which the American public identified from the first; more than any other U.S. commander, MacArthur had become a legend in his lifetime. Australian war correspondents often found him resistible, irked by such thespian props as his dark sunglasses, his corn cob pipe, his barked declaration of "Gentlemen! With Gahd's help, I shall conquer the little yellow man!" – but in the United States, MacArthur worship had reached the proportions of an industry. Luncheon counters featured MacArthur sandwiches; Hollywood starlets modelled a Scottish tartan, the MacArthur skirt; a dancing academy launched a new step, the MacArthur Glide. His birthplace in Little Rock was consecrated as a patriotic shrine; streets, bridges, dams and baseball parks were named after him, along with MacArthur Camellias and MacArthur Sweet Peas, and all, in a sense, were testimonies to that steely single-mindedness – "I shall return."

New Guinea, New Britain, the Admiralty Islands – MacArthur had seen all these as no more than stepping stones to the Philippines. "I'm going back there this fall if I have to paddle a canoe," he told General George C. Kenney, his air commander, for of all the eighty-seven amphibious landings that MacArthur staged – reputedly with less loss of life than any commander since Darius the Great – it was the Philippines that engaged him heart and soul.

Now, facing Roosevelt on this soft July night, MacArthur was conscious of conflicting emotions: anger at being summoned to Hawaii for what was in truth a presidential pre-election rally, contempt for Roosevelt as an individual – "a man who would never tell the truth when a lie would serve him just as well" – mingled with compassion for the President's grey lethargic mien. ("The mark of death is on him!" he remarked prophetically. "In six months he'll be in his grave.") Then, after Nimitz had outlined the Navy's plan, yielding the wooden pointer to MacArthur, one single thought drove out all others: to win the case for the Philippines.

And MacArthur seized his chance; not for nothing had one journalist, following a marathon two-hour conference, credited him with "the histrionic ability of Sir Henry Irving." His voice low and intense, he reminded Roosevelt that besides 7,000 starving Americans in prison camps on the largest Philippine island, Luzon, there were millions of hungry Filipinos on all the islands. "You cannot abandon 17 million loyal Filipino Christians to the Japanese in favour of first liberating Formosa and returning it to China," he chided Roosevelt. "American public opinion would condemn you, Mr President. And it would be justified."

From moral imperatives, he passed to strategy. His plan, he claimed, was foolproof. If he landed in force on Luzon's Lingayen Gulf, he would be in Manila, 120 miles south, within five weeks of the initial landing. Manila – that was the key! From the Philippine capital, he could cut off Japan from her raw materials in Indochina, Malaya, Siam, Burma and the Dutch East Indies. From Manila his army and air force could join Nimitz in overwhelming the Japanese on nearby Formosa.

To Fleet Admiral William D. Leahy, Roosevelt's Chief of Staff, it seemed that the President's chairmanship, that evening, showed a fine impartiality. As the hours wore on, his skilful questioning elicited the fact that Nimitz was arguing King's case, rather than his own: Manila Bay, he agreed, could not fail to be useful, while an attack on Formosa could only pay off if fighter strips and anchorages had been set up in the central and southern Philippines. At midnight, when Roosevelt adjourned the conference until morning, the odds seemed marginally in favour of MacArthur.

But at 10:30 a.m. next day, Roosevelt was having second thoughts. In Europe, the casualty lists were lengthening daily, and MacArthur's plan to hit Luzon with 100,000 men might cost thousands of young American lives. "Douglas, to take Luzon would demand heavier losses than we can stand," Roosevelt argued. "It seems to me we must by-pass it."

MacArthur was implacable. "Mr President," he retorted, "my losses would not be heavy, any more than they have been in the past! The days of the frontal attack are over. Modern infantry weapons are too deadly, and direct assault is no longer feasible. Only mediocre commanders still use it. Your good commanders do not turn in heavy losses."

In truth, as Roosevelt knew full well, MacArthur was the living embodiment of this creed. To date, his entire war had been a text book example of what he called "hit-'em-where-they-ain't" and "leave-'em-die-on the vine": this tactic of "leapfrogging," leaving whole island chains cut off from communications and supplies, had transformed the by-pass manoeuvre into a new art of war. By constantly flanking the Japanese, giving them a line of retreat which might yet lead nowhere, MacArthur's gains far outweighed his losses. Told that certain strongpoints could not be taken with limited forces, MacArthur had replied: "Well, let's just say that we don't take them. In fact, gentlemen, I don't want them!" "The jungle! Starvation! They're my allies," he had exulted to General Kenney at Port Moresby.

As MacArthur finished his peroration there was total stillness; more than one man was taking thought of those accomplishments. Bowing gravely to the President, the General prepared to withdraw. Passing round the end chair, he felt Admiral Leahy pluck at his sleeve and the old seadog's hoarse stage whisper broke the silence: "I'll go along with you, Douglas!"

It was a verdict, which Roosevelt, too, was swift to endorse. "Well, Douglas, you win!" was his final pronouncement. "But I'm going to have a hell of a time over this with that old bear, Ernie King!" To his aide, as they departed for Hickam Field, MacArthur was, for once, succinct. "We've sold it!"

For the Philippines, the die was cast, and soon, in the bazaars of Manila, a message of hope was whispered from friend to friend like a password: "*Malabit nang dumating si kanô* – The American is coming soon."

—

All over the world, as August dawned, this sense of imminent liberation was in the air – and nowhere more than in the Polish capital of Warsaw. For two weeks now, intense excitement had gripped the 380,000 members of the *Armja Krajowa* (the Home Army), a nation-wide resistance movement commanded by Lieutenant-General Tadeusz Bor-Komorowski, a bald pensive ex-cavalry officer. After three long years, the Moscow radio station, "Kosciusz-ko," the mouthpiece of the Kremlin, had at last signalled the onset of Operation Burza (Tempest).

Through June and July, thirteen separate appeals had urged the citizens of Warsaw to rise up against the German occupation troops; by 30 July, the call to battle took on an irresistible urgency: "Warsaw trembles from the roar of guns. The Soviet Armies are pushing forward and are nearing the Vistula. They come to bring you liberation, PEOPLE OF WARSAW TO ARMS!"

For thousands, this stirring battle-cry had come in the nick of time; only recently Himmler had ordered the conscription and dispatch to the Reich of all males between 15 and 60. And in the grassy tree-lined streets, parched and yellow in the sultry heat, the sound of the Russian guns, twenty miles from the suburb of Praga, on the Vistula's eastern bank, grumbled like distant thunder.

In London at 6 p.m. on 26 July – while Roosevelt and MacAfthur conferred in Hawaii – Premier Stanislaw Mikolajczyk, en route to Moscow to seek a meeting of minds with Stalin, set the seal on the insurrection: the Home Army could rise up at a moment of their own choosing.

As decreed by General Komorowski, that moment – to coincide with the rush-hour traffic – would be at 5 p.m. on Tuesday 1 August. The logic was impeccable. – yet due to a fatal flaw in timing thousands of combatants had no word of warning.

Not until 6 p.m. on 31 July, did General Antoni Chrusciel, commanding Warsaw District, receive his first orders – but to code and despatch them to his group commanders was impossible, given an 8 p.m. curfew. Thus only at 8 a.m. on the day of the rising, were the sub-sector commanders alerted – with district commanders in the dark until 1 a.m., partisan commanders only warned at noon, platoon commanders given hasty notice at 2 p.m., suburban commanders at 4 p.m. and even later.

In the early afternoon Warsaw was a city divided – often with lesser fry completely in the know and top commanders totally oblivious. Stefan Korbonski, a leader of the Polish Peasant Party, had the news on the street from his wife, Zosia; his first indignant reaction was "Don't talk nonsense – don't you think I would know of it?" Hastening to his office he was more baffled still, for even then no word had come. Maria Dangel, a resistant's wife, reported to her unit's headquarters on Szpitalna Street, to find that she alone of 1,200 freedom fighters was privy to H-Hour. At 24, Zhuravia Street, Bernard Goldstein, a leading resistant, had casual word from his landlady; a Jewish businessman, Michael Zylberberg, heard the news from a nun in an ominously deserted restaurant.

Many were as completely in the dark as Colonel Jan Klepacz, lingering over a late lunch at the house of the Piekalkiewcz family. News of the rising reached him so precipitately he couldn't even reach his own apartment – yet as General Komorowski's Chief Quarter-Master he should have been briefed a whole day earlier.

For those whose eyes were sharp enough the signs were there to see. Along Marszalkowska, Stefan Korbonski was suddenly aware of a shimmering sea of bicycles; boys in windcheaters and top boots, were pedalling as hard as their legs would go, ferrying arms to the assembly point in their rucksacks – some with rifle barrels clumsily wrapped in newspaper protruding from the flaps. En route to his headquarters in the Kammler tobacco factory, in the working-class suburb of Wola, his pistols cached in a portable gramophone case, General Komorowski noted similar signs: everywhere hurrying pedestrians, their jacket pockets, briefcases, even women's handbags, bulging grotesquely with hidden grenades.

Yet first impressions were deceptive. Incredibly, at this eleventh hour, before a battle that would have taxed three well-armed divisions, no more than six per cent of the insurgents had arms of any kind. Like the Trojan War of 1250 B.C., the rising would be geared less to vital objectives than to seizing German weapons and ammunition.

At the tobacco factory, where the owner, Lieutenant Kammler, was reporting to Komorowski, the position was typical:

"How many men are here with you?"

"Thirty-three actually on the spot."

"And what arms?"

"Fifteen rifles, maybe forty grenades, and a few *filipinki*" (lethally-explosive home-made grenades).

Weapons were sadly lacking, so, too, were ammunition, food and supplies. But they had the wrathful courage of a threatened people and only twenty miles away was General Konstantin Rokossovsky's Second Belorussian Army Group. And promptly at 5 p.m. on 1 August, that courage was made manifest.

From the tobacco factory roof, General Komorowski had a grandstand view: a flashing like that of innumerable heliographs as thousands of windows were flung wide. All over the city, a hail of fire from those windows riddled German-held buildings and cut down marching formations. As if by magic, civilians vanished from the streets. From dark doorways and cellars, Home Army troops, sporting their distinctive red-and-white armbands streamed forth to attack. Within fifteen minutes, all Warsaw – more than a million inhabitants scattered over fifty-four square miles – was engulfed in the fight. All traffic had ceased, and the battle for the city was on.

It was a city vital to Russians and Germans alike, for seven main arteries traversed it, crossing the 600-foot-wide Vistula over three road and two railway bridges: a highway to the Eastern Front for the Germans, a highway to the cherished prize, Berlin, for the Russians. Thus for 63 days and nights thereafter the fighting would be bitter indeed.

Towards 8 p.m., after his troops had staved off a furious attack that cost the Germans thirty-five dead, Komorowski heard wild shouting from the roof-top. Hastening up the narrow stone stairway, slippery with blood, he found an excited guard, saluting rigidly. "The flag, sir!" he stammered out, "the Polish flag."

It was a moment too deep for tears. From the top of Warsaw's tallest edifice, the sixteen-storey Prudential Building, the white-and-red flag of Poland – raised by a consumptive officer-cadet – streamed above the city for the first time in five years. As Komorowski scanned the horizon, other flags were rising: from the dome of the Town Hall, from the tower of the Post Office Savings Bank, from other roofs and towers with every passing minute. Over the city, a giant mushroom of smoke, tinged red from leaping fires, hung motionless; the roar of battle grew palpably louder, but still discernible, above the whine and crackle of fire, were the poignant notes of Chopin's *Polonaise*, amplified from the Town Hall's radio station.

But no rising could be long sustained without additional arms or supplies and to this end Komorowski, on 2 August – and again on 5 and 7 August – had radioed London: "Exceedingly urgent that mass dropping of ammunition and weapons on Warsaw be done today." As yet, though, the rank-and-file – holed up in attics with telescopic rifles, holding their own behind primitive street barricades of overturned tram cars, telegraph poles and felled trees – felt no undue alarm. Stefan Korbonski summed up the mood of most: "It will be necessary to wait a few days before the Soviet troops enter Warsaw."

At 27, Topiel Street, Irena Orska, a tobacconist, was less certain. By 3 August, the insurgents had liberated one-third of the city – yet although Irena listened intently only total silence reigned on the far side of the Vistula. Later, General Komorowski charged that Russian troops stood fast on the opposite bank, their rifles stacked, oblivious to the plight of the Poles.

Here there is confusion. As General Rokossovsky told it, a spirited attack by four German armoured divisions drove his Army Group back 65 miles – at the same moment that Komorowski and his troops "butted in *kak ryzhy v tsirke* – 'like the clown in the circus who pops up at the wrong moment'," a claim supported by *Generaloberst* Heinz Guderian. Yet all Churchill's and Roosevelt's pleas to Stalin to furnish supplies and munitions fell on deaf ears. Cynically, ignoring the radio appeals that had sparked off the Rising, Stalin, on 16 August, dismissed it as "a reckless and fearful gamble," and six days later, his condemnation went further still: "Sooner or later the truth about the handful of power-seeking criminals who launched the Warsaw adventure will out." For Poles who gave their allegiance to the London Government in exile, Stalin could spare no pity.[22]

The Allies were in a quandary. As Air-Marshal Sir John Slessor, R.A.F. Commander in Italy and the Mediterranean pointed out, from Italy to Warsaw was a 700-mile flight, as against 100 miles for Russian supply planes; of 13 planes despatched on 5 August, five had failed to return. "If we are to drop supplies with the necessary accuracy for this job," Slessor stressed, "it means coming right down to 1000 feet and we know all German formations have plenty of light guns which are lethal at this height." He summed up bleakly: "I do not intend to send aircraft to Poland again in full moonlight."

"The Russians wanted to see us rise and bleed," one Home Army soldier claimed with justified bitterness, for whatever the Red Army's setbacks, even crippled Allied aircraft with wounded aboard were forbidden the use of Russian airfields. Yet such was the spirit of Warsaw no man or woman, although faced with the fire-power of five German divisions, contemplated surrender.

Shortages gave rise to infinite ingenuity. One sixteen-year-old sentry stood guard armed only with a scythe; other combatants, lacking hand-grenades, lobbed old socks stuffed with nuts, bolts and scrap-iron. In printer Waclaw Zagorski's unit, the men pillaged a stock of sun helmets to protect their heads when crawling through narrow tunnels. When bandages ran short, a public-spirited tie-vendor put his entire stock at the resistants' disposal. Others fashioned grenade throwers from water pipes and flame-throwers from street hydrants; surgeons operated in dimly-lit vaults by the light of car headlamps. Even the problem of prisoners was solved; Waclaw Zagorski, after stripping a group of Germans to prevent them escaping, covered their nakedness by reclothing them all in clean pyjamas.

Strongpoints changed hands with bewildering frequency. On 5 August, the Germans re-took the Vistula bridges; by 28 August, the insurgents following a 24-hour battle, had seized the telephone exchange, recaptured the Bank of Poland and lost the Town Hall. Five days later, they had ceded up the Bank premises but gained Police Headquarters. But in this battle for smoking piles of rubble and littered streets, where combatants on both sides grew floury white like millers with drifting plaster-dust, fixed lines of defence lost all distinction. Often the Germans held the basement and ground floor of a house, while the Poles clung tenaciously to the upper storeys.

Yet despite all, life of a sort went on among the ruins. A new issue of postage stamps, bearing portraits of fighting men and the letters "AK," celebrated the Rising, and Polish Boy Scouts stood in as mail carriers, along with twenty-two deaf mutes from the Deaf and Dumb Institute on Three Crosses Square. At peak, hand-presses were cranking out thirty-two journals and magazines, and many, in off duty periods, repaired to the Palladium Cinema on Zlota Street to see their own prowess celebrated in contemporary newsreels. But as the weeks wore on, fatigue became a factor as deadly as any mortar barrage: to wash often entailed a six-hour queue at a standpipe, and even for front-line combatants, sustenance had scaled down to four daily ounces of boiled barley. At her Red Cross station, the tobacconist Irena Orska kept going for 58 hours with shots of caffeine before collapsing; often men fell asleep from sheer exhaustion in mid-sentence.

For the opposition they faced was brutally repressive. "Wipe them out!" was Hitler's concise command when news of the rising reached him, and two Himmler units in particular followed the instruction to the letter: the SS Assault Brigade "RONA" under a Russian turncoat, *Brigadeführer* Mizieslaw Kaminski and a 1,700 strong penal brigade under *Oberführer* Oskar Dirlewanger. As early as 5 August, Dirlewanger's men, rampaging through the women's cancer wards of the Curie-Skiodowska Radium Institute in the suburb of Wola, raped both patients and nurses impartially, before shooting them out of hand. In the streets of Wola, 2,000 corpses were piled in obscene layers, drenched in petrol then ignited. That night all Wola was engulfed in a sea of fire.

Forced to pull out of the Kammler tobacco factory, General Komorowski had shifted his headquarters to a schoolhouse in Stare Miasto (the Old City), a district of narrow streets and high cramped medieval houses. For the only time in World War Two, the fate of the defenders now hinged on a city's sewerage system, for on 11 August, and again on 16 August, the Germans kept up an 11-hour mortar barrage and aerial attack on the quarter. By 31 August, the Old City was swallowed up by flames. The sewers of Warsaw – sixty years old, in some places seven feet wide, in others only three feet high and two feet wide – now offered the one escape route for the 2,000 defenders.

It was a nightmare journey. Often the bravest of streetfighters, faced with the darkness, the putrid sludge, collapsed in stark terror after a hundred yards. Sharp debris, thick on the bottom, made crawling on hands and knees impossible; travellers used short stakes, like pogo-sticks, to progress in jerky froglike jumps. On one stage of the journey, the Aleja Szucha, the Germans covered every manhole, ready to toss down hand-grenades at the slightest sound. Though Stare Miasto lay only a mile from central Warsaw, the journey took the defenders nine hours.

By 27 September, Komorowski knew that Warsaw could hold out no longer. To the north, the newly-created suburb of Zoliborz was under pressure; to the south, the Germans had regained the district of Mokotow. Food reserves were exhausted; water was cut off. That evening, Komorowski sent one last appeal to General Rokossovsky – a message confirmed as received by the radio operator at Soviet Headquarters. But no answer ever came.

Two days later, Komorowski sent peace envoys to the German Commander, S.S. *Obergruppenführer* Erich von dem Bach-Zelewski. On 2 October, the day of surrender, one scant consolation remained, after 63 days of bloodshed that had cost the lives of 250,000 Poles: the Germans could not capture Warsaw again. For the Warsaw for which her citizens had fought no longer existed.

It was Air Marshal Sir John Slessor, far away in Italy, who summed up the lesson of the rising in one contemptuous sentence: "How, after the fall of Warsaw, any responsible statesman could trust any Russian Communist further than he could kick him, passes the comprehension of ordinary men."

–

Every day now, history was in the making. For war correspondents, the problem was to record it in sober and balanced prose.

On a hot August Sunday, the first party of Allied newsmen came to Majdanek Camp, a mile from the Polish city of Lublin, which the

Russians had liberated on 27 July. This in itself was a milestone, for never before had newsmen, Allied or otherwise, set foot in one of Heinrich Himmler's concentration camps.

"They called this 'the road of death'," their guide Dmitri Kudriavtsev, of the Soviet Atrocities Committee, told them, and *Time's* Moscow correspondent, Richard Lauterbach, duly noted that fact. He noted, too, the 200 grey-green barracks, systematically spaced for maximum light, air and sunshine, the winding roads, the vegetable plots, and then the jarring realities: the 14 machine-gun turrets jutting towards the blue sky, the 12-foot high double rows of electrically-charged barbed wire, the kennels which had housed the gaunt and hungry guard dogs.

Dutifully, the London *Daily Express*' Alaric Jacob in turn took note of the fourteen compost heaps, each 50 feet long, high grey-brown mounds made up of manure, human bones and human ashes from the five massive red brick coke-fired ovens. They could disintegrate 1,900 people a day, their guide told them. Close by were the cabbages, big leafy cabbages, covered with sooty grey dust. "This is German food production," Kudriavtsev explained. "Kill people; fertilise cabbages." Jacob nodded politely, like any horticultural correspondent, taking note of that, too.

When they came to a wooden warehouse, the newsmen stopped short. "There are 820,000 pairs of shoes here," Kudriavtsev led off, as prompt with statistics as any model guide. "They represent twenty-two nationalities." Well, that was something, thought Raymond Davies of the New York daily *P.M.*, that you had to take on trust. You could not count the shoes. But the total seemed credible.

The warehouse was an engulfing sea of shoes. They were piled haphazardly, like chunks of coal in a bin, halfway up the walls, and somehow the sight of them brought Majdanek home as no other sight could have done. Shoes, boots, rubbers, leggings, slippers, children's shoes, soldiers' shoes, old shoes and new. Shoes from Warsaw, Vienna and Antwerp, from Athens, Belgrade and Kiev and Minsk. High heels, low heels, red, grey and black shoes; evening slippers, beach sandals, pumps, Oxfords and Dutch clogs. A tiny pair of white shoes, to fit Correspondent Lauterbach's youngest daughter. A dangerous thought, that, one to be put aside.

Correspondent Davies recalled a recent instruction from his editors: "Cable only if death rolls unusually large or deaths themselves unusually gruesome." Since Majdanek had claimed a million and a half victims, this condition was amply met – but how did you lead in such a story? How did you angle it? How did you convey the enormity of Majdanek to a peaceful citizen of New York?

All of them, on that Sunday, felt the same. They would become veterans, no doubt, given time – but just then Majdanek was a sunlit nightmare that had no precedent at all.

-

It was a battlefield that decided the fate of France, and no German who survived it was ever to forget it. For 10,000 of their number did not survive; they died in the battle for the Falaise-Argentan pocket.

"The battle should never have taken place," Montgomery was to comment later. "It wasn't meant to take place." S.S. *Gruppenführer* Josep "Sepp" Dietrich, once the staunchest of National Socialists, was in full agreement. "There was only one person to blame for this stupid impossible operation – that madman Adolf Hitler."

By 7 August, the German Seventh Army was boxed in a rectangle bounded by the Norman market towns of Falaise, Vire, Argentan and Mortain. The one escape route now remaining was the ten-mile gap between Argentan and Falaise. But "retreat" was not a word in the Führer's military lexicon. The hapless *Feldmarschall* von Kluge, Rommel's successor, was ordered to counterattack at Mortain.

It was a costly error, for at the height of the battle rocket-firing Typhoons swooped down upon the German panzers. Remaining on the ground only long enough to re-load, they strafed the battlefield all that day until almost a hundred tanks had been shot into smoking scrap-metal. On 10 August, when Hitler reluctantly ordered "Disengage," barely 100,000 men remained to obey this command.

Now the Seventh Army were trapped inside a monstrous killing ground, twenty-two miles wide by eleven miles deep: what one survivor termed "a Stalingrad in Normandy." British and Canadian artillery, Typhoons and U.S. Flying Fortresses pounded the pocket day and night, cratering it like a lunar landscape. "I shall talk with him (Hitler) again tonight," Kluge assured a colleague. "…I owe this to the troops and to the German people. One way or another." Instead, learning that the *Führer* was supplanting him with *Feldmarschall* Walter Model, Kluge wrote Hitler a farewell letter, then swallowed a cyanide capsule.

Now a bitter controversy arose. On the evening of 12 August, Lieutenant-General George S. Patton's Third Army, officially activated on 1 August, had already reached Argentan – moving so fast that his forward tanks were obtaining their gasoline by parachute. A thrusting self-dramatising poseur who used his armour like poniards – "Flanks are something for the enemy to worry about" – Patton, who practised martial frowns in a mirror, was as famed for his shrill-voiced profanity as for his biting contempt of his fellow commanders – "I can outfight that little fart any time," was his verdict on Montgomery, while Bradley was "a man of great mediocrity". Now to Patton's fury, his two *bêtes-noirs*, Bradley, acting on Montgomery's orders, had halted him at Argentan.

"Monty is too tidy," grumbled his Chief-of-Staff, Major-General Freddie de Guingand, for Montgomery's motives, while obscure, seemed to have stemmed from a desire to avoid an overlapping front. Yet as Patton saw it, this failure to close a ten-mile gap to the east, which tenacious S.S. men kept open for five days – until 19 August – allowed perhaps 50,000 Germans to escape.

Yet the devastation wreaked on all those left behind was indescribable. "It was as if an avenging angel had swept the area bent on destroying all things German," one aghast U.S. observer noted. Prisoners emerging from the battlefield moved with glassy unseeing eyes like the walking dead of Haiti, for here were small smouldering piles of black metal that had been vehicles with passengers, royal blue farm carts spattered with fresh blood, their dead drivers stiffened in postures of terror, a scatter of dark grey blankets, loads of bread green with mould, flasks of wine, radio sets, typewriters, wallets stuffed with banknotes, dead cows "like overturned rocking horses," everywhere corpses in shabby grey, slumped as if in sleep.

Near Sainte-Eugénie, the massive ancient evil smell of 2000 putrefying horses penetrated even to the cockpit of Prince Jean of Luxembourg's Piper Cub; hastily he gained height to escape it. In the seven kilometres between Coudehard and Tournai, villagers were unable to set foot on solid ground; handkerchiefs pressed to their noses, they trod a squelching carpet of dead soldiers, dead cattle, dead horses, "wading in blood".

"Under such conditions," the same U.S. observer concluded "there are no supermen – all men become rabbits looking for a hole."

The lesson was not lost on those reliable bellwethers of European public opinion, the neutrals. Turkey broke off all diplomatic relations with Germany. Sweden reduced the flow of high grade iron ore – up to 10 million tons in 1943 – to a trickle. Invoking their insurance underwriters, they pleaded that Allied bombs henceforth made German ports unsafe for Swedish ships.

In London, six months of patient negotiations between British, U.S. and Swiss diplomats ended in a deal – with Germany once more the losers. In exchange for permission to import some of her own stores of cotton and wool shut off by the Allied blockade, the Swiss slashed their $60 million annual sales of machinery and precision instruments by one-third, cutting sales of ball-bearings to ten per cent and ammunition by five per cent.

And in Madrid's Pardo Palace, U.S. Ambassador Carlton J. Hayes noted a significant change of décor in the handsomely furnished study of General Francisco Franco. The large autographed photographs of two of the *Caudillo*'s favourite heroes, Hitler and Mussolini, had vanished from the scene.

Only the irreproachable features of Pope Pius XII now adorned Franco's desk.

—

Churchill was out of humour as August dawned. He, who in January, after recuperating from virus pneumonia, had astonished King George VI's Private Secretary, Sir Alan Lascelles, by disdaining the lift and taking the stairs at Buckingham Palace two at a time then cocking a snook like an urchin, was now a tired and disillusioned man. Mentally fatigued, he now demanded that every option must be boiled down to no more than half a sheet of notepaper. More and more his physician, Lord Moran, observed, he succumbed to what he called "Black Dog" – prolonged fits of depression.

Increasingly he found himself at odds with Roosevelt, who rarely let slip the opportunity for sententious moralising on world affairs. Bitterly condemnatory of the Argentine regime of General Edelmiro J. Farrell and his strong-arm man Colonel Juan Domingo Perón, who still maintained Axis ties, the President never ceased urging the

Premier to sever diplomatic relations – although one-third of Britain's meat supplies came from Argentine abattoirs. When Roosevelt withdrew the U.S. Ambassador, Churchill, in the interests of Allied unity, grudgingly followed suit – though commenting tartly, "I do not myself see where this is leading or what we expect to get out of the Argentines by this method." But Roosevelt could not resist the last word: "We would do nothing to prevent your getting a new (meat) contract ... I hope, however, that you will, in very firm, clear, disgruntled tones of voice let Argentina know beyond a doubt that we are all fed up with her pro-Axis sentiments and practices." When he again took exception to a favourable reference to Franco in the House of Commons, Churchill's reply was an icy put-down: "I do not know whether there is more freedom in Stalin's Russia than in Franco's Spain. I have no intention to seek a quarrel with either."

Thus, in search of rest, sunshine and a tour of an operational theatre, Churchill, on 11 August, departed for Naples, installing himself in the "palatial though somewhat dilapidated Villa Rivalta," with its fine view of Vesuvius and the Bay, for his first meeting with his new protégé, Marshal Josip Broz Tito of Yugoslavia.

Since June, affairs in the Balkans had marked time. Tito, a hunted man in Yugoslavia, had been transported by a British destroyer, H.M.S. *Blackmore*, to new headquarters on the Dalmatian island of Vis, disembarking mellow with the wardroom's gin and cherry brandy, blissfully reciting "The Owl and the Pussy Cat". In London, King Peter II, under relentless pressure from Churchill and Eden, had appointed Dr Ivan Subasic, a former *Ban* (Governor) of Croatia as his Prime Minister; thus while the King recognised Tito, Tito had agreed only "not to raise the question of the final state system during the war."

For Churchill, the meeting – soon after noon on 12 August, in a sitting room of the Villa Rivalta – was a disappointment. "My confidence in Tito ... was weakened when I met him at Naples," he was to write later, for the Marshal was wary and sweating in a too-tight woollen uniform, stiff with gold braid, scarlet stripes and oak leaves, worn to prove him a statesman in his own right rather than a cave-dwelling Communist brigand. ("I did not tell him that anyhow it was only Lend-Lease," Churchill chuckled later.) All through the meeting, Tito's twelve-man bodyguard armed with sub-machine guns, hovered outside the door, along with the Marshal's ferocious Belgian sheep-dog, Tiger. His interpreter, Olga Nincić, one of the few card-carrying

Communists to have graduated from an English finishing school, noted that her chief was, unusually for him, on the defensive.

Puffing on a cigar, Churchill asked blandly: "Is it not true that there is a large portion of the Serb peasantry who would not be very glad to see the Communist system introduced?"

Tito's reply was hard, almost aggressive. "We do not intend to impose any such system. I have often stated this publicly."

Churchill was reasonableness itself. "Yes, I remember. But I was interested to hear it from your own lips. Would you allow individual freedom in your country after the war?"

"Why, yes. That is our basic principle – democracy and the freedom of the individual."

"I mean, will a man be free to choose what work he does and where he does it? Will strikes be allowed?"

"Not as long as the war lasts."

"That's the same with us. Mr Bevin has passed strict legislation against it. But we must see to it that after the war the workers enjoy their full rights."

The interview was drawing to a close. "I have been asking most of the questions," Churchill told Olga. "Please tell the Marshal to ask me anything he likes – even the awkward questions."

Tito paused. Then the former note of petulance crept once more into his voice. "I am rather concerned by all the questions that are constantly being asked about Communism in Yugoslavia," he complained. "I have stated quite categorically that we don't intend to introduce it. There are many reasons for this. All the countries of Europe must have a democratic system after the war and Yugoslavia will be no exception."

In the end, neither man preserved any illusion concerning the other. Churchill, writing wanly to Eden, commented on Britain's enormous responsibility in supplying Tito with arms with which he could subjugate Yugoslavia – "We hardly needed this reminder," Eden commented frostily. "He's a big devil." Tito, for his part, commented to Milovan Djilas, his emissary to Stalin. "He wants to foist King Peter on us."

Three days later, on Tuesday 15 August, Churchill was more disenchanted still: from the bridge of the destroyer *Kimberley*, seven miles offshore, he could see little though he knew with mounting bitterness that more than 2,000 Allied aircraft, 6 battleships, 21 cruisers and

100 destroyers were pounding the 70-mile stretch of southern France between Toulon and Cannes. Heading for the ancient tranquil towns of Provence came a new breed of American tourists, fighting through the cork oaks and the oleander bushes alongside the Frenchmen of General Jean de Lattre de Tassigny, impeccable from his képi to his pigskin gloves, sometimes called "the MacArthur of France".

It was 5 a.m. and the 286,000 men of Major-General Alexander M. Patch's Allied Seventh Army were pouring ashore in the most misguided and fruitless campaign of the war – "Operation Anvil," rechristened "Operation Dragoon," for as Churchill commented furiously, "I have been dragooned into it."

Not only Churchill had inveighed against "Dragoon" – originally intended to chime with "Overlord" and now delayed by fully 10 weeks. It had been an invasion all along opposed by King George VI, Field Marshal Jan Smuts, the South African Premier, by Montgomery, Bedell Smith, Mark Clark, Alexander and Brigadier-General Lauris Norstad of the Mediterranean Allied Air Force. For Patch's Army was landing 500 miles south of Eisenhower's advance; not until mid-November would they join up with the main force and in the meantime their advance northwards diverted not a single German division.

All these men saw the logical goal of the seven divisions stripped from Alexander – 3 American and 4 Free French – as eastwards: through Yugoslavia's Ljubljana gap, to aid Tito, then onwards to Vienna, Budapest and Trieste. Even Eisenhower had grown increasingly uncertain of "Dragoon's" necessity; in the end he had been persuaded largely by the implacable insistence of Roosevelt and General George Marshall. "For purely political considerations over here I would never survive even a slight setback in "Overlord" if it were known that fairly large forces had been diverted to the Balkans," was Roosevelt's cynical confession, and to Churchill's ire, he even descended to persiflage: "I always think of my early geometry. A straight line is the shortest distance between two points."

Sunk in gloom, the Premier faced up to the bitter truth that he had voiced to Roosevelt on 1 July: "Dragoon" was "in my humble and respectful opinion, the first major strategic and political error for which we two have to be responsible."

Central Europe might yet be saved, but from this day forward the Balkans were lost. Between them Roosevelt and Stalin had seen to that.

In Paris, Monday 14 August was a day of scorching sunlight. Along the *quais*, thousands of carefree boys and girls had transformed the waters of the Seine into a vast swimming pool. On this breathless blue summer morning, the second of the three-day Assumption holiday, it was a time to savour picnics in the *Bois*, the comforts of a folding deck-chair, above all, to forget *la sale guerre*. Eleven days earlier Paris had remarked its 1,503rd day of German occupation.

Like a woman before a multi-faceted mirror, Paris now presented many aspects. At Maxim's and the Lido, caviare and champagne were still plentiful but many residents bred rabbits for the pot in their bathtubs; the city's shame was 25,000 under-nourished babies. Fashionable women sported the *Mode Martiale* of Lucien Lelong and Jacques Fath – broad shoulders, wide belts, short skirts – and twenty theatres were still in business, along with the racetracks at Longchamps and Auteuil. Yet Parisiens travelled like indigents, on bicycles, in fiacres, or vélo-taxis towed by bicycles; the staple fare of the boulevard cafes was ersatz coffee ground from acorns and chick peas. Chronically short of gas and electricity, housewives cooked with damp scraps of newspaper; a six-page paper set a litre of water boiling in twelve minutes. Most citizens, lean and fit after four years of trudging and cycling, subsisted largely on the rutabaga turnip fed to cattle.

But on the surface, there was nothing to suggest that three contending forces were preparing a battle for the soul of the city.

In his first-floor office at the Hôtel Meurice in the Rue de Rivoli, the tubby monocled fortress commander of Paris, *Generalleutnant* Dietrich von Choltitz, whom Hitler had appointed one week earlier, was facing a difficult decision. Minutes earlier *Hauptman* Werner Ebernach, of the 817th *Pionier Kompanie*, had fished from his tunic pocket a piece of blue paper signed by Jodl as Chief of Operations. Stamped "KR Blitz – top priority" it was an order to destroy all 45 bridges that spanned the Seine in Paris: the historic Pont de la Concorde, the Pont de Neuilly, the fourteenth-century Pont de la Tournelle. "The Seine would be damned from one end of Paris to the other," Ebernach explained, with a technician's justifiable pride.

Von Choltitz listened impassively. This plan of a "limited scorched earth policy" had been expounded to him earlier by *Generalleutnant* Günter Blumentritt, chief of staff to the Commander-in-Chief, West, and for the best reasons; in Allied hands, the vast industrial complex of Paris would be turned against the Third Reich. Choltitz had raised but one objection. His orders from the Führer were to defend, not destroy, the city: the time for that would come if and when the *Wehrmacht* pulled out. Premature destruction would not only drive the factory workers into the arms of the Resistance; it would set the populace against his own troops.

Thus, while Ebernach was given the green light to "go ahead" no final demolitions were authorised without von Choltitz' "personal approval". "We have the whole world watching us here," he cautioned, "not just a handful of generals."

Von Choltitz did not know it, but the Allies had no plans for Paris at all. In his command caravan, code-named "Shellburst," two miles inland from the Normandy beachhead at Granville, Eisenhower had resolved on one thing: to by-pass Paris altogether. His reason was primarily logistical. To reach the city would call for thousands of gallons of gasoline; to administer it would swallow up an equivalent of eight divisions of civil affairs officers. To feed its citizens would call for 75,000 tons of food and medicine and 1,500 daily tons of coal.

To avoid these commitments, what Eisenhower planned, by contrast, was an American drive for Reims, 98 miles north-east, and a British push from Amiens, 82 miles north, to entrap Paris in a giant pocket – not earlier than 15 September, not later than 1 October.

In Algiers, in a cool tree-shaded villa, *Les Oliviers*, General Charles de Gaulle had other plans for Paris. De Gaulle, like Eisenhower, wanted no Warsaw-style insurrection – but he was convinced his bitter enemies, the French Communists, were planning just that. Already he estimated they numbered 25,000 armed men. But here de Gaulle faced a dilemma; his Paris military representative, 29-year-old Jacques Chaban-Delmas did not control the Resistance. The Communists did.

To effect this reality, de Gaulle planned a counter-coup: on a hasty trip to London, Chaban-Delmas had conferred with General Joseph-Pierre Koenig, commanding the French Forces of the Interior (FFI), and his orders were plain. A short twenty-four hour rising to boost civilian morale, was permissible when the Allies reached the city gates – but if the Communists forced an earlier rising, de Gaulle's limited forces, alerted by the message, "*As-tu bien dejeuné, Jacquot?*" would seize control of key-points, Operation Prise de Pouvoir.

There was little time to lose. Dubious as to their loyalty, von Choltitz had, on 17 August, disarmed the 20,000 strong Paris police force – and the *flics*, egged on by the Communist leader, "Colonel Rol," a coppersmith named Henri-Georges-René Tanguy, had promptly gone on strike. Whether they would follow Communist orders, Tanguy did not know – but as he himself was to assert, "Paris is worth 200,000 dead."

By 7 a.m. on Saturday 19 April, Tanguy, to his chagrin, had his answer. Under 34-year-old Yves Bayet of the Gaullist faction, the police had seized the great brown-stone fortress of the Préfecture, within the shadow of the Cathedral of Nôtre-Dame. The most important public building in all Paris was firmly in de Gaulle's grasp.

One day earlier – fearing an Allied advance that was still no more than a fertile figment of de Gaulle's imagination – the Vichy Ministry of Marshal Henri-Philippe Pétain's government, had fled the capital, leaving a power-vacuum in their wake. Now not only the police but the railways, the Metro, postmen, switchboard operators, even the Bank of France, had gone on strike. Paris was now a silent city, waiting for no one knew what: no factory whistles blew, the boulevards were innocent of bicycles, no barges moved on the broad face of the Seine.

It was a challenge no Communist could feasibly resist. At 7 a.m. – the same hour that the Gaullists seized the Préfecture – Tanguy set the key-note for all that was to follow, ordering: "A chacun son Boche". As some FFI men moved to take over the morgues, post offices, the *Mairies* of Paris' twenty arrondissements, even the Comédie Française, others were engaged in bloodier work: the hunting down and slaughter of lone German soldiers. With sinking heart de Gaulle's political representative, Alexandre Parodi, realised that the Communists had even now stolen a march on him. Where they led, the Gaullists had no choice but to follow.

In the Hôtel Meurice, *Generalleutnant* von Choltitz heard the first casualty reports with mounting anger: 50 of his men had been killed, 100 had been wounded. His first instinct was to attack the seeming seat of the insurrection, the Préfecture, but before risking his tanks on two exposed bridges, the Pont Saint-Michel and the Pont Neuf, he wanted a Luftwaffe dive-bombing attack: promptly at 5:51 a.m. on Sunday 20 August.

Now an unlikely emissary entered the story: the Swedish Consul-General, Raoul Nordling, a plump grey-haired *bon viveur* who as managing director of the S.K.F. ball-bearing factories had been a Parisien by adoption since 1912. At sunset on 19 August, Nordling, concerned that the Luftwaffe's near-misses would fall on Nôtre Dame, proposed something that von Choltitz had not then considered: a temporary cease-fire to pick up the dead and wounded.

No desk-bound administrator, von Choltitz was a fighting soldier who had seen service at Cassino and in Normandy; never yet had he granted or requested a cease-fire. Yet with only three divisions available to him, he could see the merits. A Luftwaffe attack would be tantamount to a declaration of war. A cease-fire would free his troops from the unpalatable task of stemming an insurrection.

"I have one thing to ask you," he murmured to Nordling. "Don't associate my name with your truce." The fire-eating *Feldmarschall* Walter Model, he thought, von Kluge's successor, might interpret the gesture as "against the orders," he had received for Paris.

Nordling had bought precious time for de Gaulle's battle for the soul of Paris.

Early on Sunday, a Lockheed Lodestar, code-named *France*, skimmed across the choppy Channel waters to land on an improvised fighter strip at Maupertus near Cherbourg, with only 120 seconds of fuel left in the reserve tank. Once more Charles de Gaulle had returned to France – this time for good and all.

In Cherbourg's Préfecture, the General, sharing a borrowed razor with his aides, heard from Koenig that the Paris rising was an accomplished fact. His reaction was immediate: to seek an appointment with Eisenhower at his Granville headquarters and endeavour to change his mind.

"From the strategic point of view," he told the American, after studying his charts, "I don't see why you cross the Seine at Melun and Mantes and Rouen – in short, everywhere – and yet at Paris, and Paris alone, you do not." And he stressed with urgency: the fate of Paris was of fundamental concern to the French Government. He begged that at least French troops should be sent: the Second Armoured Division of General Jacques Philippe Leclerc. If need be, he, de Gaulle, would not scruple to withdraw the division from the Allies and despatch it to Paris on his own authority.

Eisenhower smiled politely, not believing a word of it – unaware that Leclerc, on his own initiative, had for three days now been hoarding rations, ammunition and gasoline, for just this eventuality. In an act of blatant insubordination, Leclerc was preparing to send Lieutenant-Colonel Jacques de Guillebon, with 17 light tanks, 10 armoured cars and two platoons of infantry to wrest Paris from the Germans.

In the capital, Nordling's fragile truce – which the Communist Tanguy had denounced as "treason" – was falling apart, as Communists everywhere opened fire on unsuspecting German patrols. All over the city, Gaullists and Communists, from sheer self-preservation, organised for insurrection. In the cellar of the Préfecture, Frédéric Joliot-Curie, armed with sulphuric acid and potassium chlorate, borrowed from the laboratory where his mother-in-law had discovered radium, settled absorbedly to manufacture Molotov cocktails. Overnight, restaurants converted themselves into resistants' soup-kitchens. In the famous market of Les Halles, the refrigerators now stood in as morgues; a sewage station in the Rue Gay-Lussac became a casualty-clearing station, along with the Comédie Française, where a 39 year-old stretcher bearer, Jean Paul Sartre, opted for night duty. In the tranquil small hours, he would find time to record his impressions.

By the Monday, the age-old cry of the Paris streets – "*Aux barricades!*" – had travelled like a leaping fire across the capital, and at every crossroad, they sprang up like mushrooms on an autumn morning, 400 of them in all; everything from burnt-out trucks to paving-stones, grand pianos and a five-man *pissoir*. The Communist Tanguy, requesting the Builders' Union to work on barricades, met his match: the members would comply – for a bonus payment of red wine. At the Comédie Française, the actors, versed in crowd psychology, ringed a skimpy barricade with canning jars, labelled them "*Achtung Minen*" and experienced no trouble at all.

One devout Gaullist, a 26-year-old trade unionist, Yves Morandat, was so convinced of the General's imminent arrival, he resolved on seizing the Hôtel de Matignon, the residence of the prime ministers of France – then in embarrassment, realised that he didn't know where it was. Directed to the Rue Varenne, he found the 100-strong bodyguard of the departed Premier, Pierre Laval, drawn up in the courtyard – where their commander first called his men to attention and the white-gloved maître d'hôtel ushered him to the Green Room, the premier's personal bedroom.

When Morandat next took over the Ministry of the Interior in the Place Beauvau, the major domo was less forthcoming: Morandat's plan of a dinner party for twelve resistants was deemed impossible. The former Minister had decamped with all the silver.

Meanwhile, to de Gaulle's inestimable advantage two commanders were wavering fatally – Eisenhower and von Choltitz. By the evening of 21 August, sweating and wakeful in a blacked-out bedroom overlooking the Tuileries garden, von Choltitz had not issued orders to destroy even one factory – and that afternoon had even refused to receive *Hauptmann* Ebernach. The impatient Ebernach, who with 12 tons of explosives planned the demolition of the Eiffel Tower, the four-century-old Palais de Luxembourg, the Chambre des Députés and the Quai d'Orsay, home of the French Foreign Office, was told merely to "stand by for further orders".

That same evening, Eisenhower, too, was in two minds – for Bradley's intelligence chief, Brigadier General Edwin Sibert, had not long concluded a thought-provoking interview with Major Roger Gallois, an emissary sent by the Communist Tanguy to solicit American arms. But Gallois, undergoing a change of heart, had pleaded that what Paris needed was not American weapons but the American presence – "or there is going to be a terrible slaughter."

This heart-cry, coupled with a further written appeal from de Gaulle, gave Eisenhower cause for concern. Unlike Roosevelt and Churchill, he respected de Gaulle as a soldier and a man; if the Frenchman was anguished for Paris, Eisenhower knew that anguish to be valid. At his morning conference of Tuesday 22 August, his brow wore the familiar frown that had preceded the decisions for D-Day. "Well, what the hell, Brad," he sighed finally. "I guess we'll have to go in."

Within hours, the word was passing: the French 2nd Armoured Division, soon to be backstopped by the 4th U.S. Infantry Division, was ready to roll. As excited as a schoolboy at end of term, the tall austere General Jacques Philippe Leclerc bolted for his Piper Cub to hail his G.2 Major André Gribius, *"Mouvement immédiat sur Paris."* Captain Raymond Dronne, a tank commander with the Regiment of Chad, and the first French soldier to enter Paris for four years, took the news more calmly; first he must trim his bristly red beard to look his best for the Parisiennes. The crew of the tank-destroyer *Simoun*, celebrating a comrade's birthday with a roast duck, heard in a way that all boulevardiers would cherish: "Pack it up, we're moving. This time it's Paname."[23]

In the capital, on this same day, a bizarre conference took place between von Choltitz and the indefatigable peacemaker, Raoul Nordling. "Your truce, Herr Consul General," von Choltitz remarked, "doesn't seem to be working very well." It was an understatement, as Nordling knew; harassed increasingly by the FFI the Germans had been forced to retreat into ten heavily-fortified strong-points.[24] Nonetheless, the Swede expressed his regrets. The FFI, he explained, obeyed only one man: Charles de Gaulle. Then von Choltitz made an astounding proposal: "Why doesn't somebody go to see him?"

Nordling was flabbergasted – but by degrees the situation grew clearer. Since the truce had broken down, von Choltitz must soon carry out his demolition orders or be relieved of his command. Only one factor could save the face of Paris: the speedy arrival of the Allies.

In truth, the party von Choltitz eventually despatched – two Gaullists, two Allied intelligence experts and Nordling's brother, Rolf[25] – arrived too late to affect the outcome. De Gaulle was already at Rambouillet, thirty miles from Paris. And through driving rain 4,000 vehicles of Leclerc's armoured division each decked out for identification with a bright pink square of oilcloth, were carrying 16,000 men towards Paris from the south-east, bent on bypassing German tanks by entering the city via the Porte d'Orléans.

It would be a near-run battle, even so. All over Paris, in railway stations, power plants, along the forty-five bridges the deadly charges had been placed in readiness. Across the Seine, on the left bank, one minor building, the Saint-Amand telephone exchange, was already a smoking cloud of debris. How much longer, von Choltitz wondered, would he stave off the decision?

At 9:22 p.m. on Thursday 24 August – 1,532 days, three hours and 52 minutes after the first *Wehrmacht* troops had entered Paris in June 1940 – Captain Raymond Dronne unwittingly set the German commander's mind at rest. With a rush his lead tank swept through the Port D'Italie, to pull up smothered by weeping cheering Parisians, outside the Hôtel de Ville. At the Préfecture, now almost out of ammunition, a message dropped from a low-swooping Piper Cub, gave the defenders fresh courage: "*Tenez bien. Nous arrivons.*"

For the Americans, few of whom had ever seen Paris, these were electric hours: would her heart, they wondered, recalling the old song, still be young and gay? To war artist John Groth, who had hitched a ride with Dronne's column, it seemed that it would: so many girls were already astride the tank turrets he thought of "floats in a Rose Bowl parade." Lieutenant Jack Knowles, of the 22nd Infantry Regiment, knew how special this occasion must be: for the first time since leaving

England, his men had been ordered to wear neckties. Captain Billy Buenzle, of the 38th Cavalry Reconnaissance Squadron, who had vowed to race the French into Paris, radioed his commander, Colonel Cyrus Dolph, that he had made it. When the old soldier asked how he knew Buenzele whooped, "Dammit, Colonel, I'm looking right up at the Nôtre-Dame."

From one of the first ambulances to bump through the Porte d'Orléans, a trim khaki-clad redhead pushed through the throng of Maquisards clad in dirty sweaters and Basque shirts for a heartfelt reunion with her parents: Private 75954 Lily Sergueiev had returned, like the bannering Tri colours on the skyline, to the city she loved. "I'm no longer alone," she told them blissfully. "I've got the whole army with me."

An early arrival in the American ranks was Lieutenant-Colonel Saul K. Padover, of the Psychological Warfare Division, who months ago had been set the task of ascertaining what motivated the German nation. Now "stunned by the delirium and the hysteria of the reception," Padover wondered as to the task that lay ahead of him. None of the French men or women who seized his hand or kissed him fervently, ever used the word "German": instead, in undertones of dread, they spoke of "the Boche". It was all, Padover decided, a far cry from London or Washington, D.C.; a young Frenchman, armed with a Sten gun, to whom Padover offered a lift in his jeep, replied in answer to his query, "I am not, really what you would call a soldier, I am what they called a terrorist."

He would somehow need to adjust his perspective, Padover thought, in the weeks that lay ahead.

All that night and throughout the next day, Paris was a strange city – "like separate sets at a movie studio," noted the war correspondent Alan Moorehead perceptively. From thousands of open apartment windows the strains of *La Marseillaise* from radios and tinny gramophones mingled with the crack and splatter of snipers' bullets as Germans and FFI battled each other from the roof-tops, sounds at times overwhelmed by the joyous pealing of the bells from 146 churches – bells clearly audible to *Generalleutnant* Dietrich von Choltitz, attending a farewell dinner with his staff. "Gentlemen," he told them scathingly, "I can tell you something that's escaped you here in your nice life in Paris. Germany's lost the war, and we have lost it with her."

From his darkened office von Choltitz placed a final call to the Chief of Staff of Army Group B, *Generalmajor* Hans Speidel. "Listen," he said, extending the receiver into the night, "Do you hear that sound?"

"I do," Speidel replied. "It sounds like bells."

"It *is* the sound of bells, my dear Speidel. The bells of Paris, ringing to tell the city the Allies are here."

Speidel was silent. Then von Choltitz spoke again, silkily, this time. Everything was prepared for destruction, as ordered. Could Army Group B "extricate them" from the city once that work was completed? Speidel had to admit it. "I'm afraid not, *Herr General*."

At Rastenburg, Hitler was by now in a frenzy. Over and over, as if possessed, he demanded of Jodl: "*Brennt Paris?* Is Paris burning? Jodl, I want to know – is Paris burning right now, Jodl." But it was already much too late. On the first floor of the Hôtel Meurice, a Frenchman armed with a sub-machine gun saluted firmly before General von Choltitz: "Lieutenant Henri Karcher of the Army of General de Gaulle. Are you ready to surrender?" "*Ja*," the General replied.

"Then you are my prisoner."

And suddenly surrender was in fashion. Outside the Hôtel de Crillon bar, 176 Germans surrendered to Lieutenant-Colonel Ken Downs and Lieutenant John Mowinckle. Bored, Mowinckle told them all to check their arms in the cloakroom. In the barricaded Ministry of Posts, Telegraphs and Telephones, *Gefreiter* Alfred Hollesch, and his men found an original way to give up; smashing a fire-alarm box in the cellar they surrendered to the first fireman who answered.

More and more liberators were pouring into the city: Tuaregs from the French Sahara, Africans from the jungles of Cameroun, GIs from Nebraska, Maryland and Georgia; Leclerc, to receive von Choltitz' formal surrender in the billiard room of the Préfecture; even Ernest Hemingway, checking in at the Ritz to demand seventy-three dry martinis for two truckloads of grimy FFI. Appropriately, it was Captain Raymond Sarniguet of the Fire Brigade, who on 13 June, 1940, had brought the Tricolour down from the Eiffel Tower, who climbed the 1,750 steps to the summit to hoist it once again.

Lastly came de Gaulle. On Saturday 26 August, all Paris would honour him: from the Arc de Triomphe, where he laid a wreath of red gladioli at the tomb of the Unknown Soldier, he moved on down the Champs-Élysées followed by Koenig, Juin and the rest – "*Messieurs*, one step behind me" – to a "*Te Deum*" service in Notre-Dame. But on the Friday there was municipal business to transact; priorities to be established.

From Leclerc's temporary headquarters in the Gare du Montparnasse, he passed briefly by his old offices – which had once been Clemenceau's – in the Ministry of War. His next priority was made plain. He would visit the Préfecture, a symbol of Gaullist resistance – and hence the state – before visiting the Hôtel de Ville, where many Communists, cheated of their *fait accompli*, held sway. Unknown to them his next ploy would cut the ground from under them: disarmed of their personal weapons and outfitted with regulation uniforms, they would be absorbed into the Regular Army under martial discipline.

At the Hôtel de Ville, the resistants awaited him with angry consternation: a prior personal visit to the police was an intolerable affront. But worse was to come. In a naive attempt to present themselves as the General's "sponsors," the Committee of National Resistance had drafted a proclamation for him to read to the massed crowds below. Thus he would appear not as the leader of Free France but as the Committee's executive officer.

Shaking no hands, only curtly acknowledging introductions, de Gaulle exchanged courtesies with the President of the Municipal Council, Georges Bidault. Then Bidault cleverly sprung his trap: "General, would you step to the balcony and solemnly proclaim the Republic before the people here assembled?"

De Gaulle surveyed him coldly before replying: "No. The Republic has not ceased to exist. I myself am President of the government of the Republic. Why should I proclaim it now?"

And when he stepped to the balcony and spoke briefly to the crowd, the chanted shockwave of "De Gaulle, De Gaulle" that drifted towards the Seine gave the Communists their answer. It was he, not the Resistance, who spoke for France.

"The iron was hot," de Gaulle summed it all up later. "I struck it."

In the Hôtel de Ville that day, a disgruntled Communist on the spot was equally to the point. "It's simple. We've been had."

De Gaulle's was a lone victory. Captain Mikhail Koriakov, the Russian officer unjustly accused of holding a requiem mass for the deceased patriarch of Moscow, saw this ever more clearly as autumn approached. The Communist advance was like a creeping floodtide: if one breach in the dyke was plugged, another fissure would soon appear.

For two months after that drumhead interrogation by the implacable Major Rutman, Koriakov had remained in limbo. Still officially a military correspondent attached to the 6th Red Air Force, he was not permitted to work, but neither was he dismissed. His former friends shunned him like a plague victim; he slept apart, ate apart. All meals were brought from the Headquarters Mess to his billet, an attic in a peasant woman's cottage, where Koriakov passed the solitary hours reading books by Russian émigré writers. Not until August did Lieutenant-General Boris Polynin, the 6th's commanding officer, pronounce the verdict: Koriakov had been found "ideologically unfit to serve as military correspondent."

But equally for ideological reasons, his shame, to avoid any hint of martyrdom, was never promulgated. Neither the men nor the civil population were informed of his transfer to the 32nd Reserve Officer Infantry Regiment near Lublin, virtually a holding unit of Army riff-raff that had served time in penal battalions. It was here that the news of the Red Army's latest irresistible advance – prompted by a random Royal coup – reached Koriakov.

At 3 p.m. on 23 August, the patience of 22-year-old King Michael of Rumania snapped abruptly. Seven days earlier, tiring of the endless inconclusive negotiations of Prince Barbu Stirbey in Cairo and London to bring his country out of the war, the King had authorised an emissary, General Aurel Aldea, to conclude an armistice with the Red Army. Two days later, the Russians, ignoring the offer overwhelmed the Rumanian border town of Jassy.

The King wasted no more time. At 2 p.m. on 23 August, he summoned both the Head of State, the Axis-oriented Marshal Ion Antonescu and the Foreign Minister, the Marshal's brother Mihail. Following his custom, the Marshal arrived an hour late, leaving his bullet-proof automobile, a gift from Hitler, in the courtyard. A warning that Hitler had given him as recently as 5 August – "Antonescu! On no account set foot inside the King's castle!" – went unheeded.

"I have a wire from the front and the situation is disastrous," was the King's opening gambit. "What are you going to do about it? Are you or are you not going through with the armistice?"

"There are certain conditions to be met," the Marshal maintained. "I want a guarantee from the Allies that they will land in Rumania and guarantee it for us against the Russians."

"That is so absurd it is not worth discussing," the King retorted. "How can you expect the Allies to guarantee us against their own Allies?"

When Antonescu refused, the King delivered his ultimatum: "You, I know, consider me to be a stupid, stammering child; my Rumanians will judge of that. You will have to make an armistice or resign. This time you have gone too far."

Turning, the Marshal now saw that he was cornered. From an adjacent room the Marshal of the Court, Baron Ion Mocsonyi Stircea and the King's secretary Mirce Ionittiu, had emerged, and both were levelling drawn revolvers. Before the King had even stretched his foot towards a push-button beneath the carpet, a posse of soldiers trooped in.

"You miserable people!" Antonescu cried angrily. "Tomorrow you'll all be shot!" But the King's soldiers, unheeding, bundled both the Marshal and his brother into a fireproof vault where Michael's father, the exiled King Carol, had kept his stamp collection.

The Marshal's bodyguard, invited in for coffee, proved even easier prey. As they lifted their cups for the first sip, Palace servants deftly slipped their revolvers from their holsters.

On 12 September, an armistice was duly signed with Moscow.

What followed was truly predictable as Koriakov well knew. On a 200-mile front from the Carpathians to the Black Sea, the signal flashed to all Red Army units: head for Rumania. In their wake came death and destruction: the bodies of dead Germans choked the ditches, but peasant villages were there for the burning and Rumanian women there for the raping. The roads were jammed with columns of infantry, tanks and artillery, driving herds of Rumanian cattle and horses away to the north. Almost a million men, part of the Southern Army Group of Marshal Feodor Tolbukhin crawled like a gigantic grey-brown snake along the highways, moving at fifteen miles an hour, stripping every tiny village of chickens, hogs, towels, blankets, even wooden spoons.

In Bucharest, the capital, panic reigned. Heavy iron window shutters on the boulevards and on the Street of Victories came clanging down. Windows were boarded up, doors and garden gates were secured by iron bars and padlocks. Children were hastened indoors and women shunned the streets. Now, for the sake of amity, the police took a hand: victory flags must be displayed, not only the blue, yellow and red tricolour of Rumania but the red flag – neatly converted from Hitler's swastika flags by dint of removing the white circle and the black hooked crosses. All were in place to greet the first Russian combat troops, stocky sweating men with ashen hair stubble and flat weatherbeaten faces now filing into the city.

"Soviet Government do NOT wish ... to claim any further rights than that Soviet troops and those of the Allies should be able to move freely across Rumanian territory in all directions," Eden assured Churchill, and certainly the troops were moving: on to Bulgaria, to Hungary, to Yugoslavia. Yet a limited tyranny was early apparent: Rumanians were forced to exchange the rouble at the rate of 100 Rumanian lei, ten times the rouble's value. An 8 p.m. curfew was clamped down. In police stations and *Prefecturas*, portraits of King Michael and Queen Mother Helen – still nominally the country's rulers – gave place to genial likenesses of Stalin. The telephone-tapping centre was enlarged to five times its former size: in Bucharest, rigid censorship of letters imposed a three week delay between mailing and delivery. Into the seat of power moved the first of Stalin's exiled *apparatchiks*, 51-year-old Ana Pauker, a squat, grey-haired harpy, addicted to such capitalistic trivia as nylon stockings and good food, who within four years would swell the Rumanian Communist Party to 500,000.

"The Soviet Government may decide that it will pay them best to break all the rules," Eden mused at about this time, "to take full advantage of post-war disorder in Europe, to come out in open antagonism of everything which Russian propaganda has associated with 'capitalism' and 'imperialism'...".

But this, he thought, was "far less likely": for "a minimum of five years and probably much longer," the Soviets would "embark on a policy of collaboration with ourselves and the United States (and China) whether within the formation of a World Organisation or without it."

It was an illusion Mikhail Koriakov had once cherished – but a long time ago now, in another life.

7

"Stop! I Have Made a Momentous Decision"
1 September–15 October, 1944

"What are we going to do, Sarge?" Corporal Ralph Driver asked, "That water sure looks deep."

Staff-Sergeant Warner W. Holzinger, who headed the five-man patrol, was silent. The ruins of the wrecked bridge, which the Germans had blown only hours earlier, sprawled untidily across the brown fast-flowing River Our – effectively blocking the advance units of the U.S. 5th Armoured Division. It was almost dusk on Monday 11 September – and back in Luxembourg, the commander of the 500,000 strong U.S. First Army, Lieutenant-General Courtney Hodges, urgently needed information.

"Okay, men," Holzinger ordered his little band, "We're going across," then, to their French guide, Delille, "You follow after me." Decisively, his carbine raised to chest level, he slid into the racing river. At the half-way mark, the water had reached his thighs, but still the opposite bank remained silent in the thickening dusk. Very far away, as the men floundered onto the muddy bank, guns were rumbling.

"Okay, men," Holzinger told them, "spread out! We're going to check out those buildings up there – and then we're gonna get the hell out of here *quick*!" Cautiously, tensed for action, they groped their way up a steep slope – advancing towards what seemed to be a group of abandoned farm buildings.

But appearances were deceptive. Drawing closer, they found they had chanced upon a clutch of twenty cleverly-camouflaged concrete bunkers – one of them housing an abandoned chicken-coop – which had plainly been deserted a few hours before. It was 6:05 p.m. and darkness was falling: time to report that this section of the West Wall (the Siegfried Line to the Allies) near Stolzemburg, Germany, a few miles north-east of Vianden, Luxembourg, was no longer tenanted.

Ten minutes later, the men had plashed back across the river and were doubling for their parked half-track. Thirty minutes later, their discovery was made known to the 85th Reconnaissance Squadron. One hour after that, General Hodges was privy to the secret.

For the first time since Napoleon's day, an enemy soldier had set foot on German soil in the midst of war. Unbeknown to Adolf Hitler, Staff-Sergeant Warner Holzinger had returned to the fatherland of his ancestors.

—

In those last heady days of August and the first weeks of September, the names of falling towns told the story: Cannes, Troyes, Rouen, Meaux, Soissons, Amiens, Arras, Verdun, Lyons. The speed of the British advance was breathtaking: did the Allies, one German commander pondered, have seven-league boots? Often Royal Army Service Corps drivers were at the wheel for 72 hours without sleep. By 23 August, No 45 Royal Marine Commando, near Drubec, Normandy, had abandoned the phrase "digging in"; with the *Wehrmacht* in full retreat, they bivouacked at their leisure. It was the same with the 50th (Northumbrian) Division; between D-Day and 15 November, only once – for forty-eight hours – were they absent from the Order of Battle. In one three-week period alone they advanced 500 miles.

A dizzying euphoria prevailed. On 3 September, Major-General Sir Alan Adair's Guards Armoured Division rolled into Brussels as dusk was falling after covering 93 miles in fifteen hours. From the carnival atmosphere, the liberators retained brief but enduring impressions: a line of masked street lights hung above the centre of the Chaussée Ninove "like a green necklace suspended in the sky," the smell of cheap perfume and cigars, "like incense," the great dome of the Palais de Justice, burning like a flambeau in the night, everywhere rapturous crowds chanting "It's a Long Way To Tipperary," convinced that this was the British national anthem. One day later, Major-General "Pip" Roberts' 11th (U.K.) Armoured Division, streaking into Antwerp, found the same sense of surprise, the same uproarious welcome; the first Germans they saw were sipping beer in outdoor cafés. Here, too, the 6000-strong garrison offered scant resistance, and Lieutenant-Colonel Ian Reeves proposed housing them in the local zoo – officers in the lion-cages, other ranks in the monkey house, Belgian Fascists in the tiger-pens.

When Brigadier J. B. Churcher protested, "The animals must be half-starved and will eat them," Reeves updated him on the facts of life in hungry Europe: "The people are half-starved and have eaten the animals long ago."

Yet Antwerp was a useless prize without the 54-mile Scheldt Estuary and its strongpoint, Walcheren Island, which the Germans still commanded. Not until 28 November did Antwerp function again as a port.

In the American lines, the same cheerfulness prevailed; to the fourteen-strong unit of Lieutenant-Colonel Saul K. Padover, who had now reached the city of Luxembourg, "it was all over but the shouting". The 39-year-old Padover was less convinced; to one colleague, Major Paul Sweet, he quoted Napoleon's dictum: "An enemy is not defeated until he thinks himself defeated". For did the Germans falling back beyond the West Wall by now *think* themselves defeated?

"If we had really known," Padover commented dryly later, "we would have realised it was all over but the shooting."

In a roomy office building near the city centre, Padover and his colleagues found Luxembourg what they styled "an Eldorado," for thousands of Luxembourgers had fled from the Third Reich into their liberated homeland: lawyers, policemen, industrialists, dentists, engineers. By late September, after analysing hundreds of personal testimonies, Padover had compiled the first-ever report on the state of the German nation.

Some of the findings gave cause for Allied comfort – in a negative way. Defeatism was rife throughout Germany, the Luxembourgers reported; there was no evidence of last-ditch sentiment. Most were hoping for a quick end to the war, even readiness to accept an Allied occupation and to pay the price of defeat. Accepted, too, was the concept of *Vergeltung* (retribution); German civilians were unlikely to offer resistance.

Yet, Padover stressed, "no informant has mentioned a breaking point". People were tired, war-weary, probably exhausted, "but even bad news, bad food and bad housing do not cause any overt action against the regime. One assumes that as long as the Germans have enough to eat the majority of them will go on with the work and the war in hand. But there are many notable fissures and it is our task to discover and report them..."

But the Germans were rallying. Around this time, on Saturday 16 September, Hitler was in secret session with four men in an inner chamber at the *Führersperrkreis*: Keitel, Jodl, *Generaloberst* Heinz Guderian and *General* Werner Kreipe of the Luftwaffe. Jodl was summing up the current position: the palpable treachery of Rumania, Hungary and Bulgaria. While nine million Germans were under arms, the last three months had seen 1,200,000 casualties – more than half of them on the western front. "In the west," Jodl pointed out, "we are getting a real test in the Ardennes" – the thickly wooded area of Belgium and Luxembourg that had marked the highway to German victory in 1940.

Now, hearing the word "Ardennes," Hitler was galvanised. "Stop!" he commanded suddenly, and Jodl fell silent. Then, his eyes blazing like the Hitler of old, his shoulders squared like those of a younger man, he confided his Wagnerian dream: "I have made a momentous decision. I am taking the offensive. Here – out of the Ardennes!" His left fist came down on the unrolled map like a hammer blow. "Across the Meuse and on to Antwerp!" The others stared at him in silent awe. Was this once more the Führer of 1940 – who could galvanise the German people to victory, exorcising the apathy that Padover was reporting?

Hitler did not know it then – but the Allies, in their abundant optimism, were about to entrust thousands of hostages to fortune.

-

It was one of the boldest gambles of World War Two and it failed tragically – at the cost of more than 17,000 Allied casualties and perhaps 3,300 German, including 1,300 dead.

Yet the object in view was in itself admirable: to end the war speedily by surrounding the 4000 square mile industrial area of the Ruhr and forcing Germany to sue for peace.

To its euphoric architects, the plan seemed foolproof. Almost 9000 airborne troops and 1100 glider pilots were to drop and crash-land in broad daylight – to reverse the errors of Normandy – forming a 60-mile long airborne carpet to secure the bridges spanning five major water obstacles: the Wilhelmina Canal, twenty miles beyond the Dutch frontier, the Zuid Villemsvaart Canal, ten miles farther north, then three approximately parallel rivers, the Maas, the Waal, and the Neder Rijn (Lower Rhine). Once these were seized, Lieutenant-General Brian Horrocks' XXX (U.K.) Corps were to punch through the German units on the Dutch frontier and roll down the airborne path to the Zuider Zee. Then the full weight of Allied might would be turned upon the Ruhr.

To Montgomery, newly-promoted Field Marshal, whose concept this was, speed was of the essence. Running his finger up the long wall maps in his advance Belgian command post, tapping each bridge in turn, he stressed to Lieutenant-General Frederick "Boy" Browning, the deputy Allied air commander: "It is of the utmost importance that you drop as many men as possible to quickly seize the bridges". In reply, Browning pointed with concern to the northernmost tip of the carpet: the bridge at the market town of Arnhem, Holland.

"How long will it take our tanks to reach us here?" he asked. "Two days," Montgomery estimated. Still staring at the map, Browning guaranteed: "We can hold it for four." As an afterthought he added: "But I think, sir, we may be going a bridge too far."

Others, too, had their misgivings – among them Major-General Walter Bedell Smith, Major-General Kenneth Strong, Eisenhower's intelligence chief, and Lieutenant-General Sir Miles Dempsey, commanding the British Second Army. But both Montgomery and Eisenhower – in what Lieutenant-General George S. Patton styled "the most momentous error of the war" – brushed their objections aside.

If the dapper ambitious Browning had his doubts, he swiftly contrived to stifle them. At 6 p.m. on Sunday 10 September, a full-dress conference was attended by 27 men at the Sunningdale Park, Ascot, headquarters of the First Allied Airborne commander, Lieutenant-General Lewis Hyde Brereton. Focussing on Major-General Robert Urquhart, of the First Airborne Division, Browning, "with a grand sweep of the hand," drew a large circle on the talc-covered map, announcing, "Arnhem Bridge – and hold it."

To Brigadier-General James M. Gavin, of the U.S. 82nd Airborne, the entire conference had the basic unreality of a peacetime exercise: Brererton was seeking a commitment for four days hence, yet maps and ammunition had still to be issued, and artillery and supporting arms allocated. And as Urquhart outlined his drop and landing zones, located six to eight miles west of Arnhem, Gavin couldn't believe his ears. He whispered to his G–3, Colonel John Norton, "My God, he can't mean it." "He does," replied Norton grimly, "and he is going to try it."

Soon enough Gavin saw the reasons: Urquhart was a victim of R.A.F. obstructionism. Unwilling to risk the heavy flak near Arnhem Bridge, the R.A.F. were equally leary of that at Deelen Airfield, several miles north. The closest they could venture to Arnhem was six miles west – condemning Urquhart to battle his way through the suburbs and the city before ever reaching the bridge. Moreover, due to a shortage of planes, Urquhart would have to receive his troops, who would never fight as a cohesive division, in three separate lifts – what airborne men called "feeding Oxo cubes to the lion one by one."

It was with good reason that the commander of the Polish Parachute Brigade, Major-General Stanislaw Sosabowski, more than once enquired loudly, "But the Germans, General, how about the Germans, what about *them*?"

For the Germans were indeed a force to be reckoned with, as no one knew better than Major Brian Urquhart (no kin to the General), the intelligence chief at Browning's First British Airborne Corps headquarters. To the irritation of his superiors, his apprehensions regarding the newly-christened "Operation Market-Garden" were increasing daily. At Bletchley Park, 40 miles north of London, the experts of Hut 3, studying the German "Ultra" intercepts, had already charted several significant troop movements. On 5 September, the staff of II S.S. Panzer Corps had been transferred to Eindhoven, forty miles south of Arnhem and clear in the path of Horrocks' XXX Corps; by first light on 14 September, *Feldmarschall* Walter Model had shifted the headquarters of his Army Group B to Oosterbeek, on the outskirts of Arnhem.

Neither Urquhart nor Horrocks were ever briefed on these changes of disposition – and when Major Urquhart did furnish reconnaissance photos of German armour near Arnhem, Browning promptly dismissed them. "They're probably not serviceable, at any rate," was his astonishing comment. Not long after, Major Urquhart was sent home on enforced sick leave, suffering from "exhaustion".

As the target date – 17 September – drew closer, anything but total faith in the mission's success became tantamount to disloyalty. "Militarily, the war is won," Bedell Smith told a press conference early in September; Post Exchange officials had already astonished Brigadier-General Gavin by arranging to return all Christmas parcels – now in the mail – to the United States. Moreover, the need to use the airborne troops, the most highly-trained of the reserve, in some role was seen as imperative. In 40 days, eighteen different airborne operations had been set up then cancelled; the armies had moved too far and too fast.

But "Market-Garden" was by no means the summit of Montgomery's ambition. On 10 September, in a stormy conference held aboard Eisenhower's private plane in the airport at Brussels, the Field Marshal had bitterly criticised the American's policy of advancing on a broad front – as opposed to the narrow rapier-like thrusts advocated by Montgomery. Patton's drive to the Saar River, he complained, was robbing him, Montgomery, of vital supplies; "jerky and disjointed thrusts" were equally impeding both armies and achieving nothing. At one point his language grew so unrestrained that Eisenhower, reaching out, patted Montgomery on the knee and rebuked him, "Steady, Monty! You can't speak to me like that. I'm your boss".

Montgomery's mounting anger cooled. "I'm sorry, Ike," he said quietly.

But Eisenhower remained wedded to the broad front concept. "What you're proposing is this," he told Montgomery incredulously, "if I could give you all the supplies you want, you could go straight to Berlin – right straight to Berlin? Monty, you're nuts. You can't do it… you'd have to throw off division after division to protect your flanks from attack… Suppose you did get a bridge across the Rhine, you couldn't depend for long on that one bridge to supply your drive…"

As Eisenhower later recalled it, Montgomery argued: "Just give me what I need and I'll reach Berlin and end the war." Patton, equally cocksure, boasted, "If Ike stops holding Monty's hand and gives *me* the supplies, I'll go through the Siegfried Line like shit through a goose."

Thus the stage was set for disaster from the first.

Strangely, though, few men, from divisional commanders to combat troops, had premonitions. For Private Donald Burgett, veteran of D-Day, who had twice been slightly wounded on 12 June, Sunday 17 September stood out as "a parade-ground jump" – everything would go exactly as planned. Chary of scattering his troops in penny packets, Major-General Maxwell D. Taylor had selected three major landing-zones as near to the 101st's objectives as possible: the bridge across the Zuid Villemsvaart Canal and the bridge across the Wilhelmina Canal at Zon.

For Burgett that Sunday was remarkable, too, for his first-ever glimpse of the cliffs of Dover, "really white in the sun." Somehow it seemed a good omen for all that was to follow; he was convinced he would "come through".

At mid-morning, as the Controller's green flag signalled the "Off" on 24 airfields, others, on the ground and in the air, took comfort from such everyday sights: a Salvation Army's bass drummer, thumping out a V-for-Victory in Morse code, the peaceful village streets of England, thronged with people, the fluttering of white handkerchiefs waving farewell. Lieutenant-Colonel John Frost, whose 2nd British Parachute Battalion, had been assigned Arnhem Bridge, was glad that at the last moment he had besought his batman, Wicks, to pack his gun, cartridges, golf clubs and dinner jacket – all to follow with the heavier baggage.

Many, like Burgett, took comfort from the rock-steady demeanour of the transport pilots, keeping their planes on course through even the deadliest ack-ack. One U.S. glider pilot, Flight Officer Gale Ammerman, grabbed his phone to alert his tow-pilot that gasoline was streaming from his right wing tanks. There was a long pause before the pilot replied: "We're going towards the drop zone as long as the engines keep going." The day was marked by such nonchalance. As Flight Officer John L. Lowden headed his glider for a fenced area, the airborne sergeant beside him remarked diffidently, "I wouldn't presume to fly for you but I think you're about to land in a minefield." Just in time, Lowden stretched his glide to the stalling point, barely clearing the danger area. In another glider, an airborne trooper, noting the rising flak, promptly removed his helmet and wedged it into his crotch. "Hell," he explained calmly, "if I'm hit there I'm dead anyway."

For many men, their first sight of the Dutch countryside exercised a tranquilising effect: the pleasant summer villas of the rich burghers from Amsterdam and Utrecht, peaceful in the lush and slumbering countryside. Towards them, a never-to-be-forgotten sight, streamed the tanks, half tracks and armoured cars of Horrocks' XXX Corps, spread over every field and road. The CBS correspondent Ed Murrow noted that "all the houses seemed to be covered with red tiles ... the spire of a magnificent old Dutch church rises clear above the little houses that surround it". As he watched the first men to drop he remarked them descending "beside the little windmill near a church, hanging there very gracefully ... like nothing so much as khaki dolls hanging beneath green lampshades."

As the main armada neared the drop zones, other sights swam into view: clusters of burgeoning colour, khaki, white, orange, blue and yellow, floating harmoniously down like one great moving canopy; scores of fawn-coloured gliders with broad black and white wing stripes, scattered like a plague of locusts across the ploughed fields; the small town of Oosterbeek, perched neatly beside the dark calm ribbon of the Neder Rijn.

It was a day when many, once on Dutch soil, felt that nothing could go wrong. Sergeant Major Les Ellis, holding a dead partridge aloft, explained to Sergeant Norman Swift: "I landed on it. It'll be a bit of all right later, in case we're hungry." Lieutenant Leo Heaps, a young Canadian, landing west of Arnhem, found action so lacking he called in at the Wolfheze Hotel for a mug of tea, promising to return that evening for champagne. Few men had as keen a sense of priorities as the British paratrooper whom Second Lieutenant Arthur Kaplan unearthed in a barn; although barely an hour on the ground he, with a willing Dutch maiden, was briskly fornicating in the hay loft.

Forty miles south of Arnhem, the Americans' first conviction of success abruptly gave place to disquiet. Although Private Burgett and his outfit had dropped from 1500 feet without incident, to march unmolested from the drop zone, no sooner had they struck the road for Zon than the Germans "opened up".

For the first time Burgett encountered a deadly weapon which all desert war veterans had learned to dread: Flak 88 mm guns, levelled now for use against men and tanks, whose 22-pound shells could tear holes as big as basketballs in targets a mile away. The leader of "A" company, Captain Milton O. Davis, fell gravely wounded; the medic attending him, "Doc" Derek Saint, was hit, too. "They just about wiped out my company," Burgett was to recall. Four times in all Davis was hit, yet still his calm Texan drawl rallied the medic, whose arm was streaming blood: "Ya better hurry, boy. They're gainin' on ya." Now only two young officers were left, 2nd Lieutenant Borrelli and 1st Lieutenant Retan, a "repple-depple" (a new man lacking combat experience). Accordingly, Borrelli took over. Emerging from woods, the 506th saw three 88s on their side of the water, still menacing them; at once Borrelli ordered a frontal assault with fixed bayonets.

Pounding for the piled sandbags, Burgett scaled them like a hurdler; his bayonet was wedged against a German's breastbone as the man gave up. Fighting their way towards the bridge, they were barely fifty yards distant when it blew up.

For Colonel Robert F. Sink, commanding Burgett's regiment, this was a major setback; his orders were to take Eindhoven and its crossings not later than 8 p.m. But American can-do, Burgett recalls, saved the day. Aided by a sergeant, Major James LaPrade strung ropes across the remains of the bridge and Burgett and the others, teetering on one rope, hanging like grim death to the other, inched their way across – no mean feat when Burgett was laden with a 42-pound 30-calibre air-cooled machine gun.

Within ninety minutes, engineers, utilising black market timber and the bridge's centre trestle, had spanned the canal. The way to Eindhoven was clear.

There was no way of knowing that at Arnhem "Operation Market Garden" was already falling apart.

Almost from the first, due to an unforeseen chain of accidents, Urquhart was in difficulties. His plan called for a four-troop squadron of the First Airborne Division Reconnaissance Unit, under Major Freddie Gough, to race for the bridge in heavily-armoured jeeps, ahead of Lieutenant-Colonel Frost's foot-slogging 2nd Battalion. But when Gough sought his transport, due to be ferried in by glider, the news was bad; an entire squadron's transport, roughly 22 jeeps, had not arrived.

Worse, the No 22 radio sets, with a radius of barely three miles, refused to function; cut off from Gough's squadron, Urquhart was equally out of touch with his Divisional headquarters. For better, for worse, he decided to stay put with Brigadier Gerald Lathbury's 1st Para Brigade – to lose all control of the battle for thirty-nine hours.

Next, disaster overtook one troop of Gough's unit – attempting a dash for the Arnhem Bridge with such vehicles as remained. At Wolfheze, where Lieutenant Heaps had so lately taken tea, an ambush was waiting in force: men of the 9th and 10th S.S. Panzer Divisions, of which "Ultra" had all along warned. Pinned down by accurate fire, the men of "C" Troop were forced to surrender. Trooper Arthur Barlow would always remember the desembodied voice of the Control operator, crying distractedly from the discarded headsets of a wireless set: "For Christ's sake, Oboe Two, give us your position."

By 8 p.m., Frost and his headquarters company were within sight of the great steel girders of the 400-yard long bridge, moving cautiously through dusk, rapping covertly at the doors of all the tall buildings grouped at the northern end. Consternation was swift to follow: as the red-bereted paratroopers moved in to rip down curtains, using their rifle-butts to stove in windows, before barricading them with antique furniture, householders alternately pleaded, cajoled and raged at the oblivious soldiers. Thus, as midnight approached, one end of Arnhem Bridge was firmly British – the other as solidly German.

Though taken by surprise the Germans had lost no time. At noon, *Feldmarschall* Walter Model, in Army Group B's headquarters at Oosterbeek's Tafelberg Hotel, was enjoying a pre-luncheon aperitif; in the *Kasino*, the waiters, wearing white jackets over field-grey uniforms, were laying the tables for the *Wehrmacht*'s traditional Sunday lunch: thick green pea soup with chunks of pork. In his whitewashed cottage at Vught, *Generaloberst* Kurt Student, commanding the 1st Para Army, was still working quietly at his desk.

Suddenly Student was aware of a steady insidious hornet-drone: repairing to his balcony, he saw a vast unending stream of troop transports and gliders passing overhead. For Student, the man who had planned the airborne assaults on Rotterdam in 1940 and Crete in 1941, professional pride drove out any thoughts of danger. His lament to his Chief of Staff was heartfelt: "Oh, how I wish that I had ever had such a powerful force at my disposal."

Model's reaction was higher-keyed; giving orders for his headquarters to evacuate both the Tafelsberg Hotel and the nearby Park Hotel at Hartenstein, he ran to his bedroom to cram a suitcase with belongings. As he raced for his waiting car, the suitcase burst open; shirts and shaving kit, spilling into the street, had to be hastily repacked. "Which is the way to General Bittrich's headquarters?" Model shouted to a passing S.S. major.

It was a cogent question. *Generalleutnant* Willi Bittrich's 9th and 10th S.S. Panzer Divisions were bivouacked in the Arnhem area but purely by chance – "it was a peaceful sector where nothing was happening," Bittrich explained later. By nightfall, Model would allocate him more troops yet; the real threat, both men adjudged, would come more from the advancing XXX Corps and the Americans to the south than from the airborne at Arnhem. "Almost before the British had touched the ground," Bittrich commented later, "we were ready to defeat them."

It might have seemed an empty boast – but within nine days, Bittrich, a cultured musicologist far removed from the traditional S.S. stereotype, was to make it good.

Late on the Sunday afternoon, an undamaged briefcase found in a shot-down Waco glider was rushed to *Generaloberst* Student, who was bemused to find it contained the entire operational plan for "Market Garden". Although it took Student ten hours to locate Model and transmit the document to him by radio, the objective of the assault, a thrust for the Ruhr, was now plain – and so, too, was the timing and location of the second air drop. Thus, on the Monday afternoon, on both zones west of the Wolfheze Railway Station, paratroopers and glider-borne infantrymen dropped into a raging fire-fight.

None of this was then known to General Urquhart; all through that Monday, after narrowly escaping German panzer grenadiers, he was holed up in the attic of No 14, Zwarteweg, feeling "helpless and absurd," while his entire Division, uncoordinated, fought a battle around him. Many other key figures were equally cut off; Major Anthony Deane-Drummond, of First Airborne Divisional Signals, spent three days, along with four others, locked in the lavatory of an abandoned house.

At Divisional headquarters, Brigadier Philip Hicks, who had temporarily assumed command, was equally in the dark, for only one unit, Major Dennis Munford's Light Battery of No 1 Airlanding Light Regiment, in an attic near Frost's headquarters, linked him with the bridge. All that was plain was that Frost, though twice driven back from the bridge's southern end, was holding his ground – but where was the vanguard of XXX Corps? And how were the Americans faring?

In fact, the Americans had reached Eindhoven by early on 18 September, and Private Donald Burgett's squad was already in the process of "hunting Germans" – by the simple expedient of taking the elevator to the top of each tall building and working their way down. Farther north, Gavin's 82nd Airborne were stalled before Nijmegen – and not until nightfall on 18 September did the first contingent of Horrocks' Corps, the Irish Guards, reach Eindhoven.

Nor was this surprising. "This is a tale you will tell your grandchildren," the lean insouciant Horrocks had joked at their final briefing, "and mighty bored they'll be!" – yet the tale, when told, would be one of endless and crippling frustration. From Nijmegen on – which the Corps would not reach until 20 September – their progress slackened to a crawl, for the soft swampy soil made it impossible for their 20,000 vehicles to leave the single narrow causeway.

Cut off in cellars and attics, blasted by mortars and 88 mm guns, men survived as best they could, on iron rations or apples scrounged from outhouses, and somehow preserved their sense of humour. Radio operator J. L. Cull always recalled tuning in to the B.B.C. after a night of non-stop shelling, to hear an announcer's voice: "You have been listening to Frank Sinatra's latest record, *I Couldn't Sleep A Wink Last Night*." "Well, Padre," Sergeant "Jack" Spratt greeted Frost's chaplain, Father James Egan, at the height of one bombardment, "they're throwing everything at us but the kitchen stove." With those words, the ceiling fell in, bringing a torrent of debris – and a kitchen stove.

"I knew the bastards were close," said Spratt in mock-wonder, "but I didn't believe they could hear us talking."

Not until around 7:25 a.m. on Tuesday 19 September, after a frantic jeep-ride through debris-littered streets, did Urquhart break through to Divisional Headquarters, the Park Hotel at Oosterbeek – to find that virtually every unit save Frost's was operating on their own initiative. Already XXX Corps were twenty-four hours behind schedule. All wireless links had broken down; though the landing zones allotted to the third air drop were now in German hands, no word of this could be passed to London. Nor had any link been established with General Browning near Nijmegen.

And as tanks and 40 mm guns pounded the British-held houses to rubble, the perimeter was shrinking hourly. Clouds of white and choking dust swirled through the shattered masonry, tinged with the acrid reek of phosphorus shells. Even at night, Frost recalled, it was like daylight in the streets – "a curious metallic daylight," lit by the fierce fires consuming the church towers of St Walburg and St Eusebius. "The world was a red glow smelling of smoke and death," remembered Private James Sims, of Frost's battalion, for whom Arnhem would always be a "physical and spiritual auto-da-fé".

By Wednesday, Urquhart had faced up to the truth: there was no more hope of sending reinforcements to the men cut off at the bridge, where Frost, wounded in both legs, had passed over command to Major Freddie Gough. Now it was barely possible to distinguish between German and British positions: in some areas German bullets fired at one end went straight across and out the other side. Many felt the desperation of animals trapped by a forest fire; eyes red with lack of sleep, they crouched in cellars or foxholes, faces blackened by firefighting, bristling with three days' growth of beard, "whitened again with thick plaster".

At 7:15 p.m. on Wednesday 20 September, help seemed at hand, for the great multi-spanned Nijmegen Bridge had fallen, and the first tank squadron of the Irish Guards rolled across it. Yet this was a squadron in name only, down to six tanks – and few squadrons were in better shape. Only eleven miles away lay Arnhem, but Horrocks, short of both petrol and supplies, deemed it best to wait for the infantry of the 43rd Wessex Division – who were still eight miles south. Not until first light on the Thursday did XXX Corps' advance resume.

They would come too late. At 9 a.m. unknown to Urquhart, holding his morning conference in the Park Hotel's wine cellar, the Germans, using stick bombs and automatic rifles, had already driven the 150 survivors at the northern end of the bridge from their last boltholes. The fighting was savage, for every foot of bloody stairway and smoke-stained cellar was contested. But by 9 a.m. it was all over; Frost and his garrison were now prisoners of war.

At 10:30 a.m. on Monday 25 September, Urquhart convened his last "Market Garden" conference in the dusty wine-cellar. Plainly, the troops remaining could hold out no longer; that night, on the password "John Bull," they would pull out of Arnhem. It would be a fraught withdrawal, for the British now held little more than 600 yards of river bank; any hint of an exodus would place them at the mercy of German artillery.

At 10 p.m., a night of high wind and teeming rain, the great retreat began. The survivors stumbled through blackness, fumbling their way along taut lines of tape, groping for one another's parachute smocks, boots muffled "with rags and sacking and the torn trousers of the dead". From across the Neder Rijn, the heavy guns of XXX Corps, alerted to the pull-out, poured a storm of diversionary fire into the German lines. Filing into wooden Canadian storm boats with outboard motors and British collapsible assault boats paddled by engineers, all that was left of Urquhart's ragged dead-beat army were heading for Nijmegen and the south.

Private Donald Burgett, helping to cover their retreat at Opheusden, between the Neder Rijn and the Waal, remembered that as "the loneliest day of my life". There was no sound after the troops moved back: only a silence like sorrow, "silence until you could hear ringing in your ears."

Some of the British felt lonely, too. Sergeant "Andy" Andrews, a glider pilot, arrived back at a Wiltshire airfield, to a Nissen hut with a cheerful fire and comfortable-looking beds with sheets and blankets – "two of us alone in a hut that held twenty-six beds." It was too much. "Without a word we dumped our kit and rifles on the bed and left."

It was H.R.H. Prince Bernhard of the Netherlands, then Commander-in-Chief of the Netherlands Forces, who supplied the bitterest epitaph for "Market Garden": "My country can never afford the luxury of another Montgomery success."

—

While the soldiers fought and died, the statesmen talked. Often, it seemed, their sentiments were pitched to the listening ear of history. Three conferences in the autumn of 1944 – resolving little – would be succeeded by three more – resolving less – by the late summer of 1945.

At Dumbarton Oaks, a handsome mansion set in a 16-acre estate in the fashionable Washington suburb of Georgetown, 39 delegates, American, British and Soviet, pondered the problems of postwar security organisation. Meeting from the third week of August to the end of September, they agreed on little more than their right to disagree.

Was Russia to be trusted for the peace of the world, as Roosevelt believed? Or was Churchill's rhetorical question nearer the mark: "What are we going to have between the white snows of Russia and the white cliffs of Dover?" As the weeks wore on, it seemed that deadlock on preserving the peace had been reached even as the Allies were winning it.

"This will blow off the roof," exclaimed the Secretary of State, the ailing 71-year-old Cordell Hull, who was to resign early in October in favour of Edward Stettinius, a prematurely white-haired glad-hander, a former cheer-leader of the University of Virginia. For early in the proceedings, Stettinius reported to Hull that the Soviet delegate, Andrei Gromyko, had insisted that all sixteen republics comprising the U.S.S.R. should be members of the new United Nations organisation. Thus Russia would claim sixteen votes.

In vain, Stettinius, Hull, even Roosevelt himself in a personal interview, sought to change Gromyko's stance – this was tantamount, the President argued, to all forty-eight states of the Union demanding admission. But Gromyko, impassive and pasty-faced, was unyielding. And now, another vexed question arose: that of the veto. Assuming that the Big Four were always unanimous, Gromyko proposed, then a Big Four power could veto Council action intended to protect a lesser nation or another Big Four power.

When the Allies protested that a party to a dispute, great or small, should not be allowed to vote on the question, Gromyko flatly rejected any limitation on the veto.

On Thursday 28 September, when the conference broke up, one factor was plain: Russia's haunting sense of isolation would make for intolerable tensions in the foreseeable future.

At Quebec, between 11 September and 16 September, primarily a military conference, no Russians were present to quench what Churchill termed "a blaze of friendship" – though the initial gaiety of ships dressed overall in Halifax Harbour, screeching sirens, packed ranks of Canadian Mounties and fire-boats playing their hoses, all too soon gave place to acrimony.

The bone of contention was a plan dreamed up by Secretary of the Treasury, Henry Morgenthau, for the permanent pastoralisation of post-war Germany, destroying her future war potential by stripping whole areas of the Saar and the Ruhr and converting them to agriculture – what the London *New Statesman* called "a ruined no-man's land in which no wheel turns". The plan, initially approved by Roosevelt, was at first opposed by Churchill. "You cannot indict a whole nation," he insisted; he looked on the Treasury plan as he would on "chaining himself to a dead German". But when his Scientific Adviser, Lord Cherwell, known always as "The Prof," who hated Germans as bitterly as Morgenthau, came out in favour, Churchill promptly switched his allegiance.

Both Eden and Hull were appalled. "It was as if one were to take the Black Country and turn it into Devonshire," Eden objected, and Hull's reactions were typically intemperate to this "plan of blind vengeance". "In Christ's name," he burst out to Stettinius, "what has happened to the man?" while Eden, unusually for him, took Churchill to task in public: "You cannot do this. You and I have said quite the opposite."

Such was the calibre of Roosevelt's thinking that he later told Stimson that he had "no idea how he could have initialled the memorandum." The plan was quickly shelved – although enough of its intent leaked out to provide valuable grist for Göbbels' propaganda mill.

"Everything we have touched has turned to gold," was Churchill's joyous reaction, over the final luncheon in Quebec's Citadel, but Roosevelt, sunk in lassitude, made no response. In less than two weeks' time he was to begin his election campaign for an unprecedented fourth term of office: the problems of the world had been put aside.

But for Churchill they had by no means receded; still unresolved, for one, was the plight of the Polish Government in Exile. Assuming an American withdrawal from Europe – "I am absolutely unwilling to police France and possibly Italy and the Balkans as well," Roosevelt had warned him as far back as February – what the Premier now sought was an accommodation with Josef Stalin: a finite partition of Europe into British and Soviet spheres of influence.

"*Kto eto?*" (Who is that?) curious Muscovites asked one another, as the silver-grey Rolls Royce from the British Embassy sped down Gorky Street, for the faces of the passengers were undoubtedly familiar. On Monday 9 October, five plane-loads of 50 Britons, headed by Churchill and Eden, had swooped down on Moscow's Tushino Airport, intent on resolving these pressing problems.

They were questions that the Premier and his Foreign Secretary had long debated. "Are we going to acquiesce in the communisation of the Balkans and perhaps of Italy?" Churchill had put it to Eden as far back as 4 May, to which Eden replied: "It will not be easy to show that they have embarked on a policy of communising the Balkans and Italy even if we suspect that this is their long-term objective … it is an unfortunate fact that communists seem to make the best guerilla leaders…"

Thus Churchill lost no time. That same day, after dinner, he sat down with Stalin in the dictator's Kremlin study, in an attempt to redraw the map of Europe once for all. "Let us settle about our affairs in the Balkans," he told the dictator roundly. "Your armies are in Rumania and Bulgaria. We have interests, missions and agents there. Don't let us get at cross-purposes in small ways."

Promptly, he scribbled down figures on a half-sheet of paper, giving percentages, of respective Russian and British "predominance" throughout the Balkans: Rumania, Russia 90 per cent, the others 10 per cent; Greece, Great Britain (in accord with the USA), 90 per cent, Russia 10 per cent; Yugoslavia and Hungary, 50 per cent apiece; Bulgaria, Russia 75 per cent, the others 25 per cent.

This done, he pushed the paper over the table to Stalin; after a slight pause, the dictator picked up his blue pencil and flicked a large tick on the document before tossing it back. Now Churchill felt a twinge of conscience. "Might it not be thought rather cynical," he asked Stalin, "if it seemed we had disposed of these issues, so fateful to millions of people, in such an offhand manner? Let us burn the paper." "No," Stalin replied shrewdly. "You keep it."

Despite Churchill's shame-faced pride that he could play the power-game with the best of them, Stalin's tick meant nothing at all. The next day, faced with a draft of the discussion, he carefully erased all phrases suggesting spheres of influence – a truth which Churchill excluded from his memoirs. This, as the British Ambassador Sir Archibald Clark-Kerr had noted, was a new Stalin, Stalin, the Marshal, the natural heir of the Tsars: a Stalin no longer clad in a pepper-and-salt gabardine tunic but in a trim champagne-coloured uniform with gold braid, a Stalin who had replaced the great enlarged photos of Marx and Engels – "After all, they weren't Russians" – with oil portraits of the great commanders, Suvarov and Kutusov.

This new Stalin, pursuing what one Soviet commentator called a policy of "socialist Caesarism," was content to bide his time, with no intent of Bolshevising Eastern Europe – provided always that the Communists polled the biggest share of the votes. As George F. Kennan, of the U.S. Embassy, pointed out: "There is no border zone of Russian power." If the voters failed in their duty, then the Communist lackeys would move in: following Ana Pauker in Rumania, the frog-faced Mátyás Rakosi in Hungary, Vlko Chervenkov in Bulgaria, Enver Hoxha in Albania.

The next day, Eden took his Soviet counterpart, Vyacheslav Molotov, severely to task: on 21 September, without even consulting his British sponsors, Marshal Josip Broz Tito had left the island of Vis for secret consultations in Moscow. ("This graceless behaviour," Churchill fumed, for Tito had left partisan sentries guarding his cave to suggest that he was still in residence). Molotov, for his part, made light of it – "All you could expect of a Balkan peasant" – without revealing that Stalin had read the Yugoslav leader and his emissary Djilas a series of curtain lectures.

Stressing the need to reinstate King Peter, the dictator told them brusquely: "You need not restore him forever. Take him back temporarily, and then you can slip a knife into his back at a suitable moment." The partisans' mode of dress came in for criticism, too: "What do you need red stars on your caps for? You are frightening the British." He inveighed against the two Allies who between them had supplied the Red Army with $10,212,000,000 worth of Lend-Lease goods: "Churchill is the kind of man who would pick your pocket of a kopeck[26] if you don't watch him... By God, pick your pocket of a kopeck!... Roosevelt is not like that. He dips in his hand only for bigger coins. But Churchill? Churchill – will do it for a kopeck."

But nothing of this showed in his demeanour at 9 p.m. on 11 October when the dictator, for the first time ever, set foot inside a foreign ambassador's residence: the British Embassy on the Sofiiskaya Embankment, overlooking the Moscow River. Arriving in a black armour-plated Packard with dark-green bullet-proof glass windows three inches thick, escorted by 400 NKVD men in a fleet of Lincolns, the dictator was geniality itself. He was lavish in his praise of the English-style dinner of roast turkey and sucking-pig. Staring at a portrait of the late King George V, he remarked curiously: "Is that our Nicholas II?" Apparently revelling in his intimate contact with Churchill, he pooh-poohed the chances of the British Labour Party in any general election – "they're a bunch of Mensheviks." Afterwards he and the Premier, their noses glued to the french windows, watched a mammouth firework display, accompanied by the thunder of guns celebrating the Red Army's "liberation" of Cluj, in Rumania. Flocks of crows, agitated by the racket, wheeled against the searchlights – "the descendants of the same crows," said Churchill happily, "that protested the coming of Napoleon Bonaparte."

Two days later, the fate of the Poles was debated for the first time.

For Stanislaw Mikolajczyk, the affable slow-spoken Polish Premier, the meeting was one of the most traumatic he could ever recall. Arriving in Moscow on 12 October, with his Foreign Minister, Tadeusz Romer, he was greeted in Molotov's office next day by Stalin, Churchill and Eden. Holding a watching brief for Roosevelt was William Averell Harriman, the American Ambassador. To Mikolajczk's surprise, Molotov invited him to open the meeting.

Mikolajczyk came speedily to the point: the Soviet-sponsored Polish National Council, soon to be known as the Lublin Government, was far from representing the will of all Poles. "To find a solution," the Polish Premier conceded, "we propose that the postwar Polish government includes all parties, including the Communists."

"The Lublin government should have a bigger share in the future Polish government," Churchill cut in, and now Stalin spoke for the first time: "If any Polish government wants relations with the Soviet Union it must recognise the Curzon Line as an actuality."

Mikolajczyk was stubborn. "I cannot accept the Curzon Line. I have no authority to yield 48 per cent of our country, no authority to forsake millions of my countrymen and leave them to their fate. If I agreed, everyone would have the right to say, 'It was for this that the Polish soldiers fought – a politician's sell-out'."

Now Stalin grew angry. "Who is threatening the independence of Poland?" he thundered, "Soviet Russia?".

Narrowly, Mikolajczyk bit back a resounding "Yes!"; whatever his feelings, he must strive to negotiate calmly. Instead he continued to resist the Curzon Line argument, until Molotov roughly stopped him short. "But all this was settled at Tehran!" he barked.

Mikolajczyk was stupefied. He looked first to Churchill, then to Harriman, but both men were silent.

Calmly, levelly, Molotov recapitulated. "If your memories fail you, let me recall the facts to you. We all agreed at Tehran that the Curzon Line must divide Poland. You will recall that President Roosevelt agreed to this solution and strongly endorsed the Line. And then we agreed that it would be best not to issue any public declaration about our agreement."

Still Mikolajczyk could not believe it. No Poles had attended the Tehran conference, but as recently as June, on a visit to the White House, Roosevelt had assured him that the Curzon Line was negotiable, and that Mikolajczyk could at all times count on his "moral support". The Premier had believed this implicitly – not realising that with seven million Polish voters in the United States, Roosevelt was out to sidestep all commitments until after the November election.

Now Mikolajczyk turned to Harriman, but the ambassador, his gaze rooted on the carpet, did not meet his eye. Then – "I confirm this," said Churchill quietly.

In his anger, Mikolajczyk cast aside all discretion. "I didn't expect to be brought here to participate in a new partition of my country," he shouted.

Vainly Churchill essayed the role of peacemaker. "But you can at least agree that the Curzon Line is the temporary frontier," he pleaded, but Stalin's patience was exhausted. He rose indignantly from the table. "I want this made very clear," he announced gruffly, "Mr Churchill's thought of any future change in the frontier is not acceptable to the Soviet government. We will not change our frontiers from time to time. That's all!"

Later that same day, Churchill and Eden met up with the Lublin Poles. For both men it was a depressing experience: as far back as 23 July, just as Harriman had warned the State Department, the Russians had announced that these men, while not considered as the government of Poland, might in due course form the nucleus of a provisional government. Faced with their prize protégés, Boleslaw Bierut, formerly a Soviet agent named Krasnodewski, with what one source called "quick greasy hard sly eyes like a tough Bradford businessman," and Edward Osobska-Morawski, a sharp-nosed locksmith's son, both men despaired of Poland's future. "The rat and the weasel," Eden muttered, and Churchill grunted his assent.

For five days thereafter, Churchill sought to sway Mikolajczyk – it was with reason that Sir Archibald Clark-Kerr's diary entry for 14 October was a laconic: "Bullying Poles". "You cannot defeat the Russians!" Churchill urged, "I beg of you to settle upon the Curzon Line as a frontier." He grew more vehement still: "Unless you accept the frontier, you're out of business forever! The Russians will sweep through your country and your people will be liquidated." In his rage and frustration, he stooped to personal abuse: "You ought to be in a lunatic asylum. I don't know whether the British government will continue to recognise you."

All was in vain. Though Mikolajczyk proposed a compromise – a recognition of the Curzon Line in return for the city of Lwów (now Lvov) – he failed to gain the assent of his hard-line colleagues in London. On 24 November, sick at heart, Mikolajczyk resigned. By February, Stalin's nominees had been accepted as Poland's provisional government.

Everything, it seemed, had come full circle. Although Churchill defended the settlement in the House of Commons, a score of Conservative M.P.s – former supporters of Neville Chamberlain – voted against a motion to approve it. "Churchill," noted the diarist, Harold Nicolson, "was as amused as I am that the warmongers of the Munich period have now become the appeasers ... the appeasers have become the warmongers."

While the statesmen conferred in Moscow, and the diplomatic bags grew bulkier by the week, Wing-Commander Roland Beamont, no longer pitted against V-1s, was battling on the Western front.

"Here the targets fight back, you know," Air Vice-Marshal Harry Broadhurst, of the 2nd Tactical Air Force, warned him, and Beamont, for one, was glad that they did. To the old menace of the V-1s had been added the new menace of some 500 V-2s, rockets 46 feet long, weighing more than 13 metric tons: an ordeal that from 8 September onward cost the lives of more than 2,700 Londoners. But against them a Tempest pilot was powerless: Beamont welcomed a target which did "fight back".

"Pleasant scrap with 15–20 Focke-Wulf 190s over town," ran a typical log-book entry, following a low-level patrol over Nijmegen, "Huns tried to dive away. Caught one at 510 m.p.h., and shot him down in flames near Cleve. Much flak."

Ironically, it was to prove his last victory.

Yet only the obstinate streak in his nature prevented Beamont from a return to the comparative tranquillity of civil life: on 10 October had come the chance to return to Hawker's Aircraft Factory at Langley, Buckinghamshire, as No 2 experimental test pilot. But Beamont hesitated. He had done 94 sorties over German-held territory now; it would be satisfying to round off the century.

On 12 October, Beamont, breaking for once his own golden rule, paid the penalty.

Time and again he had cautioned his pilots: "The ground strike policy is a single surprise attack ... there is to be no more than one pass over the target." But that afternoon, travelling west of the railway line between Nijmegen and Bocholt, Beamont and the others spotted an exceptionally long and tempting troop train. It was too good to miss.

"Hello, Corncob aircraft," he rallied them, "Echelon for attack to port, go!"

Already the train was pulling up, in a hissing miasma of steam, tiny ant-figures spilling from its doors to hit the dirt beside the track face down. Raking the train steadily with a glinting shower of tracer, Beamont pulled out from the dive on the far side, watching the Tempests of No 3 Squadron peel off one by one, swooping like switchback railways into the attack. And now he told himself that the train was so very long and so packed with soldiers that a second attack seemed justified.

"Hello, Corncob aircraft," he called, "Anyone out of ammunition orbit five miles south. The rest follow me in again."

Now, in this second attack, small arms fire crackled up at them, but there was no sense of apparent damage. His ammunition exhausted, it was time to pull back for the home base, Volkel airstrip, but now a fatal curiosity overtook him. Just how much damage *had* they done?

For the third time he dived low, skimming the full length of the train, and then, quite unexpectedly, the flak truck opened fire at point-blank range. He felt no impact as the bullet entered his radiator, but his No 2 had seen the danger signs: "Corncob leader, you are streaming smoke."

He was thirty miles from the British lines, and he knew from the outset that there was no hope of reaching base. He held the Tempest in a glide, watching the branches of the tall trees rising to meet him, arm braced hard against his gun-sight, miraculously winging down past the perilous trees, to the sanctuary of a grassy paddock. The Tempest bucketed across it, juddering heavily over a ditch, then slewed to a halt.

Determined to survive, Beamont first fired the aircraft with an incendiary bomb, then headed west toward the setting sun. If he struck the Rhine he could hide up in the woods until the Allies crossed the river. Abruptly he stopped short. A teenage boy, wearing the black shirt and shorts of the Hitler *Jugend*, was shadowing him on a bicycle.

Striking into the woods, stumbling over tree-roots and rough ground, Beamont endeavoured to shake him off. At last, looking back, he felt a glow of relief; the boy had vanished. And he was wearing a gaberdine golfing jacket over his uniform; with luck he might yet pass off as a civilian. He struck off into a lane, trudging steadily.

Then, rounding a bend in the road, he knew it was all up: once more, the teenager on the bicycle, only now accompanied by ten *Wehrmacht* reserve soldiers from an older war, led by a young corporal, and all with guns at the ready.

Beamont raised his arms. The first man to break silence spoke in laborious English. It was a cliché that had echoed many times from the sound track of a cinema, but one that he had never thought to hear: "For you the war is over."

—

Soon after noon on Saturday 14 October, the war was over for another fighting man: *Feldmarschall* Erwin Rommel.

The end had been a long time coming. Back on 1 August, when Rommel, following a low-level strafing by a Spitfire, was still undergoing treatment for a fractured skull in the Luftwaffe hospital at Bernay, *General* Alfred Jodl was noting in his diary:

> 1700 hours. The Führer allowed me to read Kaltenbrunner's report on Oberstleutnant Hofacker's statement regarding conversations with K(luge) and R(ommel) (i.e. on their involvement in the 20 July plot) The Führer is looking for a new C-in-C West. He intends to interrogate R(ommel) when he is fit and then dismiss him without further ado.

In truth, Rommel was guilty of nothing more than keeping his own counsel. Like Kluge, like Guderian, he had sensed that a plot was in the wind — and though no man was witness to his conversation on 9 July with Hofacker, adjutant to the military governor of Paris, he seems always to have rejected assassination. Instead, with or without Hitler's consent, he favoured peace feelers to his "friendly enemy," Montgomery. Yet, aware of a plot, he had kept silent. For Hitler, this was complicity enough.

On 13 October, Rommel learned by telephone that *General* Wilhelm Burgdorf, Hitler's newly-appointed chief adjutant, and *Generalmajor* Ernst Maisel, head of the army personnel branch's legal section, would be calling at his Herrlingen villa between noon and 1 p.m. next day.

Rommel was under no illusions. On the morning of 14 October, during a long tramp in the woods with his son, Manfred, Rommel told him, "Today will decide what is planned for me, whether a People's Court or a new command in the East." "Would you accept such a command?" Manfred asked. Rommel took his son's arm. "My dear boy, our enemy in the East is so terrible that every other consideration has to give way before it... Of course I would go." The generals arrived punctually at noon: Burgdorf, burly and florid, Maisel, shorter, with a beaked nose. Both men, though the souls of courtesy, declined Lucie Rommel's invitation to lunch. It was, they explained, official business. All three retired to Rommel's ground-floor study.

They had no Eastern Command to offer Rommel, only a choice: a People's Court or a poison capsule, to be followed by a state funeral with full honours. (The wreath had already arrived at Ulm railway station, nearby). Though testimonies obtained under Gestapo duress had falsely implicated him, the Desert Fox was too precious to German legend to perish through a garotte of piano wire.

There were brief restrained farewells with Lucie and Manfred. Then, shrugging into his topcoat, firmly clasping his field marshal's baton, Rommel passed from the villa, to climb into the back of Burgdorf's small Opel. The driver, S.S. *Hauptscharführer* Heinrich Doose, let in the clutch and the car cruised 200 yards down the road before pulling up on Burgdorf's orders. Following instructions, Doose and Maisel sauntered slowly down the road.

Five, perhaps ten minutes later, Burgdorf called them back. In the rear seat, Rommel was unconscious, but not yet dead – "slumped down and sobbing," Doose was to recall, "not a death-rattle or groaning but *sobbing*."

Solicitously, the S.S. man helped the Field Marshal to sit bolt upright, as a soldier should. Then, carefully, he replaced Rommel's fallen cap.

–

Just as they had done when the year was young, his reluctant satellites were giving Adolf Hitler nothing but trouble.

Bulgaria had always been an ally unstable as water – the more so since King Michael of Rumania's coup had allowed the Russians to reach the Bulgarian frontier so speedily. For two weeks in August, the Führer learned with disgust, a former speaker of the Bulgarian parliament, Stoicho Moshanov, had been besieging the British Embassy in Ankara, demanding to know the Allied terms for pulling out of the war. Shunted on to Cairo for talks with Allied representatives, Moshanov heard, on 5 September, that a new right-wing government under Konstantin Muraviev had declared war on Germany – at the same time that Russia had declared war on Bulgaria.

Thus for five-and-a-half hours, Bulgaria was in the invidious position of being at war with Russia and Germany simultaneously, before begging Moscow for an armistice – "all very Balkan," sniffed a Foreign Office mandarin. From that time on Bulgaria would become increasingly a Communist fief – "they are of course willing to punish Bulgaria for her many offences, but only in the spirit of a loving parent, quote this hurts me more than it hurts you unquote," as Churchill relayed to Hopkins.

Finland, too, had proved the weakest of reeds in Hitler's long battle against Russia, despite a defiant stand summed up by an old Finnish "magic song": *Just this much they will get from me: what an axe gets from a stone, a stump from slippery ice, or death from an empty room*. The brave words availed nothing. In Moscow, on 19 September, Premier Antti Hackzell submitted tamely to a harsh peace that took Finland out of the Axis camp – but cost her the Karelian Isthmus, the port of Petsamo, and reparations amounting to 300 million American dollars in gold, to be paid within six years. What a later generation would call "Finlandisation" was already in the offing.

With faint-hearted Hungary, just as in March, Hitler's tactics were bold, brutal and initially effective.

Towards the end of September, Admiral Nicholas Horthy had finally taken "the humiliating step of appealing to Moscow," speeding three emissaries to the Russian capital to begin negotiations. On 11 October, a tentative agreement was initialled – but Hitler, who was in on the secret, struck first.

To this end he entrusted the capture of the Citadel, Horthy's power-base, and the complete occupation of Budapest to two S.S. men well-suited to the task: *Obergruppenführer* Erich von dem Bach-Zelewski, who had forced Warsaw to capitulate, and *Sturmbannführer* Otto Skorzeny, Mussolini's liberator. With these tasks accomplished, Horthy was to be deposed and replaced by Ferenc Szálasi, leader of the Nazi-oriented Arrow Cross party, who claimed to receive all inspiration through visions of the Mother of God.

The coup was planned for Sunday 15 October – the same day that Horthy planned a defiant broadcast setting out the armistice terms.

It was a dramatic race against time. Unknown to Horthy, his son, Nicholas, had that morning contracted a rendezvous on the Pest bank of the Danube with men he believed to be Titoist envoys – in reality German undercover agents. Seized by a squad of Skorzeny's men and rolled up in a carpet – a ruse Skorzeny had borrowed from George Bernard Shaw's play *Caesar and Cleopatra* – young Horthy was flown to Vienna and thence to Mauthausen concentration camp.

The Admiral had given a precious hostage to fortune – and he knew it. At noon, when the German Minister in Budapest, *General* Edmund Weesenmayer, arrived at the Citadel, he found Horthy in a towering rage, demanding the release of his son. At 2 p.m., while the men were still wrangling, the armistice announcement was broadcast. At this point, Ambassador Rudolf Rahn, one of Ribbentrop's ablest diplomats, arrived to appeal to Horthy's conscience. "Horthy was crying like a little boy, kept clutching Rahn's hand and offering to call everything off," reported the S.S. commander in Budapest, *Obergruppenführer* Otto Winkelmann. Soon after, a proclamation was broadcast declaring Horthy's announcement null and void.

That same evening, a deal was offered to Horthy: if he would resign, legally transfer power to Szálasi, and leave the country, under Hitler's protection, for Schloss Hirschberg, near Weilheim, then his son would be restored to him. Failing this, at 6 a.m. on 16 October, 25,000 German troops would storm the Citadel.

Given this *fait-accompli*, Horthy gave in. Szálasi took over as "Leader of the Nation," retiring to an estate near Sopron to complete his memoirs, a carbon-copy of Hitler's *Mein Kampf* which became required reading for all newly-wed couples.

Three months later, after the fall of Budapest, the last of Hitler's military satellites changed hands yet again. For the duration, Hungary agreed to put eight divisions at Russia's disposal to fight against Germany – on the eastern front.

―

The fate of Hungary was no longer of pressing concern to Dr Gisella Krausz in Auschwitz. The need to survive had established new priorities, new yardsticks. It had taken a piece of string to shake her from her apathy, to vow to herself that she would never be engulfed in "that swamp of human depravity."

For months on end she had gone barefoot, at the two daily roll-calls and during her hospital duties, for all civilian clothing was stripped as a matter of course from new arrivals – consigned to the warehouse strangely called "Canada," where the deportees' clothing was stored. As her feet grew swollen, pitted with sores, Gisella grew panic-stricken. Suppurating feet were reason enough for *Obersturmführer* Dr Josef Mengele to jerk his thumb to the left: the crematorium. Shoes became a priority – shoes at any price.

The price, in fact, was two days' bread ration, gladly exchanged for a pair of men's shoes, size ten, which a woman working near the crematorium had stolen for her. Beside the benison of the shoes, the hunger pangs meant nothing; now her feet were protected from the mud, from the sharp gravel of the camp's paths, from the hot, shifting ashes yielded up by the dead. But the shoes were so large she was reduced to hobbling. She needed shoe-laces – at best a piece of string.

The thought of this filled her waking hours, until someone in her block mentioned that a Polish workman employed on the latrines had come by a piece of string. At once, snatching up that day's bread ration, Gisella sought him out: a short stocky pock-marked man with staring eyes. Holding out the bread, she begged for string.

The man looked her over very carefully from head to foot. Then, grabbing her by the shoulder, he hissed: "I don't want your bread… you can keep your bread… I will give you a piece of of string, but first I want you…"

For a second Gisella didn't understand. "Please give me a piece of string… my feet are killing me…"

The man was not listening. "Hurry up… hurry up," he growled, and the hands, smeared with human excrement, groped with obscene haste for her vagina. Then suddenly Gisella was running, stumbling in her unwieldy shoes, away from the man, away from the gross indignity, forgetting the shoes, considering only how deeply she had sunk: how high the price of a piece of string had soared.

That night, with her shoes padded out with rags, she saw the string as a turning-point. She was going to remain a human being, to preserve her dignity in the face of every humiliation, every torment.

Instead of sleeping, she began to talk to those around her: of her old life in Marmaros Sziget, about her work, her husband, the books they had read, the music that had stirred them. To her intense gratification, others took up the theme: Dr Olga Schwartz told of her life as a Budapest pediatrician, Dr Ella Lingens of her student days in Vienna. As the nights wore on towards autumn, they recited poetry, recalled the plots of books they had read and treasured, traded recipes from memory – "if you'll give me your Pepper Tokány, tomorrow I'll give you my Rákóczy cheese cakes" – or played the game, "I am a lady" – "What shall I do today? Maybe I'll do some shopping. I haven't had a new dress, a new hat in weeks…"

In time this game had spread from block to block until every woman in Auschwitz was participating. Though the odds were all against them, it had come home to them that it was their duty to fight.

There was much to fight against: the fear of being transferred to the S.S. brothels, where all the inmates were dressed as nuns, the fear of falling sick and being shipped to the diarrhoea room, where the patients strained through twenty motions a day, the fear of typhus, for Mengele had a sure cure for typhus. Once he had nipped an epidemic in the bud by sending 1500 infected Jewesses to the gas-chamber.

Above all, there was the fear of Mengele himself, with his wild eyes and his sharp wolf's teeth and his unholy obsession with eugenics: his curiosity concerning twins was exceeded only by his fascination with dwarfs and hunchbacks. All twins were automatically exempt from the gas-chamber, but if they died they were earmarked for the Pathology Laboratory and instant dissection. Could Mengele stumble on the secret of reproducing untold numbers of "pure" Germans, with German mothers bearing as many twins as possible?

In search of the mystique of "twinhood" Mengele recklessly grafted glands and removed spinal marrows; if the patients died, the answer was more grafts, more spinal surgery. Dwarfs and hunchbacks, though equally an *idée fixe*, did not survive as long, for Mengele's research here had only one object: to demonstrate the degeneracy of the Jews.

Still, by a hair's breadth, Gisella Krausz and those round her kept the horrors at arm's length. "What shall I do today? Go to the hairdresser? Meet my friends at the café? I'm certainly not going to the office…"

8

"You Could Hide An Army In These Goddamned Woods."
16 October–16 December, 1944

He returned as a saviour – and for exactly two years, seven months and three days, this was the way he had planned it. Now, at 10 a.m. on Friday 20 October, he stood on the bridge of the 10,000-ton light cruiser, *Nashville*, proud and erect in freshly pressed khaki, his corn-cob pipe pointed over the glassy green waters of Leyte Gulf, towards Leyte's capital, Tacloban. Around him, as the Higgins boats, fast high stout-bottomed assault craft, churned towards the shore, rode the mightiest fleet (718 ships) ever assembled in the south-west Pacific, General Douglas MacArthur had come back to the Philippines with a panache that was all his own.

It was no clandestine venture. Ahead of him, as if in defiance of Leyte's 30,000 Japanese defenders, had gone leaflets, trinkets, even match-boxes, bearing the legend "I Shall Return". Yet at first resistance was slight: the Japanese, expecting a heavier naval bombardment, had retired inland. Sprinting through the milky surf and dropping flat on the hard coral sand, the first infantrymen, by long habit, lay doggo, clinging like barnacles to the jeeps, only green helmets and faces showing above the froth as the surf boiled through their uniforms. Soon, facing no opposition, they had risen sheepishly and were moving inland. Thinly, from within the palm groves, familiar Japanese *banzai* calls greeted them: "Surrender, all is resistless," and "F.D.R., eat shit." Turning to his Chief of Staff, Lieutenant-General Richard Sutherland, MacArthur, slapping him jubilantly on the back, exclaimed, "As Ripley says, believe it or not, we're here."

In the early afternoon came a moment for history. Sitting bolt upright in the stern of the *Nashville*'s landing barge, Macarthur was fifty yards from the shore when it grounded in shallow water. (He had expected to tie up at a pier, but a crotchety hard-pressed naval beachmaster had growled, "Let 'em walk."). Angrily descending to his midriff in the surf, MacArthur had splashed forty wet strides to the beach, destroying his immaculate creases. Snapped by a photographer, he immediately sensed the dramatic impact; next day, for the benefit of the press, he waded ashore all over again, for a shot that became immortal.

At the revelation that MacArthur could not walk on the water, some expressed irreverent surprise.

"They are waiting for me up there," MacArthur had proclaimed on Morati, 300 miles from the Philippines. "It has been a long time." But it would be longer still – April 1945 – before all pockets of Japanese resistance had been wiped out on Leyte. Despite a decisive defeat, handed their fleet in the naval battle of Leyte Gulf, when Admiral Takeo Kurita's attempt to destroy MacArthur's amphibious shipping cost Japan more than 300,000 tons of combat ships, heavy rains and bitter resistance by 45,000 Japanese reinforcements, slowed MacArthur's progress to a crawl.

"Marvellous country to raise rice," growled MacArthur's chief engineer, Brigadier-General Leif Sverdrup, for daily, under sodden skies which yielded 24 inches of rainfall in 30 days, the war was bogging down in a porridge of mud. Pilots like Captain John A. Tully, of the 475th Fighter Group, had to be towed from the dispersal area, to take off at full throttle without even a magneto check; on touching down, with a splash that drenched both plane and pilot, they were again towed clear of the runway.

Yet the Battle of Leyte Gulf raised disturbing implications for many Japanese, among them Cadet Pilot Ryuji Nagatsuka – for at least two dozen planes had been lost through their pilots' own volition.

Before Saipan had even fallen, Nagatsuka and his entire intake had left Kanumaruhara airfield for Mibu, 50 miles north of Tokyo, to begin training in deadly earnest, on the yellow Akatonbos.

The sense of dedication there grew daily more insistent. "Your hearts must be as pure as the sky," Lieutenant Komorizono, Commander of the 1st Squad, told them, "When you're piloting a plane, the least impurity will fester and lead you to your death. Forget your family, your girl friend, your studies... nothing is more futile than to get yourself killed during a training flight."

From that day on, they flew in monotonous circles over the airfield: one tour of seven minutes, five tours each day. With six months training still to go, none of them had thus far flown solo, and the thought nagged them daily: would they be ready in time to confront the B-29s? With Saipan fallen, raids on Tokyo were now a foregone conclusion.

As August dawned, Nagatsuka, with nine hours dual control flying to his credit, was permitted his first solo flight.

All went well until the touchdown. Climbing to 750 feet, Nagatsuka felt his spirits soaring, watching the faint diaphanous clouds drifting towards the far-off mountains. Steering his plane into the glide path, he checked his angle of descent, approaching the tarmac at the lowest possible speed: thirty feet, fifteen feet. The touch-down must be made at three points, he reminded himself, both wheels of the undercarriage and the tail wheel. He pulled gently on the stick and the plane rolled smoothly down the runway.

Proudly, he reported to Lieutenant Komorizono: "Cadet Pilot Nagatsuka. Overhead circling flight completed. All in order!"

"No!" Komorizono shouted at him. "The tip of your wing was over the dividing line between the take-off area and the landing area! If there had been a plane taking off just then you would have collided. A disastrous fault!".

Then, lashing out with his fist, he sent Nagatsuka spinning to the floor. As the young cadet sprang to his feet, Komorizono was once again adjusting his binoculars, alert for other infringements of duty. "Do you understand?" he said coolly. "Good! You may dismiss."

That set the pace for all that was to follow. "We had forgotten how to smile," Nagatsuka recalled later. "There was no time." From 4:30 a.m., reveille, to 9 p.m. curfew, every minute of free time was devoted to polishing flying boots, cleaning goggles, burnishing swords. All day long, there was training in aerobatics: looping the loop, inverted flights, the Immelmann roll, the horizontal roll, the slow barrel.

Then late that autumn, as formation flying began, came two disturbing items of news. For ten days, all flight training was suspended: fuel supplies, an early symptom of Japan's collapsing economy, were almost exhausted. From then on, normal aircraft fuel was out; instead the "beetles," as ground crews were called, used "A-Go" fuel – petrol mixed with alcohol – whose flash-point was dangerously low.

But it was the Battle of Leyte Gulf and a new phenomenon called the *Kamikaze*[27] (divine wind) that caused Nagatsuka to think furiously.

On 18 October, two days before MacArthur's Leyte landing, Vice-Admiral Kimpei Teraoka, in Manila, on the eve of turning over command of the First Air Fleet to Vice-Admiral Takijiro Onishi, noted in his diary the onset of a new kind of warfare:

> "Time is against us. Available aeroplanes are limited in number. We are forced to take the most effective method to fight in this operation. The time has arrived for consideration of Admiral Onishi's crash dive tactics."

Thus, by dawn on 20 October, at Mabalacat airfield, Central Luzon, the first 24 volunteers of the Special Attack Corps, under Lieutenant Yukio Seki, had already assembled. Five days later, the attack began: while American sailors watched with appalled fascination, a Zero fighter dived with guns blazing at the carrier, *Santee*, striking the forward end of her flight deck, blasting a hole 15 feet wide by 30 feet long. Another, diving for the *St. Lo*, burst through the flight deck to hose the hangar deck below with flaming gasoline, exploding seven torpedoes, blasting the elevators and entire aeroplanes high into the air. A third *Kamikaze* struck the *Kalinin Bay*, severely damaging the flight deck.

Other planes, narrowly missing their target, crashed into the sea — but the shape of the battle to come was clear from that day on.

It was a concept with which Nagatsuka was totally at variance. When one of his intake, Cadet Pilot Furukawa spoke warmly of Petty Officer Nonaka, who had crashed his Toryu fighter into a B-29 over Leyte, Nagatsuka was censorious.

"That's the very best method to bring down these damned planes." Furukawa insisted. "All we have to do is follow his example!"

"Nonaka should have found some other means of destroying the bomber," Nagatsuka disagreed. "Wasn't he carried away by his impetuosity?"

"Rubbish! He fulfilled his duty," Furukawa snapped back.

But as yet it was a philosophy Nagatsuka could not bring himself to embrace. In his heart he could not believe that Japan's plight was so desperate. "If so, his thinking was gravely mistaken," he replied sombrely. "Death leads nowhere!"

By late 1944, the war against Japan could make or break. In the southwest Pacific, Douglas MacArthur's star was in the ascendant. From China, as testimony to Roosevelt's bankrupt policy in that theatre, "Vinegar Joe" Stilwell was going home.

In a sense, Stilwell had been his own worst enemy: crammed with undying grievances against "frogs," "limeys," "niggers," "wops" and "huns," he was in antagonism with all the world. Stilwell, like Anthony Trollope's Mr Crawley, "could tell the truth, though that should ruin him." Early on 18 September, Stilwell told it to Generalissimo Chiang-kai-shek and thereafter all lay in ruins.

From Quebec, on 16 September, a hard-hitting 600-word telegram from Roosevelt, prompted by Chiang's threat to withdraw his forces across the Salween River and protect the important supply base of Kunming, had been routed to the Chinese leader.

In part it read:

> "I have urged time and again in recent months that you take drastic action to resist the disaster which is moving closer to China and to you. Now, when you have not yet placed General Stilwell in command of all forces in China we are faced with the loss of a critical area in east China with possible catastrophic consequences ... I am certain that the only thing you can now do to prevent the Jap from achieving his objective in China is to reinforce your Salween armies immediately and press this offensive, while at once placing General Stilwell in unrestricted command of all your forces..."

A tactful man might have softened the wording, but Stilwell was far from being that. In typically crude language he recorded how he had "handed this bundle of paprika to the Peanut (Chiang) and sank back with a sigh. The harpoon hit the little bugger right in the solar-plexus and went right through him."

Chiang was now in a quandary. If Roosevelt foisted Stilwell on him against his will he might do likewise in the matter of Chiang's true enemies, the Communists – whom Stilwell had already suggested should fight the Japanese with American arms and ammunition. His one problem now was to get rid of Stilwell without risking the cessation of lend-lease supplies with which to fight the Communists.

On 25 September, the Generalissimo called Roosevelt's bluff and the President duly fell for it. His demand – that Stilwell should summarily be stripped of his three-fold command[28] and recalled to the United States – met with no speedy answer, but on 11 October, Major-General Patrick J. Hurley, a loud-mouthed reactionary Oklahoma lawyer, soon to be U.S. Ambassador to China, put in his oar: "If you sustain Stilwell in this controversy, you will lose Chiang-kai-shek and possibly you will lose China with him."

Caught in the swirling cross-currents of global politics, Stilwell – who described himself as "a fugitive from a Chiang gang" – had been washed off his feet. On 18 October Roosevelt issued orders for his recall. Ten days later, his successor, Major-General Albert C. Wedemeyer, reported the China situation as "unfavourable but not irretrievable."

But what purpose was the United States now serving in China? To help win the fight against Japan? To create a strong China? To prop up Chiang-kai-shek? As Roosevelt was soon to admit to Churchill:

"We can do very little to prepare China to conduct a worthwhile defence." Secretary of War Stimson saw the Communists as "the only live body of military men there is in China at the moment."

But to the end Roosevelt continued to dream an impossible dream: a fusion between Chiang's armies and what he always styled the "so-called Communists". This dream was abetted by the ebullient Hurley, a figure of fun to both Nationlists and Communists alike: one faction dubbing him "The Second Big Wind," the other "Little Whiskers". Proud of legal work he had once undertaken for the Choctaw Indian tribe, he was given to piercing tribal war-whoops; it was thus, descending from his aeroplane on a visit to Communist headquarters at Yenan, that he greeted the dignified Mao-tse-tung and Chou-en-lai.

Though the British Ambassador, Sir Horace Seymour, more realistically, foresaw imminent civil war, Hurley's advice was both disastrous and predictable: no arms should be promised to any forces of whom Chiang did not approve, and there should be no Stilwell-like attempt to pressurise the Generalissimo. But all his efforts to reconcile Chiang – whom he called "Mr Shek" – and Mao – who in Hurley's pronunciation was "Moose dung" – were in vain. Convinced that his five-point plan for the unification of China would be acceptable to Chiang he flew back to Kuomintang headquarters in Chungking with high hopes; the Communists had accepted all his tenets and were indeed, as Stalin termed them, "radish Communists – red outside and white inside".

Chiang and his entourage greeted the document with barely-concealed derision. "The Communists have sold you a bill of goods," the Generalissimo's brother-in-law T. V. Soong, told Hurley. "Never will the Nationalist Government grant the Communist request." The coalition government Hurley proposed would soon be dominated by the Communists; the Chinese would see coalition as a total defeat for the Kuomintang.

It was scant consolation to Roosevelt that his insistence on treating Chiang as an ally, as a chief of state, as one of the Big Four, had been halfway right. China would indeed emerge as a great power, but not the China of the President's dreams.

-

This was the shape of a soldier's life as winter closed in on the West Wall. Days when all a man's hopes centred on sustaining the "million-dollar wound" – a clean hole in an arm or a leg that would heal but would put you out for a long time. Days when the world's vista shrank to little groups of wooden-faced men, carrying their rifles at the high port: reluctant heroes, moving ten paces apart. Nights rendered restless by the screech and hammer of Spandaus, by sudden bursts of machine-gun fire, ripples on a great pool of silence.

It was not a world much concerned with strategy: with single thrust or broad front. It lived by its own definitions; a battlefield shorthand. A veteran was a man who had lived a week in combat and survived. A rest area was anywhere back of the second hedgerow from the front line. To be driven back 150 yards equalled six houses, hard-won in street fighting, then lost.

All its fears were private ones, tacitly acknowledged, never discussed: the fear of the "Bouncing Betty," a three-pronged mine that leaped from the ground to explode against the genitals, the fear of finding darns in freshly-laundered uniforms, signifying a bullet hole and thus bad luck. The fear of any sight or sound evoking a gentler way of life: a British corporal in an Ypres billet, sobbing his heart out because a shining lavatory pan reminded him of home. That was the sure way to "C.E.," which stood for "Combat Exhaustion," otherwise "psychoneurosis".

Whatever the battle front, each army, men noted, carried its own distinctive smell. Hodges' and Patton's men bore with them the smell of industrial America: clouds of carbon monoxide, burnt gunpowder, Spam, baked beans and chewing gum. The British brought with them the smell of overcooked cabbage, boiled ham and milky tea from their field-kitchens; the French the smell of bistros, rough red wine and Gauloise cigarettes. Moving west, the Russians carried the smell of fresh black bread, newly threshed-corn and the earthy tang of the farmyard. The Germans seemed to smell of "sweat, sauerkraut and impending death."

In November, in the Hürtgen Forest, the close-ranked firs towered 100 feet high, and even the brightness of noon was muted to an eerie twilight, filtering onto spongy brown pine needles and rotting logs: a fathomless sea of darkness. The battle raged for ten weeks: the forest changed hands eighteen times, the forest village of Vossenack twenty-eight times.

Stolberg was a blustering maelstrom of sound, where gin and grapefruit juice kept the medics on their feet; at the 3rd Battalion Aid Station, 415th Infantry, a boy with a Red Cross brassard slumped on a chair, babbling, "Noise, too much noise, all noise, too much noise." In Geilenkirchen, the only noise was of the rain, cold non-stop rain, drumming pitilessly against the sides of tanks and vehicles.

Walcheren Island was a lonely battle, where a howling wind brought the endless gossip of machine-guns, a land of sheep grazing the rich black polder land, and Dutch peasant women in their white winged lace bonnets, spreading salvaged onions to dry. It was a campaign the war correspondents relished, for when night fell a man could take a street-car back from the front to Antwerp's Century Hotel for dinner served by waiters in white tie and tails. Not so the Regina Rifles of Canada, who could not leave their Walcheren slit trenches to eat: rations were heated in a central dugout then lobbed into space like grenades, so that one isolated rifleman was heard to yell: "Why the hell do I keep getting marmalade?"

Lastly there was Aachen, the first pitched battle in which Lieutenant-Colonel Saul K. Padover had participated, however briefly.

Padover came late to the battle because at Homburg Barracks, a camp for evacuated German civilians half way between Eupen and Aachen, he and the team had "struck pay-dirt". Day after day they evaluated for the first time citizens who all too soon would become stereotypes: Wilhelm Geller, a labourer in a garment factory, who professed himself "*ein kleiner Mann* – don't think I'm a Nazi!" Had he ever done anything against them? Padover wanted to know. "We have a saying that with the wolves one must howl," was Geller's reply.

There was Käthe Raab, a bank official's daughter; at 19, she had never heard of the German Federal Republic. "But there was unemployment and nothing to eat and then came the Führer who gave them work and food." Next, Adolf Gladding, fifteen, a mechanic's apprentice, bitterly ashamed of a Communist father. When, he asked Padover, would the United States join Germany to fight against Russia?

Nothing in any of these interviews, Padover thought, suggested a conviction that would contest Aachen to the death – yet equally nothing indicated a willingness to accept collective responsibility for an Aachen.

From the Forward Observer Post of a chemical mortar company, codenamed Camel Red, sited in the attic of a palatial mansion on the outskirts, Padover and Major Sam Gittler, a colleague, saw the end of Aachen. By then the ancient city of Charlemagne, which the French had known as Aix-la-Chapelle, was "a sterile sea of rubble," for the battle had raged for six weeks with unparalleled ferocity. Caught in a classic bear-hug by the two arms of Hodges' First U.S. Army, the fortress commander, *Generalleutnant Graf* Gerhard von Schwerin, had first contemplated only passive resistance, burdened as he was by the presence of 40,000 civilians. Then Hitler, on 14 September, had promoted Aachen to "fortress" status.

What the Führer sought now was the first of many Stalingrads – "there will be twelve other 'Aachens' on German soil," Stimson had warned – for the city was not only an age-old spa but a modern textile and coalmining centre, the route to major industrial cities like Essen, Dortmund and Düsseldorf.

In the attic, crouched beside a corporal with a brown leather-encased field-telephone, Padover silently accepted the loan of a pair of field-glasses and "pulled the dead city into the concentrated focus of startling proximity. One could almost reach out and touch it". As night fell, it became a city "as dead as yesterday," haloed by a dull red mist which shimmered as new fires were added to the old. At 12:05 a.m. on 21 October, the last defender of Aachen, *Oberst* Gehard Wilck, gave up.

Later, when his driver, Private Joe Dorferlein, inched the jeep through the city, beneath a sea of white fluttering flags, Padover was conscious of nothing so much as silence, "a silence that is louder than a scream, an utter silence that shrieks violent death."

Across the Belgian border, the headlines of *La Nation* wrote the epitaph of Aachen: "Aix-la-Chapelle n'existe plus." An elderly woman, trudging to the safety of a U.S. refugee camp, saw the devastation as all quite pointless: "If only the English had given in in 1940 none of this need have happened."

-

On 26 September, as a positive response to the attrition of Aachen, Adolf Hitler made it official: there were no more German civilians.

Just as Stalin had mobilised the factory workers of Moscow and Leningrad in 1941, Hitler, following a suggestion by *Generaloberst* Guderian, now decreed the formation of a *Volkssturm*, a people's army, involving every able-bodied man between 16 and 60, to battle for every yard of German soil. No uniforms were available – the conscripts were distinguished by red armbands and mostly equipped with hunting-rifles – but as a symbol the *Volkssturm* did give fresh scope to Göbbels and his slogan writers: "Hard time, hard hearts!" "Save our women and children from the Red beasts!"

Not all rallied to the cause. In sceptical pragmatic Berlin, doctors came near to writer's cramp, faking electric cardiograms, "making invalids by affidavit"; drugstores were besieged for Atebrin, an anti-malaria drug whose abuse turned the malingerer a bright jaundiced yellow. But here the Nazi Party leaders, whose writ ran larger than the local Army commander, held a trump card: in Berlin, those who did not register were threatened with the non-renewal of their ration cards.

On Wednesday 18 October – chosen as the anniversary of the 1813 Battle of Leipzig – Himmler, announcing the formation of "the last and most dangerous secret weapon," conjured up visions of "death-defying volunteers" who would "like werewolves, injure the enemy and cut his lifelines". "A nation rises up, the storm breaks loose!" was the vaunted slogan, as the inductees took the oath with hands placed upon the "blood banner," for this was in the cherished traditions of Nazism: a classless band of fighting men.

Yet as Saul Padover might have predicted this desperate attempt to rally the nation to a last-ditch onslaught had come too late. The *Volkssturm*, a rag-bag militia at best, could never alter the course of the war now. An American company commander with the 4th Armoured Division, recalled them with something of admiration and something akin to pity: "old men … who had old rifles and hearts full of hate."

—

The night of Monday 4 December was bitter. A chill wind scoured the wide gritty plains of Strasbourg's Place de la Gare. From the far side of the Rhine, artillery rumbled and flickered, like a slowly-wakening volcano. Though Strasbourg had fallen to Patton's Third Army on 15 November, this was still a front-line city.

In an abandoned house near the city centre, two men were working late, following an improvised dinner of cold K-rations. The room was cloaked in shadows, lit by the hesitant flicker of candles and the glow of a compressed gas lamp. At a table in its centre, a group of sleepy GIs had settled to a game of cards. The two sprawled in easy chairs at the side, intently scanning files.

Although ostensibly civilians, both men, as part of a U.S. military mission, wore battledress with an unique insignia – an alpha sign in white, transfixed by red forked lightning. The lightning symbolised atomic power, for both Dr Samuel A Goudsmidt, a nuclear physicist from the Massachussetts Institute of Technology, and his colleague, Fred Wardenburg, were atomic spies.

Their mission had been set up in November 1943, under Colonel Boris Pash, described as a "Zorro in uniform," a onetime athletics teacher at Hollywood High School, whose sole claim to fame was discovering Lana Turner at a soda-fountain. But since August 1944, when Pash's unit, code-named "Alsos," had moved into Paris, to meet up with Frédéric Joliot-Curie, its personnel had been in search of a new kind of discovery: German atomic scientists. Now, after three months of promises and false starts, they were closer than they had ever been.

At three sites scattered across the United States – Oak Ridge, Tennessee, Hanford, in the state of Washington and Los Alamos, New Mexico – physicists and technicians of many nations had, since October 1942, been involved in a $2 billion project which might or might not work: the creation of an atom bomb. Now, in November 1944, the question was: how far were the Germans ahead of the Allies in this field?

Chance had favoured Goudsmidt's quest. On entering Strasbourg, the swashbuckling Pash had promptly interned seven physicists and chemists from the University, among them Dr Rudolf Fleischmann, a Heidelberg physicist who had sought to separate uranium isotopes by gaseous and thermal diffusion. Fleischmann and the others had refused to co-operate – but Carl-Friedrich von Weizsäcker, Strasbourg's Professor of Theoretical Physics, had fled, leaving many files behind. His office door had yielded to an axe – and Goudsmidt was now studying the fruits of his labours.

Almost from the beginning, the picture seemed complete. There was a postcard from Professor Walther Bothe in Heidelberg, lamenting slow progress with the production of large uranium plate. There was draft correspondence between Weizsäcker and Dr Werner Heisenberg, a Nobel Prize-winner, on the long delay of the latter's uranium pile. Evidence in plenty showed that far from being ahead of the Allies, the Germans were at least two years behind. They had no factories for the production of Uranium 235 or Plutonium 239, necessary for chain-reaction in the bomb.

Goudsmidt and Wardenburg looked at one another then, and almost as one let out a triumphant whoop.

"Drawn the lucky number, doc?" a sleepy soldier mumbled from the card table.

"Looks like it," Goudsmidt called back in barely restrained excitement. "We shall soon win the war now."

—

At 6:30 p.m. on 12 December, gathering with the Chiefs of Staff in Churchill's Map Room, in the Annexe below London's Whitehall, Eisenhower felt the same. As the Supreme Commander saw it, a buoyant future divided into two main phases: Phase One, opening with an operation to straighten the right flank of Montgomery's 21st

Army Group. Following this, Bradley would extend his left flank to Montgomery's south, releasing four British divisions for an offensive in the north. Come January, Montgomery and Bradley would launch major attacks for the clearance of the left bank of the Rhine below Bonn. At the same time, Patton would strike north-east towards Mainz, ready to cross the Rhine by the spring.

Most German divisions were weak either in armour or in personnel, Eisenhower summed up, and a large proportion were badly trained. The army opposite Patton, he thought, was on the verge of cracking.

On that same day in a bunker at Ziegenberg, near Giessen, Hitler, like an ageing matinée idol undertaking one more "farewell performance," was holding his last great war council. To the assembled generals the legacy of 20 July was manifest in more ways than one: not only were they compelled to leave their briefcases and revolvers in an antechamber, but the Führer confronting them was "a stooped figure with a pale puffy face ... hunched in his chair, his hands trembling, his left arm helplessly twitching". All through the meeting, S.S. guards, burpguns at the ready, maintained a cold-eyed scrutiny: as *Generalmajor* Hans Waldenburg, of 116 Panzer Division later recalled, "it was a very uncomfortable feeling ... not daring to reach into a pocket for a handkerchief for fear of being shot."

Yet the old fervour which had sustained Hitler ever since 16 September, was nowhere lacking. "The coalition between the ultra-capitalists and the ultra-Marxists is breaking up," he harangued them. "Even now they are at loggerheads ... their antagonism will grow stronger from hour to hour. If we can now deliver a few more blows this artificially bolstered common front may suddenly collapse with a gigantic clap of thunder..."

It was a bold yet carefully calculated gamble. Three armies, the Fifth, Sixth and Seventh Panzer – some twenty-eight divisions in all – were to strike through the Ardennes Forest along a 50-mile "ghost front," heading from Antwerp, Brussels and the Givet-Luxembourg line. And though Von Rundstedt, now restored as C-in-C West, had scoffed "Antwerp! If we reach the Meuse we should go down on our knees and thank God!" Hitler had brooked no opposition.

For three months now, his generals had tried vainly to convince him: even if Antwerp were reached, how was it possible to hold on to the ground covered by the advance? By contrast, they favoured a "partial solution," the recapture of Aachen, with the possibility of destroying up to fifteen American divisions, a quarter of the United States forces in Europe. Hitler was unconvinced. Von Rundstedt's final plan was scored with the Führer's handwritten *diktat*: "Not to be altered *in any detail*," and like a zealous quartermaster, Hitler had overseen every detail of the great offensive: everything from the infantryman's winter boots and blankets to the marshalling of formidable Jagd-Tiger tanks with 128 mm guns.

The clues were not lacking – yet were oddly ambiguous. Early in December, Ultra intercepts at Bletchley Park had reported some 200 trains unloading in the Eifel and Saar districts, with a further 40 destined for Alsace: all 6th Panzer Army formations were enjoined to observe strict punctuality lest the prescribed rail time-table went awry. For those same units, Army Group B was demanding adequate air cover – and from 10 December on, all S.S. units were observing wireless silence. Yet equally the Allies could deduce that Von Rundstedt was prudently preparing for the next Allied attack.

In fact, Hitler's code-name for the advance preparations – *Herbstnebel* (Autumn Mist) had been well chosen, for, unnoticed, 250,000 men, 900 guns, 970 tanks were being assembled on the 50-mile front between Monschau and Echternach.

Two men did have qualms, but these were brushed aside: both Colonel B. A. "Monk" Dickson, head of intelligence for U.S. First Army and Brigadier E. T. "Bill" Williams, of the British 21st Army Group were wary. "The enemy is capable of a concentrated attack with air, armour, infantry and secret weapons at a selected focal point at a time of its own choosing," Dickson reported on 7 December – but Bradley, in his Luxembourg headquarters, felt that any such attack would be in no great strength. "If the other fellow would only hit us now," summed up Bradley's gung-ho approach.

Few others had forebodings. At 10 p.m. on the night of Friday 15 December, the American troops at Echternach, Luxembourg, the southern anchor of the Ardennes front, preparing for bed in yellow patrician houses with dormer windows and mansard roofs, saw no cause for alarm; by 10:30 p.m. most were asleep. The entire front was held by six divisions – three of them grass-green, three of them suffering from battle fatigue. Echternach itself was held by a single company of riflemen.

In the historic border town of Monschau, the northern end of the front, the few cavalrymen guarding the town had also retired early in thick feather beds: ahead lay the coldest Christmas Europe had known for 54 years. Nowhere did the GIs feel safer than in Monschau: rumour had it that the young Hitler had cycled through its cobbled streets and on becoming Führer had ordered that the entire town be preserved as a museum.

To the passengers of a lone American military jeep, travelling the main highway between Liège, Belgium, and Sedan, France, the sound of their engines in the frosty Ardennes night, dislodging shifting veils of snow, did strike an eerie note. "You know, Corporal," Sergeant Donald Brownlow told his driver, "you could hide an army in these goddamned woods and no bastard would ever know it."

It was a prophecy swiftly fulfilled. Soon after 4 a.m. on 16 December, in his forward command post at Waxburg, *General der Panzertruppe* Hasso von Manteuffel, commanding Fifth Panzer Army, was well-pleased with the last-minute weather reports. This would be a dawn without sun; a rolling fog would make the element of surprise greater than planned. Now the diminutive (5ft 2ins) Manteuffel, his peaked hat cocked to one side, addressed his massed troops: "We begin the attack! The heavily encircled homeland and our comrades at the front expect that we do our duty. Forward! Leap to the march!"

Along 50 miles of front, surprise was total. In Lanzerath, Lieutenant Lyle Bouck, 99th Divisional Intelligence, watched in horror as "the whole horizon erupted": with his platoon he hit the bottom of a foxhole just in time. In St Vith, as the first 16-inch salvoes landed, panic-stricken scantily-clad civilians, clutching their children, fled for their cellars. A jeep bounded down the cobbled Haupstrasse, heading for the schoolhouse headquarters of Major-General Alan Jones, commanding the green 106th Infantry Division, the "Golden Lions". Jones was worried, and with reason; like most of his raw GIs he had never yet fired a shot at an enemy. The lack of training proved fatal: of 16,000 "Golden Lions" who moved into the forests, only 4000 returned.

From hundreds of cannon (including 14-inch railroad guns) launching platforms and mortars a storm of shell and rocket fire burst upon the American lines, wrecking telephone communications from one end of the sector to the other. Flames seared through the splintered trees, bathing the snow-bound woods in leaping light. Closely in their wake came searchlights, a drenching blue-white glow through which ghostly figures seemed to stumble. By degrees the wraiths grew substantial: hundreds and hundreds of white-clad bucket-helmeted German soldiers, advancing with ominous steadiness, twelve and fourteen abreast. Behind them lumbered 60-ton tanks, their tracks debauching the fine powdered snow to black icy slush.

Already some American units had been cut off and surrounded. Others were fighting desperate rearguard actions. Many were in headlong flight, clogging the narrow winding roads, their vehicles bumper to bumper. Along and behind a crumbling front all was confusion.

In Paris, an icy rain washed the leafless trees: to Lieutenant-General Omar Bradley, leaving the Ritz Hotel for a 2 p.m. conference at Eisenhower's Versailles headquarters "the city looked cold and cramped under its lifeless chimneys". More chilling still was the news that arrived in mid-afternoon, brought by the deputy of Major-General Kenneth Strong, Eisenhower's British Intelligence chief: "This morning the enemy attacked at five separate points across the First Army sector."

At first Bradley was inclined to dismiss it as a spoiling attack; the Germans were merely buying time, forcing the Allies to pull Patton's Third Army out of the Saar region.

Eisenhower objected. "This is no local attack, Brad. It isn't logical for the Germans to launch a local attack at our weakest point."

"If it isn't a local attack, what kind of an attack is it?" Bradley countered.

Eisenhower was resolute. "That remains to be seen. But I don't think we can afford to sit on our hands till we've found out."

It was Lieutenant-General Carl "Tooey" Spaatz, the wry freckled Pennsylvania Dutchman commanding the U.S. Strategic Air Forces in Europe, who spotlit the stumbling-block that lay ahead.

Mindful of the fog blanketing the Ardennes front, Spaatz opined: "If the Germans are going to put on a counterattack, now is the time for them to do it ... I don't think we'll be able to put a plane in the air for three days."

9

"No Game Is Lost Until The Final Whistle"
17 December, 1944–19 February, 1945

In Spa, Belgium, most famous of all world health resorts, the curfew bell was tolling, a harbinger of ill tidings for the first time in months: henceforth all civilians must remain behind closed doors. Spa was once again a front-line town.

No man was more taken by surprise than Lieutenant-Colonel Saul Padover. For weeks now he had almost forgotten there was a war on; absorbed in the interrogation of fugitive Germans at Eupen, near Aachen, his sole knowledge of the battle-front was from out-of-date copies of *Stars and Stripes*. On 18 December, he was visiting Spa purely by chance, to look up colleagues at First Army Psychological Warfare Headquarters.

In the Headquarters War Room, a grim faced intelligence officer, silently studying a wall-sized map of the front, seemed almost as if in shock. "They're still advancing," he muttered, as if to himself, "still advancing." Who was advancing? Padover wanted to know. Hodges? Patton?

The explosive answer came as a shock: "Rundstedt!"

Yet beyond this basic fact, the man knew nothing. How many divisions did Rundstedt have? Where were they – and where were they heading? The news had scarcely penetrated when Lieutenant Salvatori, head of the P.W.D. Unit, arrived with "a face like Job".

"Generals and Colonels," he said dryly, "are stumbling over each other like chickens with their necks cut off." Almost casually, Salvatori added: "We must begin to pack. The Germans are somewhere outside of this town."

"Retreat?" It was a word that Padover, at this stage of the war, had not thought to hear.

Salvatori nodded. "They are pushing ahead somewhere between Malmedy and Monschau. I shouldn't think your town of Eupen would be a safe place for very long."

Back at Eupen, Padover's first impression was reassuring: American tanks and tank destroyers were roaring through the streets so precipitately that windows were rattling and cobblestones shaking loose. A closer look and his spirits sank: the armour travelling at such break-neck speed was marked not "I A" but "I X A," going not east towards Malmedy but south towards Luxembourg. Lieutenant-General William Simpson's Ninth Army, readied for an offensive out of Holland was now speeding into Belgium to rescue Hodges' First Army before Rundstedt cut it in two.

Around noon next day, a company of combat troops began digging foxholes and setting up machine-gun posts in the gardens around Padover's office. "What the hell you guys doing here if you aren't fighting?" an officer asked Padover and his colleague, Major Paul Sweet. "This is the front line."

Hastily packing their duffel bags, Padover and Sweet reached a decision: they would head for Paris, via Luxembourg, and arrive in time for Christmas. Their route lay through ghostly Aachen, to Heerlen, in Holland, thence via Liège, the Meuse and the Ardennes. Here their troubles began. Fog lay like a folded shroud over the wooded hills and rocky fields of south-eastern Belgium, and out of this fog loomed trigger-tense sentries, their guns pointed purposefully at the stomachs of the jeep's passengers.

Identification papers and dog-tag checks were only a beginning. The sentries asked questions that only an American would know how to answer.

"Where you from?"

"Detroit."

"What state is that in?"

"Michigan."

"What's the main street in Detroit?"

"Woodward Avenue."

"Where did you skate in Detroit?"

"In the Arena."

"Where's that?"

"On Grand River Avenue, near Grand Boulevard."

"Okay."

All along the "Ghost Front" the same bewildering questions were posed: Who won the World Series last year? What is Babe Ruth's first name? What is South Bend famous for? Who is Micky Mouse's girl friend?

Soon enough, Padover knew why: a hand-picked force of volunteers under the scar-faced *Obersturmführer* Otto Skorzeny, known as Armoured Brigade 150, had infiltrated the American lines dressed as GIs, to misdirect reserves, sever telephone lines and generally spread moral chaos. To Skorzeny himself, forced by Hitler to oversee the operation by radio from 6th Panzer Army HQ at Schmittheim, the whole affair was a sorry farrago: for the 300 men selected he had only two serviceable Sherman tanks, a dozen camouflaged Panthers and four U.S. scout cars. Only 50 per cent had U.S. rifles and uniforms were woefully lacking.

Yet as a crippling blow to American morale in those first days, Operation Greif (Grasp) was an unwonted success. Even at Versailles, a rumour that a Skorzeny column was converging on Paris's Café de la Paix with a view to assassinating Eisenhower kept the Supreme Commander unwillingly confined to quarters for days – until "Ike," rebelling, stormed from his office declaring: "Hell's fire, I'm going out for a walk. If anyone wants to shoot me he can go right ahead."

One man was early determined to restore order from this chaos. At No. 10, rue Auxerre, Nancy, Lieutenant-General George S. Patton had at first bitterly resented Bradley's commandeering his 10th Armoured Division to serve with Major-General Troy Middleton's VIII Corps up north. The 10th Armoured had been a vital link in a break-through Patton had planned at Saarlautern on 19 December. But now before any orders were received, Patton saw his troops might have a vital role to play in what became known as the Battle of the Bulge – after the dent inflicted in Hodges' First Army line. Late on 16 December, he told his staff: "I want you, gentlemen, to start making plans for pulling the Third Army out of its eastward attack, change the direction ninety degrees, moving to Luxembourg and attacking north."

It was a major masterpiece of logistics. Within five days, Patton's transportation officer, Colonel "Speed" Perry, standing before a map day and night and working mostly from memory, had assigned new roles to 133,178 motor vehicles, moving combat and supply units more than 1.6 million miles. Colonel Walter J. Muller's G-4 set up scores of new depots and dumps, shifting 62,000 tons of supplies in exactly 120 hours. Using 20,000 miles of field wire, Colonel Elton F. Hammond's signalmen set up a whole new communications network.

Pointing to the Bulge piercing the thin blue lines on the war map, Patton exulted to Bradley, "Brad, this time the Kraut's stuck his head in a meat-grinder." Then, with a twist of his wrist, he added: "And this time I've got hold of the handle."

Thus, at 11 a.m. on 19 December, in the barren boardroom of a French barracks at Verdun, Patton was in euphoric mood. "There will be only cheerful faces at this conference table," Eisenhower greeted his senior commanders, though as Patton's aide, Colonel Charles Codman noted, "I have seldom seen longer faces." Almost at once it was Patton's turn.

"George," Eisenhower ordered, "I want you to go to Luxembourg and take charge of the battle, making a strong counter-attack with at least six divisions."

Patton, with only three divisions immediately available, merely answered, "Yes, sir."

"When can you start?" Eisenhower asked.

Patton was seraphic. "As soon as you are through with me."

Eisenhower was taken aback. "What do you mean?" he asked and the others shifted uneasily in their chairs: Patton's misplaced flippancy was a byword.

"I left my household in Nancy in perfect order before I came here," Patton explained, "and can go to Luxembourg right away, sir, straight from here."

"When will you be able to attack?" asked Eisenhower patiently, and Patton answered, "The morning of 22 December – with *three* divisions."

"Through the room," Codman noted, "the current of excitement leaped like a flame," but it entirely failed to galvanise Eisenhower. "Don't be fatuous, George," he replied curtly.

Patton was unruffled. His arrangements were made and his staff were "working like beavers ... to shape them up." And though he could not attack with more than three divisions, he would attack on 22 December, lest the element of surprise was lost.

Where Patton led, Montgomery was not slow to follow. On the morning of 20 December, the normally optimistic Field Marshal despatched a telegram that for the first time showed Churchill and Alan Brooke the gravity of the situation: German advance units were within 15 miles of Liège. "The situation in American area is not – not – good." Montgomery warned. "There is a definite lack of grip and control and no one has a clear picture as to situation ... I have heard nothing from him (Eisenhower) or Bradley ... my own opinion is that ... the American forces have been cut clean in half."

Losing no time, Churchill at once called Eisenhower in Versailles; despite the Arnhem débâcle, the Premier still saw Montgomery as the man to command the whole northern wing of the battle – eighteen American divisions plus the sixteen divisions of his own 21st Army Group. Eisenhower concurred – for under pressure from Walter Bedell Smith he had just reached the same decision.

It was a ukase hotly resented by Omar Bradley for although he would command the southern battle area, one American army, General Simpson's Ninth, would hereafter remain under Montgomery's control for almost the duration of the war. "I cannot be responsible to the American people if you do this," he stormed, and fortwith threatened to resign.

When the need arose, Eisenhower could yet show a Supreme Commander's steel: "Brad," he said, "I, not you, am responsible to the American people. Your resignation therefore means absolutely nothing."

But Montgomery and Patton were now in their elements: free to fight their own battles without tiresome supervision from the top. Promptly at 1 p.m. on 21 December, Montgomery's large green Rolls Royce slid to a halt outside the Hôtel Bains et Perigord at Chaudfontaine, Belgium, Hodges' First Army Command Post. As Montgomery, enveloped in a bearskin, strode into the lobby, looking in one man's words, "like Christ come to cleanse the temple," First Army staffers were dismayed; the Field Marshal had brought his own sandwich box and a thermos jug of tea and the splendid luncheon that Hodges had laid on for his guest would go uneaten.

Oblivious to Hodges' magnificent wall maps, Montgomery, munching sandwiches, unrolled his own 1 to 250,000 map, rubbed his hands and announced briskly, "Now let's review the situation." If some of his phrases smacked of the pedagogue – "Come, come" – "Dear me, this can't go on," – Hodges and his staffers at least appreciated the steps he had already taken in the British sector. Horrocks' XXX Corps were now concentrated west of the Meuse from Namur to Givet; at three main crossing points – Givet, Dinant, Namur – a regiment of 50

British tanks was waiting to welcome the Germans hurtling towards the river. The "Hell-in-Kilts" (51st Highland) Division was already stationed south of Liège.

At his new command post, in Luxembourg's Hotel Alpha, Patton, too, was laying it on the line. "It's either roothog, or die," he told his staff. "If these sons of bitches want war in the raw, then that's the way we'll give it to them". And he made plain the no-holds-barred nature of the battle to come: "There are to be no reserves. Everybody fights."

The focal point of the battle was a nondescript market town (population 4,500) set at the hub of seven spokes in the southern Ardennes road network: Bastogne.

In time Bastogne would go down to American folklore, along with such proud names as Harper's Ferry, the Argonne and Valley Forge – yet its role as a pivotal point of the entire campaign was wholly fortuitous. In German plans it had figured as no more than a possible supply centre, to be by-passed by the main force and picked off by a lesser division, the 26th Volksgrenadier.

It was already too late. On 17 December, Major-General John Whiteley, Eisenhower's British Deputy G.3 (Operations) hit on the seven-road junction at Bastogne as the key-point of the Allied defences – and sold the idea to Bedell Smith. By 19 December, when Von Manteuffel realised that Bastogne "must influence all our movements to the west," the town itself and the perimeter two miles distant were defended by 11,000 Americans, under Brigadier-General Anthony McAuliffe, acting commander of the 101st Airborne, the "Screaming Eagles". Among these defiant defenders, "the battered bastards of the bastion of Bastogne," was Private Donald Burgett.

All along, the young paratrooper had had the hunch that D-Day and Arnhem had been no more than dress rehearsals for "the real thing" – and "the real thing" was Bastogne. This time there had been no long tense weeks of anticipation. On the night of 17 December, Burgett had just returned to quarters at Mourmelon-le-Grand, south-east of Reims, after three uproarious days and nights in Paris; in all that time he had not caught a wink of sleep. But at 1:30 a.m. on 18 December, he was rudely shaken awake; the 101st were to pack their "seaborne rolls" (blanket rolls with shelter hats, dry socks and pup tents) and hit the road. By noon, the 101st, supplied with K-rations, lying prone on bales of straw in a long convoy of 380 open cattle trucks was grinding towards Bastogne.

To Burgett, it was not an auspicious beginning to a battle. Many of the division were replacements who had not fought before. Their machine-guns and mortars were worn and pitted with holes: Ordnance had had no time to repair them. Some men had no helmets; others were without M.I. rifles. Under a sky hobnailed with stars, they crawled for hours, along roads clogged with refugees streaming for France. Long past midnight, they halted at Champs, five miles west of Bastogne – and bivouacked. Early on 19 December, they trekked towards the town.

On that same day, Patton, touring the front, met up at Arlon, twenty miles south of Bastogne, with Major-General Troy Middleton, commanding VIII Corps. Patton warmly approved the plan to hold Bastogne. "I don't think the enemy dare pass it without reducing it," he said.

Middleton counselled caution. The problem would be to sustain Bastogne with its 11,000 defenders and some 3000 civilians. "They'll be surrounded unless they get help," he told Patton.

"They will get help!" vowed Patton grimly.

For five days and nights thereafter, Bastogne held out, harassed by four German divisions, an island fortress in a raging sea of gunfire. On 21 December, when VIII Corps, by radio telephone, asked what the situation was, Lieutenant-Colonel Henry Kinnaird of the 101st was succinct: "Visualise the hole in a doughnut. That's us." The tough cocky paratroops summed it up another way: "So they've got us surrounded – the poor bastards!"

At Noville, 1500 yards north of Bastogne, the outermost perimeter, fog lay so thick that Burgett recalled it as "like being in a glass of milk". Towards noon, it lifted, uncloaking a landscape like a Currier and Ives print: smooth white rounded hills stippled by banks of dark forest, dotted with nestling villages. "At sunrise and sunset, the snow was pink," one eye-witness recalled, "and the forests grew smoky and soft". What Burgett remembered more distinctly was the thirst and the cold: dust from the collapsing cottages of Noville and the smell of burnt powder choked them, and the only way to slake their thirst was by melting snow in their helmets. The cold was so intense that on one day the temperature sank to 9° above zero. The medics kept their morphine syrettes under their arms to prevent them from congealing.

At 11:30 a.m. on 23 December, four Germans, led by a major, walked into the 101st's front line under a white flag of truce. With them they had brought a surrender ultimatum:

> There is only one possibility to save the U.S. troops from total annihilation. In order to think it over, a term of two hours will be granted, beginning with the presentation of this note.
>
> If this proposal should be rejected, one German Artillery Corps and six heavy A.A. Battalions are ready to annihilate the U.S.A. troops in and near Bastogne. The order for firing will be given immediately after this two hours' term.

McAuliffe, who had been touring the aid stations, to hear the wounded beg him, "Don't give up on account of us, General Mac," did not hesitate. Sitting at his debris-littered desk, he printed his reply with formal military courtesy:

> To The German Commander:
>
> NUTS!
>
> The American Commander.

Now McAuliffe requested Colonel Joseph H. Harper, of the 327th Glider Infantry, "Would you see that this is delivered?" "It'll be a lot of fun," Harper responded.

Returning by jeep with the German officers, Harper removed the blindfolds that had been secured. "If you don't understand what 'nuts', means," he told the Germans, "in plain English, it is the same as 'go to hell'. And I'll tell you something else – if you continue to attack we'll kill every goddam German that tries to break into the city."

"We will kill many Americans," one officer remarked solemnly. "This is war." "On your way, Bud," Harper retorted briskly, "and good luck to you."

Donald Burgett heard that news from McAuliffe himself, along with his buddies Private Donald Liddle, a Mormon farmer from Utah, and Harold Phillips, a Pennsylvanian Dutchman. The three men were taking a coffee break in a barn at Luzery when the General walked in and broke it to them: How did the troopers feel about it? Their volley of profanity seemed to hearten him, but Burgett and the others were astonished by the gall of the Germans' demand. Hell, the "Screaming Eagles" were winning, weren't they?

It was an uphill fight, even so. When the blizzards stopped, the wind blew and the snow drifted. Water froze in the canteens of those lucky enough to possess them: motorised troops on the move were building fires on the steel bottoms of their trucks. Each dark morning Burgett and the others climbed from their foxholes, sleepless, stiff-legged and red-eyed to fight another day. At Noville, the fighting was hand to hand in the narrow streets and in the fields; once Burgett ducked behind a haystick to dodge a tank, but the tank shelled the stack and it caught fire. He ran for the town with the tank in pursuit, leaping into the first open doorway to find Phillips and Liddle in the same house. All three burst through the back door "at the same time"; shells were toppling the building as they did so.

Somehow the hours and the days seemed to blur after that. Following forty-eight hours, Colonel Robert Sink sought permission to withdraw the 506th from Noville, and McAuliffe finally agreed: Bastogne had need of seasoned troops closer at hand. So they pulled out, felling the church tower across the road so that artillery spotters could not use it, moving towards Bastogne in fog so thick they were unaware that the Germans had captured Foy, only 1000 yards from Bastogne: a savage fire-fight ensued in the snowy ditches. Then a jeep broke loose across the fields and all of them straggled in its wake until they reached Luzery, within the perimeter. Burgett remembered machine-gun bullets "stitching towards them in the snow," and killing three more Germans, then there was a lull and "everything was quiet, like Christmas, with silver-dollar size snowflakes". The forest was beautiful, but the white ground was littered with black and lonely corpses.

Suddenly, on the day after Christmas, planes were once again airborne, and gaily-wrapped packages belatedly labelled "Merry Christmas" came floating from the sky. There were fruit cakes and candy bars but the prize package, which Burgett shared with seven others, was a tube of toothpaste and a toothbrush. Solemnly they lined up at a nearby stream, taking turns to brush their teeth.

At 6:45 p.m. on the same day, the cutting-edge of the U.S. rescue spearhead, a clanking chain of Shermans, moving on a 300-yard corridor, forged for Bastogne in a daring plunge that sent the Germans reeling. This was the 37th Tank Battalion under Lieutenant-Colonel Creighton Abrams, a unit whose GIs boasted that no man was eligible unless he could prove he had both killed his mother and been born out of wedlock.

It was the end of the beginning. All told, the Battle of the Bulge was to rage for 42 days, costing Eisenhower 80,000 casualties, but by 22 January, the Ardennes bulge had dwindled into a strip which reached only twelve miles into Belgium at the widest point, east of Houffalize. For all the panzer divisions at the front, fuel was running out. Behind them the Allies had once more taken to clear skies, blocking the roads, destroying the supply columns. Despite all the hard-won terrain, the German position was no longer tenable.

In the American camp, the post-mortems would soon begin: how had the *Wehrmacht* achieved such total surprise, caused such unmilitary panic? The Inspector-General of the First Army was to conduct investigations into dereliction of duty by the 106th Division, the 14th Cavalry Group, the 820th Tank Destroyer Battalion, and the 106th Reconniassance Troop.

None of this could detract from the legend of Bastogne. Long after, medics would tell the story of a young paratrooper, a replacement, grievously wounded in his first action: a shell fragment had sheared off his left arm below the shoulder. Carried to an aid station he sought something more specific than sympathy: "One of you guys go back and find my arm. There's a wrist-watch on it I want to keep."

—

Anthony Eden was in a towering rage. "Hell," he wrote feelingly in his diary, "I was looking forward to quiet family Christmas." At Chequers, the Premier's country residence, Clementine Churchill, who had nourished the same hope, had retired to her bedroom in "floods of tears". The cause of their chagrin was one man: an unrepentant Winston Churchill.

On 23 December, at the eleventh hour, Churchill, on an impulse, had cancelled all plans for Christmas. Instead, accompanied by the reluctant Eden, his secretary John Colville, his personal physician, Lord Moran and sundry staffers he had resolved to fly 1,500 miles to Athens, where civil war had raged for twenty days, where the citizens were burning their furniture to keep warm, and inflation had boosted the value of a British gold sovereign to 22 trillion drachmas.

Like a rick fire, the tension had been smouldering beneath the surface for months. On 14 September, Hitler, ordering a withdrawal from Greece, had an ulterior motive in view: "to kindle and fan strife between Communist and Nationalist forces". As October dawned and the Germans withdrew they left intact many arms dumps – which fell into the hands of ELAS guerillas, the Communist-dominated arm of the political movement, EAM. On 13 October, when the British reached Athens, they faced an uncomfortable reality: 75,000 well-armed ELAS troops, who were determined not to yield up those weapons.

On 7 November, the Greek Premier, the Socialist George Papandreou, announced that both guerilla armies, ELAS and the monarchist EDES, would be disbanded on 10 December. Still to be decided was whether two formations of the regular Greek Army, the 3rd Mountain Brigade and the Sacred Regiment, which had fought at El Alamein and in Italy, should be disbanded, too – or retained as the nucleus of a new Greek National Army.

On this point, Papandreou was obdurate: as the only regular Greek forces in existence, neither unit could be demobilised. But the ELAS C-in-C, General Stephan Seraphis, proved obdurate, too. ELAS could not disarm unless the regular forces disarmed simultaneously. Otherwise the "monarcho-Fascist" forces would try to restore the rule of King George II.

Although in sympathy with the King, neither Churchill nor Eden had any such intention. "It is no good blinking the fact that according to our present information he (the King) is at best a controversial issue," Eden minuted Churchill on 27th September, urging that the King's return to Athens should be resisted at all costs, likewise that of Crown Prince Paul, "for he has less brains and a German wife."

The stage was now set for a Communist power-grab. On 1 December, six Communist ministers of EAM resigned from Papandreou's government – calling a general strike for 4 December, preceded by a demonstration on Sunday 3 December in Athens' Constitution Square. Promptly Papandreou vetoed the demonstration.

On that clear bright Sunday, thousands of men, women and children, defying that prohibition, converged on Constitution Square and on the Government Palace, rallied by demonstrators with megaphones chanting "Down with Papandreou" and "Down with George Glücksburg." Crowds lining the pavements heard a clicking of rifle-bolts before Police Chief Paunias Ebert ordered his grey-clad cohorts: "Fire!"

Scores of demonstrators hit the pavements, some for safety but many with mortal wounds: twenty, according to some accounts, more than 100 by others. For more than half an hour, the shooting continued, until the police withdrew, leaving the square to lamenting relatives who stuck small crosses, made with branches torn from the pepper trees, on the pools of blood where the martyrs had fallen.

That night, and in the nights that followed, Athens was a mourning city, with all electricity cut off, its darkness pierced only by the flickering light from small bowls of olive oil. The city where democracy had first achieved political meaning had become a battlefield for two forces, each claiming to defend that concept.

Martial Law, ordered by the British commander, Lieutenant-General Ronald Scobie – "Do not hesitate to act as if you were in a conquered city," Churchill had counselled him, perhaps unwisely – and the general strike paralysed all public services. Shops closed, trams stopped, streets emptied. The shadows of strafing Spitfires flashed across the ruins of the Parthenon. The Acropolis was again a fortress, occupied now by red-bereted paratroopers of the British 6th Airborne. Only in the "Papandreou State," four square miles in the heart of Athens, controlled by the Government with British help, were civilians allowed out for two hours a day to fetch food and water.

It was to resolve this melancholy impasse that Churchill and his entourage were journeying to Athens on the eve of the Nativity.

It had been a seesaw battle from the first. The port of Piraeus was contested street by street. Only the 6th Battalion of the Black Watch Regiment kept open "The Mad Mile" – the 4-mile long Leoforos Singrou Boulevard to Kalamaki Airport, where only armoured vehicles could safely go. British troops had secured both ELAS and KKE (Greek Communist Party) headquarters on Constitution Square, but the Communist secretary, George Siantos, had eluded them.

An EAM emissary battled through to Scobie's headquarters, the Hotel Grande Bretagne, to receive the British terms for an armistice: ELAS troops in Athens and Piraeus must yield their arms and evacuate the area. Three days later, EAM countered with a three-point demand for an amnesty, an all-party government, a regency. To underline their muscle, they dynamited their way into R.A.F. headquarters in the suburb of Kifissia and stormed the formidable Averoff prison in Central Athens, capturing many political prisoners.

At 3 p.m. on Christmas Day, as his Douglas C-54 Skymaster touched down at Kalamaki, this question of a regency was much on Churchill's mind. At first he had resisted it as strongly as

King George II, who had four times refused to countenance it in December alone – would a regency automatically see the rebels disarming and Scobie's terms accepted? the King had asked rhetorically, claiming that any such agreement would be "an abandonment of the struggle".

Yet a man, acceptable to both Papandreou and EAM and approved by the British Ambassador Sir Reginald Leeper, had offered to mediate: Archbishop Gregorio Damaskinos, Primate of the Greek Orthodox Church, a strapping (6ft 4ins) priest who had graduated to the church after scoring as an all-in wrestler.

Aboard the icy plane, Churchill, dressed as an R.A.F. Air Commodore, listened in grim silence, sipping copious draughts of whisky, as Leeper, supported by Field-Marshal Sir Harold Alexander and Harold Macmillan, Resident Minister in the Mediterranean, put the case for Damaskinos.

Finally Churchill gave characteristic judgment. "Huh!" he said. "A scheming medieval Prelate. He's our man!"

Time was now of the essence, for both at home and abroad the spectacle of British troops fighting Greek guerillas had attracted trenchant if ill-founded criticism. "Democracy is no harlot to be picked up in the street by a man with a tommy-gun," Churchill had protested hotly in the House of Commons but his cable to Scobie, leaked by the State Department to the Washington gossip columnist, Drew Pearson[29] had sounded an unwontedly jingoistic note. "The lengths to which they will go to hang on to the past!" Roosevelt grumbled to his son, Elliott, and in the left-wing weekly *Tribune* H. G. Wells charged, "He (Churchill) is as much an anomalous survival in politics as the platypus is in nature."

Since the British Embassy was under siege, with Leeper confined to one corner of his study and a staff of twenty taking their meals in the main hall, the one safe billet for Churchill's party was HMS *Ajax*, an 8-inch cruiser anchored in Phaleron Bay. Sped there by armoured car, Churchill was delighted when Captain J. W. Cuthbert warned him that the cruiser might have to give the Army supporting fire. "Pray remember, Captain," he remarked blandly, "that I come here as a cooing dove of peace, bearing a sprig of mistletoe in my beak – but far be it from me to stand in the way of military necessity."

Now a complication arose: both Papandreou and Damaskinos had been summoned to *Ajax* for private consultations with Churchill. As chance had it, both men arrived at the height of the ship's "Funny Party" – a Royal Naval Christmas tradition, when sailors in bizarre fancy dress make their rounds of the ship. Papandreou, a lanky worried-looking man in a dark suit, commanded no attention, but Damaskinos, a towering black-bearded figure dressed in flowing robes, wearing a stove-pipe hat and carrying a crook, was, to the unsuspecting sailors, a one-man "Funny Party" on his own. Barely in time, a naval aide rescued the incredulous Archbishop from the embraces of a grass-skirted hula-hula "girl" with a shimmering brassiere and a white-faced red-nosed Coco the Clown, both spoiling to tug off his beard.

At 6 p.m. on 26 December – the hour when Bastogne stood on the brink of deliverance – a historic conference took place in the Ministry of Foreign Affairs. In a large ground-floor room with drawn shutters, lit only by flickering hurricane lanterns, heated by evil-smelling Valor stoves, the participants faced one another across an immense table: Damaskinos at its head, Papandreou and his government down one side, Churchill and his party down the other. Only the ELAS seats were vacant.

"Your beatitude," Churchill began, "today Greece may march with the United Nations to victory, which is not far distant. But if all our efforts fail, we shall have to bend to our hard task to save the city of Athens from anarchy..."

There was a knock on the door, and Churchill paused. At the crucial hour, the ELAS delegates had arrived: the Communists' Siantos, Demetrios Partsalides, of EAM, and ELAS' General Emmanuel Mandakis, "all muffled to the ears, like pilots coming into the mess from a winter flight," Moran noted. All three were relieved of their pistols, then the door was locked and the key handed to the ELAS men.

It was, concluded Pierson Dixon, Eden's Principal Private Secretary, the "oddest of international conferences". For half-an-hour Churchill spoke, to a mounting crescendo of gunfire, his words at times drowned by the scream of Beaufighter rockets. Next Alexander, who told the ELAS delegates, "Instead of me pouring men into Greece you ought to be pouring men into Italy to join my victorious armies against the enemy." Then the Archbishop rose: did anybody wish to speak? Yet strangely, as if overawed by Churchill's presence, the Greeks kept silence. Finally an ageing royalist, Dimitrios Maximos, of the Popular Party, rose to deliver a halting speech of welcome.

On behalf of the government, Papandreou echoed these sentiments. Finally Partsalides, on behalf of ELAS, expressed the passionate friendship of the Greeks for England.

Churchill rose heavily to his feet. "I should like to go now," he said. "We have begun the work. See that you finish it." Then, in a gesture that won him Moran's undying admiration, he paused before the Communists. He had vowed that he would never shake hands with these brigands – but there was nothing petty in Churchill's make-up. "Who," he asked, "will introduce these gentlemen to me?" And as he shook each hand in turn, a look of pleasure crossed their faces for the first time. For the Communist, Siantos, the Premier had one parting shot: "Greece for ever!"

Next day, as Churchill stepped out to watch the war, and a burst of Spandau fire hit a wall 30 yards away – "What cheek!" the Premier commented – a second session took place, one so stormy that Damaskinos adjourned the meeting before blows were struck. But from the spate of tempestuous talk, one point of unanimity emerged: all parties accepted Damaskinos as Regent. And in the tweedy seclusion of his Claridge's suite, King George must not delay his consent.

In the end, all Churchill's efforts to combat "naked triumphant Trotskyism" were temporarily vindicated. After a spirited Churchillian curtain-lecture lasting until 4:30 a.m., King George assented to the Regency. The Archbishop chose as his new Premier, Greece's No. One king-breaker, the exiled General Nicholas Plastiras, who had helped depose King Constantine in 1923, King George II, the following year. Even his left-wing critics were silenced when a delegation from Britain's Trades Union Congress, under Sir Walter Citrine, testified to mass graves housing 10,000 victims of Communist atrocities.

"We must take our decision uninfluenced by our closeness to the battle," Churchill had vowed. "We must adopt a course of action which in England will be regarded as right in fifty to a hundred years." Time alone would tell – but as 1945 dawned, Athens was once more the cradle of democracy.

–

In Germany, by contrast, the New Year had dawned bleakly. The shrinking frontiers now meant all-out mobilisation, as Josef Göbbels, appointed Reich Trustee for Total War the previous August, now made plain. Women of fifty were conscripted for labour to release more fit men for the Army. A 60-hour week became mandatory for war industries. All beauticians were drafted along with U-Bahn ticket collectors; the personnel of Berlin's Charlottenburg Opera House was set to work in the Siemens electrical plant. Theatres were closed down, periodicals suspended. As the writer Ernst Jünger noted in his diary on 5 January: "Hopelessness is the only positive aspect of the situation."

Only one man, it seemed, failed to read the writing on the wall: the Führer, Adolf Hitler.

All through the night of Monday 8 January, the command train of the Chief of the Army General Staff, *Generaloberst* Heinz Guderian, rolled westward from Zossen, south of Berlin, to Giessen, in Hesse. Under the dim blue glow of the night lamp, Guderian courted sleep that would not come. All evidence amassed by the Chief of *Fremde Heere Ost* (Foreign Armies, East) *Generalmajor* Reinhard Gehlen, suggested that in three days' time, on 12 January, Marshal Ivan Konev's First Ukranian Army Group was due to launch a pile-driving assault on Guderian's eastern front.

Tomorrow's meeting with Hitler, Guderian knew, would decide not only the fate of the front but the fate of eastern Germany.

Central to the issue were two almost forgotten German armies, the 16th and the 18th, twenty-six divisions in all, stationed in the Kurland bridgehead between the Gulf of Riga and the Lithuanian border.[30] Only their presence, the Führer fantasised, was keeping neutral Sweden out of the war – and to date all Guderian's efforts to transfer them and stiffen the eastern front had been in vain.

On the evening of 9 January, approximately twenty men gathered in Jodl's roomy study at Ziegenberg, near Giessen: among them, Keitel, Jodl, Göring, Himmler and *Generalleutnant* Paul Winter, Chief of Staff of the Southern Theatre of Operations. Hitler entered last, his left leg dragging behind him, stooping like a very old man. As an adjutant placed a chair behind him, he collapsed into it as if suddenly stricken. By custom, following the 20 July explosion that had shattered Hitler's right eardrum, Guderian was placed on the Führer's left.

For a moment there was silence, broken only by a strange unearthly rustling: the sound of Hitler's left hand, trembling uncontrollably on the maps that Guderian had brought.

"*Mein Führer*," Guderian began, "we have information that makes it certain that the Russian winter offensive, aimed at Berlin, will begin three days from now ... this is the last moment for action. I hope that our report will prompt you to transfer to the eastern front the reinforcements that are needed there – and do it tonight."

Then, as Guderian was always to recall, Hitler threw a mammoth tantrum. Following a cursory glance at Gehlen's maps and charts, he swept them to the floor. "This is completely idiotic!" he shouted. "Get rid of this man – he ought to be in a lunatic asylum!"

Now Guderian's own temper rose. "The man who made these is General Gehlen, one of my best staff officers," he retorted. "I should not have shown them to you if I were in disagreement with them. If you want General Gehlen sent to a lunatic asylum, then you had better have me certified as well."

For answer, Hitler shook his palsied fists in rage: twice Göring and General Winter had to step between the bellowing pair. "The eastern front has never before possessed such a strong reserve as now," Hitler shouted. "That is your doing, I thank you for it." "If you had studied Gehlen's reports more closely, *mein Führer*," Guderian shot back "you would have realised that the eastern front is like a house of cards. If the front is broken through at one point, all the rest will collapse, for twelve and a half divisions are far too small a reserve for so extended a front."

But at this point Hitler wound up the conference, exclaiming like an irrational child: "The eastern front must help itself and make do with what it's got."

In fact, the situation was graver than even Guderian suspected. On Friday 13 January, dawn on the rolling plain of southern Poland broke like many another – a grey blending of snowy night with snowy day. For the Germans huddling in their trenches west of the Vistula, nothing seemed likelier than another day of wary waiting. The earth was soft and sticky, and no planes would fly.

On the Red Army side of the line, patrols were already moving stealthily into the haze, as many patrol squads had done before. But these were no mere patrols.

Like a stupendous explosion of trapped lava, the 25-mile Russian line erupted in a huge arc of gunfire. Along every mile Marshal Konev had hid 300 to 400 guns – long-barrelled giants, stubby deep-throated howitzers, batteries of *Katushas*, the rocket-projecting pride of Soviet artillerymen, whose boast was "Where *Katusha* strikes, nothing lives."

But much more was at stake than the city of Berlin, precious prize though that might be. Within the week the Red Army had pierced the German lines for 40 miles and had spread the breach to a width of 65 miles. Their first major target, Kielce, had fallen, and only 40 miles beyond Cracow, the ancient fortress of Poland's Kings, was a prize second only to the Ruhr: the 6,000 square kilometre industrial complex of Silesia.

At the end of November 1944, Konev, a bald austere man who liked to quote the Roman historian Livy to his staff officers, was summoned by Josef Stalin to the Kremlin. Pointing to a giant relief map of the area, Stalin, circling Silesia with his finger, uttered just one word: "Gold."

Konev took his meaning perfectly. The area, studded with industrial installations — most of which would later be removed bodily to Russia — was to be enveloped to the north and south but otherwise by-passed. Each artillery battery was to be assigned a specific sector, accurate enough "to hit a mosquito in the eye," and to avoid combat in the industrial zone Konev would permit the Germans "a golden bridge," an escape corridor to the south-west.

Machinery and equipment would thus be sacrosanct, but not as Captain Mikhail Koriakov soon discovered, human life.

In the months since his demotion from correspondents' duties, Koriakov had found the trumped-up charge of the Requiem Mass rankling increasingly — and, paradoxically, was drawing closer to Catholicism. During his time with the 32nd Reserve Officer Regiment he had prayed in the Church of Our Lady of Lublin: a prayer that in 1945 he might witness a miracle.

There was little to choose, he decided, as Konev's First Ukrainian Army forced the Oder River, leaving besieged Breslau behind them, between Hitler and Stalin.

On 19 January, Stalin had issued an order proscribing the behaviour of Red Army troops in German territory. On 27 January, Konev had issued a similar order, citing fearsome instances of debauchery and rape: one tank crew had been so far gone in drink they had opened fire on the Russian lines, destroying four gun emplacements.

But Konev's Draconian orders had been in vain. Along the wide asphalt Breslau-Berlin highway, a stream of traffic flowed as on a river bed: grimy bespattered tanks decked out with brightly coloured rugs, straddled by dirty tankmen in uniforms soaked in machine oil, swigging from bottles: caissons lined with soft silk cushions, their gun crews playing accordions inlaid with mother-of-pearl; looted landaus packed with drunken officers, wearing top hats and ogling the troops through looted lorgnettes.

In the small Silesian town of Bunzlau, Koriakov saw with his own eyes what liberation, Russian-style, could mean.

In a tiny square near the city centre, dominated by its statue of Field-Marshal Kutuzov, who had routed Napoleon's armies, Koriakov was musing on Russia's past glories, when a piercing shriek turned him cold. A girl in torn dress, with damp dishevelled hair, had come running into the square: one stocking had slipped down round her ankle, blood was running from a cut on her knee. She stopped short, and Koriakov went forward to meet her.

In that moment, Koriakov saw the cause of her terror: two young and panting soldiers, their revolvers lodged in their belts for ready use, both of them wearing black Tank corps helmets and leather belts. Seeing Koriakov, they stopped and grinned cheerfully.

"Are you from the 3rd Army?" Koriakov asked.

"Yes, Comrade Captain," they chorused in unison.

The question was pertinent, for Colonel-General Pavel Rybalko's 3rd Guards Tank Army had from January on become a by-word for rapine and slaughter. For two years Rybalko had grieved for his daughter, whom the Germans had abducted from the Ukraine: on 12 January, on the banks of the Vistula, he had told his men: "The long awaited hour, the hour of revenge, is at hand! We all have personal reasons for revenge; my daughter, your sisters, our mother Russia!"

From that time on, Koriakov knew, revenge had taken many forms and one of them stood before him now: a plump pale-skinned girl with grey and hunted eyes.

Now two other tankmen, one of them a drunken sergeant, grinning wolfishly, had joined the group. "What's the matter? What are you waiting for?" the new arrivals asked.

"What do you want her for?" Koriakov parried, playing for time, and the sergeant answered insolently. "We want her and that's all!" Another, more pacific, explained, "She will work in the kitchen for us, in our company kitchens…"

"She is not going to work for you," said Koriakov decisively, then turning to the girl, "*Kommen Sie mit mir.*"

The sergeant was truculent; he grabbed the girl's arm. "No, no, she has nothing to do with you. We have our own officers. They are waiting for her…" Koriakov, tight-lipped, called his bluff. "Get in the car! We'll go to the military police headquarters and find out about this girl."

The gambit worked. "Come on! Forget it!" the soldiers urged the sergeant. "We'll find another one." Sulkily the man gave up. "A headquarters rat!" he taunted Koriakov. "Think you can frighten us with police headquarters? We burn alive in tanks, while you ride about in a car! We should check your papers, find out who you are!"

Her name was Helen Springer, and she no longer had a home: home had been the house of an elderly relative, who had been killed by a bomb that morning, and the house had been burnt out. She had salvaged a suitcase from the ruins, she told Koriakov, as they drove through burning Bunzlau, flames pouring from its windows, black burning embers spraying into the air.

He took Helen with her suitcase to stay the night with friends, the former Mayor of Bunzlau, *Burgermeister* Wunsch. Before they parted, Koriakov printed several signs. "This house occupied by commissioned officers" "Unauthorised entry forbidden." These he hung on the doors and windows, knowing the standing joke in the Red Army that January: the first wave gets the wrist watches, the second wave gets the girls, the third wave gets what's left.

Three weeks later Koriakov returned to find Helen weeping and distraught. The second wave had caught up with her. In that time she had been raped by at least 250 men. *Frau* Wunsch had been raped before her husband's eyes. Even the Mayor's aunt, the frail and emaciated 78-year-old *Frau* Simon, had not escaped the Red Army.

Appalled, Koriakov took the girl to the military police commandant, Major Lavrenov, an elderly and humane man. "Two hundred and fifty men!" the Commandant sighed. "She cannot last more than two or three weeks. If she hasn't some disease already, she will have. As soon as she admits that she is sick someone will shoot her in self-defence, so she will not contaminate others."

It transpired that Helen had an aunt in Liegnitz, farther to the rear of the front. "Take her there, if you can spare the petrol," the Commandant advised. "Better find a Red Army greatcoat and disguise the girl."

Koriakov followed this advice, but after that he did not see Helen again. Later, passing back through Liegnitz, he called at her aunt's house to find that she had left a message, as arranged, scratched on the garden gate. "We are being taken somewhere on 14 March, but I do not know where. Thank you for all the kind things you have done for me. I hope that God will bring us together again in this life. Lenchen."

Numb at heart, Koriakov wandered through the empty house. It was as if an army of vindictive apes had been turned loose: everything had been ransacked, despoiled. Clothes bearing the imprint of soldiers' boots were piled on the floor: jam from a broken jar had been smeared all over the table. Near the window the last man to loot the house had been careful to leave his calling-card: a spreading puddle of urine.

Mikhail Koriakov could not know it, but Bunzlau was merely the tip of the iceberg. Terror was riding on the cold wet wind with the sound of Russian guns, fuelled by memories of Nemmersdorf, the first town in East Prussia to be overrun by General Ivan Galitsky's 11th Guards Army.

That had been on 22 October, 1944, and five days later, when the Fourth Army of *Generalleutnant* Friedrich Hossbach drove the Russians out, scarcely a single inhabitant remained alive. Women had been nailed to barn doors and farm carts. Tanks had crushed those who had tried to flee. Children had been shot – along with French prisoners of war and German Communists.

Now the appalling cruelties which the Russians had endured at the hands of the *S.S. Einsatzkommandos* had at last produced a backlash in which the innocent would suffer along with the guilty.

Now the great flight westward began, long lines of carts, wheelbarrows and prams, and by the end of January millions had reached the Polish ports of Gdynia (which Hitler had re-named Gothenburg), Danzig and Pillau. Almost five years later, the stage was now set for Germany's own "Dunkirk".

On the icy morning of 30 January, one link in the vast seaborne evacuation, which by 8 May was to lift more than 2 million refugees beyond the Red Army's grasp, set sail from Gdynia: the liner *Wilhelm Gustloff*, 25,484 tons, a peacetime cruise ship whose 400-strong crew had waited on the whims of the 1,465 minor Nazi party officials, who were their passengers. But on 30 January, no less than 8,000 refugees were crammed aboard the *Wilhelm Gustloff* – many of whom had used babies as tickets, carrying them aboard only to toss them down again as passports for other members of the family.

Of twenty-two lifeboats which should have hung from her davits, ten had been requisitioned for harbour duties – and the *Gustloff*, with no warships available to escort her, wallowing at a cumbersome 16 knots, was thus ill-equipped to combat trouble.

At 11:08 p.m. on 31 January, trouble, in the shape of the Russian submarine S13, commanded by the brilliant if rumbustious Captain Third Class Alexander Marinesko, found the *Gustloff*. Three torpedoes – predictably labelled "For the Motherland" – "For the Soviet People" and "For Leningrad" – struck her port side. At 11:09 p.m., the S13's log noted: "Target began to sink."

Under the pressure of thousands of tons of ice-laden Baltic water, bulkheads and watertight doors gave way. Within sixty seconds the great liner had capsized on to her port side, her funnel level with the water: two thousand refugees trapped on the Lower Promenade Deck never stood a chance. Others recalled moments of apocalyptic horror: a teenager, 13-year-old Gunther von Maydell, ran to the boat-deck to find sailors vainly trying to operate winches: the machinery had frozen stiff. Another, 17-year-old Gertrud Agensons, fled from her cabin to find herself thigh-deep in water: in consternation, she saw the body of a dead girl floating past, followed by a tray of sandwiches. Eve Luck, 16, trapped with her family in the Music Room, watched appalled as the grand piano "went berserk," barrelling across the crowded room to crush women and children to pulp.

Seventy minutes after the first torpedo struck her, the *Gustloff*, her siren howling like a lost soul, boiled beneath the Baltic waters.

Some, crying aloud with cold terror, survived by clawing aboard rafts and lifeboats; others found refuge aboard the torpedo boat T.36, pursuing a parallel course with 250 refugees, the torpedo boat *Löwe*, and the freighter *Gotenland*. All told, some 964 people were plucked from the sea, some of whom died later from exposure – but at least 7,000 people were lost: a death-toll five times greater than that of the *Titanic*.

The Soviet Navy's Red Banner Fleet of 218 submarines, the world's largest and to date the least efficient, had scored their only notable victory.

-

At Yalta, on the south coast of the Crimea – "the Riviera of Hades," Churchill called it – a myth was born between 1 February and 11 February. It was to prove a durable myth, a long time a-dying, and its substance was this: that between them Roosevelt, Churchill and Stalin, conspired to divide up the territorial spoils of Europe.

Yet most of Yalta's major issues – the dismemberment of Germany, the problems of Poland's post-war borders, how to organise an international peace-keeping operation – had been aired as far back as Tehran. And from Tehran on, the military balance in Europe had shifted irrevocably in Stalin's favour: by February 1945, the vanguard tanks of Marshal Georgi Zhukov's First White Russian Army were less than 40 miles from Berlin. No matter how the talks had gone, Stalin held eastern Europe in the one way that counted.

The hands of the clock of history had moved ahead to a later hour; the Poles had been sold out long ago.

No one was more conscious of the futility of the exercise than Churchill – a conference that General Ismay was to describe as "from the military point of view, unnecessary ... from the political point of view, depressing." "Christ," Churchill remarked to his daughter, Sarah Oliver, after an hour's journey along rutted roads on the six-hour drive from Saki airfield, "five more of this," and to pass the time he began intoning Byron's *Don Juan*. Although the Russians had installed a double bed for him at the British headquarters, Vorontsov Palace, and Yalta was a balmy paradise of orange groves and palm trees, nothing could reconcile Churchill to Yalta; the British Military Mission's suggestion that "plenty of flea-powder and toilet paper be issued to all ranks" proved the soundest of advice. "If we had spent ten years on research we could not have found a worse place in the world," he told Hopkins glumly.

For the victors, the time had come to set their sights on the future of the world – but, as Joan Bright of the British War Cabinet Secretariat pointed out, "there were three cameras held by three powers with three different viewfinders". For Roosevelt, who had triumphed over the Republican contender, Thomas Dewey, to win an unprecedented fourth term on 7 November, what counted was to induce Stalin to share his dream of the United Nations and to participate in the war against Japan: everything else was to be "loose," to be bargained. Yet Roosevelt, had he realised it, held all the aces, for the entire Soviet offensive in the east was largely dependent on U.S. lend-lease equipment: enough woollen cloth to make twenty million uniforms, enough telegraph wire to reach thirty-eight times round the world. Moreover, the Russian stance had already made it plain they would invade China and Japan as and when they chose – with or without American sanction.

The cogent suggestion of George F. Kennan, of the American Embassy in Moscow, that plans for the United Nations be buried "as quietly and quickly as possible," rather than commit the United States to defending "a swollen and unhealthy Russian sphere of power," sounded no warning bell in the President's mind.

What impressed most of Yalta's 700 participants was the Russians' efficiency as capitalists. In the Vorontsov Palace, just as in the 50-room Livadia Palace, the former summer house of Nicholas II, where Roosevelt's party was quartered, the staffs of three Moscow hotels had been drafted to turn the clock back to the days of the Tsars. Fireplaces crackled with burning logs; walls were hung with paintings from Moscow art galleries. More than 1,000 Red Army soldiers had restored roads, rebuilt and painted houses, replaced broken windows and planted gardens. Nothing was too much trouble. Joan Bright's casual admission over luncheon that she had never sampled Chicken Kiev produced a plate of it on her desk within the hour – with a proud butler standing by to make sure that she ate it. When Sarah Oliver mentioned that lemon juice improved caviare, a huge lemon tree burdened with fruit appeared as if by magic in the Vorontsov orangery – and at Livadia too.

At Livadia, to the secret joy of the irreverent, the aloof General George C. Marshall and the crusty Fleet-Admiral Ernest King were bedded down in the Tsarina's suite, but less illustrious guests fared more leanly. Sixteen American Colonels sharing one dormitory was commonplace, and at Vorontsov Eden's Principal Private Secretary, Pierson Dixon, shared a bathroom with thirty others or repaired to a communal wash-room whose taps yielded only cold water.

To the observant, evidence of Russian paranoia was swiftly apparent. At all times, Stalin was flanked by a bodyguard of eight generals, one of whom doubled as a waiter at banquets, and in the ornate grounds, guards were posted every ten yards. Since every one of them insisted on inspecting a pedestrian's pass, Fleet-Admiral King swiftly abandoned his customary afternoon stroll.

From the first, the days fell into an unvarying pattern. Each morning, the Foreign Ministers conferred in private. Then, at 4 p.m., the Grand Ballroom at Livadia Palace, where all plenary sessions were held, overflowed with delegates, for meetings lasting three to four hours, followed by dinner an hour later. Cablegrams carried by specially laid landlines to the U.S.S. *Catoctin* shuttled to and from Washington, 5,700 miles away, London, 3,000 miles distant, and Moscow, 900 miles to the north.

Of eight plenary sessions, Churchill was later to stress, seven were devoted to Poland – with the Western Allies staunchly insisting that the Lublin government be reorganised to include non-Communists, and "free and unfettered elections" held. "How long will it take you to hold free elections?" Roosevelt enquired, and Molotov replied promptly, "Within a month's time."

In fact, the election, which was not "free" by any Western standard, was held twenty-three months later, on 19 January, 1947.

Here Roosevelt had faltered, for no firm guarantees had been extracted from the Soviets that free elections would indeed be held. Churchill's long argument that a three-power commission be set up to monitor Polish voting was firmly rebuffed by Stalin. "The Poles are an independent people," the Marshal insisted, "and they would not want to have their elections supervised by outsiders." But although the British were stubborn in their insistence, Roosevelt would not ultimately support them. He feared that to raise doubts about Stalin's intentions might prompt a Soviet pull-out from the Grand Alliance.

On the eve of his sixty-third birthday, which he had celebrated at sea, Roosevelt seemed very close to death – "he was transparent," Churchill noted later, in an unpublished aide-memoire. Yielding to Stalin's insistence that he could not leave Russian soil at this critical stage of the war, Roosevelt had undertaken the long fatiguing journey to the Crimea, a voyage which was to hasten his end. "He has all the symptoms of hardening of the arteries of the brain to an advanced stage," Lord Moran told the State Department's Stettinius clinically, "So I give him only a few months to live." The British interpreter, Major Arthur Birse, found him "worn-out and almost disinterested": to Eden he was "vague and loose and ineffective". To the dismay of James F. Byrnes, soon to succeed Stettinius as Secretary of State, the President, on the outward voyage, had signally failed to study his State Department briefings.

Yet when the stakes were high enough, the old devious Roosevelt was once more in the ascendant. For his intervention in the Far East, Stalin was demanding a stiff price, which Roosevelt – unknown to Churchill, Eden or even Stettinius – was prepared to pay. On Thursday

8 February, in a secret session with Stalin, the President agreed to yield up to Russia the southern sector of Sakhalin, an island off the east coast of Siberia, held by Japan since 1904, the Kurile Islands, and Manchuria, as well as assuring them "pre-eminent interests" in the commercial ports of Dairen and Port Arthur.

All this was done not only without consulting China but without informing China – in the words of the former Ambassador to Moscow, William C. Bullitt, "no more unnecessary, disgraceful and potentially disastrous document has ever been signed by a President of the United States."

The price of admission to the San Francisco World Security Conference, tentatively set for April, would prove onerous indeed.

Yet Eden, too, with Churchill's assent, paid a shameful price: an agreement to forcibly repatriate some two million Soviet prisoners of war, held by the Allies and the Germans, many of whom faced instant execution or a lingering death in "the Gulag Archipelago," their ideological taint, through contact with a capitalist society, being automatically assumed.

These shameful decisions apart, what characterised Yalta was the ducking of every real issue: "the outward appearances were preserved, as they had to be," Eden wrote later. Missing from the agenda were any plans for occupying Berlin: unsettled, too, was the question of German reparations, though Stalin, his knuckles turning white with anger, demanded $20 billion – "we have already lost 4 million soldiers – and they are human beings you know!" There was Roosevelt's last-minute Declaration on Liberated Europe, to which Stalin surprisingly agreed – and which so woefully misfired within weeks.

For all other questions likely to provoke controversy or dissent – the fate of war criminals, the future of the British Empire – a tactful solution was found. The matter was referred to the Foreign Ministers for "further study".

Yet on the last day, Sunday 11 February, when the delegates assembled for photographs on the sunlit terrace of Livadia, most felt a sense of achievement: that the curtain of double-talk had, in spite of all, preserved unity. Stalin was in high good humour, parroting his four phrases of English – "So what?" – "You said it!" – "The toilet is over there!" and "What the hell goes on around here?" Churchill, by contrast, seemed disgruntled, referring to the joint communiqué as "this bloody thing," and dismissing the Conference out of hand,

"Anyway that's done with and out of the way." Yet later, in tranquillity, he was to muse, "We had the world at our feet. Twenty-five million men were marching at our orders by land and sea. We seemed to be friends."

The public at large viewed it all with euphoria. "It will offer a great hope to the world," former President Herbert Hoover proclaimed. William L. Shirer hailed it as "a landmark in human history." Raymond Gram Swing enthused: "No more appropriate news could be conceived to celebrate the birthday of Abraham Lincoln." Harry Hopkins, so frail that he had lost 18 pounds in weight since the conference began, summed up: "We really believed in our hearts that this was the dawn of the new day that we had all been praying for and talking about for so many years."

And Roosevelt? Despite his forcedly jaunty mien, those closest to him saw hints that he harboured private doubts. She was disappointed, his wife, Eleanor told him, when he returned to the White House, and even rather shocked that Esthonia, Lithuania and Latvia had been left with the Soviet Union, instead of regaining their independence and freedom.

The President's reply somehow summed up the whole future of Europe in chains: "How many people in the United States do you think would be willing to go to war to free Esthonia, Latvia and Lithuania?"

–

Increasingly, the percipient noted, Adolf Hitler and his entourage had lost all gift for prophecy. On the late afternoon of 27 January, in a conference attended by twenty-four men, Hitler speculated, "Do you think that deep down inside the English are enthusiastic about all the Russian developments?" And Göring agreed vehemently: "They certainly didn't plan that we hold them off while the Russians conquer all of Germany. If this goes on we will get a telegram in a few days." "If the Russians really proclaim a national government," Hitler elaborated, "the people in England will really start to be scared ... That will make them feel as if someone had stuck a needle in them."

In Berlin, on 6 February, Yalta was the main topic on the agenda; the Big Three, the Führer prophesied, intended to "crush and annihilate Germany". "We have reached the final quarter of an hour," he said gravely. "The situation is serious, very serious. It seems even to be desperate." Yet still he believed that his troops, defending the Fatherland step by step, could wrest victory from defeat – "if Churchill were suddenly to disappear, everything could change in a flash!" He rallied his intimates: "While we keep fighting there is always hope, and that, surely, should be enough to forbid us to think that all is already lost. No game is lost until the final whistle."

Later, those with long memories would recall that in his earlier years, the Führer's predictions had been closer to the mark: "Give me five years and you will not recognise Germany again."

—

For seventy-two days now, the bombs had fallen without surcease. But this was only the beginning. For three days the bombardment group of the U.S. Fifth Fleet, under Rear-Admiral William Blandy, pounded the defences with the worst they could deliver, and still the defenders hit back. On the fourth day, new battleships added their 16-inch salvoes to the devil's chorus – but the defenders were still unbowed.

Monday 9 February dawned bright and clear over a calm sea black with ships: 800 craft under Vice-Admiral Richmond Kelly Turner, the hard-driving conqueror of Guadalcanal, New Georgia, Tarawa and Saipan. With Turner on the bridge of his command ship, U.S.S. *El Dorado*, stood Lieutenant-General Holland M. ("Howlin' Mad") Smith, commanding the Fleet Marine Force. Loaded on the surrounding transports were the men of Major-General Harry Schmidt's V Amphibious Corps: the 4th and 5th Marine Divisions.

Ahead of them stretched a bloodier battle than Americans had fought since Pickett's Charge up Cemetery Hill, Gettysburg: a sustained 36-day amphibious assault against the pork-chop shaped island of Iwo Jima, in the Western Pacific, 750 miles from Tokyo, 700 miles from the Marianas.

From the airfields of tiny Iwo, five miles by three, Japanese fighters had attacked both the B29s and their fields on Saipan: thus, whatever the cost – a total of 28,648 killed, missing and wounded up to 27 March – Iwo must be secured. Then the Americans would be as close to the Japanese heartland as Bermuda was to New York.

It was an awesome yard by yard advance, and the first men ashore, sinking to their calves in black volcanic ash, faced a nightmare soon familiar to others, "each man leaving behind him footprints which might have served an elephant, the heavy loose underpinning tugging at his legs like a quicksand." "Tanks were clustered," another man wrote, "...like so many black beetles struggling to move on tar-paper." Over all, hung the pungent sulphurous odour of rotting eggs, so that one man griped with feeling: "All I want to take away from this place is a faint recollection."

It was a cynical deck-hand aboard the carrier U.S.S. *Saratoga*, blazing from *Kamikaze* attacks, who set the keynote for the weeks that would follow. A confused pilot, touching down narrowly on her deck, remarked thankfully as he alighted: "Gee, I'm glad I'm not on the 'old Sara'. All hell's broken out there!"

"Take a good look around, brother," the deckhand consoled him. "This *is* hell!"

10

"When We Step Down, Let The Whole World Tremble"
20 February–30 April, 1945

The island was alive, and the Japanese were waiting and all too soon the defenders knew it. They were on the terraces above the beach and on the tabletop airstrips and all through the ridges of the island in pillboxes, bunkers and blockhouses. To overrun Iwo in three to four days – the over-confident aspiration of both Smith and Schmidt – was to ask too much even of the U.S. Marines.

The 21,000 Japanese under Lieutenant-General Tadamichi Kuribayashi, boosted by Radio Tokyo as "a short squat brown man of fifty-four, whose slightly protuberant belly is full of fine fighting spirit," knew exactly what they had to do. The beach landings were to go unopposed but once the Marines were 500 yards inland automatic weapons and artillery would open up, and from that moment on men would begin to die. One of them, the General fully expected, would be Kuribayashi himself; "Do not plan for my return," he had written to his wife.

For four days, the bitter bone of contention was an extinct volcano, Mount Suribachi, 556 feet high, which the Marines dubbed "Son-a-bitchie," for Suribachi alone had 1,000 fixed defence points. At dawn on 23 February the Marines once more resumed their assault, knifing their way into pillboxes and underground galleries, until forty men under First Lieutenant Harold Schrier had reached the summit. Someone found a long piece of iron pipe and at 10:30 a.m., with due solemnity, an American flag, 54 X 28 inches, was secured to the pipe and raised by Schrier and five men. At noon a larger flag was procured from an LST and plump little Joe Rosenthal, the Associated Press photographer, using another group of Marines as stand-ins, snapped a picture that went round the world.

On the beach-head, General Holland Smith, the tears streaming down his face, heard Secretary of the Navy James Forrestal assure him, "Holland, the raising of that flag on Suribachi means a Marine Corps for the next 500 years." Simultaneously, a loudspeaker announcement made it official: "Fine work, men. We have only 2,630 yards to go to secure the island."

"Only," muttered one disgruntled Marine, "*only*..."

Within a week, Iwo Jima had become the most densely-populated slice of real estate in the world, its 8 square miles choked with 10,000 men per square mile – and by 5 March, every Marine on Iwo was within range of Japanese guns. But just as in the Italian campaign of 1943, the forbidding terrain proved as great an enemy as the defenders: a stone jungle like a miniature Grand Canyon, where ridges loomed as high as three-storey houses and where one gorge alone might take eight days to subdue. Burrowing like gophers, the Japanese created ridges of death even a mile behind the front lines, and only flamethrowers, their long tongues of flaming liquid searing along the curving walls of the tunnels, drove them from cover.

But within nine days of the first landings, all three of Iwo's airfields had been secured, and on 8 March, nineteen days before Kuribayashi's ritual *hara-kiri* marked the end of resistance, P51 Mustangs were flying their first missions. At a fearsome cost Iwo was secured.

It was a wounded Marine on Iwo who voiced what thousands felt: "I hope to God that we don't have to go on any more of these screwy islands."

The hope was unfounded. There was one more "screwy island" yet and its name was Okinawa.

—

Exactly fifteen days after the Yalta agreements, the Russians reneged on them for the first of many times.

Striding through Customs and Immigration at Bucharest's Băneasa airport went a puffy bespectacled man with a shock of grey unruly hair and a nervous tic in his left cheek: Andrei Januari Vyshinsky, Soviet Vice-Commissar for Foreign Affairs. The tigerish ex-prosecutor of the Moscow Old Bolshevist trials was embarking on another witch-hunt.

For two weeks, Rumania's Premier, General Nicolai Radescu had defied every effort by the small but vociferous pro-Communist

National Democratic Front to drive him from office. Denunciations, demonstrations, and minor riots in four cities had failed to force Radescu's resignation. But where bully-boy tactics had failed, Vyshinsky was determined to succeed.

On the day of his arrival, he at once sought an audience with King Michael and his Foreign Minister, Constantine Visoianu. Radescu, he claimed, could not maintain civil order behind the front and must therefore be dismissed. Vyshinsky was asked to return next day.

King Michael was outwardly co-operative. He was, he told Vyshinsky on 27 February, consulting party leaders to select a new Premier. Vyshinsky dismissed this as "unsatisfactory". Glancing at his watch he told the King that by 8 p.m. – in two hours and five minutes time – a successor must be chosen and named. When Visoianu noted that the King "must observe constitutional procedure," Vyshinsky flared at him: "Shut up!" In leaving he slammed the door of the royal apartment so hard that the plaster cracked round the lintel.

Still the King remained placatory. He besought Prince Barbu Stirbey, that long-time peace envoy, to form a government, but Stirbey's attempts to woo the Communists proved fruitless. Now Vyshinsky showed his teeth: the Soviet choice for the new Premier was Dr Peter Groza, of the trouble-making National Democratic Front, a small-time politician who proclaimed himself the greatest tennis player since Tilden and the greatest lover since Casanova. When the king demurred, Vyshinsky was final: failure to accept the Groza government could mean the end of Rumania as an independent state.

Both in London and Washington, alarm bells sounded. Learning that Radescu had fled to the British Legation, Eden instructed: "You are authorised, in the event of an attempt to seize General Radescu, to open fire in his defence in the last resort..." "I feel sure that you will be as distressed as I am by recent events in Rumania," Churchill cabled Roosevelt. "The Russians have succeeded in establishing the rule of a Communist minority by force and misrepresentation." To the War Cabinet, his old distaste for Communist machinations was once more apparent. "They are Christians without Christ, Jesuits without Jesus."

In the twilight of his life, Roosevelt belatedly saw that the longtime warnings of his Ambassador in Moscow, William Averell Harriman, had made rock-ribbed sense. At a White House luncheon on 23 March, with one of his most trusted advisers, Anna Rosenberg, the

President, angrily banging his fists on his wheel-chair, announced: "Averell is right. We can't do business with Stalin. He has broken every one of the promises he made at Yalta."

Almost before the ink was dry, the Declaration on Liberated Europe, like much else glossed-over at Yalta, was emerging as the hollowest of shams. "Is it any use to go to San Francisco in these conditions?" Eden lamented to Churchill. "How can we lay foundations of any new World Order when Anglo-American relations with Russia are so completely lacking in confidence?"

—

On battle-fronts 6,000 miles apart, events now moved as swiftly as an unravelling spool of film.

Before dawn on Wednesday 10 January, a thousand anchors churned the waters of Lingayen Gulf, on the main Philippine island of Luzon, to white froth: with one giant step 100,000 men of MacArthur's troops, to be followed by a back-up force of a further 100,000, had been transported 2,000 miles from Leyte. On 1 February MacArthur instructed Major-General Verne Mudge, commanding the 1st Cavalry Division: "Get to Manila! Go around the Japs, bounce off the Japs, but get to Manila!"

This 120-mile hell-for-leather dash across Japanese-held rice paddies and ploughed fields was essentially a mercy mission, for the prime objective was the liberation of 3,500 American internees held in Manila's Santo Tomás University, plus 1,000 POWs in the city's Bilibid Prison and 2,000 more in Los Banos Prison Camp, 40 miles south. By 9 p.m. on 3 February, advance elements of the 1st Cavalry had entered north Manila, and a tank christened "Battling Basic" had splintered through the high wooden gates of Santo Tomás.

Then the battle for the city raged for thirty days and nights, among the pink, blue and green stucco houses massed with bougainvillea, until roofs were scattered "like spilled packs of playing cards" and the old inner city of Intramuros, its walls forty feet thick and twenty-five feet high, lay in ruins. No other city, save Warsaw, suffered more than Manila, but the early liberation had spared the internees much hardship, for in Santo Tomás, Red Cross supplies were reduced to bandages, gentian violet and Vaseline.

After months of stagnation, the front had come alive in Burma, too: in January, Akyab fell, and farther to the north Lieutenant-General Sir William Slim's "forgotten" Fourteenth Army crossed the Irrawaddy River in February, and seizing Meiktila en route, had reached Mandalay before the end of March. By May, they would seize Rangoon.

In Europe, following the Ardennes setback, the advance was forging ahead and the big industrial towns were falling like ripe fruit: München-Gladbach, Krefeld, Rheydt. On 1 March, Patton, despite orders to bypass it, took Trier.[31] Towns burned like torches for a night, smouldered for a day, then lay blackened and dead. Great centres like Frankfurt and Mannheim were becoming ghost cities, stark in their architectural wreckage. "When the heart breaks, all breaks," the London *Observer* noted, "and Germany now is Heartbreak House."

It was a house with many mansions, and Lieutenant-Colonel Saul K. Padover was no stranger to any of them. Jeeping through North Rhine-Westphalia, it was hard to distinguish one broken town from another; Padover looked for other yardsticks. München-Gladbach was a town plastered with slogans; all told Padover totted up more than two dozen within the hour. Always the keynote was exhortation: TUST DU FUER DEN SIEG (What are you doing for victory?) JEDE STUNDE UNSEREM FUHRER (Every hour for our Führer).

Yet the citizens were promenading the streets, the women gaily dressed and smiling, and some of them waved to the GIs as they passed through. Near Rheydt, Göbbels' home-town, refugees from the Ruhr asked Padover eagerly, "Did you bomb Berlin and Düsseldorf today?". When he replied yes, their acclaim was wholehearted: "Wonderful! Flatten everything. Don't leave the swine in peace!"

Krefeld was the town where 150 *Volkssturm* had given up in disgust without firing a shot, where the only Nazis to be found, as in all the other towns, were *muss*-Nazis – those who had joined the party under pressure. The way to get conversation flowing, Padover found, was to lead off, "And when did you *have* to join the Nazi party?" Time and again the reply would come "I'm so glad you understand that one *had* to join the party ... if one didn't the *bonzen* (politicians) would make it uncomfortable for you. How they lied to us and deceived us, these Nazis. They promised us victory. They promised us plenty of work. They promised us everything. And we fell for it."

"Hitler," Padover concluded to his driver, Private Joe Dorferlein, "is the greatest man of all time." And when the GI goggled, Padover elaborated: "I've never been more serious. They're all against Hitler. They've always been against Hitler. So that means that Hitler alone, without help or encouragement from anybody in Germany started the war, licked all Europe ... murdered five million Jews, set up 400 concentration camps, created the biggest army in Europe and made the trains run on schedule. It takes a pretty good man to do all that by himself."

"I getcha," said Joe laconically. "For a moment I thought you was kiddin'."

Sooner than he knew, still in diligent search of avowed Nazis, Padover would cross the Rhine.

Only the steep-walled Rhine itself now shielded the heart of Germany from nine advancing Allied armies – and now, around 3:50 p.m. on Wednesday 7 March, there came one of the great lucky chances – perhaps the greatest – of the European war. Or, as *Feldmarschall* Albert Kesselring put it from the German viewpoint: "Never was there more concentrated bad luck at one place."

Thus far, all units to reach the Rhine had found the bridges destroyed – but at that hour on 7 March a squad of the 3rd Platoon, Company A, 27th Armoured Infantry Battalion, reached the great Ludendorff Bridge at Remagen, a double-track railroad bridge just over 1,000 feet long, spanning the Rhine between Bonn and Coblenz. To the astonishment of the first men on the spot, Sergeant Alex A. Drabik and Second Lieutenant Karl Timmermann, the bridge was intact.

Both men knew one thing: there was no time to lose. Explosive charges must have been set, and the bridge could blow at any moment. (In fact, *Hauptmann* Karl Friesenhahn, the engineer commander, had timed the moment for 4 p.m.). Pounding at the head of his platoon Drabik reached the bridge's western edge then pelted hard, under heavy small arms fire, down the middle, his men following in squad column on the other side. "We took cover in some bomb craters," Drabik explained later. "Then we just sat and waited for the others to come."

And come they did: within ten minutes 100 Americans led by Timmermann, the first officer, had crossed the Rhine.

The news was swift to travel. The first senior officer to hear, the First Army's Lieutenant-General Courtney Hodges, at once called Bradley. "Hot dog, Courtney," Bradley exulted. "This'll bust the

Krauts wide open," and he in turn lost no time in calling Eisenhower's headquarters at Reims. "Brad, that's wonderful," was the Supreme Commander's first reaction, and when Bradley urged pushing all the neighbouring forces to the east bank of the Rhine, Eisenhower was in full agreement. "Sure, get right on across with everything you've got. It's the best break we've had."

It was no exaggeration. Within twenty-four hours 8,000 Americans had crossed at Remagen; within five days, several divisions. By then, floating Treadway bridges, transportable in sections and laid from bank to bank within a day, were taking the brunt of the heavy military traffic. The Ludendorff, weakened by German air and artillery attack, had served its purpose: it at last collapsed on 17 March.

The role of the front-line infantryman is often lost to history, but on the night of 7 March an anonymous reporter from the Omaha *World Herald* sought to set the record straight. Placing a call to the Goldenrod Café, in West Point, 75 miles northwest he informed Mrs Mary Timmermann, a waitress, that her son, Karl, was the first officer over Remagen Bridge.

A German war bride from World War One, Mrs Timmermann's English was uncertain at all times: in confusion she handed the phone to Proprietor Bill Schafer. "Karl is all right," Schafer told her, after listening impatiently, "Now talk to the man."

The disembodied voice again: "Your son Karl has just crossed the Remagen Bridge. You know what it means?"

"I know what it means to me: Is he hurt?"

"No, he's not hurt. But listen to this: Karl Timmermann was the first officer of an invading army to cross the Rhine River since Napoleon."

On behalf of all mothers, Mrs Timmermann put the matter in perspective: "Napoleon I don't care about. How is my Karl?"

-

Crouched above the uncertain flames, Allen Dulles energetically plied the bellows. The wood sputtered, then caught. Towards 10 p.m. on 8 March, the courtly 51-year-old former diplomat, head of America's top-secret Office of Strategic Services, was as absorbed as he had ever been. Kneeling before the library fireplace of a rented ground-floor apartment on Zurich's Genferstrasse, he sought to coax a pinelog fire into a merry blaze.

As the flickering light wavered and danced on the rows of morocco-bound books, Dulles momentarily relaxed. If a big conference was on the agenda, he set tremendous store on holding it round a wood fire – it had the subtle effect of making the participants feel at ease, shedding their inhibitions. And if you yourself needed time to answer, a fire helped in the by-play of lighting a pipe. Tonight, Dulles was especially anxious that everyone should be at their ease. After tortuous months of negotiation, he at last glimpsed the end of the war in Italy.

Hastily he checked his watch: five minutes to go. Once more he ran through the handwritten document before him, which his guest-to-be had sent via an intermediary earlier that day – one of the most astonishing documents Dulles had ever seen in his career as an intelligence agent. As he said later, it was more the kind of *curriculum vitae* a man prepares when applying for a job with a company – though in a sense his visitor was:

KARL WOLFF

S.S. Obergruppenführer and General of the Military S.S., Highest S.S. and Police Leader and Military Plenipotentiary of the German Armed Forces in Italy.

Information about the above person can be given by:

1. The former Deputy of the Führer, Rudolf Hess, at present in Canada.

2. The present Pope: Visit in May, 1944 ... he stands by to intercede, if desired, at any time.

There were pages more of it, together with letters of reference from prominent churchmen supporting claims that Wolff had saved precious paintings from Florence's Uffizi Gallery, had stopped general strikes without bloodshed, helped *Feldmarschall* Kesselring avert the destruction of Rome, and protected Italian partisans from German labour round-ups. As Dulles summed up to his aide, Gerd von Gaevernitz, "He wants to show us just who'll vouch for him in case we have any wrong ideas."

And promptly at 10 p.m., when Wolff entered the library, along with Professor Max Husmann, a stocky Swiss headmaster who had helped put Dulles in contact with both Italian industrialists and

German top brass, the general, significantly, wore a grey civilian suit. To Dulles, he repeated what he had already stressed to Husmann on the train journey from the Italian border town of Chiasso to Zurich. "Neither Hitler nor Himmler," he emphasised, "know anything of this trip."

Pouring Scotch, Dulles proposed that Husmann should first summarise the facts that had emerged on the five-hour journey. Meanwhile he studied his man – a distinguished 45-year-old with slightly-receding blond hair, whose sharp green eyes never quite met his interlocutor's.

"He concedes," Husmann wound up, underlining the lesson of Remagen, "that the war for Germany is irrevocably lost."

Dulles studied the dancing flames, covertly watching the stiff-necked Wolff relax little by little, lulled by warmth and Scotch. Casually he invited him: "Suppose you state your own position fully and frankly." Wolff came directly to the point. "Until last year," he told his intently-listening audience, "I had complete faith in Hitler. But I realise the war is lost and that to continue it is a crime against the German people. Now *I* control the S.S. forces in Italy – I am willing to place myself and my entire organisation at the disposal of the Allies to terminate hostilities."

Although Dulles and a staff which had grown to thirty had begun undercover operations from Berne's American Legation as long ago as November 1942, it was not until late 1944 that Milan industrialists had begun to make peace feelers, conveyed throughthe Cardinal Archbishop, Ildefonso Schuster, to Monsignor Bernardini, Berne's Papal Nuncio. The tenor of every approach had been: if the Germans withdrew from Northern Italy without destroying vital industrial plants the Church might act as middlemen to keep the growing army of partisans in check. One month back, an envoy from Rudolf Rahn, German Ambassador to Mussolini's Republic of Salò and the mastermind behind the plot, had visited Switzerland to spell out the message all over again.

As an earnest of his intentions, Wolff had already released Resistance Chief Ferruccio Parri, a saintly white-haired World War One hero who had fought the Fascists for twenty years, from Verona Gaol – and Dulles was now hiding him up in a Zurich clinic. In the event of a German retreat from Italy, Wolff now assured them, he had given orders to carry out only token sabotage of industry.

But, Wolff emphasised, the S.S. in themselves were not enough. He had to win over the commanders of the German Armed Forces. Already he had talked with his old friend Kesselring and thought he might be persuaded. If Dulles could assure negotiations at the level of Field-Marshal Sir Harold Alexander, now Supreme Commander, Kesselring or a deputy might visit Switzerland to parley a surrender.

A self-confessed eternal optimist, Dulles christened this bold plan to remove 800,000 pawns from the board at one stroke "Operation Sunrise".

But now an hour had ticked by and Dulles felt that for tonight they had gone as far as they could. Much now depended on Kesselring's attitude. But one last question was mandatory: was Mussolini a party to these plans?

For almost the first time Wolff looked him squarely in the eye. "Mussolini knows nothing," he told the American, "and he will know nothing. This much is certain – we can't trust Mussolini."

Rarely since the days of Genghis Khan had humanity known such devastation. All over the world the fires raged unchecked; entire cities were put to the torch; human beings with brains and lives and destinies renounced all future, shrivelled to the size of dolls.

On 20 January, when Major-General Curtis E. Le May took over the XXI Bomber Command on Saipan, his most pressing problem was how to "bomb the Japanese into the Stone Age". Results to date had been unimpressive, even though the only night fighters Japan could call on were Gekko Navy planes. After long thought, Le May decided to "throw away the book". To increase their payload his B-29s would be stripped of almost all armament. Since 90% of Japanese cities were of tinder-box construction, the planes would carry incendiaries: 7 to 8 tons per plane. They would not fly formations, they would go in by night and attack from as low as 5,000 feet.

At 5:36 p.m. on 9 March, the first B-29 of a wave 334 strong thundered down the runway of North Field on Guam, in the Marianas, to be followed, fifty seconds later, by another. Their destination was Tokyo, whose wartime population had swollen to seven million people. Of these, 750,000 low-income workers were crammed together in the three-by-four mile downtown sector.

Precisely at 12:15 a.m. the first pathfinders zeroing in on the quarter, dropped the first of 50,000 bombs: M-47 missiles, which split apart 100 feet above the ground to scatter two-foot-long napalm sticks, spreading a creeping carpet of flaming jelly.

As plane after plane homed in from Saipan along the "Hirohito Highway" what followed was what firemen call a "sweep conflagration": literally a tidal wave of fire. Leaping from building to building like a living creature, the fire exploded as it went, whipped by 28 m.p.h, surface winds, until the temperature reached an incredible 1,800 degrees Fahrenheit; soon the thermals soaring upwards were tossing the bombers like spillikins 4,000 feet higher.

Houses exploded like ovens charged with gas. Tree trunks caught fire like giant logs in a fireplace. Thousands who took refuge in shallow ornamental lakes and canals were literally boiled to death. Thousands more were charred beyond identification; to the crews of the last bombers over the target, the stench of burning flesh turned the stomach even at 5,000 feet. More than sixteen square miles of Tokyo were gutted, and within six hours perhaps 84,000 perished in the flames.

It was no lone exception. Three weeks earlier, on the night of 13 February, the R.A.F. and the U.S. 8th Air Force had also played their part: almost 2,000 Allied bombers dropped 3,000 tons of bombs, including 650,000 incendiaries, on the centre of Dresden, on the Elbe River, fuelling a conflagration that wiped out 135,000 people.

The *Volkssturm* slogan, "Hard times, hard hearts," had never been more apt. On the night of that raid, Air Marshal Arthur Harris, C-in-C of R.A.F. Bomber Command, arrived to dine with Churchill. The Premier's secretary, John Colville, found him, brooding and alone, in the Great Hall at Chequers. "What is the news of Dresden?" Colville asked.

With no apparent emotion or regret, Harris answered: "There is no such place as Dresden".

—

The concept of devastation was much on Adolf Hitler's mind. But it was not the devastation the Allies were wreaking on Ruhr and Rhineland that now obsessed him. It was the planned and systematic destruction of a Germany that had failed its Führer.

"If the German people cannot wrest victory from the enemy then they shall be destroyed," he told *Brigadeführer* Walter Schellenberg, of the Reich Security Service, passionately. "Yes, then they deserve to perish for the best of Germany's manhood will have fallen in battle. Germany's end will be horrible and the German people will have deserved it."

This was no mere rhodomontade. On 18 March, Hitler's Minister of Armaments and War Production, Albert Speer, submitted an urgent memo which insisted: "We have no right at this stage of the war to order demolitions which would affect the future existence of the German people." Hitler's nihilistic reply mirrored his prophecy to Schellenberg: "On the contrary, it is better ourselves to destroy such things, for this nation will have proved itself the weaker and the future will belong exclusively to the stronger Eastern nation."

On 18 March, to Speer's horror, this "scorched earth" policy became official. Not only industrial plants were to be razed but all facilities that could sustain life: food supplies, sewerage systems, long-distance cables, telephone exchanges. Even historic monuments and works of art were not exempt from this Gothic *Götterdämmerung*: castles, churches, theatres and opera houses would all be swept away.

Although the order stripped Speer of all powers, he did not yield lightly. All told, by his own calculations, he committed some sixty separate acts of high treason. Making the Ruhr his top priority he skilfully enlisted the aid of the industrialist Walther Rohland in thwarting the Nazi Party Gauleiters charged with destruction: all dynamite, blasting caps and fuses were to be thrown into the sumps of the coal mines, to prevent them flooding. A master of dissimulation, Speer even gave written orders for demolitions – then mailed them in towns about to fall to the Allies. On 30 March, he wheedled Hitler into granting him total demolition powers – but failed to order a single act of sabotage.

There was no lack of collaborators. As Chief of Staff of the Armed Forces High Command, *Generalmajor* Walther Buhle consistently refused to authorise the issue of any explosives. On 30 March, *Grossadmiral* Karl Dönitz, the Navy C-in-C, also won a valuable concession: no wrecking of harbours or dockyards would take place without his orders.

Unknown to the conspirators, Eisenhower, on 28 March, had reached a decision that would render their task that much harder.

Instead of launching his last offensive across Northern Germany, as originally planned, he would now strike directly across the centre of the country. Lieutenant-General William Simpson's Ninth Army, reverting to Bradley's command, would now have the major role. The main thrust would take place in the area Erfurt-Leipzig-Dresden, to join hands with the Russians 100 miles south of Berlin.

Since he was authorised to liaise directly with the Russians on matters of military co-ordination, Eisenhower requested Major-General John Deane, head of the U.S. Military Mission in Moscow, to pass on this news to Stalin.

Five days after that signal, Churchill belatedly woke to life; he saw trouble ahead, and its emblem was a hammer-and-sickle. Moscow was reacting with vehemence to Dulles' "Operation Sunrise," charging that a separate peace was in the offing. Sixteen Polish nationalists, invited to Moscow for talks, had mysteriously disappeared. Berlin, Churchill now insisted, must be saved from the Red Army, and not only Berlin but Prague, Vienna, north Germany and Denmark. "I deem it highly important that we should shake hands with the Russians as far east as possible," he signalled Eisenhower, and he likewise urged Roosevelt, "Should Berlin be in our grasp we should certainly take it."

Eisenhower could not see it. "That place has become, so far as I am concerned, nothing but a geographical location," embodied his thinking, for Bradley estimated that taking Berlin could result in 100,000 casualties – a stiff price to pay when Berlin was within the zone assigned to the Russians by the European Advisory Commission.

Above all, the Supreme Commander's *volte-face* was prompted by the credulous acceptance of a myth.

On 11 March, SHAEF G-2 drew up what, with hindsight, was recognised as one of the war's worst intelligence estimates: that Hitler was bent on establishing a mountain retreat in the Bavarian Alps to direct continuing nation-wide resistance. "Here, defended by nature and by the most effective secret weapons yet invented," was a sample of its purple prose, "the powers that have hitherto guided Germany will survive to reorganise the resurrection ... a specially selected corps of young men will be trained in guerilla warfare, so that a whole underground army can be fitted and directed to liberate Germany..."

The truth was more prosaic. The project, envisaged by an O.S.S. contingency report in September 1944, had been intercepted by *Gauleiter* Franz Hofer, of Bregenz, on Lake Constance, who pronounced it "the best idea that the Americans have had in this war." By degrees, the chimera took shape, received with rapture by Göbbels for its propaganda potential, with qualified enthusiasm by Hitler for its nuisance value.

Thus, in February 1945, work of a kind had begun: 2000 Todt organisation workers under Hofer were drafted to build fortifications in the twenty miles between Bregenz and Feldkirch. Yet the myth grew faster than the concrete was poured; by the end of March, Ernst Kaltenbrunner, Chief of the Reich Security Service, had taken charge, anxious both to exploit Allied fears and gain better occupation terms from the Allies. Though the British were sceptical, the National Redoubt was no figment to Lieutenant-General Alexander Patch's U.S. Seventh Army. Their estimates envisaged up to 300,000 fanatical S.S. men, and ultimately Patton's Third Army was despatched to uncover the truth behind the legend: the backwash of a defeated army, ninety per cent of them non-combatants.

One man had long known the National Redoubt for the sham that it was: *Generaloberst* Heinz Guderian. But at 2 p.m. on Wednesday 28 March, one hour before Eisenhower drafted his cable to Stalin, that knowledge became immaterial. The man who pioneered the panzer techniques of 1940, the last of Hitler's top-flight generals, bowed out of the war.

By now the Führer's obsession with "fortresses" had become paranoid – what Albert Speer was to describe as "a cruel phantom war game". Divisions were switched hither and thither according to whim. By mid-April, no less than twelve towns and cities south and east of Berlin had been accorded "fortress" status. Heads rolled as under a military guillotine; in January *Generalleutnant* Friedrich Hossbach was replaced as Fourth Army commander by *General der Infanterie* Friedrich Wilhelm Müller. When Königsberg fell, Müller was in turn banished, giving place to *General* Dietrich von Saucken.

On 28 March, Guderian fought a losing battle on behalf of *General* Theodor Busse, whose Ninth Army had failed to break through to the defenders of Russian-encircled Küstrin, on the eastern bank of the Oder River.

In Hitler's offices at the Berlin *Reichskanzlei*, a score of men grouped round the huge map table, a single slab of blood-red marble striated with the beige and white cross-sections of an ancient coral reef, at first listened in silence as Busse gave his report. Suddenly Hitler cut in: "Why did the attack fail? Because of incompetence! Because of negligence!" He rounded on Guderian: "If Busse didn't have enough ammunition as you claim – why didn't you get him more?"

"I have already explained..." Guderian began, but already Hitler was ranting, deaf to all reason. "Explanations! Excuses! That's all *you* ever give me." Guderian's temper snapped. "Nonsense!" he shot back. "This is nonsense!" His face grew dangerously purple. "Busse is not to blame! ... He followed orders! Busse used all the ammunition that was available to him! All that he had! ... Look at the losses! The troops did their duty!"[32]

"They failed!" Hitler screamed, like a voice from a padded cell. "They failed!"

So violent was the interchange that followed that few could afterwards retail its exact sequence or pinpoint more than highlights. The General Staff had "misled," "misinformed" and "tricked" him, Hitler bellowed. "Exactly when," Guderian shouted back, "do you intend to evacuate the Kurland Army?" "Please! Please!" Jodl begged, tugging at the insensate Guderian's arm. "Calm down!" Suddenly Hitler slumped exhausted into a chair, Keitel hastening to his side. At this point, *Major* Freytag von Loringhoven, Guderian's tactful aide, saved the day. Hastening to the Ambassador's Room, the tapestried antechamber to Hitler's office, he called *Generalleutnant* Hans Krebs, Guderian's Chief of Staff, at Zossen. Without difficulty, he persuaded Krebs to summon Guderian to the phone and hold him in conversation until he had calmed down.

The ruse worked to perfection: in the fifteen minute interval that elapsed, Hitler, too, calmed down. Returning, Guderian found him conducting the conference as if nothing had ensued. On Guderian's entry, the Führer told every man save Keitel to leave the room. "*Generaloberst* Guderian, your physical health requires that you immediately take six weeks convalescent leave," he ordered icily. "I'll go," Guderian replied, his voice showing nothing of what he felt.

After that there was little left to do. Since Krebs was appointed his sucessor, Guderian briefed him accordingly, then retired to his private quarters to pack. Only his wife Gretl was privy to the secret; first they would stop off at a sanatorium near Munich, where Guderian would seek treatment for a heart condition. And after that, where could be better to convalesce than the one peaceful region remaining in Germany: the Bavarian Alps?

Unlike Eisenhower, Guderian knew that nothing was going on down there at all.

-

The Marshals arrived on Easter Sunday, 1 April, one field-grey sedan following another through the western gates of the Kremlin's fortress walls. Near the white brick bell tower of Ivan the Great they slowed to a halt outside a long three-storey mustard-coloured building. On the clock face of the great Saviour's Tower guarding the entrance the gilt hands showed close to 5 p.m. Marshals Georgi Zhukov and Ivan Konev were on time for their date with Josef Stalin.

In the second-floor conference room, lit by heavy chandeliers, the full State Defence Committee, the decision-making arm of the Soviet war machine, were already assembled. Barely had they taken their chairs, before Stalin's short stocky figure emerged from his private office. Few greetings were exchanged, Konev recalled later, for Stalin had a matter of moment on his mind: Allied treachery.

No mention was made of the Eisenhower signal that had so irked Churchill, and for one good reason: Stalin did not believe a word of it. Merely, in his low sing-song Georgian accent, he announced quietly "The little Allies (*soyuznichki*) intend to get to Berlin ahead of the Red Army".

Momentarily he yielded the chair to the Operations Chief, General Sergei Shtmenko, who gave an evaluation all his own: Eisenhower's forces might be advancing on Leipzig and Dresden but "just on the way" they intended to take Berlin. To seize the city before the Red Army was "Eisenhower's main aim".

A British Dunhill pipe clenched in his teeth, Stalin turned to his two Marshals. "So," he rallied them, "who will take Berlin? We or the Allies?"

"We will," Konev announced promptly, "and before the Anglo-Americans."

"So," Stalin said again, smiling. "Is that the sort of fellow you are?" But at once the questions followed thick and fast. How could Konev, to the south, re-group his forces in time? When Konev protested that this could be achieved, the stocky bull-like Zhukov cut in: "With due consideration, my First Belorussian Front needs no re-grouping. They are ready now ... We are the shortest distance from Berlin. We will take Berlin."

It was a situation after Stalin's heart: a cat-and-mouse game in which one commander would be pitted against the other. "Very well," he told them, "you will both stay in Moscow and prepare your plans with the General Staff. I expect them ready within forty-eight hours."

Both men were palpably taken aback. Many of their divisions were below strength: neither had expected to attack Berlin before early May. Given Stalin's implacable decision, it would be a race against time to solve almost insoluble logistical problems.

As the meeting broke up, Stalin returned to his office. It was time now to match duplicity with duplicity, but by 8 p.m. his reply to Eisenhower was drafted and dispatched. He agreed that the link-up with Soviet forces should be in the Leipzig-Dresden area. The date of the Red Army's attack would be "approximately the second half of May".

As for Berlin, Stalin stressed, it rated as low in his priorities as in Eisenhower's own. Berlin, in fact, had lost its former strategic importance. It was now of such small account that "the Soviet High Command therefore plans to allot secondary forces in the direction of Berlin".

Three days later, at 3 p.m. on 4 April, the commander of the newly-created Army Group Vistula, whose task was to hold the Russians on the Oder River and save Berlin, had his first meeting with Hitler. For *Generaloberst* Gotthard Heinrici, an outspoken 58-year-old whose normal attire was a moth-eaten sheepskin coat, it was a traumatic experience from the first.

Crossing the cratered gardens of the *Reichskanzlei*, littered with broken statues and uprooted trees, he and his Operations Chief, *Oberst* Hans Georg Eismann, descended 44 steep steps to Hitler's last bolthole: the *Führerbunker*, more than 50 feet below ground level, a world like a submerged ocean liner, housing Hitler and more than 600 acolytes, a complex whose cold grey concrete walls gave off a damp musty smell, isolated from the world by sixteen feet of concrete and six feet of rammed earth, with ventilators whirring monotonously day and night.

For Heinrici the entire conference was as unreal as the surroundings in which it unfolded. Hitler, shaking as uncontrollably as a victim of Parkinson's disease, his eyes red and inflamed in a grey puffy face, toying with a pair of pale green spectacles, was "a walking corpse". The small conference room was so cramped that many, Heinrici and Eismann among them, were forced to stand. Despite Hitler's presence, a subdued buzz of conversation continued throughout; to Eismann it was reminiscent of "a swarm of bees".

Mincing no words, Heinrici, as was his wont, came directly to the point. Running his finger along Hitler's map of the 75-mile-long Oder front, he pinpointed the cities where he expected the heaviest Russian attacks: Schwedt, Küstrin, Frankfurt-am-Oder. At Frankfurt, he stressed, garrison strength was low and so was ammunition. Despite its "fortress" status, he wanted the troops brought out.

For the first time, Hitler spoke, a voice harsh with hate: "I refuse to accept this."

Heinrici did not give ground. Quietly, methodically, citing reports and statistics, he outlined his case. Quite suddenly, to everyone's astonishment, Hitler, turning to Guderian's successor, said, "Krebs, I believe the General's opinion on Frankfurt is sound. Make out the necessary orders for the Army Group and give them to me today."

Heinrici and Eismann exchanged covert glances. But their victory was brief.

Suddenly, clawing bolt upright in his chair, Hitler jerked to his feet. A gabbling torrent of words poured from him, so frenzied and disconnected that few could distinguish their drift. To Eismann it emerged as a justification of his tactical use of fortresses. "Again and again," he ranted, "fortresses have fulfilled their purpose throughout the war. This was proven at Posen, Breslau... Every one of these fortresses was held to the very last man! History has proven me right and my order to defend a fort to the last man is right!" His eyes fixed on Heinrici, he screamed, "That's why Frankfurt is to retain its status as a fortress!"

He had reversed his own decision within five minutes.

To Heinrici, it was not only Hitler who lacked all concept of reality. What he regarded as the crisis point of the meeting had now approached, for he announced flatly, "My Führer, I do not believe that the forces on the Oder front will be able to resist the extremely heavy Russian attacks which will be made upon them."

The statement was the cue for what Heinrici recalled as "a sort of ghastly auction". Breaking silence, Göring now released 100,000

Luftwaffe personnel for the Oder front. Not to be outdone, Himmler's high-pitched voice offered 25,000 S.S. fighters – and Dönitz 12,000 sailors. *Generalmajor* Walter Buhle offered another 13,000 troops from the reserve army.

"There," Hitler said calmly, as if this settled the matter. "You have 150,000 men... there are your reserves."

Heinrici was aghast. None of the men so gratuitously offered, he pointed out, was combat-trained. Moreover all the battle-hardened armoured units had been removed from his command. He must have them back and without delay.

The angry voice of Hitler's adjutant, *General* Wilhelm Burgdorf, whispered in his ear: "Finish! You must finish!"

Hitler seemed momentarily apologetic. "The main thrust of the enemy attack will not be directed at Berlin – but there," he explained, and his finger stabbed at the city of Prague. "The Army Group Vistula should be well able to withstand the secondary attacks."

Heinrici was stubborn. "I cannot consider these 150,000 men as reserves," he maintained. "It is also my duty to tell you that I cannot guarantee that the attack can be repelled."

"Finish! Finish!" the voice whispered.

Hitler came once more to life. Again he struggled to his feet. "Faith!" he trumpeted, pounding the table. "Every commander must be filled with confidence! You! *You* must radiate this faith. *You* must instil this belief in your troops!"

In the aching silence which followed, the white-faced Heinrici, followed by Eismann, left the conference room. In silence they climbed the stairs to the ruined garden. A black pall of smoke brooded over the city.

"It's all of no use," Heinrici said. "You might just as well try to bring the moon down to earth. It's all for nothing. All for nothing."

–

They had long awaited the announcement, but when it came the shock was, nonetheless, overwhelming. At Kagohara airfield, forty miles north-west of Tokyo, the cadet pilots of 24th Advanced Training Squadron received a surprising summons on that spring night: all were to muster immediately in the C.O.'s office. They noticed that Commandant Suenaga was pale and tense, unable to restrain himself from pacing before the 24 pilots assembled.

"As you know," he said finally, "the army is short of pilots, petrol, planes and ammunition... We find ourselves at an impasse. There is just one last resort left to us: to crash on the decks of enemy aircraft carriers, as your comrades have done before you. Two hours ago, our squadron received the order to form a Special Attack Corps... I am compelled to ask you..."

He paused. "I could not prevent myself from shivering as if I had been slapped in the face," Ryuji Nagatsuka recalled later, waiting for Suenaga to conclude his sentence, "to... to undertake this mission".

He added hastily: "But, of course, you are free to choose. I will give you twenty-four hours to think it over."

That was at 8:30 p.m. on Saturday 31 March. At 8:30 a.m. on 1 April, an eight-mile line of craft moved towards the beaches of Okinawa, an island 70 miles long and seven miles wide, held by 100,000 Japanese under Lieutenant-General Mitsuru Ushijima.

It was the last steppingstone to Japan in the long U.S. advance across the Central and Southwest Pacific, for southern Kyushu lay less than 400 miles north, the last and greatest land battle in the Pacific War. For the men of Lieutenant-General Simon Bolivar Buckner's Tenth Army, who had coined the slogan, "May you walk in the ashes of Tokyo," every day of the 83-day battle, which cost the Americans over 49,000 casualties, was a nightmare – "like pushing a fist down a lion's mouth," one man put it.

By 2 April, a day of deceptive triumph, Okinawa was cut in two, the Japanese in the south cut off from the Japanese in the north, but on some days, like 16 May, gains were measured in yards, won, lost, then won again. It was a battle for place names that the combatants would long remember: Sugar Loaf Hill, which changed hands fourteen times, Shuri Castle, Bloody Nose Ridge. For the most part it was a battle of what Buckner, mortally wounded by a shell splinter on 18 June, called "blowtorch and corkscrew"; the blowtorch was liquid flame, explosives, the corkscrew. In the five days between 13 June and 17 June, the flame throwers expended 37,000 gallons of burning gasoline: in this period 1,000 Japanese were dying every day.

On the ships it had begun with the biggest breakfast ever: steak, fried eggs, ice cream, scalding hot coffee. In the foxholes it ended, when the rainy season brought nine inches of rain a day, with cold pork and egg yolks eaten from a can coated with soft red mud.

At Kagohara airfield, Nagatsuka and the other cadets had been momentarily beset by indecision. All that first night they had tossed and turned in their beds, filled with a desperate yearning to live. But next morning, at breakfast, Cadet Pilot Tanaka spoke up for all of them: "Look, we're all ready to accept this mission. Why don't we go to the C.O. straightaway and tell him so?"

And Nagatsuka, who had earlier nourished such grave doubts, agreed: "Suicide attacks are the only method left to us, and therefore they *must* succeed. If with our twenty-four planes we can sink eight or nine American carriers, it would give time for the pilots who follow us to undergo full training."

By evening, all but two men, rejected on grounds of ill health, had volunteered. Under Lieutenant Takagui, a Pacific veteran, the newly-christened *Kikusui* (Chrysanthemum) Group would begin one month's intensive training to die.

It was a timely gesture. For from 6 April onwards, the invaders of Okinawa were bedevilled by no less than 1,465 *Kamikaze* attacks – and on 6 April, the last ten ships of the Imperial Japanese Navy, led by the super battleship *Yamato* had sailed for Okinawa on what was virtually a mass *Kamikaze* mission, each ship carrying only enough fuel for a one-day trip. In the Japanese Navy's last sortie, all those ships were crippled or sunk.

But now Nagatsuka was close to despair. Okinawa, he knew, was a turning point in Japan's destiny – but would the battle still be raging when their training was over? For on 4 April, classes were once more suspended. Again the fuel had run out.

To the end, one man noted, it was "a conspiracy of smiles". The physician, Lieutenant-General Howard G. Bruenn, who, early in 1944, had noted his patient's appalling physical decline, sat easily on the edge of the bed but volunteered no information. The patient, Franklin D. Roosevelt, agreed he had slept well, despite a slight headache and a stiff neck, but otherwise asked no questions.

On Thursday 12 April, 1945, spring had come early to the Little White House at Warm Springs, Georgia, the site of the polio clinic of which Roosevelt had been co-founder in 1927. Dogwood and wild violets were already in bloom. Later that day, the President would attend a barbecue prepared in his honour on top of Pine Mountain, organised by Mayor Frank Allcorn and Ruth Stevens, manager of the Warm Springs Hotel: a mammoth Brunswick stew of hens, hogs' heads, vegetables and home-made catsup.

The President had breakfasted well – fried eggs, bacon, toast – and after Bruenn's departure, leafed through the Atlanta *Constitution*. The headlines reported American troops 57 miles from Berlin and that 150 Superforts had hammered Tokyo. At 11 a.m. he folded the paper carefully and laid it on the small night-table, close to his overnight who-dunnit, Carter Dickson's *The Punch and Judy Murders*, open at the chapter headed "Six Feet of Earth". His negro valet, Arthur Prettyman, arrived to help him shave and dress. Of all the White House staff, only Prettyman knew that for months Roosevelt had been unable to wield a razor, button a shirt or move his body from his wheelchair to the lavatory seat.

At noon he joined the company in the living room: his cousins Margaret Suckley and Laura Delano, and the woman he had loved unknown to the American people for almost thirty years: Lucy Mercer Rutherfurd. Present also was a portrait painter, Madame Elizabeth Shoumatoff. To do justice to the portrait that Mrs Rutherfurd had commissioned the President had dressed more formally than usual: a dark grey suit and waistcoat and a red-striped Harvard tie.

At noon, when his secretary, William D. Hassett, brought the mail pouch, he chanced on as peaceful a domestic scene as anywhere in the world. Madame Shoumatoff was busy at her easel. Margaret Suckley was crotcheting. Laura Delano was filling vases with nosegays: the smell of honeysuckle was heady in the room. Lucy Rutherfurd watched the President intently.

Roosevelt glanced through his papers, signing some, setting others apart for study. One document was a bill just passed by Congress, increasing the borrowing power of the Commodity Credit Corporation. "Here's where I make a law," Roosevelt joked to the ladies, signing with an illegible flourish.

On the other side of the room, the houseboy was setting the luncheon table. At 1 p.m. Roosevelt glanced at his watch. "We've got just fifteen minutes more," he said, then returned to his papers.

The fifteen minutes had almost elapsed when the President raised a shaky left hand to his temple, let it fall limply, then raised it again, pressing his forehead. "I have a terrific headache," he said, very softly. Then the eyes dropped, half-closed: he slumped to the left. His mouth gaped open in a long slow yawn. Madame Shoumatoff screamed shrilly, bringing Prettyman at a run from the kitchen.

A call brought Commander Bruenn, who had been sunning himself at the pool. Only with difficulty was the heavy inert body carried to the bedroom, to be stripped naked. The breathing had cut out, then started again, an anguished laboured snore. Bruenn injected papaverine and amyl-nitrate, before calling Admiral McIntire in Washington. The minutes passed: the breathing grew more painful yet, then stopped. Bruenn made one last effort: he injected adrenalin into the heart muscle. There was no response: a massive cerebral haemorrhage had stricken Roosevelt beyond hope of resuscitation. Bruenn looked at the others grouped round the bedside. "The man is dead," he said quietly. It was 3:55 p.m.

The reporters, hastening from the barbecue on Pine Mountain, were the first to hear. "Gentlemen," Hassett told them, rooted to the centre of the living room, "it is my sad duty to inform you that the President of the United States is dead..." So the news passed to Warm Springs, to the nation, and to the world.

In Warm Springs, the grief was convulsive: for almost twenty years the President had presided over the Thanksgiving dinners of the patients at the Georgia Hall Clinic, swimming with them in the warm pool, rallying them by his example. Next morning, when an Army band of 1,000 infantrymen from Fort Benning, black streamers flying from their colours, led the hearse down the red clay road, thousands were weeping unashamedly – among them Chief Petty Officer Graham Jackson, of the United States Coastguard, a squarely-built Negro, who had rated as Roosevelt's favourite musician. Now, his face a mask of anguish, Jackson's accordion rendered the one tune appropriate to this day: "Going home".

All that night, the funeral train rolled northwards, bringing the President back to the capital eighty years to the day after Lincoln was shot. In a dimly-lit compartment, Eleanor Roosevelt, who had journeyed south from Washington, sat with the President's Scottie, Fala, recalling a poem by Millard Lampell:

A lonesome train on a lonesome track,
Seven coaches painted black...
A slow train, a quiet train,
Carrying Lincoln home again...

The nation mourned. In Washington's Rock Creek Park, the British Ambassador, Lord Halifax, strolling with Roosevelt's old friend, Judge

Felix Frankfurter, knew without any need of words: church bells were tolling, filling all the air with sound, and hurrying people stood suddenly frozen, or broke into a run, or wept. In all the fire houses throughout the five boroughs of New York City, the slow toll of five bells repeated four times was sounded: a comrade had died in the line of duty. On Capitol Hill, a young Congressman, Lyndon Baines Johnson, lamented: "He was the one person I ever knew – anywhere – who was never afraid... God – God, how he could take it for us all." In the New York *Herald Tribune* building, at West 35th and Broadway, a reporter tapped out a single line: "The story is over."

All over the world, the same sense of desolation prevailed. In London, at No 10, Downing Street, Winston Churchill sat hunched in his black leather armchair for fully five minutes before uncradling the phone, saying "Get me the Palace." Lloyd's tolled the famous Lutine Bell. In Moscow, in the one compassionate gesture ever recorded of him, Stalin took Averell Harriman's hand and held it wordlessly. In Chungking, a coolie turned from the shiny black wall newspaper, muttering "*Tai tsam sso liao*" ("It was too soon that he died").

At 4701 Connecticut Avenue, Washington, the telephone rang in a second floor apartment and 20-year-old Margaret Truman, who was dressing for a dinner date, greeted the caller gaily. "Hi, Dad."

"Let me speak to your mother."

"Are you coming home for dinner?"

"Let me speak to your mother."

"I only asked a civil question!"

"*Margaret, will you let me speak to your mother?*"

The brusqueness was understandable. A 4:56 p.m. 60-year-old Harry S. Truman, the thirty-fourth Vice-President, had been sipping bourbon and water in the office of Speaker Sam Rayburn, when he received an urgent summons to the White House. There a pale but composed Eleanor Roosevelt broke the news: unknown to him, Truman, had been, for over an hour, the thirty-third President of the United States. Was there anything he could do for her, Truman asked, shocked.

Eleanor Roosevelt's reply was pertinent. "Is there anything *we* can do for *you*? You are the one in trouble now."

To Truman's critics – and at first there were many – he was no more than an apology for a chief of state: a man naive to a fault. "I don't know whether any of you ... ever had a load of hay or a bull fall on you," he greeted reporters on Capitol Hill, with tears in his eyes, "but last night the whole weight of the moon and stars fell on me. If you fellows ever pray, please pray for me." The critics poked fun, too, at his small-town persona, his snappy double-breasted grey suits and two-toned wingtip shoes, his habitual reference to his wife, Bess, as "The Boss," his nightly check of the White House windows, like any suburban householder. On an impromptu lunchtime visit to the bank, the Hamilton National at 14th and G Streets, he created one of the worst traffic snarls in Washington history; he had yet to learn that the Bank came to the President. Washington wits soon had a word for it: "to err is Truman".

Yet Truman had one advantage over Roosevelt: from the first he appreciated that Stalin had remained faithful to Lenin's precept: "It is necessary to use any ruse, cunning, unlawful method, evasion, concealment of truth." On his desk in the Oval Office, he early placed a three-sided gadget with the motto: THE BUCK STOPS HERE. Swift to make decisions, he was unhappy only when there were none to render – and one early decision, as Lord Halifax reported to Eden on 23 April, was to convey his displeasure to Molotov, who was in the United States, "in words of one syllable".

On that same afternoon, Truman made good his vow. In the Oval Office, he coldly berated the Foreign Affairs Minister for violating the Yalta Agreement to establish a freely-elected government for Poland. "We don't want to operate on the basis of a one-way street," Truman told him bluntly.

Molotov flushed angrily. "I have never been talked to like that in my life," he blustered.

"Carry out your agreements and you won't get talked to like that," Truman snapped back.

Truman was to need such resolution. Within ten days he would be faced with a decision with which no other President of the United States had ever been confronted: to use or not to use "the most terrible weapon ever known in human history."

To the Americans it had long been known as the "Manhattan Project". To the British it had masqueraded under the code-name "Tube Alloys". To the Japanese, it would, within months, be remembered for all time as "*pikadon*," which means "flash-boom".

On Sunday 15 April, the blue smoke from many fires hung thickly in the pine woods. On the road from Winsen to Celle in Lower Saxony, the young corn was green in the clearings, and buds were quickening in the hedgerows. Yet the first British contingent of 159 Brigade, advancing down this road, soon enough knew that something was wrong. "Speed five miles an hour," warned the signs. "Dust spreads typhus," and suddenly the warm wind brought "the honey-on-herring stench of death".

The zone was to be treated as neutral; the Germans had agreed to that. No shots were to be fired anywhere in the vicinity. For if a battle was fought, many of the 60,000 prisoners held in the six-square-mile barbed wire enclosure known as Bergen-Belsen, might escape and spread typhus throughout Germany. Thus the British, under Colonel Donald Taylor, of the 63rd Anti-Tank Regiment, working in concert with Brigadier Hugh Glyn Hughes, the Second Army's Senior Medical Officer, had agreed to take over the camp.

But typhus and typhoid would be the least of their worries, as no one knew better than Dr Gisella Krausz.

Towards the end of January, the crematoria at Auschwitz had closed down: Auschwitz was to be dynamited to hide the evidence of past enormities. "Hold on a little longer," Gisella told all those who had shared her "I am a lady" game, "The Russians are coming". It was a deliverance she was not destined to see. "Get ready," Mengele told her peremptorily one morning. "You are leaving Auschwitz!"

Thus Prisoner 25,404, escorted by two silent S.S. guards, had left Auschwitz for the last time – to work briefly in a Hamburg hospital before her transfer on 7 March, along with her Hungarian nurse, Olga Singer, to Bergen-Belsen. Here she plumbed the ultimate in human degradation; "Auschwitz was no more than a Purgatory. Hell was endured between the barbed wire fences of Bergen-Belsen".

In truth, Belsen was a monstrous irony: proof that Nazi Germany, far from being a soulless and efficient totalitarian regime, was a hotch-potch of feudal fiefs engaged in endless internecine war. Originally a *Wehrmacht* POW camp, it had functioned with moderate efficiency under *Hauptsturmführer* Josef Kramer, a man "with hard slaty-blue eyes ... as expressionless as a lizard," until the Allies crossed the Rhine. From then on, train loads of new prisoners from all over Germany signalled not only the death-throes of the Reich but the breakdown of Belsen. Between 4 April and 13 April, 28,000 new inmates were crammed into the camp. Bombs destroyed the electric plant which pumped the water; strafing Allied fighters blocked the arrival of food carts.

With Olga Singer, Gisella Krausz took over Block III, the "maternity block": women of all nations, lying in the cages along the walls, two to a cage, their stomachs swollen to bursting point with pregnancy and hunger, moaning, screaming, filling the building with "a constant deafening cacophony". All were suffering from typhus in its deadliest form, which brought uncontrollable diarrhoea: "blood, pus and urine formed a slimy fetid mud on the floor of the barracks". But with little water and no medicine, Gisella was almost powerless.

Soon the inmates were dying by the thousand: the compounds piled up with mountainous heaps of putrefying corpses. Ditches were choked with bodies, some of them retaining the breath of life but not the strength to struggle out from beneath their dead companions. The living tore ragged clothes from the dead, to build fires over which they boiled pine needles and roots for soup. Naked bodies with gaping wounds in their backs and chests showed where those who still had strength to use a knife had cut out the kidneys, livers and hearts of their fellow-men.

"If the heavens were paper and all the water in the world were ink, and all the trees were turned into pens, you could not even then record the sufferings and horrors," a Jewish rabbi wrote.

The first Britons inside the camp, Captain Derrick Sington, commanding No 14 Amplifying Unit of the Intelligence Corps, with his non-coms, Sergeant Eric Clyne and Lance-Corporal Sidney Roberts, would never erase the memory. Between them they spoke five languages and their task was to maintain law and order through loudspeaker announcements, but the sights were enough to strike all three dumb.

From the rows of green wooden huts drifted a smell of ordure "like a monkey-house". "A sad blue smoke floated like a ground mist between the low buildings". Breathing ghosts with staring eyes and shaven heads, in blue and white striped cotton, surrounded them. Among the silver birches, death pits 30 feet deep were choked with blackened flaccid corpses. A woman fell down and kissed a soldier's boots, begging for milk for her baby – an infant that had died days ago.

He spooned milk into its dead lips to humour her and she stumbled away in triumph, then she, too, fell dead.

Equally Gisella Krausz never forgot the arrival of the British, for on that morning Marusa, a young Polish partisan in Block III gave birth to a daughter, the first free child born in Bergen-Belsen. Then Marusa began to haemorrhage, and nothing would stop the bleeding, so Gisella, rushing from the block, her hands filthy and blood-smeared, grasped the sleeve of a tall impressive officer.

"Do you understand French?" she queried, and when he nodded, "Get me water, please, and some disinfectant… I have to perform an operation… Hurry… Hurry." And like any dutiful medical orderly, Brigadier Glyn Hughes did as he was bidden. Half an hour later Gisella was operating "not as a helpless prisoner but as a doctor": the lives of both Marusa and her daughter were saved.

Long after 21 May, when the British put the torch to the last hut in Belsen, Gisella Krausz worked on at the local gynaecological hospital, caring for bodies that Belsen had broken. Ahead of her lay many years as a successful gynaecologist in Palestine and New York: the true embodiment of a maxim Himmler had once adopted for the S.S.: "Our highest law is charity".

-

As Churchill and Truman strove to take the other's measure, one factor, above all, conspired to unite them: the clamour, from the German side, to end the war at all costs. *Obergruppenführer* Karl Wolff was only one of an ever growing line. Never had so many Nazi hierarchs sought peace so desperately.

As early as the night of 25 April, when Truman had barely dipped a toe in the Presidential waters, he and the Premier were closeted in a long-distance consultation between the White House and Downing Street. The top at issue seemed barely conceivable: S.S. *Reichsführer* Heinrich Himmler was preparing to renege on Adolf Hitler. Through the Swedish Government he had offered to surrender the German forces on the Western Front.

"Has he anything to surrender?" Truman wanted to know.

"Everything on the Western Front," Churchill said, "but he hasn't proposed to surrender on the Eastern Front. So we thought perhaps it would be necessary to report it to Stalin…"

"I don't think we ought to even consider a piecemeal surrender," Truman opined, and Churchill was vehement in agreement. "No, no, no. Not a piecemeal surrender to a man like Himmler."

The irony was that Himmler, working through Count Folke Bernadotte of the Swedish Red Cross, a nephew of King Gustav V, saw himself, because of his proven anti-Bolshevism, as the perfect plenipotentiary. In his first meeting with Bernadotte – one masterminded by the astute *Brigadeführer* Walther Schellenberg, who had been working his passage home since 1942 – on 19 February, at a sanatorium at Höhen-Luchen Himmler conceded that the Swedish Red Cross might work among the 13,000 Scandinavian internees in concentration camps.

At a second meeting, in the same venue, on 2 April, when the release of 4,000 Scandinavians into Red Cross care had been agreed, Himmler was abruptly called to the telephone. At once Schellenberg urged Bernadotte: "Couldn't you go to Eisenhower and discuss with him the possibility of capitulation on the Western Front?"

"The initiative must come from Himmler," Bernadotte replied, and this was the stance he firmly adopted throughout 78 days of the tortuous negotiations which Premier and President had now vetoed.

The number of men seeking to work their passage with the Allies was in the end phenomenal. Through other Swedish middlemen, Göring was also putting out feelers. Kaltenbrunner, employing an able subordinate, *Sturmbannführer* Wilhelm Höttl, had made tentative approaches through Vichy France's Marshal Henri-Philippe Pétain, Spain's Franco and the Portuguese dictator, Dr Antonio Salazar.

Ribbentrop, working through Sweden, Switzerland and the Allies, adopted an altogether clumsier approach, at one point "threatening" to "hand Germany over to the Russians," at another offering surrender to the West and switching the whole weight of the *Wehrmacht* to "stemming the Bolshevist flood." In Stockholm, his envoys, Peter Kleist and Fritz Hesse, spent three whole weeks in "fruitless and misguided" interviews, offering to hand over "all Jews in German-held territory, or to put them under neutral protection". This offer, received with interest by the World Jewish Congress representative, Dr Gilel Storch, found no favour with the Foreign Office; on 13 March, following the precedent of Joel Brand, they leaked it to the British Press.

Dr Josef Göbbels saw Ribbentrop as not only a liability but in pursuit of the wrong ends: as April dawned, he worked out a forty-page memorandum for the Führer, positing that since Stalin was anti-American and anti-British, the correct tactics were to combine forces with him against the West – recognising Russia's thrall over Finland and ceding her northern Norway and the Balkans. Three weeks later he learned that Martin Bormann, the Nazi Party deputy leader, had never passed it on: the war situation did not warrant such desperate measures.

All such peace moves, even on humanitarian grounds, would prove in vain. Throughout the war, Himmler's Finnish masseur, 47-year-old Dr Felix Kersten, described as a "cross between a Flemish burgomaster and an oriental Buddha," had cajoled the lives of 60,000 Jews out of the *Reichsführer* – "all the fault of my wretched health and the good Dr Kersten," Himmler was to admit, "(he) massages a life out of me with every rub." But on 1 April, when news of a Kersten mission to save 10,000 more Jewish lives reached Stockholm's British Embassy, Eden balked.

"I do not wish to be dragged into this matter," he wrote plaintively to Churchill. "It may be a Himmler plant and it may have entangling consequences ... I would prefer to say nothing to the Swedes."

"I agree," Churchill scribbled vigorously on the minute. "No truck with Himmler."

—

Lieutenant-General William Simpson was stunned. The impetus that had carried his Ninth Army all the way to the banks of the Elbe, less than forty-eight miles from Berlin, now seemed all for nothing. Early on Sunday 15 April, a sudden summons had taken Simpson post-haste to Wiesbaden, where Omar Bradley was waiting at the airfield.

"You must stop on the Elbe," Bradley told him. "You are not to advance any further in the direction of Berlin."

"Where in hell did you get this?" Simpson asked.

"From Ike," Bradley responded.

Still in a daze, Simpson returned to the Elbe. At the headquarters of the 2nd Armoured Division's Combat Command B, he ran into the commander, Brigadier-General Sidney R. Hinds. "Our crossings are going great," Hinds told him.

"Fine," Simpson said. "Keep some of your men on the east bank if you want to. But they're not to go any further."

It was Hinds' turn to be shocked. "No, sir," he said, "that's not right. We're going to Berlin."

There was a long moment of silence. Then Simpson, his voice tired and dead, said: "We're not going to Berlin, Sid. This is the end of the war for us."

—

On the western bank of the Oder, silence reigned. In a bridgehead thirty miles long and ten miles deep, the men of the battle-hardened Eighth Guards Army, the spearhead of Zhukov's drive for Berlin, waited tensely. In a hillside bunker overlooking Küstrin, the Army commander, General Vasily Chuikov, and Zhukov, himself, stared impassively into the darkness. The minutes were ticking by. On the stroke of 5 a.m. Zhukov muttered, "Now, Comrades. Now."

Three crimson flares arched into the blackness, bathing the Oder waters in a sudden lurid light. Simultaneously in the Küstrin bridgehead, a legion of 140 searchlights, stripped from the Moscow defence zone, switched on, blinding the German positions with a purer whiter glare than moonlight. There was silence, then three green flares followed upon the red, and Zhukov's guns found their voice.

A raging maelstrom of fire engulfed the German lines. In a vortex of flame, fully 40,000 guns were firing in a barrage that lasted for twenty-five minutes, uprooting trees, pulverising entire villages, powering a hot howling wind that bent saplings like divining rods and churned dust and debris into a whirling sirocco, 3,000 feet high. Thirty-five miles distant in Berlin, night staff above ground in the *Reichskanzlei* glanced apprehensively at the ceiling, eyes riveted on the swaying chandeliers.

Four days later, Hitler's fifty-sixth birthday, proved a melancholy occasion, for all save the Führer: "Not exactly a birthday situation," Martin Bormann noted glumly in his diary for Zhukov had reached Oranienburg, barely ten miles north of the city centre, and Heinrici's Army Group Vistula, a rag-bag collection of airfield staffs, sailors and convicts freed from gaol, 30,000 men with 1,000 rifles between them, were powerless to halt the tide. As early as 18 April, Heinrici had realised that the one hope for Busse's Ninth Army was to withdraw from the Oder and move north to Berlin: otherwise it faced annihilation. Hitler's response was predictable: the Ninth Army was to stand fast.

For in the throbbing twilight of the bunker – which he left for the last time at 3:30 p.m. to fasten Iron Crosses on a group of Hitler Youth – the Führer's zest for his "cruel phantom war game" was unabated. "The Russians will have their greatest defeat, their bloodiest hiding in history, before the gates of Berlin," he pronounced on this day, for as so often in the past Hitler had hit upon a miracle-man to wrest victory from defeat: S.S. *Obergruppenführer* Felix Steiner would attack towards Berlin.

Conveniently ignored was the truth that Army Group Steiner existed only on paper: Steiner had no troops with which to execute the order. His one hope was to assemble a group as and how he could of soldiers cut off from their units.

One man knew better than any that the end had come: the canny Dr Josef Göbbels. At 11 p.m. on the eve of Hitler's birthday, to the sound of wailing air-raid sirens, he and his staff assembled for their nightly conference in Göbbels' boarded-up study lit by flickering candles. Yet there was no reproach for the Führer in Göbbels' last peroration: like Hitler he saw only "treason".

"What can you do with a people whose men don't even fight when their women are raped?" he demanded, "All the plans, all the ideas of National Socialism, are too high, too noble, for such a people."

"But," he taunted his staff, "don't you gentlemen have any illusions. None of you was forced to go along with me – just as little as we have forced the German people. The people gave us their mandate. And you – why have you worked with me? Now you will have your little throats cut!"

From the door of his study, he bade them a gallows farewell. "And when we step down," he screamed, "let the whole world tremble!"

In the Führerbunker, by contrast, each passing hour was buoyed by false optimism, clouded with a sense of unreality. In the passages S.S. soldiers, cradling their guns, slumped in apathy, made listless by the stale air, but in the five-room complex that was Hitler's sanctum – a study, a bedroom, two living-rooms and a bathroom – miracles were wrought each passing minute. Were Russian attacks grounding

Luftwaffe planes, as *General* Karl Koller, Luftwaffe Chief of Staff, reported? No matter – "I insist that every bombed airfield be made ready again overnight," Hitler instructed Koller ("Just let him rave," Albert Speer counselled. "He has never in his life seen a bombed airfield.") And when would Steiner attack? At 9 p.m. on 21 April, the Führer transferred every man available to Steiner's command – though nobody knew precisely where Steiner was located.

But by 22 April, a disquieting picture was emerging: plainly Steiner, with a skeleton army of six battalions, had no intention of attacking. Instead he was avoiding Berlin by a retreat through Brandenburg. It was the same with *General* Walther Wenck, whose newly created Twelfth Army faced Simpson's static Ninth Army on the Elbe. With few weapons save rifles and hand grenades, Wenck had no more intention than Steiner of converging on Berlin. A battle for the capital such as Hitler desired meant delivering themselves up to the Russians – and both were determined to surrender to the Western Allies.

At 3 p.m. on this day, the last full-dress conference ever held in the Führerbunker began in a mood of suppressed excitement. It was to last almost five hours. With his customary skill in dealing with Hitler, Jodl opened it by dwelling on the good news: some local advances in Saxony, Italy, and the upper reaches of the Oder. But Hitler, for once, was not to be placated: what he wanted was the bad news.

"Spare me the details!" he burst out suddenly. "Spare me the trivial things! I want to know where Steiner is!"

Then Jodl told him. Steiner had been "unable to attack". Busse's Ninth Army was virtually encircled – as was Berlin. By nightfall, Konev's troops would have reached Lichtenrade, south of Templehof airport, heading for Zehlendorf and Steglitz.

The silence seemed to yawn and stretch. Hitler's face grew progressively redder. Then, in a hoarse voice, he asked to be left alone with the generals.

Aides and secretaries filed from the room. There remained only Keitel, Jodl, Krebs, Bormann, Wilhelm Burgdorf, *Generalmajor* Eckhardt Christian, Luftwaffe Operations Chief, *Oberst* Nicolaus von Below, the Luftwaffe Adjutant, *Major* Freytag von Loringhoven, Krebs' Chief of Staff, and the stenographer, Gerhard Herrgesell. Then the storm broke.

As if charged with an electric current, Hitler jerked from his seat, raving uncontrollably. One moment as pale as paper, the next purple and suffused, he shook like a St Vitus victim. In the narrow passages, the aides and secretaries, pale and shaken, listened — for half an hour, by some accounts, for three hours, by others — as Hitler screamed with a whining undertone that made the flesh creep.

He had long ago lost faith in the *Wehrmacht*. Now, because of Steiner's treachery, he had lost faith in the S.S. too. Every officer was a traitor; nobody understood his aims; they were all too small, too petty. They could leave him, and Berlin, too: only he would stay until the end and lead his Berliners into battle. Then, incredibly, sinking slowly to his chair, he collapsed into himself like a small child, sobbing brokenly, "It is all over. The war is lost. I shall shoot myself."

Five uneasy minutes passed. Then Jodl, speaking quietly but firmly, recalled him to his duties to the people and the Army. Hitler's job was to lead the troops, not stand with a flintlock in his hand, only to die in the rubble.

But Hitler was obdurate. Come what might, he would not leave Berlin.

Later that night, he made an attempt, perfunctory at first, to put his house in order. Keitel was to hasten to join Wenck on the Elbe, and take steps to amalgamate his Twelfth Army with Busse's Ninth. Jodl was to join Steiner and advance the attack on Berlin from the north. Dönitz was to assume full civil and military responsibility for the northern province.

Now, like a pocket Gneisenau, he was again shuffling maps. Mercurial as ever, his voice had taken on a new timbre. Men of whose valour he had once more convinced himself "were marching again in his mind".

-

One day later, Lieutenant-Colonel Saul K. Padover met the archetype he, as much as Hitler, had longed to meet: a self-confessed dyed-in-the-wool Nazi.

In a Luftwaffe barracks at Brunswick, Lower Saxony, Padover, along with a G-2 Colonel from Simpson's Ninth Army and a team-member, Lieutenant Hart, met up with a newly-taken prisoner of war: *Generalleutnant* Kurt Dittmar, whose wartime weekly broadcasts had served as a mouthpiece for the Army High Command.

Tall, slim and immaculate, his boots "polished to a mirror finish," Dittmar from the first recalled to Padover "the movie actor Conrad

Veidt impersonating a Junker general." He greeted them both with a smile that never left his face. "We are all in the same game," his smile said to Padover. "Sometimes one side wins, sometimes the other. You win this time, we will be victorious next time: it's all a question of sportsmanship, isn't it, gentlemen?"

He had, he told them, been much in demand as a speaker all over the Third Reich, talking to universities, clubs, factory workers. His two hour lectures had dealt with the military situation.

"And how Germany was sure to win?" Padover cut in.

"*Sicher, sicher*, (Sure, sure)," Dittmar agreed, smiling broadly.

"Did you really believe in the victory you used to proclaim in your broadcasts?" Padover wanted to know.

Dittmar was disingenuous. "Victory? Well, I would not call it that. I never really thought we could win... When the Führer messed up our strategy in Russia, I was convinced we could not win... Above all, Stalingrad destroyed confidence in our military leadership. It was all Hitler's fault, and that is why I hate him from the bottom of my soul."

His voice quivered with palpable indignation. Was he then hostile to the Führer. Padover asked him.

Dittmar recovered his equanimity. "Not at all. My criticism of the Führer is purely military. He did fine things for Germany... Hitler came forth as the champion against Versailles, and all of us, the whole nation, backed him up on that. Furthermore, his Socialist ideals attracted the German people."

A general in sympathy with Socialism? Padover was intrigued.

Dittmar had it all pat. "*Ach, nein*, we old officers are Socialists, too, of course. For example we believe in common effort and comradeship and all that – that's real Socialism. Hitler, as an old soldier, was naturally also a Socialist like the rest of us and that is why he could win over the German people."

And the National Redoubt, someone asked, what about the Redoubt?

For the first time, Dittmar showed himself genuinely nonplussed. All he knew of the Redoubt was something he had read in a Swiss newspaper back in January. In the north there were still pockets of resistance in Norway and Denmark, and one in the south, in the Italian Alps – "but that is less by intention than by force of circumstances."

Decisively he shook his head. "The National Redoubt? It's a romantic dream. It's a myth."

And a myth it was proven to be – but no greater than the myths that prevailed to the very end in the *Führerbunker*. On the morning of 23 April, as if one stroke of the pen settled everything, Hitler dismissed the errant Steiner, vesting command of his non-existent forces in *Generalleutnant* Rudolf Holste – an order which both Steiner and Holste blatantly ignored. In a fit of pique, convinced that Göring, in Bavaria, was trying to supplant him, he stripped him of all his offices, expelling him from the Party. At 3 p.m. Keitel and Jodl returned from the battlefield with little conclusive to report. Were any talks proceeding with the Allies? Keitel wanted to know. Before talks could begin, the Führer assured him, "one more victory" must be won – the Battle of Berlin.

Far from the *Führerbunker*, the battle was raging by the hour; in the ring of industrial districts and workers' suburbs to the north and east, the Russians were everywhere. Among the wreckage of the rows of dark ugly brick and stone houses of Weissensee and Pankow, S.S. troops and Nazi youth fought from flaming block to block, from the warehouses and factories turned into fortresses. Soon the Russians were on the main spokes of the wheel of *Chaussees* and wide *Strassen* that led to the hub of Alexanderplatz. From Weissensee and Pankow they inched in towards the vast Sportspalast, where Hitler had recited much of the history that had now turned to dust.

Fifty feet below ground, Hitler sometimes sat silent for hours at a time, his tunic soiled with particles of food, crumbling slice after slice of chocolate cake, saliva drooling from the corners of his mouth. Then he would galvanise himself again, and in the teleprinter complex housed in the flak tower by the Zoo, Luftwaffe *Leutnant* Gerda Niedeck found herself deciphering the same questions over and over again: "*What is Wenck's position?*" "*Where is Steiner?*" "*Where is Wenck?*"

By Tuesday 24 April, General Vasily Chuikov, directing the battle from a gloomy five-storey building on Belle Alliance Strasse, in the central suburb of Kreuzberg, knew he could relax a trifle. To date the tension had been such that Chuikov had been smoking two packs of

Kazbek cigarettes a night. But now Berlin was completely encircled, and from 5:30 a.m. shells were landing every three minutes near the *Reichskanzlei*.

Nothing and no one would escape.

—

On 16 December, travelling to Milan from Lake Garda, Benito Mussolini had still spoken defiantly of German secret weapons that could bring ultimate Axis victory. In Milan's 2,000-seater Teatro Lirico, he had given a bravura display of silver-tongued oratory, relayed by loudspeakers all over the city – "We shall defend the valley of the Po with our nails and our teeth," he vowed. As he left the theatre, women broke through ranks to thrust bouquets upon him, tearing off his epaulettes, imprinting his hands with lipstick marks. The next day, in a triumphant procession through the city, 40,000 people turned out to cheer him.

It was the dying gasp of Fascism. Already top Fascists were advancing their own version of a National Redoubt: a heroic final battle in a mountain bastion, the Valtellina, some 50 miles north of Milan. Fortifications from World War One still ringed the 44-mile-long valley. There were electric generating stations, hospitals – and direct access to Germany or Switzerland over mountain passes. Moreover, the plan promised an Italian last stand free from the German yoke. "I like this programme very much," the Duce told its progenitor, Milan's Federal Secretary, Vincenzo Costa. To go down in glory in Valtellina would preserve his legend for all time.

But Mussolini's mistress of nine years' standing, Claretta Petacci, had other ideas. Since his move to Lake Garda, the Duce's life had been a strange dichotomy, for although he resided at the Villa Feltrinelli, along with his wife, Rachele, and his children, Romano and Anna Maria, Claretta had early on been installed at the nearby Villa Fiordaliso, overseen by a young S.S. bodyguard, *Obersturmführer* Franz Spögler. From Spögler she learned of a remote spot near his own home, 6,000 feet up in the Dolomites, where she and the Duce might hide out. Twice Spögler had taken her there by sled. They talked to an old couple who occupied a hut deep in the pine forest, and got their agreement that two people might live there for years, no questions asked.

She then persuaded Spögler to broach the subject to Mussolini. The Duce listened with apparent interest, saying, "I see, I see." Encouraged, Claretta worked out every detail of the escape route. Spögler faked transit permits so that German road-blocks would not delay them.

On 18 April, telling his family only that he was off to Milan for a conference, Mussolini covertly transferred his office quarters to a three-room suite in the Palazzo Monforte, the Prefecture of Milan. Here, free from German interference, his aim was to proclaim the Salò Republic as a Socialist State. But knowing nothing of Karl Wolff's negotiations, he was still counting on the Germans to hold the line of the Po River, 50 miles southeast. It was the vainest of hopes. On 21 April, the Allies took Bologna, forging on to the northwest. Two days later, Pino Romualdi, an aide sent by Mussolini to prospect the front, returned dusty and sweat-stained. "It's disastrous," he choked out, "there's nothing left."

"But the Germans are defending the Po," Mussolini insisted.

"The Germans are defending nothing, Duce," Romualdi almost shouted. "You should order an immediate retreat to Valtellina."

"They say they're throwing flowers to the Allies in Bologna," Mussolini said, aghast. "That can't be true?"

Romualdi was dour. "Unfortunately it is. They're ready to greet anyone who brings tranquillity."

For three days thereafter, Mussolini sat squarely on the fence, unable to reach a decision. At one moment he inclined toward the Valtellina plan – then he wavered. The area teemed with Communist partisans, some advisers pointed out.

Claretta Petacci, who had followed the Duce to Milan the day after his departure, was still intent on her own scheme but fearful that the Valtellina would prevail. In any case, she *had* to be with Mussolini. Calling a Fascist friend, Asvero Gravelli, she urged him to find her a grey-green Women's Auxiliary Force uniform. Wearing it, she could perhaps follow Mussolini if he left without warning for the Valtellina. "Please, Asvero," she begged, "I'm going to die with him."

On 25 April, as a last resort, Mussolini even treated with the partisans on the neutral soil of the Archbishop's Palace in the lee of the Cathedral. An understanding, he hoped, might avoid a Milan uprising, partisan against Fascist, which could only bring appalling suffering. Even now the streets wore a sullen air, and many shops had pulled down their shutters. Outside most public buildings, the guards had blatantly discarded their uniforms, donning civilian suits.

The meeting, chaired by the frail little Cardinal Archbishop, Ildefonso Schuster, was a bitter disappointment. Not only did the partisans, led by General Raffaele Cadorna, demand unconditional surrender – but a chance remark revealed that Wolff's negotiated surrender was almost accomplished fact.

Mussolini was electrified. "For once," he stormed, mindful of Hitler's bitter reproaches at Rastenburg, "we can say Germany has stabbed Italy in the back. They have always treated us like slaves." Twice, in mindless fury, he repeated, "And at the end they betrayed *me*!"

Now, as Mussolini returned furiously to the Prefecture, all was confusion. To Vincenzo Costa, the one solution seemed to seize Mussolini and take him to Valtellina by force so that Fascism "could die in beauty". But again the Duce underwent a mercurial change of mind. All would head for Lake Como, 30 miles north.

Within minutes they had gone; although the courtyard had but one exit more than thirty cars and trucks manoeuvred into line as swiftly as if skilled garage mechanics were at the wheel. But at Como's Prefecture, the Duce's indecision continued. Much would depend on how many men Party Secretary Alessandro Pavolini could assemble to battle through to Valtellina: at least ten armoured cars would be needed. At one point Mussolini was determined to head for the Brenner Pass at all speed to join Hitler. At another he veered toward seeking sanctuary in Switzerland.

Amid reports of the fall of Milan and of partisan sorties in the mountains nearby, Mussolini, in the Prefect's flat at Como, scrawled a last letter to Rachele in blue crayon, signing his name in red: "I have come to the last chapter in my life, the last page in my book. I ask your forgiveness for all the harm I have unwittingly done you. You know you are the only woman I have ever truly loved."

Claretta, partially disguised in a man's blue overalls and a crash helmet, had contrived to catch up with him, and the old Fascist Party chiefs would stand with him, but one by one the men assembled for the last-ditch stand were slipping away. Their faith in Mussolini shaken, fearful of the partisans in the mountains, hundreds were even donning the red neckerchiefs of the Resistance.

At 2 a.m. on 27 April, in the Fascist barracks at Menaggio, the Duce faced the moment of truth. *Kriminalinspektor* Otto Kisnatt of the S.S., who had kept up with the convoy on Wolff's instructions, was awoken from sleep to find Mussolini, crimson with mortification, confronting a pale and agitated Alessandro Pavolini.

"Yes," said Mussolini harshly, enunciating every word, "here is Pavolini, and where are the ten armoured cars? He has brought only two, and old ones at that – it's shameful!"

"And how many men?" Kisnatt asked him.

"Well, tell him," the Duce railed, as Pavolini hesitated.

Pavolini had to confess it. "Twelve."

Now the Valtellina dream was shown for what it was – a Fascist fantasy, as bombastic and empty of meaning as a Palazzo Venezia speech. The Duce was left with just one decision: to honour the Axis Pact until the bitter end. "We leave at 5 a.m.," he told Kisnatt. "Let's hope we can reach the German Embassy at Merano by nightfall."

But six miles north of Menaggio, the 40-vehicle German-Italian convoy ran into trouble. In the lead was an armoured car with a 20-mm machine gun in its turret and two smaller guns at the sides, but as it snaked along the western bank of Lake Como, a three-edged nail placed in the road by partisans pierced its right rear tyre and forced it to a halt. From the Volkswagen Kubelwagon following in its wake, Kisnatt and his deputy *Untersturmführer* Fritz Birzer tumbled to the road. It was raining lightly. Thirty yards ahead loomed a barricade of tree trunks and rocks. To the left, the rocky bank rose sheer to the mountains; to the right it dropped steeply to the lake. It was a perfect spot for an ambush.

Above the low stone wall that flanked the lakeside, a white handerchief fluttered, and a three-man delegation of partisans approached the convoy. Their leader was Count Pier Luigi Bellini delle Stelle, a black-bearded Florentine nobleman, commanding the mountain-based 52nd Garibaldi Brigade. Undermanned and underarmed, Bellini was relying solely on bluff.

Leutnant Hans Fallmeyer, commanding 200 retreating Luftwaffe flak personnel, spoke for the Germans. The column was en route to Merano, he explained, and had no wish to quarrel with the Italians. Bellini shook his head. His orders were to let no man through. "You are covered by mortars and machine guns," he warned, "I could wipe you out in fifteen minutes."

How many Italians did he have with him, Bellini asked. Impassively, Fallmeyer wrote off Mussolini and his ministers. "A few civilians, who are no concern of mine. My concern is only with my men."

To allow Fallmeyer through, Bellini explained, he must have clearance from his division. If the German would accompany him and state his case, he might get leave to proceed. There was an argument in the drizzling rain, but Fallmeyer finally agreed.

With that Bellini raced to one of his men. A dispatch rider must go ahead, warning every checkpoint to have all available soldiers out on the road. "Send the others into the hills," he instructed. "But see that they keep in sight, wear something red, and look as if they're armed."

The strategem worked brilliantly. All the way to divisional headquarters at Chiavenna, 19 miles north – a ninety minute journey – Fallmeyer's binoculars picked out red neckerchiefs and armed men crouching among the rocks. Convinced he faced a superior force he accepted Bellini's orders to dissociate his own troops from the Fascists. Returning to the road block, he told Kisnatt and Birzer that the Italians in the column would have to stay put. But if the Germans moved on to the lakeside town of Dongo and submitted to a search they could proceed toward Germany. Mussolini, however, who was travelling in the armoured car, would accompany them, disguised as a German soldier.

"But when I meet the Führer and tell him I've been forced to use this trick," the Duce expostulated, "I shall feel ashamed."

"This is the one hope you've got of passing the roadblock," Birzer told him flatly.

Grumbling, Mussolini said he would "think about it." "Duce, there is no time to think," Kisnatt bellowed. "Make up your mind now because we're leaving!". Fuming, Mussolini entered the armoured car and slammed the door shut; a German soldier wrenched it open and flung in a sergeant's topcoat and a helmet.

Minutes later, Mussolini emerged, his helmet back to front, the topcoat so long it brushed his feet. Patiently his guards set the helmet right and fitted him out with dark glasses and a P-38 machine pistol. But now Mussolini protested that his ministers must come too. That was impossible, Birzer told him stonily. "Then at least my friend," the Duce pleaded, pointing to Claretta, in tears on the running board.

"That, too, is impossible, Duce." Tamely, screened from view by the Germans, Mussolini clambered aboard the convoy's third truck, and the vehicles moved off.

At 3 p.m. the vanguard of the convoy groaned onto the wharf of Dongo harbour, where a detachment of partisans waited to conduct the search. In the second truck, their leader, Urbano "Bill" Lazzaro, was leafing through German documents when a high-pitched shouting reached him. Dropping from the tailgate, he saw partisan Giuseppe Negri haring towards him. A onetime naval gunner on a ship that Mussolini had sailed on, Negri had seen the Duce face to face – and had never forgotten. "Bill," he whispered frantically, "we've got the Big Bastard!".

But Mussolini did not resist arrest. "I shall not do anything," he said in a trance-like voice as he descended from the truck. Taken to Dongo town hall, he sat there like a man in shock, asking for nothing more than a glass of water.

Bellini had no intention of letting him be harmed, but he feared a Fascist counter-coup. Nor did he trust the trigger-happy newcomers who were hourly swelling the partisan ranks – many lured by rumours of the Salò Republic's reserve funds in gold bars and foreign currency travelling with the convoy. At 7 p.m. on that Friday, Bellini personally transferred the Duce to a cell in the Finance Guards' barracks at Germasino, four miles distant in the fog-shrouded mountains.

Once there, Mussolini sheepishly begged the partisan to send his regards to "the lady held in the town hall" (where the Italians in the convoy were being detained), thus revealing her as Signora Petacci. Returning to Dongo, Bellini recognised her for the first time – this notorious woman, whom he despised as a self-seeking courtesan.

Yet Claretta's only worry seemed to be the Duce. "How long will he be in your hands?" she kept pressing him. Bellini didn't know. Word of Mussolini's capture had been telephoned to Milan, but he was still awaiting instructions.

In a sudden spasm of grief, Claretta reached out to him. "How can I make you believe that I was with him all those years simply because I loved him?" she cried, as if divining his thoughts. "You must believe me!". And she buried her tear-stained face in her hands.

Distressed, Bellini told her he would do all he could to see she suffered as little as possible.

"I never thought an enemy could be so kind and good," Claretta replied tearfully. "It encourages me to ask you a great favour. Put me with him! Let us be together. What harm is there in it?"

Bellini gently demurred. If anything happened to Mussolini, she too might be in danger. At once Claretta accused him: "I realise now you're going to shoot him!"

"Nothing of the sort!"

Claretta uncovered her face. "Promise me," she asked, "that if Mussolini *is* shot I can be near him until the last, and that I shall be shot with him. That is all I am asking: to die with him."

Bellini was profoundly moved; he felt ashamed for having despised her. "I will discuss it with my friends," he said, and it was all he could do to keep his voice steady.

Meanwhile, the partisan high command in Milan not only knew where Mussolini was but had appointed his executioner: 36-year-old Walter Audisio, known also as Colonel Valerio, a Communist victim of a penal settlement for anti-Fascists. Ironically, although the Allies wanted Mussolini alive and had dispatched an O.S.S. officer, Captain Emilio Q. Daddario, from Switzerland to locate him, it was from the unsuspecting Daddario that Audisio obtained a pass allowing him "to circulate freely with his armed escort" in Como and the vicinity.

At 7:10 a.m. on 28 April, at the wheel of a black Lancia-Aprilia, Audisio headed north, along with Aldo Lampredi, one of the most implacable of Communist Resistants, followed by a truckload of armed men.

In Dongo, Bellini received Audisio suspiciously. But – like it or not – the man had the proper credentials and was in command. "We're going to shoot every bigwig," Audisio told him brusquely. "Those are my orders: shoot the lot of them." Calling for a roll of prisoners, oblivious to Bellini's stammered protests, he began to mark it with black crosses. Benito Mussolini – death. Claretta Petacci – death.

"You'd shoot a woman?" Bellini burst out, appalled. "She was nothing but his mistress. To condemn her for that—"

"I don't condemn anyone," Audisio contradicted him. "The judgements have been pronounced by others."

The night before, worried that too many knew where the Duce was being held, Bellini had shifted him yet again: to the farmhouse of Lia de Maria, in the foothills hamlet of Giulino di Mezzegra. This time he had allowed Claretta to join him. Their room was a cold little peasant chamber, as poor as that in which Mussolini had been born almost 62 years earlier.

Now, uneasy at the haste, Bellini groped for a compromise. It would be best, he suggested, if he himself fetched Mussolini's ministers and the other prisoners from their new gaol, the barracks at Germasino. At the same time, two of his men, Luigi Canali and Michele Moretti, would collect Mussolini and Claretta. All the captives would be delivered to Audisio at Dongo.

But one item escaped Bellini; his companion in arms, Moretti, was also a fanatic Communist. Thus, when the men set out in Moretti's Fiat, in the back seat behind them sat not only Lampredi, but Audisio, muttering, "Get on with it, get on with it."

At around 4 p.m., the Fiat drew up before the farmhouse. Later, Audisio claimed that to lull the Duce's suspicions, he told him, "I've come to liberate you," and that Mussolini replied, "I'll give you an empire." But the level-headed Lampredi heard no such theatrical interchange. "Mussolini," he later affirmed, "knew perfectly well his time had come."

After they had gathered their things together, Audisio led them to the Fiat. Claretta sat in the back seat, holding tight to Mussolini's hand. Both of them, the driver, Giovanbattista Geninazza, later recounted seemed "strangely tranquil". Coasting downhill, the car moved as decorously as a hearse; Lampredi and Moretti were walking unhurriedly ahead. Audisio crouched on the right front fender, facing backward, his machine pistol pointing into the car.

Five hundred yards down the road, beyond a hairpin bend, Audisio ordered a halt near the gateway of Villa Belmonte – its stone walls topped by clipped privet hedges, screened from the village by the sharp turn. Audisio vaulted from the fender, ordering Mussolini and Claretta out, motioning them towards the villa's gate. The others stood on guard, ready to block anyone coming from either direction.

Geninazza never caught what it was that Audisio said. To the Communist, it was a formal death sentence, "By order of the High Command of the Volunteer Freedom Corps, I have been charged to render justice to the Italian people." To the driver, only three yards away, it was just a gabble of words – drowned by Claretta's sudden scream, "You can't kill us like that! You can't do that!"

"Move aside or we'll kill you first!" Audisio rasped back at her. Then, the sweat pouring down his face, he squeezed the trigger three times, but the gun had jammed. Cursing, he tore his revolver from its holster; the trigger clicked dryly, but that was all. "Give me your gun," he shouted to Moretti.

Sick to his stomach, Geninazza saw Mussolini unbutton his grey-green jacket. "Shoot me in the chest," he told the Communist distinctly. But Claretta tried to seize the gun barrel and as Audisio fired it was she who fell first, a bullet in her heart, a sprig of flowering creeper in her hand. Then, at three paces, Audisio fired two bursts – nine shots – at Mussolini. Four struck the dictator in the descending aorta; others lodged in the thigh, the collarbone, the neck, the thyroid gland, the right arm.

Faintly, thunder rumbled from the mountains.

—

They brought the bodies back to Milan in a truck, along with the bodies of fifteen other Fascist notables, among them Alessandro Pavolini. Then they dumped them under cover of darkness in the Piazzale Loreto – a grim deed planned in retribution for fifteen Resistants executed there by the Germans.

The next day, Sunday 29 April, the crowds were at first no more than curious, as they circled the bodies sprawled on the pavement. Someone had placed a flagstaff as though it were a sceptre in Mussolini's hand and his head lay propped on Claretta's white blouse. News photographers tilted the Duce's face towards the sun, supporting his jaw with a rifle butt.

Then, abruptly, a jungle savagery set in. A man darted up and aimed a kick at Mussolini's head. People began to dance and caper round the corpses. One woman fired five shots into Mussolini's prostrate body – one for each of the sons she had lost in the Duce's war. Another ripped off his shirt, lighted it and tried to thrust it in his face.

Partisan chief Italo Pietra ordered ten men to fire into the air, striving to keep the crowd at bay, but it was hopeless. Cursing, the people trampled the corpses. Even 300 *carabinieri* could not restrain them; hastily they retreated, their uniforms ripped to shreds. A fire brigade struggled to the scene, but their powerful jets of water could not extinguish the hatred.

Finally, one by one, the bodies were hoisted by their feet to the girders of a bombed-out filling station and left to hang. Claretta hung next to Mussolini, her skirt lashed into place by a partisan's belt.

At 2 p.m. that day, as all the bells of Milan were pealing, Colonel Charles Poletti of the U.S. Army made contact with the partisan command at the Prefecture. There he found Ferruccio Parri of the Action Party couldn't keep silent – not over Claretta, not over a display "like a Mexican butcher's shop". "It's ugly and unfitting," he burst out. "It will injure the partisan movement for years to come."

"It's done now," Poletti tried to console him. "Emotions run pretty high in war. But I did come to counsel you to take those bodies down and to stop stringing others up. Those are my orders."

Parri agreed. "Very well – but where shall we take Mussolini? The mob may tear him to pieces."

Poletti considered. "In America," he said, "we have something called a morgue. Don't you have a morgue?"

"We have a poor man's morgue."

"Then, fine. Take him there. Have him guarded by the partisans and let nothing more happen to him, because it's over now. Let no more harm come to that man – no more harm at all."

In Berlin, the Russian presence was almost palpable. For fifteen minutes in every hour, noted Krebs' A.D.C. *Rittmeister* Gerhardt Boldt, the *Führerbunker*'s ventilators had to be shut off; as shells crashed into the *Reichkanzlei* gardens, the ducts sucked in limestone dust and the stench of sulphur instead of fresh air. Some of the S.S. guards, Boldt saw, were drinking themselves insensible. In all eight battle sectors, older *Volkssturm* soldiers were reported as quitting their posts, seeking the safety of cellars with their wives and children.

In Siemensstadt, a young Russian lieutenant, Victor Boëv, whose German was fluent, egged on by war correspondents from *Pravda* and *Izveztia*, placed a call to the Ministry of Propaganda, and greatly daring, asked to speak to Dr Göbbels. Much to his surprise, Göbbels seemed disposed to answer questions.

"How long can you hold out in Berlin?" Boëv asked, but in Göbbels' reply, only the word "several" was distinguishable.

"Several what?" Boëv queried. "Weeks?"

Göbbels was indignant. "Oh no. Months. Why not! Your people defended Sebastopol for nine months. Why shouldn't we do the same in our capital?"

"When and in what direction will you escape from Berlin?" Boëv queried, but at this Göbbels took umbrage. "That question is far too insulting to deserve an answer," he wound up the interview.

Yet the question was relevant, for the main Russian attack at Spandau, the biggest threat to the defences in the west, now depended on a frail enough force: the Hitler Youth of Dr Artur Axmann.

Paradoxically, by 26 April, Hitler's spirits were again soaring, for word had come that Wenck's troops, battling to the relief of Berlin, had reached as far as Potsdam, ten miles distant. "If he can relieve Berlin, we shall fall back to a new line and fight on," the Führer fantasised. In truth, Wenck, like Heinrici, was retreating westwards, hoping to elude capture by the Russians.

Two days passed. By now tremors shook the bunker as if an earthquake threatened; the ventilators were cut off for an hour at a time. The lack of air became scarcely endurable: in this twilit half-world, headaches, breathlessness and sudden cold sweats were now the norm. Only a thousand yards away loomed the Russian tanks.

At 7 p.m. on 28 April came the unkindest cut of all: hurrying from the Propaganda Ministry, Heinz Lorenz, Chief of the Press Service, had picked up a B.B.C. London newscast featuring a Reuter report of Himmler's surrender bid. The man whom Hitler had dubbed *Der treue Heinrich* had been guilty of what, in a paroxysm of helpless rage, the Führer called "the most shameful betrayal in human history". "We will certainly have to shed tears this evening," Eva Braun told one of Hitler's secretaries, Gertrud Junge.

All that night, Hitler paced the bunker passageways, armed with a Berlin street map, striving to follow the course of a battle that had lost all cohesion. Towards 2 a.m. on 19 April, he dictated his Political Testament, a bitter disappointment to Frau Junge – "simply a rehash of what he had been saying for years in his speeches and proclamations." He also resolved to marry Eva Braun, and around 4 a.m., with Eva wearing the black silk dress that was the Führer's favourite, Walter Wagner, a City official from Göbbels' ministry, performed the ceremony. Afterwards, like any newly-weds, they sat chatting in an ante-room with Göbbels and his wife, Magda, Krebs and Burgdorf.

Breakfast-time brought more bad news: from a typewritten sheet of the Reuter wireless service delivered by valet Heinz Linge, Hitler learned of Mussolini's death. Now his hand shook so uncontrollably he overturned his teacup on the typescript, and Eva hastened to his side with a napkin. "You can't dry it," her husband told her harshly. "It's blood."

Monday 30 April was a morning for farewells. He told his personal pilot, Hans Baur, "On my tombstone they ought to put the words 'He was the victim of his Generals'!" before bequeathing him his favourite portrait of Frederick the Great. He added sombrely, "I'm ending it today."

Waiter Erwin Jakubek always recalled the Führer's last lunch was "spaghetti with a light sauce". Afterwards he was joined by Eva, calm and pale in a blue dress with white trimmings and a favourite gold bracelet. "Take my fur coat as a memory," she told Frau Junge. "I always liked well-dressed people." Earlier she had confessed, "I don't mind dying heroically but it must be painless."

Towards 3:30 p.m. Hitler and Eva retired to the Führer's green and white tiled study. After twelve years of glory the Third Reich had scaled down to this, a modest room, twelve feet long by nine feet wide. The man acclaimed by millions, who had invested the twentieth century with more evil than any save Nicolai Lenin, was as alone as Mussolini had been, with only the woman he loved to sustain him, alone in a monstrous vacuum of eternity, execrated by man and woman and child.

They sat together on the narrow couch with its faded blue and white upholstery, unscrewing the slim brass casings that held the small glass phials of liquid cyanide. After Eva had bitten the glass, her head sank on his shoulder, her knees contracting in agony. Hitler, too, bit down on the phial, but to make doubly sure he had raised a heavy 7.65-mm Walther to his right temple.

The trigger eased back; the world went dark.

11

"The Last Man Will See What We Saw"
1 May–6 August, 1945

Even as the fires of war were smouldering out in north-west Europe, to the east the Cold War was already dawning.

On the late afternoon of 1 May, two armies were racing for the Italian port of Trieste, the one niche of Europe where the Allies had agreed on no advance demarcation line. Up the coast of Dalmatia thrust the Fourth Army of Marshal Josip Broz Tito, determined to hold Trieste and incorporate it into Yugoslavia. Along the wide tarmac stretch of Route 14, racing at 35 miles an hour, surged the armoured cars of the British 12th Lancers, tyres hissing on the wet road surface, their commanders erect in their turrets, earphones clamped over dark blue berets.

"Tito will certainly be reluctant to evacuate the town once he has captured it," Sir Orme Sargent, of the Foreign Office, had warned Churchill that very morning, and as the cavalry screen of the 2nd New Zealand Division of the Eighth Army, the Lancers were ready, if need be, to battle for Trieste.

This was a melancholy prospect, for victory in Europe had done nothing to lessen the tension among the victors. "Tito can be left to himself in his mountain, to stew in Balkan juice which is bitter," Churchill had advised Eden, but in the matter of Trieste he was determined to back the Italian claim to the hilt, intent on saving Italy "from the Bolshevik pestilence."

It was a situation as tense as a coiled spring. For five weeks, as both sides called upon the other to withdraw, fear lay like a miasma over the seaport: outside the British headquarters, the Albergo Grande, khaki-clad New Zealanders stood guard with fixed bayonets, watched warily by partisans in red-starred caps. Plainly it was too late to save Yugoslavia from "the Bolshevik pestilence," for the exiled King Peter II, submitting to a merger of Premier Ivan Subasic's Royal Government with Tito's National Committee of Liberation, was now saddled with a 28-man Cabinet, of whom 22 were Communists. But Italy was still a test case.

In desperation, Churchill turned to Truman, confiding his latent fears of the Sovietisation of Europe. "An iron curtain is drawn down on their front," he wrote, coining the historic phrase which became so much a part of him.[33] "We do not know what is going on behind ... A broad band of many hundreds of miles of Russian-occupied territory will isolate us from Poland." It was a rare meeting of minds, for even as Churchill's telegram was en route to Washington, Truman's Telegram No 34, also despatched on 11 May, was en route to Downing Street.

Having made his stance plain to Molotov, Truman after conferring with the Chiefs of Staff and the State Department, was prepared to take a tougher line yet with Tito. "(It) is not a question of taking sides in a dispute between Italy and Yugoslavia," he wrote clear-sightedly, "or of becoming involved in internal Balkan politics. The problem is essentially one of deciding whether our two countries are going to permit our Allies to engage in uncontrolled land grabbing – tactics which are all too reminiscent of Hitler or Japan."

Thus, after five weeks of defiance, Tito, given due warning from the White House, withdrew from Trieste. Within three years, this "Truman Doctrine," the President's determination to contain Communism, would be made manifest in many spheres: the European Recovery Programme, the Marshall Plan, which offered food, tractors and hope to millions of needy Europeans, the Berlin blockade, the Korean War.

For countless thousands this American stance would come too late, but Churchill's struggle seemed less lonely now.

In San Francisco, where the delegates of 46 nations had assembled to draft a charter for a post-war organisation of "peace-loving states," a mood of veiled cynicism prevailed. In the nick of time, the neutrals and countries hitherto benevolent to the Axis were scrambling under the wire; Turkey declared war on Germany on 23 February, Argentina as late as 27 March. In the New York daily *P.M.*, a cartoonist portrayed

Hitler and the Emperor Hirohito, united for peace, chortling "You declare war on me, I declare war on you, and we both go to San Francisco."

At 4:30 p.m. on 25 April, the auditorium of the San Francisco Opera House, where all plenary sessions were held, more truly resembled a Hollywood movie set; designed by Broadway's Jo Mielziner, noted for such spectaculars as "The Gay Divorce" and "On Your Toes," it featured a sky-blue proscenium backdrop studded with three gold pillars surmounted by giant laurel wreaths, with flags of the United Nations raised on 12-foot high silver staffs. When an unseen band sounded the first bars of music, hundreds struggled to attention, striving to identify the national anthem – then shuffled sheepishly back into their seats. For reasons unknown, the musicians were rendering not *The Star Spangled Banner* but *Lover, Come Back To Me*.

It was a comic-opera overture to a tragi-comic gathering, replete with big words and cloudy labels, with one sure pattern emerging: virtually every smaller power would vote as one or other of the Big Three dictated. ("What can one do with these Russians?" lamented Czech Foreign Minister Jan Masaryk, for his country's "liberation" decreed that all Czech National Committees must be 60 per cent Communist. "You can be on your knees and that is not enough.")

In time San Francisco would be revealed for what it was: a jealous power-game, a dusty answer to the hopes and sacrifices of millions. Finally signed on 26 June, the Charter, a 145-page document in 14-point Bodoni type, bound in blue leather, had done little more than put the last dots on a mandate written for a world of power.

Much earlier, had occurred the incident that symbolised the truth behind the spurious façade. From the very beginning, both Eden and Stettinius, for the State Department, had pressed Molotov to solve the riddle that had prompted Churchill to demand Eisenhower take Berlin: what had happened to the sixteen Polish nationalists who had mysteriously disappeared while visiting Moscow for talks?

On Thursday 3 May, they finally knew. In the Soviet Consulate on Montgomery Street, Molotov, whom Halifax dubbed "Smiling Granite" was hosting a dinner that evening, and as Stettinius walked in he greeted him with the same granite smile and a cordial handshake.

"Oh, by the way, Mr Stettinius," he volunteered, as an afterthought, "about those sixteen Poles, they've all been arrested by the Red Army.[34] Hullo, Mr Eden..."

All that Saturday 5 May, rain bathed northwest Europe. Over Eisenhower's headquarters, in a red-brick technical school at Reims, the clouds hung motionless and smoke from the railway shunting-yards drifted to mingle with the clouds. At 3:30 p.m. Eisenhower was nervous, though endeavouring not to show it. In exactly one hour German guests were expected.

In Berlin, from 1 May on, everything had been cut and dried. After two days of battle, small red flags had sprouted like poppies all over the ruins of the gutted bricked-up *Reichstag*; for the Russians, this Parliament building, deserted since the fire of 1933, for which Communists had been framed, was the most symbolic in Berlin, marking the beginning of the Third Reich. The bodies of Adolf and Eva Hitler, doused in 200 litres of gasoline by Hitler's S.S. adjutant and chauffeur, Otto Günsche and Erich Kempka, had been incinerated in a shallow trench outside the bunker entrance.[35] At Chuikov's headquarters, *Generalleutnant* Hans Krebs, arriving under a white flag of truce, greeted the Russian Commander. "Today is the first of May, a great holiday for our two nations," and Chuikov, with dry restraint, replied, "*We* have a great holiday today. How things are with you over there it is less easy to say." Simultaneously, three Yak-3 fighters roared at 100 feet over the *Reichstag*, unfurling a red banner with a single word embroidered in gold: POBYEDA (Victory).

In Reims, by contrast, the situation was still confused. One day earlier, on Lüneburg Heath, Montgomery had accepted the surrender of all German forces in Holland, northeast Germany and Denmark, signing it with an ordinary Post Office pen – but in the light of Himmler's earlier offer, would the envoys of *Grossadmiral* Dönitz, to whom Hitler had passed on the torch, be empowered to surrender on all fronts?

At 5 p.m. when Admiral Hans George von Friedburg, his eyes still red with weeping, arrived with his subordinates, it was plain they would not. After a brief 22-minute parley with Bedell Smith, whose ulcer was paining him, the emissaries were left to their own devices – eating sandwiches, drinking whisky, striving to seek a way out of the impasse. Towards 10 p.m. they were allowed to transmit a message to Dönitz at Flensburg, in Schleswig-Holstein, asking him either to authorise the surrender or to despatch someone who could.

On Sunday the rain died down; the sun shone. At 5:08 p.m. *General der Artellerie* Alfred Jodl, trim and well pressed, reached Eisenhower's H.Q. to confer with Friedburg. At 6:15 p.m., they met up with Bedell Smith and Major-General Kenneth Strong. "I have to maintain the existing agreements among the Allies," Smith explained more than once. "I do not understand why you do not want to surrender to our Russian allies. It would be the best thing to do for all concerned."

"Even if you were right," Jodl replied, "I should not be able to convince a single German that you are."

Still Jodl played for time. When Smith tried the soldier-to-soldier approach, stressing the honour and prestige of the German armed forces, Jodl sought to incorporate this in a message to Dönitz. Eisenhower hotly rejected the draft. "Tear the damn thing up," he told Smith, "and tell Jodl it can never be sent in its present form."

Now Eisenhower issued an ultimatum: either the Germans signed by midnight or he would order his armies to close their ranks and accept no more surrenders. They would be left to the mercy of the Russians.

Jodl saw the light. "I shall send a radio message," he said huskily. "It is to read: 'We sign, or general chaos.'"

Eleven o'clock came, then midnight. In ones and twos Allied officers began drifting from the buildings. By now, the lingering newsmen were almost prepared to call it a night – but just in case, they lingered. Then at 2 a.m., on 7 May, the staff cars began rolling back. The reporters saw Eisenhower re-enter the building, then Bedell Smith, swinging a swagger stick, more and more men, then finally the Germans their faces revealing nothing.

Their instructions could hardly have been briefer: "Admiral Dönitz authorises signature of surrender under conditions stated – Keitel."

It was the end of the line. In the blue walled War Room of the technical school, precisely at 2:39 a.m., Bedell Smith signed for Eisenhower, Jodl for Dönitz. Although Major-General Ivan Susloparov was present to sign for Russia, he unwittingly exceeded his instructions; next day, 8 May, to satisfy Russian *amour propre*, the surrender was taken in Berlin all over again, by Zhukov. (No more was ever heard of Susloparov.) Afterwards, with "icy West Point formality," Eisenhower received Jodl in his office to demand: "Do you understand the terms of the document of surrender you have just signed?"

"*Ja, ja,*" Jodl replied.

"You will get details of instructions at a later date," Eisenhower concluded, "and you will be expected to carry them out faithfully."

As the Germans exited, Ike's Scottie, Telek, crouched beneath the desk, growled patriotically.

At 3:05 a.m., Bedell Smith, one of the first to leave, walked down the corridor, past the waiting newsmen. He was still swinging his swagger stick but holding himself erect, as if his stomach hurt him. He climbed into his car and as he did so, he said, aptly if ungrammatically, "*Fini la guerre.*"

It was over, and everybody sensed it, yet hour by hour the uncertainty grew: no official announcement had come. The reason, once again, was Josef Stalin's obduracy: the surrender was not official until Germany had formally yielded to Russia in Berlin. Thus for most of 7 May, reluctant to renege on a misconceived pledge, Churchill and Truman remained tongue-tied.

Only at 7:40 p.m. did a cautious Ministry of Information statement, sandwiched in the midst of a piano recital, give a hint that after 2,094 days and nights, the conflict in Europe was over: the Premier would broadcast at 3 p.m. on Tuesday 8 May – "and in view of this fact, tomorrow, Tuesday, will be treated as Victory-in-Europe Day … the day following, 9 May, will also be a holiday…"

In that moment, following the years of misery and pent-up frustration, the world understandably went mad.

Entire cities exploded in a bedlam of sound. Parisians fired pistols into the air from speeding cars, and planes let loose multi-coloured flares. From the Hudson River to the Thames, the sirens of tugs and rivercraft shrilled out the V-for-Victory chorus, and cabbies responded with their horns. The 11-ton Campanone of St Peter's tolled across the seven hills of Rome. In New York, 100,000 windows were flung wide, followed by a sound like the flapping of thousands of wings: with scrap paper, torn telephone directories and streamers, clerks and typists were organising their own ticker-tape celebration.

In London and scores of other cities, the lights blazed on again, and small children who had never seen their like wept in terror at the sight: a greenish glow of light picking out Nelson's Column in Trafalgar Square, the honey light that transformed the National Gallery, the ghostly blue of St Martin-in-the-Fields, the floodlit face of Big Ben, looming "like a kind moon". Searchlights wheeled and criss-crossed over the capital, blinking out the V-for-Victory sign in Morse. All over England, on the high hills, victory beacons, just as in Napoleon's time, blazed in the dark. Every city was a bannering sea of Stars and Stripes, Red Flags, Union Jacks. Outside the Royal Palace in The Hague, massed tulips spelt out the letters W, J, and B, (Wilhelmina, Juliana, Bernhard), celebrating the return of a beloved Royal Family.

They were days to blot out the stringent austerity of the past. On Stockholm's main street, Drottningaten, a second-floor restaurant liberally lowered six magnums of champagne by rope for pedestrians to help themselves. In Paris, the Garde Républicaine clattered down the Rue Royale, brass helmets gleaming, with screaming *midinettes* riding pillion on the cruppers of every horse. In London, it was like Cup Final day, with girls sporting rosettes or Kiss-Me-Quick hats, perched on the lions' heads in Trafalgar Square or snaking in an interminable Conga line down the Haymarket. At a Russian banquet at Werdau, on the Elbe, Lieutenant-Colonel Saul K. Padover, floating in "a haze of love and happiness," drank vodka toasts with a Soviet colonel, who assured him, "We certainly don't intend to bring a noble idea like Communism to such a people." Then Padover sought an empty jeep and passed out.

For military men it was a time of mixed emotions. In the Fürstenhof Hotel at Bad Wildungen, Hessen, Omar Bradley heard the news phlegmatically in a 4 a.m. call from Eisenhower. Opening his canvas map-case he smoothed out the mapboard and wrote in a new date with a china-marking pencil: D+335. Major-General Ivor Thomas, commanding the British 43rd Division, refused to credit the B.B.C. announcement: doggedly planning an attack towards Bremerhaven, he desisted only on the direct orders of Lieutenant-General Brian Horrocks. Putting aside his map, Thomas remarked feelingly: "The troops have done us damned well."

For the truly martial, it was, of course a mortal blow. At Regensburg, Bavaria, General George S. Patton and his staff, quartered in a prince's palace, ate their dinner in total silence from first course to last. Only when retiring for the night did Patton call to mind a species of whale said to spend much of its time lying in the deepest part of the ocean.

"At the present moment," he told them deadpan, "I feel lower than that whale's arse."

Victory was sweet but in Europe there were still many hurts it could do nothing to assuage.

A new acronym, born of war, entered the language: DPs, meaning "displaced persons". Were there 20 million uprooted Europeans – or 25 million? Nobody knew. The one thing certain was that many were children; in France, they slept in haystacks, in Italy, in doorways, in Greece, in woods and caves. Every day 3,000 child refugees passed through Berlin alone. The Child Tracing Department of the United Nations Relief and Rehabilitation Administration[36] (UNRRA) sought some 65,000 named children, knowing this to be but a drop in the bucket. Many, when traced, could no longer assimilate: the ghettos and the concentration camps were the only truths they knew. In homes for the war-distressed they drew only smoking chimneys, bodies dangling from the gallows, refugees driven by whips.

All of them were hungry, that much was known, a need they shared along with the adults: 70 million Europeans in all. At Brussels' *Bon Marché* department store, a bitter window display was in evidence: a cadaverous old man, staring dully at his daily rations, totalling 1,000 calories per day, marginally less than a Frenchman received, for Paris had endured four meatless weeks on end. All this paled beside the sufferings of the Dutch, reduced to 500 calories; in "the hunger winter" of 1944–45, 15,000 had died, while others survived narrowly on sugar beet, tulip bulbs and potatoes. Meat, fat, milk, sugar and eggs were as unknown as manna.

Disease was rampant – typhoid stalked Poland, malaria raged in Italy, Greece was stricken by both typhus and tuberculosis – and so, too, was destitution. Not one in ten Poles any longer had a bed to sleep in. France was in sorry shape, too, for her role as a battlefield had shattered 1,000 roads and railway bridges; two-fifths of Le Havre had been destroyed, a quarter of Rouen. Only a massive U.S. civilian lend-lease programme valued at $2,575,000,000, would see France through the ensuing eighteen months.

It was Tito who wrote the epilogue, talking with the Yugoslav diplomat, Vladimir Dedijer, on his return from San Francisco. Though Yugoslavia was on his mind, Tito spoke for all Europe.

"The houses will be rebuilt, the railways restored," he conceded, "but we can't give back 1,700,000 human lives. Each of these men had his personal life, his hopes, his hardships, his joys. This is the tremendous price we have had to pay for our freedom."

Monday 28 May was a historic occasion at No. 10, Downing Street. For the first time since 3 September, 1939, no Cabinet business was transacted. Instead the long green baize table in the Cabinet Room was draped with a white cloth, displaying such delicacies as Russian caviare, lobster patties and limitless champagne. The tears coursing down his cheeks, Churchill was bidding farewell to his 70-strong team of Ministers and those outside the War Cabinet: "We have stayed together as a united band of friends in a very trying time. History will recognise this. The light will shine on every helmet."

Soon after, when an official photograph of the group, before the ilex tree in the garden of No 10, was interrupted by a flurry of rain, Churchill cut short the proceedings with mock concern: "We had better finish this or my political opponents will say that there is a conspiracy on my part to give them all rheumatism."

With the European War three weeks into limbo, politics were once more a dominant issue. To Churchill's dismay, the Labour Party showed no enthusiasm for maintaining the wartime coalition – despite the conviction of such Labourites as Deputy Premier Clement Attlee, Minister of Labour Ernest Bevin and First Lord of the Admiralty A. V. Alexander that a solid front against Soviet puppets like Tito made coalition desirable. But on 19 May, Labour's National Executive Committee, meeting on the eve of the party conference at Blackpool, were swayed by the Home Secretary, Herbert Morrison – to the Premier "a loathsome creature with a warped mind" – to reject Churchill's plea for solidarity.

More pressing than the war against Japan or Soviet expansionism were such tempting Socialist utopias as the nationalisation of the Bank of England, fuel and power, inland transport, and iron and steel.

Accordingly, on 23 May Churchill had resigned as Coalition leader and was reappointed head of a "Caretaker" government of Conservatives, Liberals and non-party functionaries. On 15 June, for the first time in ten years, Parliament was dissolved and to the Tory war cry, "Win With Winnie," countered by a Labour slogan harking back to the economic rot of pre-war, "Ask Your Dad," the campaign was on.

From the first, passions ran immoderately high. The fiery M.P. for Ebbw Vale, Aneurin Bevan, called for "the complete extinction of the Tory Party and 25 years of Labour Government". The candidate for Pudsey and Otley, Major Denis Healey, declared flatly: "The upper classes in every country are selfish, depraved, dissolute and decadent." Not to be outdone, Churchill, in his first broadcast on 4 June, made an astonishing allegation that his wife, Clementine, had begged him to excise: "I declare to you from the bottom of my heart that no socialist system can be established without a political police. If Labour tried to carry out their full socialist programme they would have to fall back on some sort of Gestapo."

But Churchill's exhortations fell on deaf ears – a speech "composed of reach-me-downs from the tub-thumping twenties," scoffed the *Manchester Guardian*. In the two decades that stretched between 1920 and 1939, one man in every seven had been idle; as far back as December 1942, the people had been profoundly stirred by a Government report prepared by the economist, William Beveridge, whose three basic assumptions – family allowances for all children, a National Health Service, an end to mass unemployment – seemed to offer fresh hope for the future. Preoccupied, above all, with postwar jobs, postwar housing and fears of ill-health, the people made Beveridge's "womb-to-tomb" scheme a nationwide best seller, snapping up 635,000 copies.

The mood of Britain was changing fast, as none could perceive more clearly than Wing-Commander Roland Beamont. Not until the third week in May were Beamont and his fellow POWs released from Luckenwalde prison camp, near Berlin, a nightmare experience which in the last week had seen their German gaolers supplanted by Russians; only Eisenhower's direct intervention had secured their liberty.

Then had come a wearisome journey from Kassel to Brussels, where hundreds of Lancasters and Liberators were waiting to fly them home – to a total sense of anti-climax. The street parties had long been forgotten, the blackout curtains torn down, the bunting packed away. Already a gnawing fear of the future was replacing the wartime camaraderie. Arriving at No 1 Officers' School, at Cosford, near Wolverhampton, Beamont and his fellows no longer felt like returning heroes or released prisoners-of-war – "simply like men in rags."

The irony was that many Tories were fully as sensible of the national mood as Labour. Following World War one, Churchill's Minister of Reconstruction, Lord Woolton, pointed out, "We didn't allow

Tommy Atkins to starve ... we gave him just enough money to prevent him starving and left his immortal soul and his pride of capacity to perish in despair." As Lord Privy Seal, Beaverbrook was equally to the point: "The appeal to the electorate should be positive throughout, and should be based on your own slogan, 'Food, Work and Homes'. The Tory Party has need, not of a Maginot Line, but of a Second Front."

Since 1943, four loyal Conservatives had been defeated in by-elections, and on each occasion their share of the vote had fallen. Thus, until 25 July, when the ballot boxes were opened, a question-mark hung like a cloud over the Tory future. They might proclaim their good intentions with the best of them – but would they, when it came to the crunch, deliver the goods?

On the evening of 28 June, the twenty-two pilots of No 24 Advance Training Squadron at Kagohara Airfield had one thing in common: all of them had eleven hours to live.

Sitting gloomily in his dimly-lit billet, Ryuji Nagatsuka – newly promoted Ensign, like the others – felt a painful sense of finality. Only ten weeks earlier he had realised with a sinking heart that this, his twenty-first birthday, must be his last – and now the final rituals that a *Kamikaze* must observe, the paring of fingernails, the snipping of a lock of hair, brought that certainty even closer. Neatly laying out his belongings – cap, uniform, pen and paper – for his family, he labelled them "The late Lieutenant Ryuji Nagatsuka"; by tradition a *Kamikaze*'s death brought promotion to a higher rank. He settled to a farewell letter: "My dear parents, I shall depart this life at 0700 hours on the 29th of June 1945..."

Of this eventuality he had no doubts at all, for take-off was at 6 a.m. and 300 miles off the coast of Japan, in the region of Miyagui, their objective had already been sighted; the Third Fleet of Task Force 38, comprising at least five aircraft carriers plus battleships and cruisers.

In theory, after two months intermittent training, all of them were experts. "May our death be as sudden and clean as the shattering of crystal," was their watchword, but this ethereal sentiment cloaked a hard scientific approach. Carrier funnels were usually curved, so it was hard to hit them. The best approach was from the after part of the ship, from the stern or quarter, rather than from ahead or the bow. In starting a dive from 20,000 feet, it was essential to finish with the nose of the plane at an angle of forty-five degrees to the lift cages at the bow or the stern – a carrier's weakest points.

In practice, as Nagatsuka soon found, two-thirds of the battle was finding your target.

At 6 a.m. on 29 June, four fighters were found to be defective; only 18 planes, led by Lieutenant Takagui, formed the suicide sortie. But at 6:50 a.m., Nagatsuka in the cockpit of his K1-27 fighter, could see nothing. Thick cloud "like a great eiderdown" cut off all sight of the sea: nothing but rolling masses of cloud, and now rain was lashing the windshield.

In weather like this, how could they even locate Task Force 38?

At 7:05 a.m., Takagui, at the head of the formation, pointed meaningfully to the rear. At once Nagatsuka craned his head: were American Hellcats poised to bounce them? But he could see nothing, and suddenly Takagui veered his plane to the left. A second then a third plane followed his example. They were turning back.

Choking back tears like an angry child, Nagatsuka could still see the logic of it. They had fuel enough only for the outward journey: 330 miles. There was now no hope of sighting the task force – and in ten minutes they would have reached the point of no return. If they flew on they would have thrown away their lives for nothing.

Yet all the way back, remorse grappled with reason. Shouldn't he have disobeyed and flown on in search of the enemy? Hadn't Cicero said, Philosophy is nothing but a preparation for death? Wasn't he behaving like a coward? Yet, didn't he, secretly, in his heart of hearts believe that the mission was foolhardy and senseless, that the one thing that mattered was life itself?

Back at Kagohara, Takagui reported to the commandant: "Sir, I beg a thousand pardons. Mist and bad weather prevented our reaching the target." "It can't be helped," said Suenaga simply. "A pity, but you'll have another opportunity to destroy the carriers. Go to your quarters."

Nagatsuka did as he was bidden. His belongings were still piled on his bed, awaiting the sticks of incense that would have been lit before them: the personal effects of "the late Lieutenant Nagatsuka".

Abruptly he seized the paper and, shaking with rage and hysteria, tore it into a thousand fragments.

Afterwards they were all agreed – strangely unanimous for 1000 highly-complex individuals, many of them Nobel prize winners – that the worst part had been the waiting. All that night of Sunday 15 July, as the hours ticked by, the anxiety was reflected in trivial ways. To the irritation of Brigadier-General Leslie Groves, the tall handsome chief of the Manhattan Project, the Italian physicist, Enrico Fermi, was taking bets: would the explosion, when it came, merely destroy New Mexico or wipe out the whole world? Britain's Sir Geoffrey Taylor preferred to bet on the energy released: anything from zero to 80,000 tons of T.N.T.

The scientific director, the shy lanky J. Robert Oppenheimer unable to sleep, browsed through an anthology of Baudelaire. Others – Dr Vannevar Bush, head of the Office of Scientific Research and Development, sharing a tent with Groves and James Bryant Conant, president of Harvard University, tossed restlessly on their cots.

At the 2,000-square-mile Alamogordo Air Base, code-named "Trinity," all attention was focussed on the 100-foot steel shot tower, ten miles from the main Base Camp, on a hill code-named "Zero," which housed a ball of plutonium roughly the size of a grapefruit, in turn code-named "Fat Man" in Churchill's honour. For "Zero," zero-hour had been timed for 4 a.m. – but at midnight, a storm was brewing and the steel tower was perched in the parched desert like a lightning rod. Rain and wind could increase the risk of radioactive fall-out.

Within a five mile radius of the tower, the desert bristled with equipment: tiny gauges of quartz crystal, crusher gauges to measure high blast pressure, thirty high speed cameras, positioned behind bulletproof glass in bunkers 10,000 yards north and west of the tower. All told, more than 500 miles of wiring had been installed to bring "Fat Man" to life.

For almost three years, a community that had grown to 6,000 had lived an anchorite life at Site Y, the atom bomb research laboratory, a lonely mesa near Los Alamos, New Mexico: a fenced-in area where all mail was censored and babies were born unknown to their relatives. Quartered in four-apartment blocks, where they slept on Army cots, the scientists, their wives and children lived on streets without either names or street-lights, denied all telephone links with the outside world. Blue badges were accorded those who could enter the Technical Area but had no access to secrets, white badges for those who did, yet what those secrets were even their wives never knew.

Soon all this would change.

Under heavy rainfall, a seven-man arming party, among them Dr Joseph C. McKibben of the University of California, had reached the tower soon after 11 p.m. His face ashen with fatigue, McKibben went through the 47-point check list of all that had to be done before zero hour – should zero hour arrive.

At 2 a.m., the weather was improving. At 4 a.m. the rain had stopped. By now, Groves and Oppenheimer had reached the S-10,000 post – the control dugout four miles from the Base Camp, where a stop switch, which could prevent the explosion only seconds before the detonation, was sited. At 4:45 a.m., a weather report came: "Winds aloft very light, variable to 40,000 surface calm ... Conditions holding for next two hours. Sky now broken, becoming scattered."

Groves reached a decision. The explosion was set for 5:30 a.m.

Now the final phase of the arming began. At the tower connections were checked, switches thrown, all leads connected, for contrary to popular belief, no button would be pressed: at 45 seconds to zero, McKibben would set in motion timing and firing circuits through an automatic timer. This done, they switched on floodlights, which would make the tower visible by fieldglasses from the dugout. Thirty minutes before zero, they piled into jeeps, heading for S-10,000.

Far south of the tower, at Mockingbird Gap, four military policemen smoked in silence, waiting for dawn to end their vigil; by one man's calculation this was the 210th night they had drawn guard duty at Trinity. One of them vanished behind a boulder, then shambled shamefacedly back to the trench. "Too damned scared to piss," he mumbled.

At zero minus five minutes, a siren wailed. A green Very rocket arched in the sky to the south, then trailed into blackness. At Base Camp scientists and soldiers began making for their trenches. Enrico Fermi, ebullient as always, began tearing up sheets of paper and stuffing them into his pockets. "Just watch," he told colleague Herbert Anderson. "I'll know the yield before anyone."

It was a time for last minute precautions – though against what nobody knew precisely. At the Base Camp, to which Groves had now returned, everyone lay face down on the ground, feet towards the blast, their eyes closed. Even twenty miles from the tower, Dr Edward Teller, a refugee Hungarian physicist, wore heavy gloves, dark glasses, and a pair of welder's goggles. Both he and Hans Bethe, a German refugee, smeared their faces with sunburn oil to guard against ultra-violet rays.

Zero minus forty-five seconds. In the central shelter McKibben flipped the switch for the automatic timer. The robot device came to life, triggering circuits with deadly precision. Oppenheimer held on to a beam for support. Brigadier-General Thomas E. Farrell, Grove's assistant, thought of a text from Scripture, "Lord, I believe; help Thou mine unbelief." Beside him, Oppenheimer's deputy, Saul K. Allison, gripping the microphone, screamed "Zero!"

Then, in that eternity, only the croaking of desert toads was heard.

A pinpoint of light unimaginably brilliant pierced the darkness. Like a flaming gas jet it spurted upward, billowing into a vast belljar of fire.

Fifty miles northwards, in a car on Highway 85, 18-year-old Georgia Green, clutched the arm of her brother-in-law, Joe Wills, and gasped, "What's that?"; the car swerved on to the soft shoulder of the highway.

Georgia Green was blind and had been so from birth.

In that apocalyptic moment, men burrowed for the sand as frenziedly as ants. Oppenheimer's mind recalled a line from the Hindu epic, Bhagavad-Gita: "I am become Death, the shatterer of worlds." Enrico Fermi, tossing scraps of paper from his pocket, watched them swept across the sand by a shock wave equivalent to 20,000 tons of T.N.T.

At 2,000 feet the seething ball of plutonium turned yellow, then blood-red, washing the arroyos and crevasses with golden and lavender hues. At eight-tenths of a second, it had topped the Empire State Building, but it roiled on to 40,000 feet, spreading into a mile-wide ring of grey-black ash.

The impact was titanic. In Gallup, New Mexico, 235 miles northwest, houses shuddered and windows split apart. Even in Amarillo, Texas, 450 miles east, the flash was plainly visible. (The stunned public were told that an ammunition maganize had exploded.) "Zero" was now a crater 1,200 feet wide, the 32-ton rigging tower twisted like a child's toy; the sand for 400 yards around turned to a glass-like substance, glittering like pale jade. The yuccas and Joshua trees had vanished, and only the carbonised shadows of tiny animals remained.

Yet few scientists knew any other reaction than euphoria. The silent waxworks that had viewed the scene with awe, now became capering cheering figures, doing jigs of pure esctasy: what they had all along referred to as "the gadget" had actually worked. "Oppie, you owe me ten dollars!" yelled Dr George B. Kistiakowsky, a Russian émigré, seizing Oppenheimer in a bear-hug; he had bet his entire month's salary against ten dollars that the bomb would work. Few believed that the secret could long be kept: a security officer lamented, "You might as well try to keep the Mississipi River a secret." Only scientist Ken Bainbridge seems to have early suffered doubts. Looking Oppenheimer squarely in the eyes, he said softly, "Now, we're all sons-of-bitches."

The most succinct remark made by any observer was that of Harvard's Kistiakowsky. "I am sure," he said, "that at the end of the world – in the last millisecond of the earth's existence – the last man will see what we saw."

The news of that spectacle travelled swiftly. On 17 July, Groves was met by his secretary, a radiant 34-year-old widow named Jean O'Leary at Washington's National Airport. Together they repaired to the office of George L. Harrison, vice-chairman of the Interim Committee on atomic energy, to draft an encoded message that would give Secretary of War Henry Stimson some idea of the explosion. At that moment Stimson was more than 3,000 miles distant in Potsdam, Germany, participating in a conference that Truman was holding with Churchill and Stalin.

Gauging the flash in terms of the 250 miles between Washington and Stimson's estate, "Highhold" on Long Island, they related the blast thunder to the 50 miles between Washington and Harrison's farm at Upperville, Virginia, in the lee of the Blue Ridge Mountains.

The final wording was nothing if not quaint:

> DOCTOR HAS JUST RETURNED MOST ENTHUSIASTIC AND CONFIDENT THAT THE LITTLE BOY IS AS HUSKY AS HIS BIG BROTHER. THE LIGHT IN HIS EYES DISCERNIBLE FROM HERE TO HIGHHOLD AND I COULD HAVE

HEARD HIS SCREAMS FROM HERE TO MY FARM.

At the Potsdam Communications Centre, the young decoding officers, taking it at its face value, whistled in admiration: "Jeez, that old guy sure has it in him." Convinced that the 78-year-old Stimson had just become a father, they wondered if the Big Three would take a day off to celebrate.

At No 2, Kaiserstrasse, "The Little White House," in the suburb of Babelsberg, this news was of vital import to Truman. On 16 July, discussing the test and its impact on the Russians, with his new Secretary of State, James F. Byrnes, Truman had remarked, "If it explodes as I think it will, I'll certainly have a hammer on these boys." Yet more important even than this was the knowledge that one bomb could now do what thousands had done to the once gracious suburbs of Berlin. In Truman's mind there was little doubt that if the Japanese did not respond to a formal demand for surrender, a second bomb should be used without specific warning.

The President had logic on his side. On 18 June, he had set his seal on "Operation Olympic," a November assault on Japan, aimed at the southern sector of Kyushu, whose airfields and harbours could later be used to support a further thrust against Tokyo in March 1946. It was a meticulous 400-page single spaced plan, involving three quarters of a million men, but by the yardstick of Okinawa, as Stimson pointed out, the invaders would face a Japanese Army five million strong with perhaps 5,000 *Kamikaze* planes. No one expected the fighting to end until late 1946, with an estimated one million American casualties.

If an atom bomb on Japan could save a million lives, then Truman saw his duty as plain, and Churchill, apprised of the events at Trinity, was in full agreement.

But now complications arose. On 17 July, Arthur Holly Compton of the University of Chicago, forwarded a sheaf of scientists' petitions to George Harrison in Washington. One, written by the Hungarian refugee, Leo Szilard, urged Truman not to use the bomb without a specific warning to Japan. (Szilard had at first urged that the bomb should not be used at all but his now modified version attracted 67 signatures). Yet another petition had urged using the bomb only if Japan refused to surrender. Yet a third asked for a quick use of the bomb to spare American lives. Plainly the scientists were more divided than the politicians – not surprisingly, since while the scientists were unaware that Japan had for months been putting out peace feelers, the State Department had no knowledge of the atom bomb at all.

Both Stimson and Under Secretary of State Joseph C. Grew had urged on Truman that to give Japan a chance to retain Emperor Hirohito, provided they surrender, would make negotiations that much easier. Truman had promised to "bear the Emperor in mind" – but to Byrnes this smacked of "appeasement".

Thus, the first Potsdam declaration of 26 July, calling on Japan to surrender, omitted one vital sentence that Grew had drafted: "a peacefully inclined responsible government" might "include a constitutional monarchy under the present dynasty if the peace-loving nations can be convinced of the genuine determination of such a government to follow policies of peace which will render impossible the further development of aggressive militarism in Japan."

After long discussions, the Cabinet of Premier Kantaro Suzuki, who had been seeking a way out of the war since April, decided not to answer, but merely disregard, or *mokusatu* (literally "kill with silence") the ultimatum.

This ambivalence was of a piece with Potsdam, whose thirteen plenary sessions held between 16 July and 2 August, dragged on interminably in the Cecilienhof Palace, dominated by its 24-foot star of red geraniums. On the agenda the old time-worn topics loomed large – Poland, Rumania, Bulgaria, reparations – and all in the tradition of Yalta, were "referred to the Foreign Ministers for further study". And in the familiar tradition of Dumbarton Oaks, the final agreement was to disagree.

On 24 July, after receiving a full report from Groves, Truman finally decided to drop Stalin, who six days earlier had agreed to enter the war against Japan, a hint regarding "Fat Man". Strolling nonchalantly over during a break in the conference, with the Russian interpreter, Pavlov, he mentioned only that the United States had "a new weapon of unusual destructive force".

The dictator appeared quite unimpressed. "I am glad to hear it," he said, nodding, with a slight smile. "I hope you will make good use of it against the Japanese."

Outside, in the sunshine, Churchill and Byrnes, waiting for their cars, crowded round the President, eager to hear Stalin's reactions. Truman shook a disappointed head. "He never asked a single question," he replied baffled.

Stalin had had no need. As always, his agents had been working overtime.

On Sunday 3 June, a bland moon-faced 30-year-old Communist spy named Harry Gold mounted a steep flight of stairs in a run-down apartment building at 209 North High Street, Albuquerque, New Mexico. A young Army Corporal, T/5 David Greenglass, opened the door.

"Mr Greenglass?" Gold queried. "I come from Julius."

Greenglass stood aside to let him enter. Then, crossing the room, he picked up his wife's handbag and extracted one half of a box of raspberry Jell-O. In silence Gold produced the other half from his pocket. The match was perfect.

He and his wife, Ruth, had been expecting Gold, Greenglass explained, but not on that particular day. He would have to rest up at the local Hilton until information was written out. Gold, equably, rented a room and settled to a whodunnit. Thus far he had had a profitable weekend. On Alameda Street, in Santa Fe, he had been picked up by Dr Klaus Fuchs, a dreamy gifted crypto-Communist physicist, an inner member of the Los Alamos circle, and they had driven into the country in Fuchs' old Chevrolet coupe. When they parted, Gold had benefited to the extent of a thick wad of typed notes concerning the application of theoretical fission to the building of an atom bomb.

At mid-afternoon he strolled back to North High Street to take tea and cookies with the Greenglasses. As a machinist in the smallest of the top-secret technical shops at Los Alamos, Greenglass had systematically copied bomb "lenses," which helped focus detonation waves in the triggering of a bomb. He had drawn up a supplementary report, too, neatly done on 8 X 10 wide ruled white paper.

Before 10 p.m. on 5 June, Gold was back in New York. He travelled by subway far into Brooklyn, where Metropolitan Avenue meets Queens. On the quiet sidewalk, a man approached him warily: Anatoly Yakolev, of New York's Soviet Consulate. They fell into step beside one another. Like Gold, Yakolev was carrying a newspaper.

After a block, they stopped, exchanged newspapers and separated.

Gold's newspaper was empty. But Yakolev's paper contained two stout manila envelopes, one marked DOCTOR and the second marked OTHER: the fruits of Fuchs' and Greenglass's treachery.

Soviet scientists could now by-pass a costly and time-consuming experimental stage, and that was why Josef Stalin had asked no questions at Potsdam.[37]

On 28 July, as unexpectedly as understudies appearing with the rise of a third act curtain, new faces appeared at Potsdam. Two days earlier, the British Labour Party had won a landslide victory in the General Election, netting 393 seats against the Conservatives' 213, the Liberals' 12. In what Pierson Dixon of the Foreign Office described as a "strangely Hanoverian atmosphere," the newcomers to Cecilienhof Palace were Premier Clement Attlee, self-effacing but steely – "a modest man with much to be modest about," was Churchill's verdict – and Foreign Minister Ernest Bevin, an impulsive warm-hearted onetime dockers' union leader.

In Britain, Churchill grieved. "I am worried about this damned election," he had confessed to Lord Moran in June. "I have no message for them now ... I feel very lonely without a war." As the dire election results flowed in to Downing Street, he strove to make the best of it: "It is the will of the people – robust – controlled." But on 29 July, signing the Visitors' Book at Chequers, his true feelings showed through: "Finis," he wrote beneath his signature.

By 6 August, he had quit No 10 and moved into the penthouse suite at Claridge's. That was the day Truman warned the Japanese of "a rain of ruin from the air, the like of which has never been seen on this earth."

At 7:25 a.m., on Monday 6 August, a Superfortress named "Straight Flush" was a pinpoint against the sun, six miles above the Japanese seaport of Hiroshima. Flying west across the city, then turning east, the pilot, Major Claude R. Eatherly, had seen nothing but cloud – yet the city centre itself lay naked to the sun, "as though a hole had been punched in a fluffy bedspread". Now, on Eatherley's orders, the radio operator tapped out a cryptic message in Morse: "Y2 Q2 B2 C1."

South-east of the Pacific island of Shikoku, 200 miles away, another bomber, the "Enola Gay," named after the mother of the pilot, Colonel Paul W. Tibbets, Jr., took due note of the message. With the aid of a weather code sheet, Tibbets and his radioman, Corporal Richard Nelson, interpreted it: "Low cloud, 1 to 3/10ths. Middle cloud 1 to 3/10ths. High cloud 1 to 3/10ths. Advise: Bomb primary".

That counsel spelt a death sentence for the city of Hiroshima, for although two other weather-ships, circling Nagasaki and Kokura, had sent almost identical weather surveys, these were only alternative targets if Hiroshima was socked in. At Potsdam, Stimson had successfully achieved the deletion of the cultural shrine of Kyoto from the target list – but industrial Hiroshima, the lynch-pin of defence for western Japan would enjoy no such immunity.

At 1:45 a.m., Japanese time, shadowed by two B-29s, carrying scientists with instruments to measure the blast and camera crews, "Enola Gay" had rolled down the runway on the island of Tinian, in the Marianas, with a 10,000-pound uranium bomb, code-named "Little Boy," 14 feet long and 5 feet wide, secured by steel clamps in the bomb bay. Approximately one hour later, Navy Captain William S. Parsons, a tall quiet balding man, lowered himself into the bay to begin the work of arming it. First he carefully fitted an explosive charge through "Little Boy's" tail. The side of the bomb was fitted with a green plug, which shorted two electric circuits so that "Little Boy" could not detonate. Now Parsons replaced this with a red plug, fitting flush against the bomb's skin.

The electrical circuit was now completed: "Little Boy" was armed and set to go. The end product of a two-million dollar research project had been readied for use in twenty-five minutes.

It was a masterpiece of electronic know-how. When it dropped intricate timers would shut off for fifteen seconds. After this barometric gauges would signal the four radio proximity fuses, set to explode the bomb at 1,850 feet above ground. All this must take place in forty-three seconds – from the drop to the moment of explosion.

In the crew compartment, Parsons and his assistant, First Lieutenant Morris R. Jeppson, were now seated before a two-by-two black console, connected to the bomb's electrical circuits. Every half hour now, these circuits must be monitored; one incorrect reading on the panel and "Little Boy" would return ignominiously to Tinian.

In the rear crew compartment, the tail gunner, Sergeant Robert R. Caron, was on fire with curiosity; until this moment no man in the five squadrons that made up Tibbets' 509th Composite Group had any inkling of their mission. "Is it some kind of chemist's nightmare?"

he asked Tibbets. The Colonel said no. "How about a physicist's nightmare?"

"Yeah," said Tibbets grinning. "That's about right."

As the coast of Japan slid into view, Tibbets called all hands; from now on Lieutenant Jacob Beser, the radar operator, would record all intercom conversations. "This is for history," he warned. "So watch your language. We're carrying the first atomic bomb."

To most of the crew the phrase meant nothing at all.

At 6:40 a.m. "Enola Gay" now pressurised began her long climb towards bombing altitude: 31,000 feet. At 8:09 a.m. Tibbets instructed, "We are about to start the bomb run. Put on your goggles." All twelve men aboard now pulled on polaroid goggles like those worn by arc welders, admitting only one colour, purple, through the lenses.

Before covering his eyes, the co-pilot, Captain Robert A. Lewis noted in his log: "There will be a short intermission while we bomb our target."

Precisely at 8:15:17, the bombardier, Major Thomas Ferebee, sighting through the bomber's plexiglass nose, saw "Little Boy" drop cleanly from the bomb bay. Abruptly, some 10,000 pounds lighter, "Enola Gay" jerked ten feet upwards, and Tibbets swerved her into a diving right-hand turn.

At 8:16 a.m., six miles below them, "Little Boy" blew apart.

"My God," Lewis cried out. "What have we done?" for the plane was shuddering as if beaten "with a telegraph pole". Sergeant Caron, who had closed his eyes against a flash "brighter than a thousand suns," opened them again for "a peep into hell". Dust was boiling upwards, powered by a tall white column of smoke, whose summit was an almost perfect mushroom cloud, pulsing to almost four miles in height until it split apart, rising as of its own volition, to 40,000 feet. "Good God," Jeppson heard another man gasp, "could anyone live through that down there?"

Fully 78,000 people could not. Over more than 4 square miles of Hiroshima, the 500,000 citizens recalled almost universally, a blinding white flash, "the *pikadon*," a rush of air travelling at 500 miles an hour, a rumbling as of huge waggons, then a settling darkness, peppered with black raindrops as big as marbles. All impressions were subliminal. "There was no sky left," recalled Nichiyoshi Nukushina, a fire-truck driver at the Army Ordnance Supply Depot; a Methodist pastor, the Reverend Kiyoshi Tanimoto, remembered "a sheet of sun"; in the ruins of their home, 5-year-old Nyeko asked his mother, Mrs Hatsuyo Nakamura, "Why is it night already?"

In the instant of the initial flash came the heat: a fireball whose temperature at the core was 50 million degrees. It was so intense that it melted roof tiles, charred the exposed sides of telegraph poles two miles away, incinerated humans near the hypocentre so completely that only their shadows, graven into asphalt pavements or stone walls, remained; often, in an echo of Pompeii, the shadows were poised for flight or interlocked in a last loving embrace.

In the wake of the heat came the great firestorm, howling towards the centre of the explosion, increasing in force as the raging fire turned the air above the city hotter by the minute. It swept through the parks where survivors were collecting, uprooting giant trees; it lashed up high waves in the rivers, drowning hundreds who had taken to the water to escape the flames.

Strangely, there was almost no hysteria, no tears. In Asano Park, an estate by the Kyo River, designed as an evacuation area in event of a B-29 raid the pastor Tanimoto noted, above all, the terrible silence; hundreds of wounded, the clothes seared from their bodies, lay in almost total apathy. "None of the many who died did so noisily; not even the children cried; very few people even spoke."

No sights like these had ever been seen in the history of the world. "My mother was turned into white bones before the family altar," 5-year-old Sachiko Habu would remember all her life. Everywhere things which only a short time before had been human beings were seeking something to quench a thirst "like a red-hot poker in the throat"; almost the one sound heard was the chant of "*Mizu! Mizu!*" (Water! Water!). The police chief, Shiroku Tanabe, trying desperately to reach headquarters, was blocked by thousands of refugees who looked "as if they had crawled out of a pool of blood". Private Shigeru Shimoyama chanced on a sight which would haunt his dreams for years: a pale pink cavalry horse, all its skin stripped away by blast. In Asano Park, Father Wilhelm Kleinsorge, a German Jesuit priest, found twenty men slumped in the bushes, their faces so burned that their eyesockets were hollow; the fluid from their melted eyes had flooded down their cheeks. Their mouths, puffy pus covered wounds, were unable to accommodate a teapot's spout; only by adapting a grass stem as a straw could Kleinsorge help them to a drink of water.

There was no lacking of willing Samaritans, but medicines were painfully lacking. Escaping from his nightmare vision of the horse,

Private Shimoyama saw villagers laying sliced cucumbers on the burns of survivors, carrying the seriously injured to first-aid stations in vegetable carts. An Army doctor near Asano Park had only iodine which he painted on everything – cuts, bruises, burns. At the city's large up-to-date Red Cross Hospital, Dr Terufumi Sasaki, a young member of the surgical team and seven other doctors, were swamped out with 10,000 patients – with nothing to treat the worst burns but compresses of saline solution.

More puzzling still, many survivors exhibited symptoms unknown to medical science: cuts swollen out "like the lips of a savage," great sheets of skin peeling away from the tissue to hang down "like rags from a scarecrow": eyes, noses, ears and mouths burned away. Hundreds of women reported their hair was coming out in handfuls. At the Hiroshima Communications Hospital, nominally for postal and telegraph employees, the director, Dr Michikiko Hachiya, had reports of patients passing fifty bloody stools in one night.

At the Red Cross Hospital, Dr Sasaki and his colleagues, by degrees, evolved a theory: the sickness was one new to medicine, a direct reaction to the body's bombardment by neutrons, beta particles and gamma rays. Body cells had been destroyed, the white blood-cell count was dropping sharply, *petechiae* (small round spots caused by bleeding into the skin) appeared on the mucous membranes.

All over Hiroshima, on the night of 6 August, surgeons worked on as best they could by the light of leaping fires. An acrid sulphuric smell drifted from fissures in the ground, mingled with a strange odour like that of burning sardines. For four square miles it was as if a giant rake had scarified the soil, to be followed by a monster steam-roller. Of roughly 90,000 buildings in the city, 65,000 were near unusable. In the hospital corridors and stairways, the dead and dying were laid out "like so many codfish spread out," and now, as the agony took hold, the cries went up "*eraiyo*" – "the pain is unbearable; I cannot endure it!"

"The door that slammed behind man at Hiroshima had locked," noted *Time* Magazine, "...There was no choice but to grope ahead into the Atomic Age." No choice at all, and the watchword was *eraiyo*.

12

"You And I Would Be In A Pretty Pickle"
After 6 August, 1945

Ensign Ryuji Nagatsuka was as incensed as any patriotic Japanese. Three times in the space of days his country had been violated: two days after the nightmare of Hiroshima, Russia had declared war on Japan. Then, on 9 August, came a second atomic bomb on Nagasaki, wiping out 26,000 people, injuring over 40,000. In the spirit of many Japanese civilians, ready to repel the invaders with bamboo spears or to form "Sherman Carpets," over which the tanks would roll, Nagatsuka's mind dwelt only on revenge.

But the U.S. Fleet was now well beyond their range and only six Ki-43 (Falcon) fighters survived at Kagohara airfield.

On the evening of 12 August, the alert sounded stridently: ten miles south-east of the airfield, American fighter-bombers were heading for the city of Kumagaya. "Bring down as many as you can to avenge in advance all the unlucky victims of tonight's air raid," Commandant Suenaga exhorted them. "Be fierce and daring! Scramble!"

As the last six planes raced above the Kanto plain towards a horizon piled with small crimson clouds, the image of death was never far from Nagatsuka's mind. As if to atone for the shame of that abortive sortie against Task Force 38, he wished nothing more than a glorious death for the Emperor. The commissioned officer Nagatsuka, he thought wryly, had at length vanquished the French student Nagatsuka.

Then, 2,500 feet below, he saw the small grey specks that denoted the enemy: five Grumman Hellcats, bound for Kumagaya. Revenge was very close now. Lieutenant Takagui gave the signal to fan out.

Before diving to the attack, Nagatsuka glanced round – and at that moment, a few thousand feet away, more Grummans were bursting through the clouds in a near head-on collision. For a second Nagatsuka hesitated: a zoom climb, or a spiral dive to attack the other planes beneath? A dive, he decided, pressing the rudder bar to the left, but one of the American fighters had singled him out. He shivered in pure terror.

Barrel roll succeeded barrel roll, as he strove to shake off his adversary, but the American dogged him stubbornly. Glinting flecks of machine-gun fire were ricocheting from the Falcon. Suddenly it was as if a bludgeon had struck him: his right arm hung completely inert and blood was staining the shoulder of his brown silk summer suit. His mind was clouding.

Abruptly he came to: at 3,000 feet, off balance, the Falcon was falling into a spin. With all the strength of his left arm he pulled the stick against his stomach. He was out of the battle now. In frustrated rage he knew that the one hope left was a forced landing.

600 feet… 300 feet… his mind a turmoil of anxiety, he grappled to put down the landing gear. To the left of the instrument panel, a red bulb glowed ominously: immobilised by bullets the gear was out of action. The ground was coming up very fast to meet him now, trees tearing past beneath, like jetsam cast from a shipwreck, the crimson clouds jolting wildly across the sky. Then the Falcon hit a paddyfield like a stalling truck, all the sound in the world rushing towards him, and he blacked out, unconscious.

—

It was the first time in history that a defeated country had surrendered by radio and aeroplane. It was also the first time that the victors flew in to occupy an enemy terrain without having fought for it. For 100 million Japanese, noon on Wednesday 15 August, was also the first time they had ever heard the voice of the god-like Emperor Hirohito: "To our good and loyal subjects: After pondering deeply the general trends of the world and the actual conditions pertaining in Our Empire today, We have decided to effect a settlement of the present situation by resorting to an extraordinary measure…"

At this hour, the Emperor himself was closeted in an underground conference room at the Imperial Palace with the members of his Privy Council. The broadcast, relayed from Studio 8 of the Japanese Broadcasting Association in downtown Tokyo, had been recorded at midnight the previous day, in a dusty office shielded by grimy blackout curtains, in the Imperial Household Ministry. Since April, racked by insomnia, finding comfort only in his collection of pressed flowers and a childhood volume of Aesop's Fables, the 44-year-old Emperor had known that, despite his inviolate status, the time must come for him to intervene – a conviction he shared with his Lord Privy Seal, Marquis Koichi Kido and his Premier, Kantarō Suzuki.

Thus, on 10 August, a telegram from the Foreign Ministry, accepting the Potsdam Declaration – provided that the Emperor's status was unaffected – winged its way to the capitals of the Allied powers.

The broadcast was almost never delivered. In open rebellion, a group of fanatic hard-liners under Major Kenji Hatanaka and Captain Shigetaro Uehara, of the Air Academy, led a battalion of the Imperial Guard rampaging through the Palace, kicking down doors, pulling out drawers, determined to seize the disc so that the broadcast should never take place. At the eleventh hour, after General Shizuichi Tanaka, commanding the Eastern District Army, had quelled the revolt, the disc, which had been locked all night in a wall safe, was smuggled to the studio in a lunch-box.

Inevitably, since MacArthur was involved, the 16-man Japanese delegation that arrived at Manila's Clark Field on 19 August, travelled under the password "Bataan". Yet MacArthur, a canny Orientalist, knew better than to infringe on the Empire's sacred persona. "I have no desire whatsoever to debase him in the eyes of his own people," he declared.

One day later – before Nagatsuka had even left hospital, to be reunited at his parents' home at Nagoya, with his volumes of George Sand and his *Nouveau Petit Larousse Illustré*, the 24th Squadron at Kagohara was disbanded.

Unlike the war in Europe – Eisenhower's war – the war in the Far East ended with a MacArthur flourish. On Sunday 2 September, the 45,000-ton battleship, U.S.S. *Missouri*, 18 miles offshore in Tokyo Bay, bristled with scaffolding erected for war correspondents and cameramen: the red-tabbed generals, ranked in a tight packed U round MacArthur, represented nine allied nations that had fought the war – among them two survivors from a less glorious era, Lieutenant-General Jonathan Wainwright, who had yielded up Bataan, and Lieutenant-General Arthur Percival, who had surrendered Malaya.

The eleven-man Japanese delegation, led by Foreign Minister Mamoru Shigemitsu, a tall elderly man limping on a wooden leg, leaning heavily on a walking stick, arrived at 8:55 a.m., the diplomats attired in tall silk hats, Ascots and cutaways. Following the chaplain's invocation and a recording of *The Star Spangled Banner*, MacArthur strode from the wings like a matinee idol, walking between Nimitz and Admiral William "Bull" Halsey, whose flagship this was. On a green baize mess table, marred by coffee stains, lay the copies of the instrument of capitulation, one bound in leather for the Allies, the other, canvas-bound, for the Japanese. Stooping, Shigemitsu affixed his signature, followed by the Chief of the Imperial General Staff, Yoshijiro Umezu.

Now confusion arose. The Canadian delegate, Colonel Cosgrove, his eyes dazzled by sunlight, signed the surrender on the wrong line, not for Canada but for France. General LeClerc, with a puzzled Gallic shrug, signed for New Zealand – forcing Air Vice-Marshal Issit to sign for the Netherlands and Admiral Helfrich to sign for nobody at all. Deftly, Lieutenant-General Richard Sutherland, MacArthur's Chief of Staff, with a series of neatly-penned arrows, restored order from chaos.

Lastly, MacArthur. The eighteen-minute ritual over, he pulled five fountain pens from his breast pocket, to append his own signature. One pen to become a memento for Wainwright, the second for Percival; a third would go to West Point, a fourth to Annapolis. The last would be a souvenir for Jean, his wife. At 9:25 a.m., he announced in a ringing voice: "These proceedings are now closed." To Halsey, *sotto voce*, he muttered, "Bill, where the hell are those airplanes?"

It was a superb last gesture of stage management. Lighting a cigarette, MacArthur blew a long streamer of smoke – and out of that cloud, as if by magic, droned a vast armada of planes, sweeping over the warships from the south: 400 B-29s and 1,500 carrier planes, to be swallowed up by the mists cloaking Mount Fujiyama.

At the micrcophone, MacArthur now saluted the American people: "Today, the guns are silent. A great tragedy has ended. A great victory has been won. The skies no longer rain death – the seas bear only commerce – men everywhere walk upright in the sunlight. The entire world is quietly at peace."

–

It was all over – or was it? Was "the entire world" at peace?

For the seventy million people of six countries[38] "liberated" by the Red Army over three million square miles it was far from over. Nor had it ended for 14 million Yugoslavs, for Tito, ensconced in King Peter's palace in Belgrade, had nationalised 2,000 industrial enterprises and 30,000 farms.

It was still a reality to the 17 million citizens of the forcibly-imposed German Democratic Republic, of East Germany, where Marshal Georgi Zhukov had staged a revolution without barricades, creating the nucleus of a Fourth Reich.

For the British it was positively over, but so, too, was lend-lease, and the country was in dire straits: £20 billion worse off than before the war. "So far as this President is concerned Santa Claus is dead," Truman had written his wife, Bess, from Potsdam: in Washington, seeking new credit terms, the Treasury's Lord Keynes and Ambassador Halifax, noted Labour's new Chancellor of the Exchequer, Hugh Dalton, found "nothing but a row of poker faces across the table". Hoping for an interest-free loan of $6 billion and a grant in aid, they finally settled for no grant, merely a $.25 billion loan at two per cent per annum.

The "special relationship" forged to defeat Hitler had ended abruptly; the honeymoon was over.

On every side the ironies multiplied. The Poland for which Britain had gone to war in 1939 no longer existed. Instead, Stalin's determined espousal of the Lublin Poles, sowed, like dragon's teeth, the seeds of Solidarity, the brinkmanship of the Warsaw manouevures, the shadow of martial law.

Hitler had set out to destroy the Jewish race; instead he effectively created the state of Israel, and the brooding tensions of the Middle East, of which the Palestine Liberation Organisation would remain the most sinister symbol. Finland – at the outcome of World War Two a cause as emotive as Belgium in World War One – ultimately found herself on the wrong side and paid the price: a price known as "Finlandisation".

Even the gruelling and needless Burma campaign – the British sop to Roosevelt's faith in Chiang-kai-shek – reaped the British no ultimate reward. In much of south-east Asia, the Japanese slogan "Asia for the Asiatics" found favour: Burma, Malaya, India, Indo-China and Indonesia would all cast off the imperial yoke. In China it would be Mao-tse-tung – to Roosevelt "a liberal agrarian reformer" – who would inherit the land that Chiang had thrown away.

The ultimate irony would be the atom bomb. The outcry that greeted the news of Hiroshima was wholly understandable – and, so, too, was the burgeoning British Campaign for Nuclear Disarmament. Yet those who marched on Aldermaston from 1958 onwards to safeguard their children's future might ponder one final irony: was it thanks to that deterrent that their children, by 1983, had lived all of twenty-three years?

—

V. J. Day had barely dawned before the victors flexed their muscles. The war crimes trials – a procedure without precedent in legal history – began.

In France, Vichy Premier Pierre Laval – protesting with some justice – "I'm not a war criminal – I'm a peace criminal" – went on trial, and so, too, did Marshal Henri-Philippe Pétain, so bored by the proceedings that he passed the twenty-day trial ogling the ample bosom of a woman reporter. "A Premier of France dies standing," Laval declared, when offered a stool to face the firing squad in October: Pétain was exiled for life on the Ile d'Yeu. In Oslo, Vidkun Quisling, who had given his name to a whole band of "patriotic traitors," also stood trial; the life he claimed to have sacrificed for Norway was in turn claimed by a firing squad.

All these processes paled before the trials at Nuremberg, which unfolded under Big Three auspices from 20 November, 1945. In the brilliantly lit courtroom, crowded with tiny glass cubicles for cameramen, each seat equipped with a telephone headset and a dial to ensure direct translation, 400 newsmen had gathered to hear Justice Robert Jackson, the chief of counsel for the United States, open for the prosecution: "In the prisoners' dock sit twenty-odd broken men..."

Some had been infamous the world over: Hermann Göring, defiant, cynical and appreciative by turns as the evidence was heard; Deputy Führer Rudolf Hess, eyes as impassive as a sleepwalker's beneath the black bushy eyebrows; Ribbentrop, looking immeasurably weary. Others were names that the public at large scarcely knew: the handsome haughty Keitel, Jodl, Dönitz, Speer, the lantern-jawed Kaltenbrunner.

"What makes this inquest significant," Jackson went on, "is that these prisoners represent sinister influences that will lurk in the world long after their bodies have returned to dust."

At intervals, a yellow bulb flashed urgently before Sir Geoffrey Lawrence, the Pickwickian British Lord Justice; the twelve interpreters on duty were unable to keep up. Down the corridor from the courtroom, in the huge multigraph room the machines revolved endlessly churning out copies of original documents, orders, memoranda, all captured on German soil, all to be used in evidence.

"By their fruits we must know them. Their acts have bathed the world in blood and set civilisation back a century."

These documents would take a very long time to sort out. Not until 1 October, 1946, were the final sentences pronounced: for Hess, a life sentence, for Speer, twenty years, for Dönitz, ten. Ribbentrop, Keitel, Jodl and Kaltenbrunner were all hanged – but Göring, like Heinrich Himmler before him, cheated the hangmen: two hours before he should have mounted the scaffold he swallowed a cyanide capsule.

The last word was with Churchill. On the day the trial results were announced, his old friend Ismay was paying him a visit in the former Premier's country home at Chartwell, near Westerham, Kent. Together they had fought a long battle, from the crusading days of 1940, when Britain stood alone, to the squalid *realpolitik* of 1945, when nations had become no more than pawns.

"It shows that if you get into a war," Churchill pondered, "it is supremely important to win it." The old puckish grin lit up his features. "You and I would be in a pretty pickle if we had lost."

Acknowledgements

This book is the final volume of a trilogy which began with *1940: The Avalanche* and was succeeded by *The Road to Pearl Harbor: 1941*. Like its predecessors it derives in part from interviews with several hundred eye-witnesses and in part from records and archive repositories in the United States and Great Britain. Those participants whose testimonies I have used are hereby gratefully acknowledged; the details of their individual contributions are listed in the appropriate sections of the source apparatus.

Without the archivists on both sides of the Atlantic who over the years have made records available or offered valuable guidance, my task could not have been accomplished. I hope they will accept the bare mention of their names as a token of my gratitude: Corelli Barnett, Keeper of the Archives, Churchill College, Cambridge, and his assistant, Marion Stewart; Dr B. S. Benedikz, Head of Special Collections, University Library, Birmingham; Edward J. Boone, Jr, MacArthur Memorial, Norfolk, Va.; Dr Maurice Bond, Clerk of the Records, House of Lords, his successor, H. J. Cobb, and Dr A. J. P. Taylor; Dr Daniel J. Boorstin, Librarian of Congress, Washington, D.C., and Paul T. Heffron, Acting Chief, Manuscript Division; Dr William R. Emerson, Director, Franklin D. Roosevelt Memorial Library, Hyde Park, New York; Helen Langley, Department of Western MSS, Bodleian Library, Oxford; Patricia Methven, Military Archivist, Liddell Hart Centre for Military Archives, University of London, King's College, and her assistant, Bridget Malcolm; Professor David Pocock and Dorothy Wainwright, University of Sussex (Mass-Observation Archive); Angela Raspin, British Library of Political and Economic Science (London School of Economics); Dr Peter Thwaites, Department of Documents, Imperial War Museum, London, and his deputy, Philip Reed; George Wagner, Modern Military Branch, Military Archives Division, National Archives,

Washington, D.C.; John D. Wickman, Director, Dwight D. Eisenhower Library, Abilene, Kansas; Benedict K. Zobrist, Director, Harry S. Truman Library, Independence, Mo.

To the very end, a fine team of researchers and translators have supported me. Hildegard Anderson and Amy Forbert covered very many phases of my American research; Margaret Duff delved with great effect for weeks on end in the Public Records Office, London; Pamela Colman investigated many university libraries.

My English and American publishers, Christopher Sinclair-Stevenson and Alfred A. Knopf, Jr, waited with admirable forbearance for a manuscript disgracefully overdue, and for the third time I must pay tribute to the faultless editorial counsel of Roger Machell. My agents in London and New York, Anne McDermid and Emilie Jacobson, offered the kind of moral support that only a sorely-harassed author can appreciate. Elsie Couch and Ann Walker produced an impeccable typescript from material arriving at very protracted intervals. In addition, I have to thank the staffs of the Library of Congress, Printed Books Division, the New York Public Library, the Public Record Office, the British Library, the London Library and the Wiener Library for their help and courtesy at all times.

But as always my deepest debt is to my wife. Apart from typing the first draft, she ensured that the home fires were always burning and was there just when I needed her most. The book could hardly have been finished without her.

Source Apparatus

The following abbreviations apply throughout:

BL: Bodleian Library, Oxford
BU: University of Birmingham Special Collections
CAB: Cabinet Office Papers, Public Record Office
CCC: Churchill College, Cambridge
DDEL: Dwight D. Eisenhower Library, Abilene, Kansas
FO: Foreign Office Papers, Public Record Office, Kew Green
FDRL: Franklin D. Roosevelt Memorial Library, Hyde Park, New York
HHP: Harry L. Hopkins Papers, Roosevelt Memorial Library
H of L: House of Lords Records Office, London
HSTL: Harry S. Truman Library, Independence, Mo.
L of C: Library of Congress MSS Division, Washington, DC
LHMC: Liddell Hart Centre for Military Archives, King's College, University of London
LSE: London School of Economics
MacA Mem: MacArthur Memorial Library, Norfolk, Va.
PREM: Prime Minister's Papers, Public Record Office
PRO: Public Record Office
THC, MO: The Tom Harrisson Mass-Observation Archive, University of Sussex
WRB: War Refugee Board Archives, Roosevelt Memorial Library.

Chapter One: "The Devil's On My Side, He's A Good Communist"

I am indebted to my old school-fellow, Bruce Ogden Smith, for information to supplement accounts featured in Bill Strutton and Michael Pearson's *The Secret Invaders* (London, 1958), David Howarth,

The Dawn of D-Day (London, 1959) and James Ladd, *Commandos and Rangers of World War Two* (London, 1978). Anzio planning is based on Admiral Sir Manley Power's unpublished MSS (CCC), Gerald Pawle, *The War and Colonel Warden* (London, 1963) and Lt-Gen Sir Leslie Hollis and James Leasor, *War At The Top* (London, 1959).

For Ribbentrop's peace moves, see Peter Kleist, *The European Tragedy* (Douglas, Isle of Man, 1965) and James Graham-Murray, *The Sword and the Umbrella* (Douglas, I.O.M., 1964). Monckton's report is Monckton Papers, File 11/34 (BL).

Churchill's brushes with Hopkins are from Lord Moran, *Winston Churchill: The Struggle for Survival* (London, 1966) and PREM 4/74/2, Hopkins to Churchill, 24 November, 1943. For Dill to Alan Brooke, see Alanbrooke Papers, Box 003, 2(d) 14/39, Flag B, 9 February, 1944 (LHMC). On Roosevelt's motives, see F.O. 954/30, fol. 248, Halifax to Eden, 13 February, 1944. Stalin's gibe is Sir Archibald Clark-Kerr's diary entry for 29 November, 1943 (Inverchapel Papers, BL). Churchill's distrust of the Russians is in F.O. 954/26, fols. 357/358, Churchill to Eden, 1 April, 1944. For Brooke's thoughts on Tehran, see David Fraser, *Alanbrooke* (London, 1982).

Hoare's Spanish policy is outlined in F.O. 954/27, fol. 472, Hoare to Eden, 21 February, 1944. For the attitudes of U.S. civilians, see *Time* Magazine, 10 January, 1944, and Roger Butterfield, *Report From the Nation, Life* Magazine, 28 February, 1944; for British morale, see Angus Calder, *The People's War* (London, 1969), and Norman Longmate, *How We Lived Then* (London, 1971).

For Eisenhower, see Kenneth Davis, *The American Experience of War* (London, 1967), William Manchester, *The Glory and The Dream* (London, 1975), Lt-Gen Sir Frederick Morgan, *Overture to Overlord* (London, 1950), and Kay Summersby, *Eisenhower Was My Boss* (London, 1949). For Sandel, Hansen and von Roenne, see David Kahn, *Hitler's Spies* (London, 1978), Gunter Peis, *The Mirror of Deception* (London, 1977), Ladislas Farago, *The Game of the Foxes* (London, 1972) and Nigel West, *M.I.5.* (London, 1981).

Lily Sergueiev's story is adapted from *For Secret Service Rendered* (London, 1968); Saul K. Padover's from *Psychologist in Germany* (London, 1946), with additional material furnished by Bob Thompson and Dr Philip Mason of Wayne State University; Donald Burgett's from *Currahee!* (Boston, 1967), with much additional material kindly furnished to this author by Donald Burgett.

The overall picture of the Anzio landings derives from Martin Blumenson, *Anzio: The Gamble That Failed* (London, 1963), Lambton Burn, *Down Ramp!* (London, 1947), General Mark Clark, *Calculated Risk* (New York, 1950) and Wynford Vaughan Thomas, *Anzio* (London, 1961). Churchill's strictures are from PREM/3/248/4, fol. 325, Churchill to Ismay, 9 February, 1944.

For views of Lucas, see the Penney Papers, File 16, Notes for a History of the 1st Division, letters of 17 December, 1950 and 8 February, 1956 (LHMC), plus Hilary St George Saunders, *The Green Beret* (London, 1949), Raleigh Trevelyan, *The Fortress* (edn, of 1972) and *Rome '44* (London, 1981) and Peter Verney, *Anzio: An Unexpected Fury* (London, 1978). For the Rapido débâcle, see Martin Blumenson, *Bloody River*, (London, 1970). For "The Devil's Brigade," see Robert H. Adleman and Col George Walton, *The Devil's Brigade* (Philadelphia, 1966). Other views of the beachhead occur in Morris H. Kertzer, *With an 'H' On My Dog-Tag* (New York, 1947), Katharine Tupper Marshall, *Together* (Atlanta, Ga, 1946), Bill Mauldin, *Up Front* (Cleveland, Ohio, 1946) and James A. Ross, *Memoirs of An Army Surgeon* (Edinburgh, 1948).

For Cassino, see Rudolf Böhmler, *Monte Cassino* (London, 1964), Christopher Buckley, *The Road To Rome* (London, 1945), Fred Majdalany, *Cassino* (London, 1957) and Charles Whiting, *Hunters From The Sky* (London, 1975). Cardinal Maglione features in *Time* Magazine, 28 February, 1944.

Chapter Two: "We Are Putting The Whole Works On One Number"

Wing Commander Roland Beamont kindly supplied details to supplement his own book *Phoenix Into Ashes* (London, 1968) and Edward Lanchbery's *Against The Sun* (London, 1955). Mussolini material throughout derives from this author's *Duce!* (London, 1971). For Hitler's health, see David Irving, *Hitler's War* (London, 1977). Prince Stirbey's mission is from M. R. D. Foot, *Resistance* (London, 1976) and *Time* Magazine, 27 March, 1944. For Hungary, see Mario D. Fenyo, *Hitler, Horthy and Hungary*, (New Haven, Conn., 1972), Admiral Nicholas Horthy, *Memoirs* (London, 1956), Nicholas Kallay, *Hungarian Premier* (New York, 1954), and Paul Stskmidt, *Hitler's Interpreter* (London, 1950).

Dr Gisella Perl Krausz supplied much additional information in expansion of her own book, *I Was A Doctor in Auschwitz* (New York, 1948). For Joel Brand's mission, see F.O. 371/42811; Yehuda Bauer, *The Holocaust in Historical Perspective* (London, 1978) and Alex Weissberg, *Advocate For The Dead* (London, 1958). Tito is based on Fitzroy Maclean's *Eastern Approaches* (London, 1949), Milovan Djilas, *Wartime* (1977) and *Tito: the Story from Inside* (London, 1980); see F.O. 954/34, fols. 56–62, Randolph Churchill to the Premier, 27 March, 1944, fol. 28, Churchill to Tito, 26 February, 1944, fol. 38; Maclean to Churchill, 10 March, 1944. Details of accommodation at Claridge's were supplied by Rosland Elliott, of the Savoy Hotel Information Bureau.

For Greece in general, see Foot, *op. cit.*, and Elizabeth Barker, *Churchill and Eden At War* (London, 1978); for King George II, see *Time*'s profile of 24 February, 1947. Polish sources are as follows: CAB 65/W.M.(44), 6, 14 January, 1944 and W.M.(44), 20; F.O. 954/20, fols. 14–16, O'Malley to Eden, 22 January, 1944 and fols. 32–33, McCallum to Eden, 31 January, 1944, supplemented by Stanislaw Mikolajczyk, *The Rape of Poland* (New York, 1948) and Count Edward Raczynski, *In Allied London* (London, 1962).

Roosevelt's health is dealt with by Jim Bishop, *F.D.R.'s Last Year* (London, 1975) and James McGregor Burns, *Roosevelt: The Soldier of Freedom* (London, 1971). The pros and cons of unconditional surrender are discussed at length in Robert Dallek's *The Roosevelt Diplomacy and World War II* (New York, 1970) and Maurice Matloff's *Strategic Planning for Coalition Warfare, (1943–1944*, Washington, D.C., 1959). For de Gaulle, see Sir Alexander Cadogan's *Diaries* (London, 1971), Anthony Eden (Lord Avon), *Memoirs, Vol II: The Reckoning* (London, 1965), and François Kersaudy, *Churchill and De Gaulle* (London, 1981). China features in Brian Crozier, *The Man Who Lost China* (London, 1977), Herbert Feis, *The China Tangle* (Princeton, N.J., 1953), Barbara Tuchman, *Sand Against The Wind* (London, 1970) and Tang Tsou, *America's Failure in China, 1941–50* (Chicago, 1963); Chiang's mooted defection is from Robert Butow, *Japan's Decision to Surrender* (Stanford, Cal., edn, of 1965). The role of South-East Asia Command is from F.0.954–7, fols. 20–21, memo by M. E. Dening, Political Adviser. Imphal and Kohima are drawn from Anthony Brett-James, *Ball of Fire* (Aldershot, 1951), Lt-Gen Sir Geoffrey Evans (with Anthony Brett-James), *Imphal* (London, 1962) and Arthur Swinson, *Kohima* (London,

1966); overall casualty figures are from Maj-Gen S. Woodburn Kirby, *The War Against Japan* (London, 1961–1969).

For the changing face of England, see Iris Carpenter, *No Woman's World* (Boston, 1946). The author discussed many facets of D-Day planning with the following commanders, now deceased: Field Marshal Lord Alanbrooke, Lt-Gen Sir Miles Dempsey, General Dwight D. Eisenhower, Field Marshal Lord Montgomery, Lt-Gen Sir Frederick Morgan, and Marshal of the R.A.F. Lord Tedder. In addition the following sources were used: for Eisenhower and the canteen, see *Time* Magazine, 29 May, 1944; for other aspects of Eisenhower, see Stephen Ambrose, *The Supreme Commander* (London, 1971) and David Irving, *The War Between The Generals* (London, 1981). Hitler's distrust of agents is in Albert Speer, *Inside The Third Reich* (London, 1970). Hobart's creations are detailed in *Final Report on 79th Armoured Division*, Hobart Papers (LHMC). For the naval role, see Kenneth Edwards, *Operation Neptune* (London, 1946), Rear-Admiral Edward Ellsberg, *The Far Shore* (London, 1961) and Cdr Alfred Stanford, *Force Mulberry* (New York, 1951). Other aspects feature in Gen Omar Bradley, *A Soldier's Story* (New York, 1951), Wesley F. Craven and James L. Cate, *The Army Air Forces in World War Two* (Chicago, 1953–65), Milton Dank, *The Glider Gang* (London, 1971), Gilles Perrault, *The Secrets of D-Day* (London, 1965), Cornelius Ryan, *The Longest Day* (London, 1960), Lord Tedder, *With Prejudice* (London, 1966) and Warren Tute (with John Costello and Terry Hughes), *D-Day* (1974). The "whole works" is from Eisenhower to Somervell, 4 April, 1944, Eisenhower Papers (DDEL).

Chapter Three: "Take Unto You The Whole Armour of God"

Rommel material comes primarily from Paul Carell, *Invasion – They're Coming* (London, 1962), *The Rommel Papers* (London, 1953), Ryan *op. cit.* and David Irving, *The Trail of the Fox* (London, 1977). Deception tactics are the theme of Jock Haswell, *The Intelligence and Deception of the D-Day Landings* (London, 1979), Seymour Reit, *Masquerade* (London, 1979) and David Stafford, *Britain and European Resistance* (London, 1980). Prayers in U.S. churches feature in *Time* Magazine, 29 May, 1944.

For the European Advisory Commission, see Lord Strang, *Home and Abroad* (London, 1956). For Bradley, see *Time* Magazine, 1 May,

1944, and Charles Christian Wertenbaker, *Omar Nelson Bradley*, in *Life* Magazine, 5 June, 1944; for Montgomery see Alan Moorehead, *Eclipse* (London, edn of 1967) and Noel Busch, *Montgomery*, in *Life*, 15 May, 1944.

Montgomery's briefing features in ISM/II/3/238/2a, *Notes on 15 May Conference*, Ismay Papers (LHMC), in Sir John Wheeler-Bennett, *King George VI* (London, 1958), Samuel Eliot Morison, *United States Naval Operations in World War Two, Vol XI* (London, 1957), and Irving, *Generals, op. cit*. For the Premier's rekindled enthusiasm, see F.O. 954/8, fol. 74, Churchill to Roosevelt, 13 April, 1944. King George on Montgomery is President of the Board of Trade Hugh Dalton's diary entry for 1 January, 1944 (LSE).

Mikhail Koriakov's story is adapted from his book *I'll Never Go Back* (London, 1948). For Anzio and Cassino, see the sources cited for Chapter One, as well as the following: Lt Gen Wladyslaw Anders, *An Army In Exile* (London, 1949), Harold L. Bond, *Return to Cassino* (London, 1964), L. F. Ellis, *Welsh Guards At War* (Aldershot, 1946), Peter Llewellyn, *Journey Towards Christmas* (Wellington, N.Z., 1949), Lt-Col G. W. L. Nicholson, *The Canadians in Italy* (Ottawa, 1956) and D. C. Quilter, *No Dishonourable Name* (London, 1947). For Major-General Walker's manoeuvre, see Robert H. Adleman and Colonel George Walton, *Rome Fell To Day* (Boston, 1968).

The Mongtomery impersonation is recounted in M. E. Clifton-James, *I Was Monty's Double* (London, 1954) and by Stephen Watts in *Moonlight on a Lake In Bond Street* (London, 1961). The confusion on Churchill's train is in II/3/230a, Ismay Papers (LHMC). Signs and portents of D-Day are noted by Roger A. Freeman, *The Mighty Eighth* (London, 1970), Grover C. Hall, Jr, *1000 Destroyed* (London, edn of 1962), and Rex Winfield, *The Sky Belongs To Them* (London, 1976).

For the D-Day indecisions, see Gen Walter Bedell Smith, *Eisenhowers Six Great Decisions* (New York, 1946), James M. Stagg, *Forecast For Overlord* (New York, 1971) and Maj-Gen Kenneth Strong, *Intelligence At The Top* (London, 1968).

Eisenhower among the paratroopers is from George E. Koskimaki's *D-Day With The Screaming Eagles* (New York, 1970). The scene in the dance-hall is from Brenda McBryde, *A Nurse's War* (London, 1979). For the flood of French messages, see Robert Aron, *De Gaulle Before Paris* (London, 1962). For Stalin, see Milovan Djilas, *Conversations With Stalin* (London, 1962); for Churchill, see Pawle, *op. cit*.

For Rome, see Adleman and Walton, *op. cit.*, Mark Clark, *op. cit.*, John P. Delaney, *The Blue Devils In Italy* (Washington, D.C., 1947) and Denis Johnston, *Nine Rivers From Jordan* (London, 1953).

Chapter Four: "Do Not Be Daunted if Chaos Reigns"

The experiences of the French Resistance along the Atlantic Wall are based on interviews conducted by the author between Cherbourg and Le Havre with Fernand Arsène, Albert Augé, Janine Boitard, Albertine Château, Léon Dumis, André Farine, Léonard Gille, Yves Gresselin, André Heintz, Georges Mercader, Aloyse Schultz and Jeanne Verinaud.

For the assault on the bridges, see Napier Cookenden, *Dropzone Normandy* (London, 1976) and Dank, *op. cit.*, for the British airborne role in general, see Brigadier George Chatterton, *The Wings of Pegasus* (London, 1962), Gen Sir Richard Gale, *With the 6th Airborne Division in Normandy* (London, 1948) and Laurence Wright, *The Wooden Sword* (London, 1967). For the Merville Battery, see James Gleason and Tom Waldron, *Now It Can Be Told* (London, 1952) and Garry Johnson (with Christopher Dunphie), *Brightly Shone The Dawn* (London, 1980).

For hour-by-hour German reactions, see Carell and Ryan, *op. cit.*; the definitive versions of the Verlaine messages is in Farago, *Foxes, op. cit.*

For the U.S. airborne and glider role, the main sources include Gerard M. Devlin, *Paratrooper* (London, 1979), General James M. Gavin, *On To Berlin* (London, 1979), General Matthew B. Ridgway, *Soldier* (New York, 1956) and General Maxwell D. Taylor, *Swords and Ploughshares* (New York, 1972).

For the scene on the ships see, among others, Lambton Burn, *op. cit.*, Robert Capa, *Slightly Out of Focus* (New York, 1947), Martha Gellhorn, *The Face of War* (London, 1959), Ralph Ingersoll, *Top Secret* (New York, 1946), Alan Melville, *First Tide* (London, 1945), Ross Munro, *Gauntlet To Overlord* (Toronto, 1945), Norman Scarfe, *Assault Division* (London, 1947) and J. E. Taylor, *The Last Passage* (London, 1946).

Scenes on the beaches were also graphically depicted by Hanson W. Baldwin, *Battles Lost And Won* (London, 1967), John Keegan, *Six Armies in Normandy* (London, 1981) and David Howarth, *op. cit.*

Chapter Five: "What A Lot of Things Could Have Been Arranged"

For the onset of the V-1s, see Derek Wood, *Attack Warning Red* (London, 1976) and The Sunday Telegraph Magazine for 16 June, 1974; for their overall development, see Basil Collier, *The Battle of the V-Weapons* (London, 1964), Peter Cooksley, *The Flying Bomb* (London, 1979) and Richard Anthony Young, *The Flying Bomb* (London, 1978). De Gaulle's return to France is noted by Aron, *op. cit.*, Aidan Crawley, *De Gaulle* (London, 1969) and Kersaudy, *op. cit.* For British comments, see F.O. 954/8, fol. 127, Churchill to Roosevelt, 26 May, 1944 and fols. 255/256, Duff Cooper to Eden, 20 June, 1944.

The Caen stalemate is pictured by Moorehead, *op. cit.* and Henry Maule, *Caen* (Newton Abbott, Devon, 1976) Montgomery's outlining of his role is Box I, 14/1, Alanbrooke Papers, Montgomery to Brooke, 27 July, 1944 (LHMC). For the Führer conference, see Irving, Fox, *op. cit.*, and Lt-Gen Hans Speidel, *We Defended Normandy* (London, 1951).

Hitler's "fortress" obsession is featured by Lt-Gen Günther Blumentritt, Rundstedt, *The Soldier and The Man* (London, 1952) and Lt-Gen Siegfried Westphal, *The German Army In The West* (London, 1951). For the Caen battlefield see Dudley Clarke, *The Eleventh At War* (London, 1952), McBryde, *op. cit.*, Maule, *op. cit.*, and Jocelyn Pereira, *A Distant Drum* (Aldershot, Hants, 1948).

Ryuji Nagatsuka's experiences are based on his, *I Was A Kamikaze* (London, 1973). The Marianas campaign is analysed in Craven and Cate, *op. cit.*, Carl W. Hoffman, *Saipan: The Beginning of the End* (Washington, D.C,: 1950), Patrick O'Sheel, with Gene Cook, *Semper Fidelis: the U.S. Marines in the Pacific* (New York, 1947), Fletcher Pratt, *The Marines' War* (New York, 1947) and John Toland, *The Rising Sun* (London, 1971). For Mitscher, see James H. and William J. Belote, *Titans of the Sea* (New York, 1975).

Morrison's advocacy of gas is CAB 65/W.P. (44) 348, 27 June, 1944. Discussions of the use of gas and bacteria feature all through PREM 3/65, PREM 3/88/3 and PREM 3/89; much, though not all, of the correspondence has been reproduced in Robert Harris and Jeremy Paxman, *A Higher Form of Killing* (London, 1982). For the impact of the V-1s on London, the author has drawn on his own experiences at the time, as well as the following printed sources: Calder, *op. cit.*, Prof R. V. Jones, *Most Secret War* (London, 1978), Norman Longmate, *The Doodlebugs* (London, 1981), William Sansom, *Westminster*

At War (London, 1947), Elizabeth Sheppard-Jones, *I Walk On Wheels* (London, 1958) and Sir John Wheeler-Bennett, *Special Relationships* (London, 1975).

The literature of the 20 July plot is voluminous and often contradictory, but I have endeavoured to steer an even course between the following: Constantine Fitzgibbon, *The Shirt of Nessus* (London, 1956), Hans-Bernd Gisevius, *To The Bitter End* (London, 1948), Peter Hoffinan, *The History of the German Resistance* (London, 1977), Dr Hans-Adolf Jacobsen, *July 20, 1944* (Bonn, 1969), Joachim Kramarz, *Stauffenberg* (London, 1967), Roger Manvell (with Heinrich Frankel), *The July 20 Plot* (London, 1964), Sir John Wheeler-Bennett, *The Nemesis of Power* (London, 1964), Eberhard Zeller, *The Flame of Freedom* (London, 1967). For civilian reactions in Berlin, see Ruth Andreas-Friedrich, *Berlin Underground* (New York, 1947) and Joachim Fest, *Hitler* (London, 1974). The O.S.S. plans for Hitler are in Charles Whiting, *The Battle for Twelveland* (London, 1975); the Vichy France reaction from Hubert Cole's *Laval* (London, 1963).

Chapter Six: "Paris Is Worth 200,000 Dead"

Most MacArthur material derives from RG-3, RG-4 and RG-16 (MacA Mem), plus the following published sources: Teodoro Agoncillo, *The Fateful Years, Vol II* (Quezon City, 1945), Sidney L. Huff (with Joe Alex Morris), *My Fifteen Years with General MacArthur* (Philadelphia, 1964), Frazier Hunt, *The Untold Story of Douglas MacArthur* (London, 1954), D. Clayton James, *The Years of MacArthur, Vol II* (Boston, 1975), Gen George C. Kenney, *The MacArthur I knew* (New York, 1951), William Manchester, *American Caesar* (London, 1979). For naval and air conditions, see Daniel E. Barbey, *MacArthur's Amphibious Navy* (Annapolis, Md., 1969) and Joe Christy (with Jeffrey Ethell): *P-38: Lightning At War* (London, 1978).

Personal accounts of the Warsaw Rising are contained in Lieutenant-General Tadeusz Bor-Komorowski, *The Secret Army* (London, 1950), Maria Ginter, *Life In Both Hands* (London, 1964), Bernard Goldstein, *The Stars Bear Witness* (London, 1950), Stefan Korbonski, *Fighting Warsaw* (London, 1956), Irena Orska, *Silent Is The Vistula* (New York, 1946), Zbigniew Stypulkowski, *Invitation To Moscow* (London, 1951), Waclaw Zagorski, *Seventy Days* (London,

1957), and Michael Zylberberg, *A Warsaw Diary* (London, 1969). Synoptic accounts have been compiled by George Bruce, *The Warsaw Rising* (London, 1972), Gunther Denscher, *Warsaw Rising* (London, 1972), Wanda Dynowska, *All For Freedom* (Swatantrapur, India, 1946), Andrzej Pomian, *The Warsaw Rising* (London, 1945) and Janusz Zawodny, *Nothing But Honour* (London, 1978). Supply drop difficulties are outlined in PREM 3/352/12, Slessor to Portal, 6 August, 1944.

For the Falaise Gap see Carell, Melville and Moorhead, *op. cit.*, Martin Blumenson, *Breakout and Pursuit* (Washington, D.C., 1961) and the best full-length study, Eddy Florentin, *The Battle of the Falaise Gap* (London, 1965). For Montgomery's check on Patton, see Maj-Gen Richard Rohmer, *Patton's Gap* (London, 1981). Accounts of Majdanek are to be found in Raymond Davies, *Odyssey Through Hell* (New York, 1946), Alaric Jacob, *A Window In Moscow* (New York, 1946) and in *Time* Magazine, 11 September, 1944. For the neutrals, see W. M. Carlgren, *Swedish Foreign Policy During The Second World War* (London, 1977), Carlton J. Hayes, *Wartime Mission in Spain* (New York, 1945) and Ferenc A. Vali, *Bridge Across the Bosphorus: The Foreign Policy of Turkey* (Baltimore, Md, 1971).

Churchill at Buckingham Palace is from Harold Nicolson, *Diaries and Letters*, Vol III, (London, 1967). For Churchill and Argentina, see F.O. 954/14, fol. 505, Churchill to Roosevelt, 1 July, 1944 and fol. 513, Roosevelt to Churchill, 23 July, 1944. For Churchill and Spain, see F.O. 954/27, fol. 529 Churchill to Roosevelt, 4 June, 1944. For Churchill and Tito, see PREM 3/513/6, Churchill to General Wilson, 20 November, 1944, and published accounts in Phyllis Auty, *Tito* (London, 1970) and Stephen Clissold, *Whirlwind* (London, 1949). The "Lend Lease" reference is Dalton's diary entry for 5 December, 1944 (LSE).

For Anvil, see F.O.954/17, fols. 17–19, Churchill to Roosevelt, 1 July, 1944. Analyses of the operation feature in Sir John Colville, *The Churchillians* (London, 1981), Sir William K. Hancock, *Smuts: The Fields of Force, Vol. II* (Cambridge, 1968), Trumbull Higgins, *Soft Underbelly* (New York, 1968) and Sir David Hunt, *A Don At War* (London, 1966).

The fall of Paris is based on the following accounts: Robert Aron, *De Gaulle Triumphant* (London, 1963), Raymond Bruckberger, *One Sky To Share* (New York, 1952), Larry Collins and Dominique Lapierre, *Is Paris Burning?* (London, 1965), Blake Ehrlich, *The French*

Resistance (London, 1966), Gen Charles de Gaulle, *Memoires, Vol II, Unity* (London, 1959), John Groth, *Studio: Europe* (New York, 1945), Henry Maule, *Out of the Sand* (London, 1966), David Pryce-Jones, *Paris In The Third Reich* (London, 1981), Claude Roy, *Eight Days That Freed Paris* (London, 1945) and Willis Thornton, *The Liberation of Paris* (London, 1963).

For the Rumanian coup, see PREM 3/374/8, Churchill to Eden, 25 August, 1944, and *Time* Magazine, 18 September, 1944, for King Michael's interview with the Associated Press. Eden's glimpse into the future is CAB 65/W.P. (44), 436, Soviet Policy in Europe, 9 August, 1944. For Ana Pauker, see Robert Bishop and E. S. Crayfield, *Russian Astride the Balkans* (London, 1949).

Chapter Seven: "Stop! I Have Made A Momentous Decision"

The Holzinger sortie is from Charles Whiting, *Bloody Aachen* (London, 1976). For the speed of the autumn advance, see Alexander McKee, *The Race For The Rhine Bridges* (London, 1971), Bryan Samain, *Commando Men* (London, 1948), W. A. T. Synge, *The Stoiy of The Green Howards* (Richmond, Yorks, 1952) and Maj-Gen G. L. Verney, *The Desert Rats* (London, 1954). Brussels is from Pereira, *op. cit.*, and John D'Arcy Dawson, *European Victory* (London, 1946); Antwerp from J. L. Moulton, *Battle For Antwerp* (London, 1973).

Hitler's outburst is in John Toland, *Hitler* (New York, 1976). For Arnhem, the best overall picture is Cornelius Ryan, *A Bridge Too Far* (London, 1974), supplemented by Christopher Hibbert's shorter *The Battle of Arnhem* (London, 1962), but valuable supplementary detail is contained in Ralph Bennett, *Ultra In The West* (London, 1979), Lt-Gen Lewis H. Brereton, *The Brereton Diaries* (New York, 1946), Dank, *op. cit.*, Anthony Deane-Drummond, *Return Ticket* (London, 1953), John Fairley, *Remember Arnhem* (Aldershot, 1978), Maj-Gen John Frost, *A Drop Too Many* (London, 1980), Gavin, *op. cit.*, Leo Heaps, *Escape From Arnhem* (Toronto, 1945), Lt-Gen Sir Brian Horrocks, *A Full Life* (London, 1960), Janusz Piekalkiewicz, *Arnhem 1944* (London, 1977) and James Sims, *Arnhem Spearhead* (London, 1978).

On Dumbarton Oaks, I have used Burns, *Roosevelt, op. cit.*, *The Memoirs of Cordell Hull*, Vol II (London, 1948), and W. H. McNeill, *America, Britain and Russia* (London, 1953); on Quebec, Eden, Hull and Moran, *op. cit.*, Roger Parkinson, *A Day's March Nearer Home* (London, 1974) and Christopher Thorne, *Allies Of A Kind* (Lonon, 1978).

Fears on the spread of Communism are in PREM 3/66/7, Churchill to Eden, 4 May, 1944, and Eden to Churchill, 9 May, 1944. The Premier's meeting with Stalin is described in his *The Second World War, Vol VI, Triumph and Tragedy* (London, 1954); the omission is noted by Gabriel Kolko, *The Politics of War* (London, 1969). For Stalin's thinking, see W. Averell Harriman (with Elie Abel), *Special Envoy to Churchill and Stalin* (New York, 1975) and Roy Medvedev, *Let History Judge* (London, 1972). Stalin's changed persona is in File D 2054, Miscellaneous Correspondence, Inverchapel Papers, which also describes the Embassy reception (BL); other accounts are from Jacob, *op. cit.*, and A. H. Birse, *Memoirs of An Interpreter* (London, 1967); the dictator's security precautions are in Nikolai Tolstoy, *Stalin's Secret War* (London, 1981). Stalin and the Yugoslavs is from Djilas, Stalin, *op. cit.*, and Vladimir Dedijer, *Tito Speaks* (London, 1953); Churchill's anger is from F.0.954/34, fol. 184, Churchill to Hopkins, 13 October, 1944. The Polish talks are given verbatim in Mikolajczyk, *op. cit*. The comment on Beirut is from Margaret Storm Chapman's MSS diary, entry of 11 September, ref. JMON/2 (CCC).

Rommel's death is described in Irving, Fox, *op, cit,*; Jodl's diary entry is quoted in Gen Walter Warlimont's *Inside Hitler's Headquarters* (London 1964). For Bulgaria, see Elisabeth Barker, *British Policy in South-East Europe In The Second World War* (London, 1976) and PREM 3/66/7, Churchill to Hopkins, 12 October, 1944. For Finland, see John Wuorinen (ed.), *Finland in World War Two* (New York, 1948); for Hungary, see the sources quoted for Chapter Two, plus Irving, Hitler, *op. cit.*, and Otto Skorzeny, *Skorzeny's Secret Missions* (New York, 1950).

Chapter Eight: "You Could Hide An Army In These Goddamned Woods"

For MacArthur, see the sources listed for Chapter Six. The inception of the *Kamikazes* is featured in Bernard Millot's *Divine Thunder* (London, 1971) and Rikihei Inoguchi (with Tadashi Nakajima and Roger Pineau), *The Divine Wind* (London, 1959). For Stilwell, I have followed the sources given in Chapter Two, and, in addition, the following: Charles F. Romanus (with Riley Sutherland), *Stilwell's*

Command Problems (Washington, D.C., 1956) and *Time Runs Out in CBI* (1959), *The Stilwell Papers* (ed. Theodore H. White) (London, 1949) and Gen Albert C. Wedemeyer, *Wedemeyer Reports!* (New York, 1958).

Conditions along the West Wall are drawn from D'Arcy Dawson, *op. cit.*, Leo A. Hoegh and Howard J. Doyle, *Timberwolf Trails* (Washington, D.C., 1946), Horrocks, *op. cit.*, Glover S. Johns, *The Clay Pigeons of St Lô* (Harrisburg, Pa, 1958), Munro, *op. cit.*, David Rissik, *The D.L.I. At War* (Brancepeth Castle, Durham, 1953), R. W. Thompson, *Men Under Fire* (London, 1946), Whiting, *Aachen, op. cit.*, and Rex Wingfield, *The Only Way Out* (London, 1955). Aachen features in detail in Charles B. Macdonald, *The Siegfried Line Campaign* (Washington, D.C., 1963).

For the *Volkssturm,* see Andreas-Friedrich, *op. cit.*, Michael Balfour, *Propaganda in Wartime* (London, 1979), Robert E. Harzstein, *The War That Hitler Won* (London, 1979), Alan Milward, *The German Economy At War* (London, 1965) and Dietrich Orlow, *History of the Nazi Party*, Vol II (Newton Abbot, Devon, 1973). For the atom search see Samuel A. Goudsmidt, *Alsos* (London, 1947), David Irving, *The Virus House* (London, 1967), Robert Jungk, *Brighter Than A Thousand Suns* (London, 1958) and Whiting, *Twelveland, op. cit.*

For Eisenhower's plans, see Ambrose, *op. cit.*; for Hitler's conferences, E. H. Cookridge, *Gehlen: Spy of the Century* (London, 1971), David Downing, *The Devil's Virtuosos* (London, 1977), Irving, *Hitler, op. cit.*, and Westphal, *op. cit.* For Ultra intelligence, see Ralph Bennett, *op. cit.*

Accounts of the Battle of the Bulge on which I have drawn are as follows: Donald Brownlow, *Panzer Baron* (North Quincy, Mass., 1975), Hugh M. Cole, *The Ardennes: Battle of the Bulge* (Washington, D.C., 1975), John S. Eisenhower, *The Bitter Woods* (London, 1969), Peter Elstob, *Bastogne: The Road Block* (London, 1968 and *Hitler's Last Offensive* (London, 1971), S. L. A. Marshall, *Bastogne: The First Eight Days* (Washington, D.C., 1946), Robert E. Merriam, *Dark December* (Chicago, 1947), Jacques Nabercourt, *Hitler's Last Gamble* (London, 1964), John Toland, *Battle* (New York, 1959) and Charles Whiting, *Death Of A Division* (London, 1979). For Spaatz, see Brereton, *op. cit.*

Chapter Nine: "No Game Is Lost Until the Final Whistle"

Ardennes sources are as for Chapter Eight, plus the following additions: Ladislas Farago, *Patton: Ordeal and Triumph* (New York, 1964), Robert Allen, *Lucky Forward* (New York, 1947) and Charles Codman, *Drive* (Boston, 1957). For Operation Greif, see Skorzeny, *op. cit.*; the focus on Montgomery is from Carpenter, *op. cit*. The one-armed paratrooper is from *Time* Magazine, 22 January, 1945; for Abrams, see Will Lang, "*Colonel Abe*," in *Life* Magazine, 23 April, 1945.

For the overall picture in Greece, I have drawn on the following: Wilfrid Byford-Jones, *The Greek Trilogy* (London, 1946), Richard Capell, *Simiomata* (London, 1946), Bernard Fergusson, *The Black Watch and the King's Enemies* (London, 1950), Sir Reginald Leeper, *When Greek Meets Greek* (London, 1950), Harold Macmillan, *The Blast of War* (London, 1967), William H. McNeill, *The Greek Dilemma* (Philadelphia, 1947), Henry Maule, *Scobie: Hero of Greece* (London, 1975), Stefanos Seraphis, *Greek Resistance Army* (London, 1951), and C. M. Woodhouse, *Apple of Discord* (London, 1946) and *The Struggle for Greece* (London, 1976).

Misgivings on the King's return are in PREM 3/212/9, Eden to Churchill, 2 September, 1944. For personal glimpses of Churchill's visit, see Sir John Colville, *Footprints in Time* (London, 1976), Piers Dixon, *Double Diploma* (London, 1968), Moran, *op. cit.*, Pawle, *op. cit.*, and Tickell, *op. cit.*

Unpublished glimpes of Churchill at Yalta can be found in ISM/II/3/296n (LHMC). The fullest account is in W.P. (45), 157, 12 March, 1945. Other vignettes are in Joan Bright Astley, *The Inner Cirlce* (London, 1971), Jim Bishop, *op. cit.*, Sarah Churchill, *Keep on Dancing* (London, 1981), George F. Kennan, *Memoirs* (London, 1950) and Edward R. Stettinius, *Roosevelt and the Russians* (London, 1950). The extent of Russian Lend-Lease is explored by Robert Huhn Jones, *The Roads to Russia* (Norman, Okla, 1969). For the betrayal of 2 million Russians see Nikolai Tolstoy, *Victims of Yalta* (London, edn of 1979). For divergent interpretations of Yalta, see Diane Shaver Clemens, *Yalta* (New York, 1970), and John L. Snell (ed), *The Meaning of Yalta* (Baton Rouge, La, 1956). Roosevelt's comment on the Baltic is from Joseph P. Lash, *Eleanor and Franklin* (London, 1972). The Führer's optimism is from John Toland, *The Last 100 Days* (New York, 1966).

For Iwo Jima (and in Chapter Ten) I have used many sources cited for Saipan in Chapter Five, and, in addition, Don Congdon (ed),

Combat: War in the Pacific (London, 1965), Frank O. Hough, *The Island War* (Philadelphia, 1947), J. A. Isely, *The U.S. Marines and Amphibious War* (Princeton, N.J. 1951), William Manchester, *Goodbye, Darkness* (London, 1981), Lt-Cdr Max Miller, USN, *It's Tomorrow Out Here* (New York, 1945), Morison, *op. cit.*, Vol XI (London, 1960), and Cornelius Vanderbilt Whitney, *Lone and Level Sands* (New York, 1951).

Chapter Ten: "When We Step Down, Let The Whole World Tremble"

Affairs in Bucharest are charted by James F. Byrnes, *Speaking Frankly* (London, 1947) and Herbert Feis, *Churchill, Roosevelt and Stalin* (Princeton, N.J., 1957). For British reactions, see F.O. 954/23, fol. 410, Eden to Bucharest, and fol. 398 ff, Churchill to Roosevelt, both dated 8 March. Eden's doubts on San Francisco are in F.O. 954/26, fol. 586/7, Eden to Churchill, 24 March, 1945.

For the end in Manila, see the MacArthur sources listed for Chapter Six, and, in addition, Morison, *op. cit.*, Vol XIII, 1959, Robin Prising, *Manila, Goodbye* (London, 1976), John Dos Passos, *Tour of Duty* (Boston, 1946) and Robert Ross Smith, *The Approach to the Philippines* (Washington, D.C., 1953) and *Triumph in the Philippines* (1963).

Remagen is exhaustively documented in Ken Hechler's *The Bridge at Remagen* (New York, 1957). The Dulles material is based on the author's interview with the late Allen Dulles to supplement his own book, *The Secret Surrender* (New York, 1966). For the Tokyo raid see Martin Caidin, *A Torch To The Enemy* (New York, 1960) and Toland, *Sun, op. cit.*, Dresden is from Colville, *Churchillians, op. cit.*

For "scorched earth," see Admiral Karl Dönitz, *Memoirs: Ten Years and Twenty Days* (London, 1959), Walter Schellenberg, *The Schellenberg Memoirs* (London, 1956) and Albert Speer, *Inside The Third Reich* (London, 1970). For Eisenhower, see Cornelius Ryan, *The Last Battle* (London, 1966). The fortress myth is the subject of Rodney G. Minott's *The Fortress That Never Was* (London, 1965).

For the Stalin conference and Hitler's Heinrici meeting, see Ryan, *Battle, op. cit.*, and General S. M. Shtmenko, *The Last Six Months* (London, 1978). For Okinawa see the Iwo Jima sources cited in Chapter Nine, and, in additioin, Ray E. Applemen *et al*, *Okinawa: The Last Battle* (Washington, D.C., 1948), Benis M. Frank, *Okinawa: Capstone To Victory* (London, 1970) and Brigadier-General William Heavey, *Down Ramp!* (Washington, D.C., 1947).

Roosevelt's death derives from Bernard Asbell, *When F.D.R. Died* (New York, 1961), Jim Bishop and Burns, *op. cit.*, William D. Hassett, *Off The Record with F.D.R.* (London, 1960) and Turnley Walker, *Roosevelt and The Warm Springs Story* (New York, 1953). Truman's debut is in Cabell Phillips, *The Truman Presidency* (New York, 1966), Alfred Steinberg, *The Man From Missouri* (New York, 1962) and Harry S. Truman, *Year of Decisions, 1945* (London, 1955).

For the entry into Belsen, see Raul Hilberg, *The Destruction of the European Jews* (London, 1961), Richard McMillan, *Miracle Before Berlin* (London, 1946), Derrick Sington, *Belsen Uncovered* (London, 1946), and Patrick Walker, *The Lid Lifts* (London, 1945). The conversation between Truman and Churchill is reproduced verbatim in Truman, *Decisions, op. cit.* For peace moves in general, see Count Folke Bernadotte, *The Fall of The Curtain* (London, 1945), Cookridge, *op. cit.*, Graham-Murray, *op. cit.*, Fritz Hesse, *Hitler and the English* (London, 1954), Ralph Hewins, *Count Folke Bernadotte* (London, 1950), Wilhelm Höttl, *The Secret Front* (London, 1953) and Kleist, *op. cit.* For Kersten, see Joseph Kessel, *The Magic Touch* (London, 1961) and Felix Kersten, *The Kersten Memoirs* (London, 1956). The British reaction is in F.O. 954/23, fols. 596–8, Eden to Churchill, 1 April, 1945.

For Simpson, see Ryan, *Battle, op. cit.* Göbbels is from Jürgen Thorwald, *Flight In The Winter* (London, 1953). Incomparably the best account of Hitler's retreat to the bunker is still Hugh Trevor-Roper, *The Last Days of Hitler* (London, 1947), but useful data can also be found in Hans Baur, *Hitler's Pilot* (London, 1958), Gerhardt Boldt, *Hitler: The Last Ten Days* (New York, 1973), Irving, *Hitler, op. cit.*, Michael Musmanno, *Ten Days To Die* (New York, 1950) and James P. O'Donnell, *The Berlin Bunker* (London, 1979).

Chapter Eleven: "The Last Man Will See What We Saw"

For events in Yugoslavia, see F.O. 954/34, fol. 341–344, Sergent to Churchill, 1 May, 1945; PREM 3/513/6, Churchill to Eden, 11 March, 1945; and F.O. 954/30, Churchill to Truman, 11 May, 1945. A special study of the crisis is Geoffrey Cox, *The Race for Trieste* (London, 1977).

A hiliarious description of the San Francisco Conference is in File MS Woolton 16, fol. 134–137, Woolton Papers, Cavendish-Bentinck to Woolton, 26 April, 1945 (BL); see also Charles Bohlen, *Witness To History* (London, 1973). For the surrender at Reims, see Strong, *op. cit.*, Summersby, *op. cit.*, and Charles Christian Wertenbaker, *Surrender at Reims*, in *Life* Magazine, 21 May, 1945; for the end in Berlin, see V. I. Chuikov, *The End of The Third Reich* (London, 1967), Robert Jackson, *The Red Falcons* (Brighton, Sussex, 1970) and Erich Kuby, *The Russians and Berlin, 1945* (London, 1967).

V-E Day relies primarily on Norman Longmate, *When We Won The War* (London, 1977) and Molly Panter-Downes, *London War Notes* (London, 1972); see also Bradley, *op. cit.*, Codman, *op. cit.*, and Maj-Gen Hubert Essame, *The 43rd Wessex Division At War* (London, 1952). For suffering in Europe, see James J. Daugherty, *The Politics of Wartime Aid* (Westport, Conn., 1978), Dedijer, *op. cit.*, Dorothy MacArdle, *Children of Europe* (London, 1949), Walter Maass, *The Netherlands At War* (New York, 1970), Werner Warmbrunn, *The Dutch Under German Occupation* (Stanford, Calif, 1963), and Henri van der Zee, *The Hunger Winter* (London, 1982).

Churchill's farewell to the Cabinet is Dalton's diary entry for 28 May, 1945 (LSE). For full coverage of the election campaign, see Paul Addison, *The Road To 1945* (London, 1975) and Calder, *op. cit.* Woolton's advice is in File MS Woolton 15, fols. 163–172, 18 November, 1942. (BL); Beaverbrook's is in File D 421, Beaverbrook to Churchill, 15 February, 1944 (H ofL).

For the scene at Alamogordo and Los Alamos, the following are of value: Laura Fermi, *Atoms In The Family* (London, 1955), Len Giovanitti, *The Decision to Drop The Bomb* (London, 1967), Stephane Groueff, *Manhattan Project* (London, 1967), Lt-Gen Leslie R. Groves, *Now It Can Be Told* (London, 1963), Robert Jungk, *Brighter Than A Thousand Suns* (London, 1958), J. Alvin Kugelmass, *J. Robert Oppenheimer and The Atomic Story* (New York, 1953), Lansing Lamont, *Day of Trinity* (London, 1966), William L. Laurence, *Dawn Over Zero* (London, 1947) and Ruth Moore, *Niels Bohr, The Man and the Scientist* (London, 1967). Details on Gold are from Michael Amrine, *The Great Decision* (New York, 1959).

Two well-documented accounts of events over the target are Fletcher Knebel and Charles Bailey, *No High Ground* (London, 1960) and Gordon Thomas and Max Morgan-Witts, *Ruin From The Air* (London, 1977). The pioneer account of Japanese suffering was, of course, John Hersey's *Hiroshima* (London, 1946); later useful accounts are in Wilfred Burchett, *At The Barricades* (London, 1980), Michikiko Hachiya, *Hiroshima Diary* (1955), Robert Jungk, *Children Of The Ashes* (New York, 1961), Dr Orata Osada (ed), *Children of the A-Bomb* (Tokyo, 1959) and Toland, *Sun, op. cit.*

Chapter Twelve: "You and I Would Be In A Pretty Pickle"

For the last hours in Tokyo, see Russell Brines, *MacArthur's Japan* (Philadelphia, 1948), William Craig, *The Fall of Japan* (New York, 1968), *Japan's Longest Day* (London, 1968) and Leonard Mosley, *Hirohito, Emperor of Japan* (Englewood Cliffs, N.J., 1966). For the scene aboard the *Missouri*, the best accounts are Toshikazu Kase, *Eclipse of the Rising Sun* (London, 1951), Clark Lee, *One Last Look Around* (New York, 1947), Frank Legg, *War Correspondent* (London, 1965) and Manchester, *Caesar, op. cit.*

For the trials of Pétain and Laval, see Milton Dank, *The French Against The French* (London, 1974). An evocative account of Nuremberg is in Victor Bernstein, *Final Judgement* (London, 1947). Churchill's pronouncement is from Lord Ismay, *Memoirs* (London, 1961).

Notes

1. Brooke was promoted Field Marshal on 1 January, 1944.

2. Named after a nearby town.

3. Who was himself revealed in 1979 to have been a Russian agent.

4. All told, M.I.5. "turned" 47 agents in the course of the war; for divergent reasons only half were directly involved in D-Day.

5. A pseudonym.

6. Dr Paul Göbbels was Hitler's Minister of Propaganda and Enlightenment.

7. The five in question were 78-year-old Marshal Emilio De Bono, a veteran of the 1922 March on Rome, which brought the Fascists to power, Giovanni Marinelli, another veteran, Luciano Gottardi, President of the Industrial Workers' Confederation, Minister of Agriculture Carlo Pareschi and Minister of Corporations Tullio Cianetti.

8. The larger-than-life doll featured by the U.S. ventriloquist, Edgar Bergen.

9. Grant had received the unconditional surrender of General S. B. Buckner at Fort Donelson in 1862.

10. In an interview with the author, Indio, California, 3 February, 1968.

11. Although the first relief of Kohima took place on 20 April, fighting on The Ridge continued until 14 May. Imphal remained under pressure until 29 June. The casualties here totalled 12,603.

12. One item, *Yank* Magazine's simple French phrase book, featuring the gambit, "My wife doesn't understand me", caused a storm of protest from wives back in the States.

13. Security fears had lessened after the bodies of all ten "Bigots" lost on 27–28 April were recovered from the sea.

14. Elected the first President of Israel in 1949.

15. A further 18,000 Londoners were injured to some degree, and 21,000 houses daily suffered some damage.

16. Hitler's rank in World War One.

17. Britain's gas stocks, reported the Chancellor of the Duchy of Lancaster, Ernest Brown, on 25 May, stood at 35,606 tons of mustard gas and 12,238 tons of phosgene.

18. On 23 August, when Beamont shot down his thirtieth and last V-1, the figures told the story. By 5 September, as the main launching sites fell into Allied hands and the first bombardment ceased, 6,275 V-1s had left the Continent, and the R.A.F. had destroyed 1,771 – 638 of these failing to Beamont's wing. Anti-aircraft and Royal Naval gun fire accounted for 1,460; barrage balloons for 232. The assault was to continue, although on a much reduced scale, until March 1945.

19. Named after Dr Fritz Todt, the engineer who planned the West Wall, known to the Allies as the Siegfried Line.

20. Warmly approving Stauffenberg's "Valkyrie" plan at its face value, Hitler had commented, "At last a staff officer with brains."

21. Other versions have included "Long live the eternal Germany", and "Long live holy Germany".

22. All told, the Allies attempted 10 supply drops on Warsaw – mostly only partially successful – between 4 August and 18 September. The Russians began random drops on 13 September, but without benefit of parachute. Everything was smashed to smithereens.

23. The slang title for Paris, popularised in the pre-war songs of Edith "The Sparrow" Piaf.

24. Ironically, the strongpoints included several buildings on Ebernach's demolition list – notably the Quai d'Orsay, the Chambre des Députés, and the Palais du Luxembourg. Others were sited at the École Militaire, the Central Archives, the Concorde, the Opéra, the République, the Hôtel Majestic and von Choltitz' own headquarters, the Meurice.

25. On the afternoon of 23 August, Raoul Nordling had suffered a minor heart attack.

26. A copper coin, then the hundredth part of a rouble.

27. So called from the typhoon, or "divine wind" that in August, 1281, scattered the fleet of the Mongol Emperor, Kublai Khan, and saved Japan from invasion.

28. As Chiang's Chief of Staff; as Deputy to Admiral Lord Louis Mountbatten, Commander-in-Chief of Allied Forces, South-East Asia; as U.S. Commander of the China-Burma-India Theatre.

29. Proof of the deteriorating nature of Anglo-U.S. relations was that many telegrams routed through Allied Forces Headquarters in Caserta, Italy, but intended for British eyes only, were now marked "GUARD". It was the hard-pressed Colville's failure to do so that brought Churchill's "conquered city" allusion to the State Department's notice.

30. The Armies were still holding out, facing no greater enemy than boredom, when the war ended.

31. Trier was considered a task for four divisions. On receipt of his orders, Patton cabled SHAEF: "Have taken Trier with two divisions. What do you want me to do? Give it back?"

32. Some 8,000 men were lost at Küstrin.

33. Churchill first used the phrase in public in a speech at Fulton, Missouri, on 5 March, 1946. This is an earlier usage.

34. Tried in June 1945, on charges that included organising the *Armja Krajowa* and maintaining contact with the London Poles, their sentences ranged from ten years to eighteen months. Three were acquitted.

35. The Göbbels family perished similarly – although inside the Führerbunker.

36. Sometimes unkindly defined as "Unhappy Natives Receiving Ridiculous Assistance".

37. The first Soviet Atomic explosion occurred on 29 August, 1949.

38. Czechoslovakia, Poland, Rumania, Bulgaria, Hungary and Albania.